Advice After Appomattox

LETTERS TO ANDREW JOHNSON,
1865–1866

Special Volume No. 1
of the
Papers of Andrew Johnson
LEROY P. GRAF
EDITOR

Sponsored by
The University of Tennessee
The National Historical Publications and Records Commission
The Tennessee Historical Commission

The Ravages of War: Charleston, 1865.
Courtesy of The National Archives

Advice After Appomattox

LETTERS TO ANDREW JOHNSON, 1865–1866

Edited by

BROOKS D. SIMPSON

LEROY P. GRAF

JOHN MULDOWNY

Special Volume No. 1

of the

Papers of Andrew Johnson

1987

THE UNIVERSITY OF TENNESSEE PRESS

KNOXVILLE

Copyright © 1987
by The University of Tennessee Press/Knoxville.
All Rights Reserved.
Manufactured in the United States of America.
Cloth: 2nd printing, 1988.
Paper: 1st printing, 1987.

The preparation of this volume was made possible
in part by a grant from the
Program for Editions of the National Endowment for the Humanities,
an independent federal agency.

The paper in this book meets the minimum requirements
of the American National Standard for Permanence
of Paper for Printed Library Materials.

∞

The binding materials have been chosen
for strength and durability.

Library of Congress Cataloging-in-Publication Data

Advice after Appomattox.
  (Special volume no. 1 of the papers of Andrew Johnson)
  Includes index.
  1. Reconstruction.   2. United States—Politics and
government—1865–1869.   I. Simpson, Brooks D., 1957–
II. Graf, LeRoy P., 1915–   .   III. Muldowny, John, 1931–
IV. Series: Special volume . . . of the papers of Andrew
Johnson; no. 1.
E415.6.J652   1987 no. 1 [E668]   973.8′1 s   87–5961
ISBN 0-87049-536-4 (cloth: alk. paper)
ISBN 0-87049-549-6 (pbk.: alk. paper)

FOR

Milton M. Klein

MENTOR, COLLEAGUE, AND FRIEND
EXTRAORDINAIRE

Contents

Illustrations

Preface

With the winding down of the American Civil War in the spring of 1865, it became obvious to all that the principal issues facing the nation were the restoration of the southern states to the Union and the position of blacks in postwar America. Political leaders had never before confronted the problem of readmitting states to the Union. How soon? Under what terms? Set by whom? Which southern whites would participate in the process? What would be the fate of Confederate leaders, military and civil? How would loyalty be defined in an effort to reestablish a dependable electorate? Before military occupation gave way to restored civil governments, white southerners would have to demonstrate that they accepted the results of the war. Not only would they have to repudiate the doctrine of secession, they would have to bow to the fact of emancipation, not merely by accepting the Thirteenth Amendment abolishing slavery, but by revising state laws and constitutions to establish some form of civil rights for the freedmen.

But how loyal was the former Confederate population? To what extent had they accepted the outcome of the war? Would they grant full civil rights to blacks? Should they be forced to provide blacks with land from "abandoned" estates? Should they be made to accept black suffrage, both to protect the former slaves from exploitation and to foster the formation of the Republican party's southern wing? Would white southerners accept these changes willingly, or would they have to be imposed by federal fiat? Broad was the range of difference over these questions in the victorious North. But the 39th Congress had yet to assemble and President Andrew Johnson had refused to call a special session. Before that body would convene in December, many steps would have to be taken by the chief executive affecting these questions. What would he do?

While the problems may have been obvious, the solutions were not, for there was a decided lack of information about conditions in the South. Was the South ready for reunion or was it still defiant even in defeat? Was it repentant or bent on maintaining itself as if the war had never occurred? Would whites accept the fact of emancipation readily, or would they work to restrict black economic and political opportunities? Were blacks ready to exercise their new rights and responsibilities? Did emancipation simply verify white assertions that blacks required the discipline imposed by slavery to work and behave? Did blacks require a period of transition from slavery to freedom? Should the federal government supervise this transition and provide guardianship, or would it be best to let whites and blacks work out their own solutions? Differing viewpoints on these and other questions were understandable, for rumors and misinformation abounded. What emerged then was a confusing mosaic of opinion about the situation in the South.

Advice flooded the White House from all over the United States, much of it conflicting and all of it designed to gain the President's ear. In order to devise a successful policy of reconstruction—or "restoration," the term Johnson preferred—he had to arrive at a proper assessment of conditions at the South. He could draw on several sources of information. Military commanders regularly forwarded reports describing attitudes and events; white southerners, singularly or in petitioning groups, offered varying perspectives as they sought the President's intervention in redressing grievances; later, Johnson's provisional governors would transmit news of political decisions, progress in the constitutional conventions, and their own opinions on the proper course to pursue. Occasionally, even a freedman would beseech Johnson to take a more active role in protecting and promoting the fortunes of southern blacks. The chief executive was also aware of the accounts filed by numerous newspaper correspondents despatched to the late Confederate states and appearing almost daily in northern newspapers. Understandably, these accounts differed in their portrayal of postwar conditions, complicating Johnson's attempt to form a picture of life in the South after Appomattox.

In addition, during the ensuing year, the President was able to draw on the accounts of several emissaries in formulating a policy toward the defeated South. Salmon P. Chase and Carl Schurz, both renowned Radicals, volunteered their services, eager to assume advisory roles to the White House and to shape reconstruction policies. As a counterpoint, Johnson sought his trusted lieutenant, Benjamin C. Truman, close confidant Harvey M. Watterson, and the most famous man in the country, Ulysses S. Grant, to contribute their views on the situation in the South. Between May, 1865, and March, 1866, these five men toured various parts of the South and relayed observations, impressions, and recommendations to the White House. This volume, a compilation of their reports, is intended to make readily available the fruits of this effort to garner information.

The reports reveal and represent conflicting viewpoints and ambiguities about the observations and raise as many questions as they answer. Among these were the capabilities of the freedmen, the degree to which white southerners could be trusted, the differing sensibilities to interracial violence, and the purpose of reconstruction—was it intended to remake southern society or merely to restore it without slavery? In addition, the reports embody biases of the observers themselves. Each of these correspondents let his prejudices, preferences, and concerns—racial, political, and sectional—shape both his perspective of what he saw and how he reported it to Johnson. Some writers hoped to persuade

Johnson to accept their point of view, assuming that once the President shared their vantage point he would also adopt their proposed remedies. Others sought to bolster the President's confidence by reassuring him of the success of his program. A reading of the reports also reveals the difficulties inherent in assessing conflicting evidence, suggesting the frustrations of Washington policy makers in trying to balance various perspectives. As in most fact-finding missions, assessments were influenced by where the observers went and to whom they talked. Individuals who spoke to them also hoped to advance their own views and interests. Prejudices and preferences influenced every report, making it difficult for the reader to discover what was transpiring "at the South."

Such reservations about the objectivity of the correspondents do not necessarily detract from either the accuracy or value of their observations. While at times a writer selectively colored his account in accordance with his aims and hopes, each observer did describe the truth "as he saw it," and refracted through the letters a fairly accurate impression of the attitudes of whites, blacks, and military personnel with whom he spoke. Indeed, Johnson made shrewd use of his familiarity with the attitudes of his envoys, employing conservatives and moderates such as Watterson, Truman, and Grant to counter the charges made by radicals Chase and Schurz.

Gathering information is not enough, for information is only as good as the person who uses it. The recipient has to weigh and evaluate information to compose a composite picture of the situation. These reports present to the reader, as they did to President Johnson, the opportunity to evaluate differing opinions on the attitudes and conditions of the post-Appomattox South. The volume provides a glimpse of some of the raw data, impressions, and recommendations available to Johnson as he evolved what he was proudly to proclaim "my policy," a policy which entangled him in endless controversy for the rest of his presidency.

ACKNOWLEDGMENTS

This, like most editorial projects, has been a cooperative venture, each of the participants contributing to the whole. Simpson has written the introduction to each of the observers' visits, the annotations, and the epilogue; Muldowny has contributed the preface and the prologue; Graf, who originated the undertaking, has served as reader, editor, and general supervisor of the volume.

In compiling the material contained in this volume the editors are greatly indebted to several individuals and institutions for their invaluable contributions. Most noteworthy are the following: the staff of the National Historical Publications and Records Commission, especially Sara Dunlap Jackson; the staff of the Library at the University of

Tennessee, Knoxville; John Y. Simon and David L. Wilson of the Ulysses S. Grant Association; Beverly W. Palmer, editing the Correspondence of Charles Sumner; Enid H. Douglass, formerly of the Papers of Salmon P. Chase; Lynda L. Crist of the Papers of Jefferson Davis; Paul I. Chestnut and his staff at the Manuscripts Division, Library of Congress; Jean V. Berlin, the Papers of William Thornton; Christopher Berkeley, University of Wisconsin-Madison; David K. King, the Free Library of Philadelphia; Mary Ann Gundersen, New Hampshire Historical Society; Madel Morgan, Mississippi Department of Archives and History; and the New-York Historical Society.

As longtime members of the Andrew Johnson Papers Project, associate editor Patricia P. Clark and assistant editor Marion O. Smith contributed their expertise and experience toward this enterprise, including introducing neophyte editors to the tasks before them. Invaluable as always, Patricia J. Anthony labored long hours transcribing documents, making revisions, and raising questions which had escaped the editors' attention. Volunteers Ruth P. Graf and Margaret T. Taylor also aided in the preparation of the volume.

The three agencies most significantly involved in support of the Andrew Johnson Papers are the University of Tennessee, Knoxville, which provides housing for the Project, the services of its Press, and the assistance of its Development Office; the National Historical Publications and Records Commission which makes available generous annual grants; and the National Endowment for the Humanities, which provided support for one of the editors. We also gratefully acknowledge support from the Mary G.K. Fox Charitable Foundation of Greeneville, and from our longtime patroness, Margaret Johnson Patterson Bartlett, the last Johnson descendant of the third generation.

Brooks D. Simpson
LeRoy P. Graf
John Muldowny

Knoxville, Tennessee
September 13, 1986

Editorial Method

The letters in this volume come from the Andrew Johnson Papers in the Library of Congress, except for five: two from records of the War Department and one from Freedmen's Bureau records, both in the National Archives, and one each from the Carl Schurz Papers in the Library of Congress and *Senate Executive Document* No. 2, 39th Congress, 1 Session.

In transcribing, the editors have sought to combine fidelity to the original with consideration for the reader. The orthography is reproduced without change, except where confusion might occur; in such instances bracketed letters and words, or *sic*, are inserted to clarify the meaning. When, in the judgment of the editors, an excision represents a noteworthy alteration in meaning, the omitted word or phrase is printed in angled brackets. All superscript letters have been brought to the line and, except for ordinal numbers, treated as abbreviations with a period. Stationery and telegraph headings, including hours of sending and arrival, have been omitted. In order to conserve space, dateline headings, addresses, salutations, and closings have been rearranged, but nothing has been omitted. Aside from the insertion of bracketed periods or question marks, original punctuation, or lack of it, has been retained. When there is any doubt about the writer's intention with respect to capitalization and punctuation, modern usage has been followed. Information added by the editors is bracketed.

Annotation is designed to provide the reader with information about persons, events, and allusions that will clarify the text of the document. Absence of annotation means that the subject is a matter of general knowledge, that information is unavailable, or that the person or persons are judged to be peripheral to understanding the document. Footnote sources are indicated, unless the information—here introduced as a reminder to the reader—is generally known. The absence of source citations after identifications indicates that the content comes from one or more of the following works: *Dictionary of American Biography*; *Biographical Directory of the American Congress*; *National Cyclopaedia of American Biography*; Ezra J. Warner, *Generals in Blue* or *Generals in Gray*; Mark M. Boatner, *The Civil War Dictionary*; Robert Sobel and John Raimo, eds., *Biographical Directory of the Governors of the United States, 1789–1978*; or Melvin G. Holli and Peter d'A. Jones, eds., *Biographical Directory of American Mayors, 1820–1960: Big City Mayors*.

The Chase and Watterson letters have previously been edited for twentieth-century periodical publication. The former's communications, edited by James E. Sefton, appeared in *Civil War History*, XIII

(1967), 242–64, under the title "Chief Justice Chase as an Advisor on Presidential Reconstruction." Two editors have earlier made Watterson items available. As part of her "Letters from North Carolina to Andrew Johnson," Elizabeth G. McPherson, in the *North Carolina Historical Review*, XXVII (1950), 346–49, 353–55, 358–60, published the communications of June 20, 27, 29, and July 8. Martin Abbott prepared Watterson's two trips as separate articles, which appeared as "A Southerner Views the South, 1865: Letters of Harvey M. Watterson," *Virginia Magazine of History and Biography*, LXVIII (1960), 478–89, containing the letters of June 7, 20, 29, and July 8; and as "The South as Seen by a Tennessee Unionist in 1865: Letters of H. M. Watterson," *Tennessee Historical Quarterly*, XVIII (1959), 148–61, with items of September 26, October 3, 7, 14, 20, and 30.

In addition, the following publications were based on the observations and experiences that produced the letters printed in this volume:

"Report of Carl Schurz on the States of South Carolina, Georgia, Alabama, Mississippi, and Louisiana," *Sen. Ex. Doc.* No. 2, 39 Cong., 1 Sess., 2–105. Also published as Carl Schurz, *Report on the Condition of the South*, in The Arno Press and the New York Times Series *The American Negro: His History and Literature* (New York, 1969).

"A Report from Benjamin C. Truman relative to the condition of the southern people and the States in which the rebellion existed," *Sen. Ex. Doc.* No. 43, 39 Cong., 1 Sess., 1–14.

Joseph H. Mehaffey, ed., "Carl Schurz's Letters from the South," *Georgia Historical Quarterly*, XXXV (1951), 222–57 (letters to the Boston *Advertiser*, dated July 17, 21, and 25, all from Charleston, and July 31 and August 8, both from Savannah).

SYMBOLS

A. Repositories
DLC   Library of Congress, Washington, D.C.
DNA   National Archives, Washington, D.C.

RECORD GROUPS USED
RG56   General Records of the Department of the Treasury
RG94   Records of the Adjutant General's Office, 1780's-1917
RG105   Records of the Bureau of Refugees, Freedmen, and Abandoned Lands
RG107   Records of the Office of the Secretary of War
RG108   Records of the Headquarters of the Army
RG393   Records of United States Continental Commands, 1821–1920

B. Manuscripts

ALS	Autograph Letter Signed
PLS	Printed Letter Signed
Tel	Telegram

ABBREVIATIONS

GENERAL

BRFAL	Bureau of Refugees, Freedmen, and Abandoned Lands
HQ	Headquarters
Lets. Recd.	Letters Received
Misc. Papers	Miscellaneous Papers
Tels. Recd.	Telegrams Received

MILITARY

Adj. Gen.	Adjutant General
Arty.	Artillery
Brig.	Brigadier
Capt.	Captain
Cav.	Cavalry
Co.	Company
Col.	Colonel
CSA	Confederate States of America (Army)
Dept.	Department
Div.	Division
Gen.	General
Inf.	Infantry
Lt.	Lieutenant
Maj.	Major
Rgt.	Regiment
USA	United States of America (Army)
USCT	United States Colored Troops
Vols.	Volunteers

SHORT TITLES

Bancroft, *Schurz Correspondence*	Frederic Bancroft, ed., *Speeches, Correspondence and Political Papers of Carl Schurz* (6 vols., New York, 1913).
Chase Diaries	David Donald, ed., *Inside Lincoln's Cabinet: The Civil War Diaries of Salmon P. Chase* (New York, 1954).

Fleming, *Reconstruction in Alabama* — Walter L. Fleming, *Civil War and Alabama Reconstruction in Alabama* (New York, 1905).

Futrell, Federal Trade — Robert F. Futrell, Federal Trade with the Confederate States, 1861–1865: A Study of Governmental Policy (Ph.D. dissertation, Vanderbilt University, 1950).

JP — Andrew Johnson Papers, Library of Congress. JP refers to the first series only; JP2, etc., to succeeding series.

Johnson Papers — LeRoy P. Graf and Ralph W. Haskins, eds., *The Papers of Andrew Johnson* (7 vols., Knoxville, 1967–).

Long, *Civil War Almanac* — E.B. Long, with Barbara Long, *The Civil War Day by Day: An Almanac, 1861–1865* (New York, 1971).

McCrary, *Lincoln and Reconstruction* — Peyton McCrary, *Abraham Lincoln and Reconstruction: The Louisiana Experiment* (Princeton, 1978).

McPherson, *Great Rebellion* — Edward McPherson, *The Political History of the United States of America During the Great Rebellion* (Washington, D.C., 1865).

McPherson, *Reconstruction* — Edward McPherson, *The Political History of the United States During the Period of Reconstruction* (Washington, D.C., 1880).

Nieman, *To Set the Law in Motion* — Donald G. Nieman, *To Set the Law in Motion: The Freedmen's Bureau and the Legal Rights of Blacks* (Millwood, N.Y., 1979).

OR — *War of the Rebellion: A Compendium of the Official Records of the Union and Confederate Armies* (70 vols. in 128, Washington, D.C., 1880–1901).

OR-Navy — *Official Records of the Union and Confederate Navies in the War of the Rebellion* (30 vols., Washington, D.C., 1894–1927).

Reid, *After the War*

Whitelaw Reid, *After the War: A Tour of the Southern States, 1865–1866*, ed. C. Vann Woodward (New York, 1965 [1866]).

Richardson, *Messages*

James D. Richardson, *A Compilation of the Messages and Papers of the Presidents* (10 vols. [New York], 1911 [1896–1903]).

Schafer, *Intimate Letters*

Joseph Schafer, ed. and trans., *Intimate Letters of Carl Schurz, 1841–1869* (Madison, Wis., 1928).

Schurz, *Reminiscences*

Carl Schurz, *The Reminiscences of Carl Schurz* (3 vols., New York, 1907–8).

Schurz Report

"Report of Carl Schurz on the States of South Carolina, Georgia, Alabama, Mississippi, and Louisiana," *Sen. Ex. Doc.* No. 2, 39 Cong., 1 Sess., 2–105.

Sefton, *Army and Reconstruction*

James E. Sefton, *The United States Army and Reconstruction, 1865–1877* (Baton Rouge, 1967).

Taylor, *Louisiana Reconstructed*

Joe Gray Taylor, *Louisiana Reconstructed, 1863–1877* (Baton Rouge, 1974).

Tunnell, *Crucible of Reconstruction*

Ted Tunnell, *Crucible of Reconstruction: War, Radicalism and Race in Louisiana, 1862–1877* (Baton Rouge, 1984).

Welles Diary

Howard K. Beale, ed., *Diary of Gideon Welles* (3 vols., New York, 1960).

Prologue

The end came so quickly in Virginia that no one was really ready for it. On April 2, 1865, after almost ten months of sparring in the trenches south of Petersburg, Union soldiers swarmed over the Confederate positions and seized the city. Informed of the defeat, Robert E. Lee immediately advised Jefferson Davis and Confederate civil authorities to evacuate Richmond or face capture. The next day, as Lee's tattered graycoats fled westward, units of the all-black XXV Corps entered the capital, the goal of repeated northern offensives for four years. Now the only objective left was the Army of Northern Virginia, and the Yankees took off in an attempt to cut off the Rebels' escape. Within a week the chase was all over; Lee finally surrendered the remnants of his once-mighty army to Ulysses S. Grant at a farmhouse near Appomattox Court House. In the spirit of his generous terms, which required only that Confederates lay down their arms, return home in peace, and observe their paroles, Grant quelled a riotous celebration among his troops, saying, "The war is over. The rebels are our countrymen again."[1]

Grant's simple statement obscured the complexities of the process by which Confederates would become "our countrymen again." Even as northerners celebrated the news of Lee's surrender with illuminations, bonfires, and torchlight parades, many political leaders were debating the proper course to pursue in reconstructing the divided Union. In his second inaugural address, Abraham Lincoln had urged his fellow countrymen to exercise "malice toward none, and charity for all" in an effort to "bind up the nation's wounds." Certainly the terms Grant offered to Lee were a step in that direction. Not only had Grant insisted that Confederate officers retain their sidearms, he pledged that "each officer and man will be allowed to return to his home, not to be disturbed by U.S. authority so long as they observe their paroles and the laws in force where they may reside." Lincoln's approval of the terms—"just the thing!" he exclaimed upon reading them—suggested that reconciliation, not retribution, was foremost in his mind.[2]

Lincoln had been pondering the problems associated with reconstruction for some time. Always the pragmatist, he had refrained from setting down a detailed set of guidelines. During the war he had sanctioned, even fostered, the emergence of unionist state governments in Virginia, Arkansas, Louisiana, and Tennessee; his selection of Tennessee's military governor Andrew Johnson as his running mate in 1864

1. Bruce Catton, *Grant Takes Command* (Boston, 1969), 468.
2. William T. Sherman, *Memoirs* (2 vols., New York, 1875), II, 329.

seemed a vote of confidence in the success of these experiments, although only in Tennessee and Louisiana had these efforts at establishing alternatives shown signs of transcending the status of shadow governments. In December, 1863, Lincoln had announced a plan for amnesty and restoration which looked toward the rapid establishment of unionist governments. Should a tenth of the state's eligible voters declare themselves in favor of a restored government, Lincoln promised to recognize and support it. Congressional Republicans, furious at the ease with which southerners could comply with Lincoln's terms, first passed their own reconstruction bill (which the President pocket-vetoed) and then prevented the seating of senators and representatives elected under Lincoln's government in Louisiana. Other wartime measures, notably emancipation, amnesty, and confiscation, also promised to shape the course of reconstruction, for any policy adopted by the federal government had to take into account the status of over four million free blacks and the treatment of ex-Confederate leaders and followers.

Wartime discussions of reconstruction policy, however, were inevitably tied to the conduct of the war itself. Lenient offers of amnesty and civil government were designed to sap Confederate morale and encourage internal dissent among the graycoats. Emancipation and confiscation policies allowed Grant and his subordinates to strike at southern resources and employ blacks as laborers and soldiers. With Appomattox, these objectives became irrelevant; the creation of stable, loyal, and popular southern state governments became entangled with the impact of emancipation on the South's society, politics, and economy. Moreover, the Washington policy makers had to balance their desire for reconciliation with the demand that "justice" be served, that the freedmen be protected, and that the South not merely be restored but reconstructed, perhaps including punitive measures advocated by some Republicans. With peace at hand, what would Lincoln do? What would congressional Republicans do? And how would white southerners respond?

If his efforts to construct loyal state governments during the conflict seemed hasty and excessively lenient to many Republicans, with the end of the war, Lincoln, conscious of the impact of his wartime experiments, appeared ready to move toward a more comprehensive and rigorous policy which encompassed civil and some qualified political rights for the freedmen. On the day after Lee's surrender, he told Francis Pierpont, governor of the unionist Virginia government, "that he had no plan for reorganization, but must be guided by events."[3] The next evening, addressing a crowd assembled on the White House grounds, Lincoln remarked that reconstruction "is pressed much more closely upon our attention." Acknowledging not only that the issue "is fraught with

3. LaWanda Cox, *Lincoln and Black Freedom* (Columbia, S.C., 1981), 142–43.

great difficulty," but also that northerners disagreed "as to the mode, manner, and means of reconstruction," the President, while defending his efforts in Louisiana, suggested that "so new and unprecedented is the whole case, that no exclusive, and inflexible plan can safely be prescribed as to details and colatterals."[4] In the meantime, prompted by cabinet members Edwin M. Stanton and James Speed, he had had second thoughts about a plan to convene Virginia's Confederate legislators and called off the meeting. On April 14, at his last cabinet meeting, Lincoln urged his counselors to mull over a proposal for reconstruction submitted by Stanton, remembering "that this was the great question now before us, and we must soon begin to act."[5]

The nation's uncertainty about federal policy toward the South was further magnified by the news of Lincoln's assassination. Immediately there was speculation about the response of the new President, Andrew Johnson, to those questions. At his oath-taking ceremony, the new President made only a few brief statements, which, while not very illuminating as to future policy, did make his cabinet, according to Hugh McCulloch, feel "hopeful that he would prove to be a popular and judicious president."[6] Republicans took heart upon recalling some of Johnson's previous public statements. In October, 1864, he had promised Nashville blacks that he would be their "Moses leading them from slavery to freedom";[7] at other times he spoke of breaking up large southern landholdings and distributing them to individual farmers. Nor did Johnson's well-known staunch unionism seem abated. On April 16, after meeting with the congressional Joint Committee on the Conduct of the War, Johnson reiterated to Senator Benjamin Wade that "treason is a crime, and the crime must be punished. Treason must be made infamous and traitors must be impoverished."[8] Although somewhat uncertain, moderate Republicans could be reassured by the President's promise to make some provision for some civil rights for blacks.

Both conservative Republicans and northern Democrats also had reason to believe that Johnson could be counted upon as their ally. With support both in the cabinet and from personal advisers, these two groups hoped that because of the President's previously expressed anti-black biases, his Democratic roots, his affinity for Andrew Jackson, and his penchant for the word restoration rather than reconstruction, he would foster a quick reconciliation of the Union, discourage efforts to enfranchise blacks, and welcome a return of the Democrats to power. Montgomery Blair commented that "the Democracy if they are true to

4. Roy P. Basler, ed., *The Collected Works of Abraham Lincoln* (8 vols., New Brunswick, N.J., 1953), VIII, 399–405.

5. *Welles Diary*, II, 281.

6. Hugh McCulloch, *Men and Measures of Half a Century: Sketches and Comments* (New York, 1888), 376.

7. *Johnson Papers*, VII, 251–53.

8. Allan Nevins, *The War for the Union* (New York, 1971), IV, 342.

their own principles must sustain Andrew Johnson."[9] Finally, while many southerners, regarding Johnson as a turncoat, dreaded the thought of the Tennessean in the White House, others held the conviction that the same statements which had encouraged northern Democrats could also be interpreted as suggesting that reconstruction might be rapid, lenient, and accompanied by minimal social and political change.

With every political group and faction interpreting his statements to fit its own particular hopes and desires, the President quickly moved forward in an effort to formulate postwar policy. Immediately after Johnson's inauguration, Stanton presented him with the two plans of reconstruction which the secretary had drawn up at Lincoln's request. One for Virginia called for the recognition of the Union government established during the war; the other for North Carolina called for a much more comprehensive plan of reorganization which ultimately would set the pattern for all southern states not organized under Lincoln's 10 percent plan.[10] Although the President made no commitments, Radical Republicans were pleased that he at least seemed sympathetic to their objectives.

They were further heartened on the evening of April 21 when Stanton, at Grant's urging, had Johnson hastily call a cabinet meeting to consider an urgent communication from General William T. Sherman in North Carolina. Sherman had just signed an armistice with General Joseph E. Johnston which proposed to end the last Confederate resistance east of the Mississippi. Beyond outlining terms of surrender, his communique provided for federal recognition of existing state governments as soon as their officials swore an oath of allegiance to the United States. Going even further, Sherman's terms called for a general amnesty, a guarantee of property and voting rights for all white southerners, and reestablishment of federal courts in the South. In effect, it turned over political control of the South, at least temporarily, to former Confederates.[11] Johnson immediately dispatched Grant with instructions for Sherman which called for repudiation of the agreement. Stressing that the general had overstepped his bounds, Johnson called for the same surrender terms that Grant had submitted to Lee.[12] For many Radicals, Johnson's response to Stanton's orchestrating of the rebuke to Sherman was further convincing evidence that the President would do their bidding. In addition, the conspicious role which Stanton played in the first weeks of the new administration—his assidious

9. Montgomery Blair to S.L.M. Barlow, April 18, 1865, cited in LaWanda Cox and John H. Cox, *Politics, Principles and Prejudice, 1865–1866* (New York, 1969), 57.

10. Albert Castel, *The Presidency of Andrew Johnson* (Lawrence, Kans., 1979), 22–23.

11. Michael Les Benedict, *A Compromise of Principle: Congressional Republicans and Reconstruction, 1863–1869* (New York, 1974), 101–2.

12. *Welles Diary*, II, 295–96.

pursuit and arrest of the Lincoln conspirators, the capture of Jefferson Davis, and the subsequent preparation for the military trial of the assassins—further reinforced the Radicals' belief that the new administration would be favorable to their cause.[13]

Another prominent Republican who tried to woo Johnson to the Radical cause was Massachusetts senator Charles Sumner. Beginning almost immediately after the inauguration, the abolitionist advocate seized any pretense to press his views on the new President, and described the President's attitude as "excellent and even sympathetic, without any uncomfortable reticence." Often Sumner was accompanied by Chief Justice Salmon P. Chase. On one such visit the three men discussed the question of black suffrage. Once again Sumner came away confident that "our ideas will prevail."[14] Despite the senator's optimism, Johnson took no immediate steps to implement black suffrage; believing that only the states could confer voting privileges. Nevertheless, even though the President had stopped short of advocating the ballot for blacks, Sumner and other Radicals felt confident that they still had the President's ear.

On several occasions Johnson denounced traitors and treason most vehemently, increasing the apprehension of southern whites. On April 21, speaking to an Indiana delegation led by Governor Oliver P. Morton, the President seemed to reiterate his previously announced intention that "treason must be punished and impoverished, . . . their social power must be destroyed." But he tempered his comments by adding that "leniency, conciliation, and amnesty" should be extended "to the thousands whom they [the leaders] have misled and deceived."[15] Several times during April he repeated these remarks to other delegations, but he was always careful to differentiate punishment of the Confederate leadership and the rank and file.

Democrats and Republicans were equally certain that Johnson was their friend. Almost all northern newspapers, whether Republican or Democratic, praised him and clamored for his favor. Part of this great public outpouring of trust and confidence was based upon his record as wartime governor of Tennessee, part from his reputation as a staunch unionist, and part from the hope that, like a previous Tennessean, Andrew Jackson, he would provide a strong hand for control of the postwar South. In the early months of 1865 the Democratic party was in the doldrums following the vindication of Republican policy both at the polls and on the battlefield. By the end of April it had virtually adopted Andrew Johnson as its new source of political strength. Democratic

13. Benjamin P. Thomas and Harold Hyman, *Stanton: The Life and Times of Lincoln's Secretary of War* (New York, 1962), 405–17.

14. Edward L. Pierce, *Memoir and Letters of Charles Sumner* (4 vols., Boston, 1893), IV, 241.

15. *Johnson Papers*, VII, 612–13.

senators and congressmen called upon the President, the northern Democratic press sang his praises, and Democrats everywhere began to rally to his side. While some Republicans expressed misgivings about the possible influence of Democrats with the President, Johnson retained his popularity with all factions of both political parties.[16]

Northern Democrats, conservative Republicans, and southerners hailed the President's utterances, while moderate Republicans considered them to be at least a promising beginning. Only the Radicals might have been disappointed by his failure to mention black suffrage, but they still held out hope that they could persuade Johnson to advocate at least limited enfranchisement of the freedmen. Too, he enjoyed the support of many of the Union army's most prominent generals. In short, Andrew Johnson seemed to be the man of the hour.[17] At this time of great personal popularity, numerous offers of advice on the southern question came in from both extremists and moderates, Republicans and Democrats. To make wise decisions he, like others, felt the need for fuller information about conditions in the defeated South. As the Chicago *Tribune* reminded readers, "the most important feature attending the regeneration of these States is the temper and disposition of the Southern people."[18] Only days before the assassination, Lincoln had expressed his concern that he "could get no information as to the feeling of the people."[19] During the year following Appomattox five men— Salmon P. Chase, Harvey M. Watterson, Carl Schurz, Benjamin C. Truman, and Ulysses S. Grant—traveled through the South with the purpose of providing the President with observations and advice. The dispatches which follow constitute the results of their labors.

16. Eric L. McKitrick, *Andrew Johnson and Reconstruction* (Chicago, 1960), 67–76.
17. J. Michael Quill, *Prelude to the Radicals: The North and Reconstruction During 1865* (Washington, D.C., 1980), 44–53.
18. Chicago *Tribune*, April 26, 1865.
19. Charles H. Ambler, *Francis H. Pierpont: Union War Governor of Virginia and Father of West Virginia* (Chapel Hill, 1937), 257.

Advice After Appomattox

LETTERS TO ANDREW JOHNSON,
1865–1866

Salmon P. Chase:
The Quest for Influence

Among the individuals vying for Johnson's attention during the new President's initial weeks in office was Chief Justice Salmon P. Chase, well known for his advocacy of emancipation and black equality. Indeed, his entire political career mirrored the emergence of antislavery as a political issue.[1] As a Cincinnati lawyer, he gained renown for defending blacks; as a politician in the Liberty party and its successor, the Free Soil party, he won election to the U.S. Senate in 1849 and was elected Ohio's first Republican governor in 1855. His chief contribution to the cause was the formulation of a political and legal argument against slavery, demonstrating his preference for legislative action over moral preaching as the primary tool to achieve abolition. His reading of the intentions of the framers of the Constitution convinced him that they had no desire to use that document to offer protection for slavery. Given this interpretation, he urged abolitionists to strike at slavery wherever it was subject to federal action—including territorial expansion and the interstate slave trade—to achieve "the absolute and unconditional divorce of the Government from slavery."[2] Not only did such an interpretation spur political action against slavery, it encouraged northerners whose antislavery leanings were held in check by a belief that the Constitution protected slavery to join the movement without the anxiety that they were betraying fundamental law. He also helped popularize the notion of a "slave power conspiracy," asserting that slaveholders were subverting republican institutions for the benefit of "the peculiar institution," most notably when in 1854 he coauthored the "Appeal of the Independent Democrats," affixing the conspiracy label to Stephen A. Douglas's plan for territorial organization.[3]

The Republican triumph of 1860 meant further advancement, for Lincoln offered him the opportunity to head the Treasury Department. In the cabinet he constantly pressed for emancipation, taking especial interest in the establishment of a black colony on the Sea Islands off the coast of South Carolina and in the reorganization of Louisiana. As Lin-

1. Basic sources for Chase's life include Robert B. Warden, *An Account of the Private Life and Public Services of Salmon Portland Chase* (Cincinnati, 1874); Jacob W. Schuckers, *The Life and Public Services of Salmon Portland Chase* (New York, 1874); Albert B. Hart, *Salmon Portland Chase* (Boston, 1899); David Donald, ed., *Inside Lincoln's Cabinet: The Civil War Diaries of Salmon P. Chase* (New York, 1954).

2. Eric Foner, *Free Soil, Free Labor, Free Men: The Ideology of the Republican Party Before the Civil War* (New York, 1970), 79.

3. *Ibid.*, 87–98, 255–56; see also Richard H. Sewell, *Ballots For Freedom: Antislavery Politics in the United States, 1837–1860* (New York, 1976).

coln noted, Chase was "a man of unbounded ambition . . . working all his life to become President"; the two men clashed repeatedly over war policy, and in 1864 the railsplitter accepted his secretary's resignation with relief. Despite their personal differences, Lincoln respected Chase's legal knowledge. With the death of Chief Justice Roger B. Taney late in 1864, the President saw an opportunity to replace the author of the Dred Scott decision with a man whose commitment to ending slavery was unquestioned. Despite reservations that Chase might "neglect the place in his strife and intrigue to make himself President," Lincoln submitted Chase's name as Taney's successor on December 6, 1864; the Senate immediately confirmed the nomination. With Chase as chief justice, Republicans felt they could rest assured that the Supreme Court would no longer obstruct either the war effort or emancipation policy.[4]

By 1865 the chief justice had formulated a rather simple plan for reconstruction based upon the enfranchisement of the freedmen. Armed with the ballot, blacks could not only protect themselves through legislation, they could also overcome the votes of white secessionists and join with southern unionists in creating a loyalist majority. He had pushed for the adoption of his policy in Louisiana during the war; now, with the end in sight, he redoubled his efforts to ensure that his views would win wide approval. Some proponents of black suffrage had suggested that black soldiers had earned the right to vote by demonstrating their loyalty on the battlefield; by assuming that all blacks were necessarily loyal, Chase expanded on this justification to advocate enfranchisement. While he asserted that the measure was one "of simple justice," he preferred to cite its advantages in assisting reconstruction, adhering to both legal and practical reasoning to drive his point home.[5]

In pursuit of this goal Chase was considering a tour of the Atlantic seaboard, ostensibly to make arrangements for the reopening of federal courts and the reestablishment of trade, but in reality to take a first hand look at conditions and prospects in the South. Others were interested in accompanying him, notably the Reverend Richard Fuller, pastor of the Seventh Baptist Church of Baltimore. Once a proslavery advocate and owner of a plantation on the Sea Islands, Fuller had recanted his views and was curious to see how his former hands were prospering as freed people. Visiting the minister at his Baltimore residence in early April, the chief justice repeated his opinion that "the only solid foundation of social order and political prosperity was universal suffrage," basing his argument on the need to establish loyal southern state governments: "To deny to those who had been loyal to the country—and eminently loyal—a right to a voice in the affairs of the country they had helped to save would be condemned by all impartial men;

4. *Chase Diaries*, 223–25, 260.
5. *Ibid.*, 264.

while the securing to them of the ballot would save us from much discord, violence and disorder."[6]

Events in southern Virginia were about to force the hands of Washington policy makers. On April 9 Ulysses S. Grant accepted the surrender of Robert E. Lee and his army. Two days later, while most Washingtonians celebrated the news, Chase decided to take up his pen and inflict Lincoln once more with his views on the future of the South, claiming that the "easiest & safest way" to inaugurate reconstruction would be "the enrollment of the loyal citizens without regard to color." Such an approach, he argued, was recommended by its "simplicity, facility, & above all, justice." In line with his constitutionalist approach, he silently refused to use the term "black suffrage" or any of its variants: by basing his proposal upon "loyalty" he attempted to slide around the issue of race through careful use of language. The chief justice elaborated his argument in a second letter composed the next day, this time with emphasis upon Louisiana, whose readmission had been a pet project with him. In the meantime he had read Lincoln's April 11 address on Louisiana, and while he was glad that Lincoln was now publicly pondering whether to enfranchise literate blacks and black veterans, he was sorry that the President "is not yet ready for universal or at least equal suffrage."[7]

Returning from Baltimore on April 14, Chase thought of going to the White House to discuss reconstruction with Lincoln, but "felt reluctant to call lest my talk might annoy him and do harm rather than good." Events that night at Ford's Theater meant that he would have to begin anew in his quest for influencing the formulation of policy. Of Andrew Johnson he knew little beyond the outlines of the Tennessean's public career, although he had witnessed Johnson's bumbling speech during the inauguration ceremonies in March. Still, he had missed no opportunity to flatter the self-proclaimed plebeian in the past, making sure to applaud his strong unionism. "God offers men opportunities: those who wisely use them are great," he had written Johnson in 1863. At the time he was urging the military governor to assist blacks as they began to work as free people in Tennessee; now he would try to ingratiate himself with the incoming President to secure black suffrage. After Chase swore in Johnson on April 15, the new chief executive asked whether he should make some remarks. The chief justice seized the opportunity, advising Johnson to issue a brief public statement, and dashed off to prepare some comments at Johnson's suggestion. When Chase returned an hour later, he discovered that the gathering had moved to the Treasury Department to hold a cabinet meeting. That evening Chase read that Johnson had responded to the assemblage after

6. *Ibid.*, 264.
7. Chase to Lincoln, April 11, 12, 1865, Lincoln Papers, LC; *Chase Diaries*, 266.

Salmon P. Chase.
Courtesy of The National Archives

the chief justice had departed. The President's action—asking for advice without promising to abide by it—was a hint of things to come. Undeterred, Chase enclosed his draft in a note to Johnson the next day: "It may be of no use to you, but will show my wish to serve you."[8]

Over the next two weeks the chief justice visited Johnson several times, always with reconstruction in mind. He came away from his first visit to Johnson's room at the Kirkwood House convinced that the new President "seems thoroughly in earnest and much of the same mind with myself." Several days later he returned with Massachusetts senator Charles Sumner, another leading Radical. They once again pressed the topic of black suffrage. Johnson replied that "all loyal people, without distinction of color, must be treated as citizens, and must take part in any proceedings for reorganization." He thought, however, such a movement "should appear to proceed from the people," to avoid party strife. Chase seized upon Johnson's reservations. The chief justice mentioned his forthcoming trip along the South Atlantic seaboard. Why not use this tour to drum up support for such a movement? The President agreed, and, according to Sumner, permitted Chase "to say . . . what the President desires, and to do everything he can to promote organization without distinction of color." As the two Radicals prepared to depart, Johnson declared, "There is no difference between us."[9]

Believing that the news of Joseph E. Johnston's surrender on April 26 "put a new face on affairs," Chase went to see Johnson once more before leaving, carrying with him the draft of a speech on reconstruction for the President to peruse. Once more he reiterated his desire that "the loyal colored men" be recognized as citizens "entitled to the right of suffrage." Johnson asked Chase to read the draft out loud, then commented that while he agreed "to all you say," he thought it impossible to issue "such a document" at the moment: "I am new and untried and cannot venture what I please." Despite Chase's pleading and prodding, Johnson refused to budge, but Chase came away from the meeting optimistic about the future. "I almost hoped the President's reluctance was conquered," he wrote in his diary. Writing to abolitionist editor Theodore Tilton, Chase was more reassuring, reporting that Johnson "does not materially differ from me except as to the time of action. My time is *now*. All good men should try, by cordial support and friendly cheer, to make him feel that *now* is the safe time and best time." Perhaps evidence gathered from the tour and skillfully presented would do the trick.[10]

8. *Ibid.*, 266, 269; Chase to Johnson, September 4, 1863, *Johnson Papers*, VI, 365; Chase to Johnson, April 16, 1865, *ibid.*, VII, 564.

9. *Chase Diaries*, 269; Edward L. Pierce, *Memoir and Letters of Charles Sumner* (4 vols., Boston, 1893), IV, 242–43.

10. *Chase Diaries*, 271–72; Chase to Theodore Tilton, May 1, 1865, New-York Historical Society.

Sumner freely admitted that Chase's journey, far from being a mere tour of observation, was motivated by the need to win Johnson over. To English liberal John Bright he wrote that the chief justice "will on his way touch the necessary strings, so far as he can. I anticipate much from this journey. His opinions are fixed, and he is well informed with regard to those of the President." Incautiously he made a similar explanation to Secretary of the Navy Gideon Welles; "Sumner assures me Chase has gone into Rebeldom to promote negro suffrage," the gruff cabinet officer scribbled in his diary. "I have no doubt that Chase has that and other schemes for Presidential preferment in hand in this voyage."[11] Probably he confided his suspicions to his superior.

On May 1 Chase and his entourage—including his daughter Nettie, the Reverend Dr. Fuller, special treasury agent William P. Mellen, and reporter Whitelaw Reid of the Cincinnati *Gazette*—departed Washington on the *Northerner* for Norfolk. Reid was prepared to furnish his Radical organ with a first-hand account of the expedition: the next year he would publish his observations, along with the results of subsequent journeys, in book form under the title *After the War: A Tour of the Southern States, 1865–1866*. First stop was Norfolk, Virginia. Chase conferred with General George H. Gordon about the transition from military to civil rule. He also met with Lucius H. Chandler, U.S. district attorney, who expressed concern that the unionist minority in the state needed to be protected from a rebel resurgence in politics. Disfranchisement seemed the only answer; and yet, as Reid noted, "it remains to be seen how long a minority, however loyal, can govern, in a republican country." The reporter also followed Chase to Fortress Monroe, where they visited a black school. Like many Americans, the chief justice saw education as a panacea for the freedmen; books and ballots would be the keys to advancement and self-protection. Reid also thought that it would imbue blacks with responsibility; they "need to be taught—that liberty means, not idleness, but merely work for themselves instead of work for others; and that, in any event, it means always work." They had to be left "to take care of themselves." There was no hint here of government intervention, political or economic, or an expanded federal responsibility to oversee the transition from slavery to freedom.[12]

Transferring to the revenue cutter *Wayanda*, Chase and company soon departed Virginia for Beaufort, North Carolina. There the chief justice encountered state senator Michael F. Arendell, described by Reid as "a large, heavily and coarsely-built man" with "the inevitable bilious look, ragged clothes and dirty shirt." Anxious to discover Johnson's policy, Arendell sought out the chief justice for a talk. Chase, disclaim-

11. Pierce, *Sumner*, IV, 242; *Welles Diary*, II, 304.
12. Chase to Tilton, May 1, 1865, New-York Historical Society; Reid, *After the War*, 12–18, 20.

ing knowledge of the President's plan, wanted to probe his visitor for signs of resurgent unionism. "Oh, well, Sir, we all went out unwillingly, you know," Arendell replied, "and most of us are very glad to get back." Although the legislator admitted that the South was "whipped," when Chase asked whether the former Confederates would submit to whatever terms Johnson proposed, the state senator sputtered, "No, sir-oh, ah-yes, any terms that could be honorably offered to a proud, high-minded people!" One of Arendell's compatriots then made it clear that such conditions did not include allowing blacks to vote: "I'd emigrate, sir. Yes, sir, I'd leave this government *and go north!*"[13]

A comparison of the accounts of this exchange offered by Chase and Reid illustrates how the observers' objectives and prejudices affected their description of the conversation. The chief justice informed the President in his first letter that while his visitors wished to retain control over reorganization, they "did not dissent" from returning the right of suffrage to North Carolina freedmen that had been taken away in 1835; furthermore, "they would acquiese in any mode of reorganization rather than see any more rebellion." Obviously he was trying to coax the President into extending suffrage to blacks by suggesting that he had total freedom of action and that southerners would not resist whatever policy he imposed. While he admitted to Secretary of War Edwin M. Stanton that whites "would all like that restoration best which would give *them* most power & place . . . they will just as clearly accommodate themselves to any mode of reorganization," including black suffrage. He added, however, "It is clear to me that the national Government must *take* or *suggest* the initiative." Reid, seeking to uncover signs of continued rebel recalcitrance, discerned that the phrase "honorable terms" reserved to southerners the right to reject "dishonorable terms." Further, "It was easy to see that the old political tricks were not forgotten, and that the first inch of wrong concession would be expected to lead the way to many an ell." And, far from concluding, as did Chase, that Arendell and friends "did not dissent" from the idea of black suffrage, Reid made it clear that they did indeed dissent—vehemently.[14]

Bad weather forced the *Wayanda* to remain in Beaufort Harbor. There Chase was joined by General William T. Sherman, who had also decided to wait out the storm before continuing on to Washington. The general was still fuming over Stanton's treatment of him in abrogating his surrender agreement with Joseph E. Johnston. "I fancied the country wanted peace," he growled. "If they don't, let them raise more soldiers." The chief justice was more interested in persuading Sherman of the need for black suffrage than in placating his wounded pride. The warrior demurred: "I am not yet prepared to receive the negro on terms

13. *Ibid.*, 23–27.
14. Chase to Johnson, May 4, 1865; Chase to Stanton, May 5, 1865, Stanton Papers, LC; Reid, *After the War*, 24.

of political equality for the reason that it will arouse passions and prejudices at the North" and "will revive the war and spread its field of
operations." Sherman, for one, had had enough of war. He knew that
racism still ran deep in many whites, North as well as South: "we cannot combat existing ideas with force."[15]

Unable to convert Sherman, Chase began to work on General John
M. Schofield, who had remained in North Carolina in command of occupation forces. The chief justice set forth the policy favored by him
and others "who think as I do," including (so he believed) Andrew
Johnson. The President, according to Chase, "desires the earliest possible loyal reorganization of the late insurgent states," including the suffrage requirements in force before 1835 in North Carolina—which
would enfranchise freed blacks.[16] The chief justice was engaging in a
rather sly attempt to establish policy, telling his correspondents in the
South that Johnson supported Chase's concept of reconstruction while
writing the President that black suffrage was not only feasible but necessary, hoping thereby to create a consensus for his policy where none
existed. Ironically, Johnson and generals such as Sherman and Schofield
did share many assumptions on the proper course of action, but their
perception of the situation did not encompass Chase's vision.

Schofield wanted nothing to do with Chase's policy. True, he agreed
that southerners "are now in a mood to accept anything in reason,"
and that civil reorganization should take place under military supervision. But "anything in reason" did not include black suffrage. Two
days after sending Chase a non-committal thank you note, he confided
to Grant his belief that the chief justice's policy "would, in my opinion,
lead to disastrous results," due to its lack of constitutional legitimacy
and the "absolute unfitness of the negroes, as a class, for any such
responsibility." Indeed, the freedmen "do not even know the meaning of the freedom that has been given them, and are much astonished
when informed that it does not mean that they are to live in idleness
and be fed by the Government." Enfranchising blacks would also
alienate white unionists, weakening the prospect for a successful re-
habilitation of the southern states. "Yet if a policy so opposed to my
views as that proposed by Mr. Chase is to be adopted," he told his
commander, "I respectfully suggest that I am not the proper person to
carry it out."[17] It was a measure of Chase's capacity for self-delusion that
the chief justice told Johnson that Schofield would "be well trusted"
with command of North Carolina.[18] The President could indeed trust

15. *Ibid.*, 32; Chase to Sherman, May 6, 1865, W.T. Sherman Papers, LC; Sherman
to Chase, May 6, 1865, *OR*, Ser. 1, Vol. XLVII, Pt. III, 410.

16. Chase to Schofield, May 7, 1865, *ibid.*, 427.

17. Schofield to Chase, May 8, 1865, *ibid.*, 440; Schofield to Grant, May 10, 1865,
ibid., 461–62. Grant endorsed Schofield's views: Grant to Schofield, May 18, 1865,
ibid., 529.

the general to carry out a conservative policy; it was Chase's trust that was misplaced.

Determined to find support for his views, Chase continued to move south along the coast with mixed results. At Fort Fisher, he conferred with General Joseph R. Hawley, a Connecticut Republican, who agreed that most southerners would accept any terms and were anxious to discover what Johnson wanted.[19] But others offered less hope. Reid listened as J.S. Pennington, editor of the Raleigh *Progress*, conceded that whites would accept black suffrage only as a last resort if the alternative was continued uncertainty and delay in restoring civil government.[20] Bartholomew F. Moore, a prominent Whig lawyer, pushed for a program which would not only exclude black suffrage, but would allow southern states to frame legislation regulating black labor. A third North Carolinian, Colonel John A. Baker, also spoke with Chase and Reid. Apparently Baker believed he could play a leading role in the restoration process, for he had already corresponded with noted legal theorist Francis Leiber on black suffrage and Sumner had read Baker's letter to Johnson.[21] Here again accounts differ: the chief justice proclaimed that Baker was ready "to take an active part in the regeneration of North Carolina on the basis of universal suffrage," while the reporter merely recorded that Baker was not "so peremptory in his condemnation of negro suffrage" as Moore. Indeed, at least one northern reporter at Raleigh questioned the entire purpose of interviewing only a few self-selected citizens, expressing doubt "as to the possibility of ascertaining the true state of public feelings in the state by such means, so as to be able intelligently to shape any future policy upon it." And sometimes opinions changed. Within weeks Pennington came out foursquare against black suffrage, claiming that he told Chase that white southerners "would be opposed to giving the right of suffrage to the freed negro, and that should the general government attempt to force it upon them, they would feel aggrieved and mortified."[22]

Satisfied in his own mind that North Carolinians would accept black

18. Chase to Johnson, May 17, 1865. The chief justice thought that most military commanders advocated black suffrage. "Of course those who entertain it feel different degrees of certainty or expectation, but with almost all it is quite strong." Chase to Stanton, May 20, 1865, Stanton Papers, LC.

19. Hawley to J.A. Campbell, May 11, 1865, *OR*, Ser. 1, Vol. XLVII, Pt. III, 471–72.

20. Reid, *After the War*, 43–44. Pennington was less cooperative concerning other aspects of Yankee occupation, especially the presence of bluecoat soldiers; within days Schofield reprimanded him for publishing editorials critical of military rule, arguing, "Such grumbling is intolerable ingratitude." Schofield to Pennington, May 10, 1865, *OR*, Ser. 1, Vol. XLVII, Pt. III, 458.

21. Reid, *After the War*, 43–45; Pierce, *Sumner*, IV, 423.

22. Chase to Johnson, May 8, 1865; New York *Tribune*, May 13, 1865; Howard P. Raper, *William W. Holden: North Carolina's Political Enigma* (Chapel Hill, 1985), 71.

Whitelaw Reid.
Courtesy of The Library of Congress

suffrage, Chase departed for South Carolina, where blacks made up over half the adult male population. After interviews with white and black leaders at Charleston, he attended a meeting of blacks at Zion Church, where General Rufus Saxton had assembled thousands of freed people, "with the flattest noses and the wooliest heads, I ever saw," scribbled Reid. Unable to resist the temptation to speak, Chase delivered what Reid characterized as a "familiar and fatherly talk to helpless negroes." A look at the speech, however, suggests that it was more than that. After immodestly outlining his own central role in advocating emancipation, he argued that since blacks had participated in the struggle to save the Union, they should "partake of its fruits" as well. "Shall not the ballot—the freedman's weapon in peace—replace the bayonet—the freedman's weapon in war?" He urged his audience to work hard and "make proofs of honesty, sobriety, and good will" to "save yourselves and fulfill the best hopes of your friends." As Chase concluded his remarks, the blacks cheered and applauded him. Reid overheard one announce, "'T isn't only what he says, but its de man what says it. He don't talk for nuffin, and his words hab weight." One white staff officer preferred to compare the chief justice to the speaker who preceded him, Major Martin L. Delaney, a black officer, concluding that it "made almost as striking an argument against the equality of the races as I ever saw."[23]

Chase and others preferred to emphasize the distance blacks had traveled from slavery to freedom. The party soon headed toward the coast south of the city to survey the black communities at Port Royal. As secretary of the treasury under Lincoln, Chase had been instrumental in establishing free black communities on the Union-occupied Sea Islands. Now, some three years later, he was able to judge the result first hand. The first stop was Dr. Fuller's old plantation at Beaufort. Fuller remarked that he "never saw the slaves of Beaufort so well clad, or seemingly so comfortable." The freed people clustered around their former master, greeting him enthusiastically and listening attentively as he reiterated Chase's message of hard work. The chief justice chimed in, advocating black suffrage once more. Convinced that the free labor experiment was indeed proving successful, the company traveled to other settlements aboard Captain Robert Small's *The Planter*, and then de-

---

What Pennington actually *did* say to Chase became a point of contention in North Carolina. See the Wilmington *Herald*, June 20, 1865.

23. Reid, *After the War*, 79–83, 581–86. Saxton's brother later estimated the crowd at 6,000. J.W. Saxton Diary, May 14, 1865, Saxton Family Papers, Yale University; Worthington C. Ford, ed., *War Letters, 1862–1865, of John Chipman Gray and John Codman Ropes* (Boston, 1927), 488. Gray, stationed at Hilton Head, also reported, "I heard Judge Chase say that he was authorized by the President to declare that he (the President) would like to have negro suffrage established, but he would not say that he would not admit the states without it." *Ibid.*, 486.

parted for Savannah. Entering Savannah harbor the next day, they passed a steamer taking Jefferson Davis north to Fortress Monroe.[24]

At Savannah, Chase observed a repetition of his experiences at Charleston, although he did manage to forego addressing meetings. White leaders wanted to retain power, while black leaders asked for the vote, assuring the chief justice, "We know who our friends are!" Ex-Confederates eagerly awaited news of the President's policy, assuming that their submission would halt the confiscation process. "The simple truth is," wrote Reid, "they stand ready to claim everything, if permitted, and to accept anything, if required." From Savannah, Chase toured the Florida coast, and was flattered to administer the oath of office to Fernandina's new mayor, Adolphus Mot, who had once tutored Chase's children. The chief justice was pleased to note that blacks had voted in Mot's election. Then it was off to Cuba for a short excursion, with plans to return to Mobile. "I begin to be very anxious to get back to the North," Chase wrote Johnson.[25]

As Sumner had warned Welles, Chase's letters to Johnson consistently stressed the chief justice's belief that enfranchising blacks was essential to the success of reconstruction. Suspecting that the President might hesitate advocating such a bold policy, Chase sought to portray the measure as safe, necessary, and constitutional, and minimized considerations concerning the reaction of southern whites by asserting that they would accept whatever terms Johnson offered. "You *can* do what you think right & do it safely," he concluded, no doubt hoping that the President shared his notion of what was "right."[26] In the process, Chase freely interpreted his conversations with southern whites in order to discover support for black suffrage. An ex-rebel's silence was reported as a lack of dissent; a willingness to consider the proposition was cited as evidence of enlightenment and loyalty. By assuring the President that southern whites would accept black suffrage, Chase strove to allay what he perceived as Johnson's reluctance to act.

Aware that opponents of black suffrage questioned the ex-slave's ability to act responsibly and intelligently, the chief justice presented evidence to contradict these charges and to counter reservations about the freedmen's intelligence, willingness to work, and desire for self-improvement. He capped his plea for black enfranchisement by asserting that only black votes could assure the formation of loyal state governments in the former Confederacy, allowing blacks to resist resurgent disloyalty as well as offering protection for themselves and their white allies. In his attentiveness to black suffrage, Chase neglected the question of land redistribution. True, he testified to the freedman's willingness to work hard and praised the black farms surrounding Port

24. Reid, *After the War*, 121, 134.
25. *Ibid.*, 142–43, 150–52, 155; Chase to Johnson, May 23, 1865.
26. Chase to Johnson, May 4, 1865.

Royal, but said little about helping blacks obtain more land. Perhaps he believed that enfranchisement was the key, with economic power following political power. In this respect he differed from many of his Radical friends, who gave land redistribution equal billing with political privileges. The chief justice also apparently envisioned a rather rapid reconstruction under military supervision, with the explicit acknowledgment "that the arrangement is temporary & only auxiliary to reorganization."[27]

Chase was not the only person writing to Johnson about his trip. Letters made their way to Johnson's desk which warned the President that Chase was planning a run at the White House. "From this man you have more to fear than any other man in the nation," one businessman wrote. "He is a restless perturbed spirit, whose vaulting ambition knows no bounds," a man who acts "upon the principle that corruption *wins more* than honey."[28] Conservative unionist Harrison Reed told Montgomery Blair that the chief justice's trip to Florida "was for no other purpose than to revive the effort to secure this state for his future purposes & against the policy of the administration." According to Reed, Chase was filling federal posts with "his corrupt tools" ready to carry out "his nefarious plans," including the imposition of black suffrage. Blair forwarded Reed's missive to Johnson, noting, "These Chase vermin he speaks of should be squelched out summarily."[29] Even an observer who relayed to the President Chase's "sincere friendship for you" wondered whether "the Chief Justice was looking forward to the vote of Florida one of these days."[30]

Newspapers had been speculating on the reasons for Chase's trip. First reports had stated that he was simply interested in getting a head start on reorganizing federal district courts. Given the chief justice's reputation for political intrigue, however, it was not long before reporters assigned a more personal motive to the tour. On May 20, the New York *Herald*, citing a letter Chase wrote to an Ohio politician, speculated that the chief justice was attempting to foster a realignment of parties by uniting Radicals and Democrats with liberal racial views, bringing together men who shared views on economic issues such as the tariff and monetary policy. "The fact of the matter is, he is in search of his old friends in the South." News of Chase's Sea Islands speech appeared to confirm this analysis. The *Herald* criticized the speech, and described the black audience as "promiscuous": two days later it denounced the chief justice as "the great negro-worshipper," and characterized the trip as a "stumping tour." The Democratic New York *World*

27. Chase to Johnson, May 12, 17, 21, 1865.

28. R.W. Latham to Johnson, June 21, 1865, Johnson Papers, LC.

29. Harrison Reed to Montgomery Blair, June 26, 1865, and Blair endorsement, n.d., *ibid.*

30. J. George Harris to Johnson, June 9, 1865, *ibid.*

jumped all over Chase for "perambulating a disquieted portion of the country, making harangues on a disturbing question," citing the action of blacks in breaking up a meeting of Charleston whites opposed to black suffrage just prior to his arrival.[31]

"I could write a great deal more, but it would do no good," Chase told the President during his tour.[32] He did not suspect how close he was to the truth. The chief justice and his entourage visited Cuba in late May and returned to Mobile just in time to receive word of Johnson's two May 29 proclamations, setting forth his pardon policy and reconstruction program. Chase was disappointed: the President had ignored his advice about enfranchising blacks, and had bypassed other recommendations. He gave up submitting more reports, concluding that it would be a fruitless exercise.[33]

Although he ceased writing Johnson, Chase continued his tour through Mobile, New Orleans, and then up the Mississippi and Ohio rivers to Cincinnati in June. There he wrote Sumner that he was "profoundly impressed" that the President had committed "a great mistake" in failing to include blacks in the restoration process. "The vanquished rebels were ready to accept, though of course reluctantly, universal suffrage—a large portion of the loyal whites regarded it essential to their own safety." Two weeks later he told his private secretary that Johnson "in saying that the loyal people constitute the state & must reorganize it & then saying that the loyal blacks shall have no part in the reorganization . . . seems to me to contradict himself."[34] Of course the President saw no such contradiction; his definition of "loyal" simply did not include the freedmen. Despite the clever arguments presented in his letters, Chase had in no way modified the President's convictions.

31. New York *Herald*, May 2, 20, 22, 24, 1865; New York *World*, May 22, 1865.

32. Chase to Johnson, May 12, 1865. Chase had also asked Stanton to look at the letters: "They give the best views I am able to form." Chase to Stanton, May 20, 1865, Stanton Papers, LC.

33. Sumner to Carl Schurz, October 20, 1865, Bancroft, *Schurz Correspondence*, I, 276.

34. Chase to Sumner, June 25, 1865, and Chase to J.W. Schuckers, July 7, 1865, Chase Papers, LC.

Letters

Beaufort, N.C. May 4, 1865.

My dear Sir,

I was at Norfolk on Tuesday Evening & left Fortress Monroe Wednesday Morning.

Gen Gordon[1] at Norfolk seemed a good deal embarrassed by the peculiar relations of the civil & military authorities. He was much gratified to learn that the loyal government of Virginia under Gov. Pierpont[2] was to be recognized and sustained. Gov. P— had written to him to know whether he saw any objection to the resumption of their jurisdiction of the State Courts, and he desired to know my opinion concerning this. I felt that it was not a matter free from doubt; but said that I could see no objection to it so long as the Courts did not oppose themselves to the military authorities; but that these, in case of conflict, must be supreme, until the President should see fit to declare the insurrection at an end & the civil government fully reestablished[.] This, I supposed, the President would do as soon as in his own judgment & in that of the Executive of Virginia, the actual State of affairs should warrant it. In the meantime, I suggested, that he should write to Gov. Pierpont for a copy of the Amended Constitution and have a large edition printed for general distribution, in order that the people generally might be informed in respect to the fundamental law under which they were to live.

It seems to me that the sooner Gov. Pierpont goes to Richmond now, & the fact is made known to Every body that the people are expected to respect the loyal government, the better.[3] They cannot know too soon that Neither Governor, Judges or Legislators—neither the Executive, the Judiciary or the Legislature—deriving state existence from any source while the state was in rebellion can be recognized by the National Government.

We reached this place this morning. Dr. Fuller,[4] the celebrated Baptist Clergyman of Baltimore who is with me & with whose history I suppose you are acquainted went into the town a few moments after we came & met several of the inhabitants. He says that they are all with inconsiderable exception, anxious for peace & for the restoration of state government and looking to the National Government to tell them how it is to be restored. Two of the principal men have since called on me— one a State Senator[5] under the rebel government & the other the Clerk of the Court.[6] The Ex Senator has just come back to our lines, having been in the Legislature up to the time it was broken up. Both were extremely anxious to know what is to be done at Washington. I told them that I, of course, had no authority to speak; but that I thought that, in some way, the people would be expected to reorganize their own government; and said that as the colored people had been made citizens by enfranchisement it might be desired that they should take part as voters in the work of reorganization. The first part of this proposition they liked but not the last. The idea of blacks voting was evidently distasteful. The Clerk asked why the Govt. might not convene the Legislature and let it call a Convention, repeal the Ordinance of Secession, & confirm Emancipation by adopting the Amendt.[7] To this I replied that this would not be beginning with the people & besides it might be considered as settled that no functionaries who derived their powers from rebels can be recognized in any way by the national government. The Doctor—ExSenator—said he saw that this was likely to be the case, & seemed to take it as much a matter of course. As to voting I reminded them that the blacks in North Carolina had the right to vote until about thirty years ago;[8] and that nothing could be more natural than that, as the right was taken away in the interest of slavery it should be restored by the interest of Freedom. They did not dissent from this—but my general conclusion was that they would *prefer* to have the reorganization in their own hands & those of *their friends*; but that they would acquiesce in any mode of reorganization rather than see any more rebellion.

You *can* do what you think right & do it *safely*. In my judgment the most decided & prompt action is safest.

Faithfully Yours S P Chase

The President

ALS, DLC-JP.

1. George H. Gordon (1823–1886), head of the Department of Virginia since November, 1864, was frustrated in his efforts to discern the boundaries of civil and military authority. "For a time there was no method in the work," he later recalled; "it was a jumble of collisions." He expressed relief when directives from Washington "resolved chaotic elements into a more orderly arrangement, and commanding officers used their power to restore the civil machinery which had so long been trampled out of sight under the feet of contending armies." George H. Gordon, *A War Diary . . . 1863–1865* (Boston, 1882), 418.

2. Francis H. Pierpont (1814–1899), a Virginia Whig and unionist who had supported Lincoln in 1860, had served as provisional governor of Virginia since 1861.

3. On May 9 Johnson recognized the Pierpont administration, then located at Alexandria, as the legal government of Virginia. Pierpont arrived in Richmond on May 26. Ambler, *Pierpont*, 263.

4. Richard Fuller (1804–1876), renowned for his scriptural defenses of slavery, had maintained a Sea Islands plantation worked by 200 slaves while serving as pastor of a church in Baltimore.

5. Michael F. Arendell (b. 1819), a doctor, Whig politician, and state legislator both before and during the war, had been a staunch unionist prior to Sumter. *Cyclopedia of Eminent and Representative Men of the Carolinas . . .* (2 vols., Madison, Wis., 1892), II, 564–65.

6. James Rumley (b. c1813) had been county court clerk for nearly three decades at the time of Chase's visit. 1860 Census, N.C., Carteret, Beaufort, 148; Reid, *After the War*, 24.

7. Currently in process of being submitted to the states, the Thirteenth Amendment abolishing slavery was ratified December 18, 1865, having been approved by North Carolina on December 1.

8. North Carolina's 1776 constitution did not mention race as a barrier to exercising the suffrage, allowing the vote to all freemen owning a 50-acre freehold for six months who had resided in the state for a year. This clause was amended in 1835 to exclude free blacks and mulattoes. Reid, *After the War*, 25–26.

Beaufort Harbor, May 7, 1865.

My dear Sir,

We are still here and my first letter which was sent on board of Maj-Gen. Sherman's Steamer Russia[1] to be forwarded from Fortress Monroe is here also. Gen. Sherman[2] like myself has been detained by the gale which now appears to be subsiding. The Russia & Wayanda[3] will probably both go out this evening.

General Sherman is greatly dissatisfied with the publication of the projected Convention with Johnson,[4] & the reasons for disapproval;[5] and also with the order of Gen Halleck.[6] He has written General Grant on the subject and you have doubtless seen the letter.[7] He has shown it to me in confidence. It is not in the right spirit; but will, I doubt not, be considered with every allowance for his wounded sensibilities: He is thoroughly persuaded of the superior merits of the plan of reorganization, which was initiated by General Weitzels[8] order at Richmond, & applied more extensively by the proposed Convention.[9] He does seem to take into account the great changes produced by the conversion of slaves into free citizens; which alone are sufficient to make honorable reorganization through rebel authorities impossible.[10]

My detention here has enabled me to see a good deal of the Citizens. I have been at Newberne & have seen some there & have conversed with a number of the leading men of Beaufort. All agree that slavery is at an end, & acquiesce fully in the order of Gen. Schofield,[11] which I enclose,[12] declaring that all persons in North Carolina, who were held as slaves, were made free by the Proclamation of Emancipation and must be upheld in their rights as freemen. As to the Extension of suffrage to loyal blacks I find that readiness & even desire for it is in proportion to the loyalty of those who express opinions. Nobody dissents, vehemently; while those who have suffered from rebellion & rejoice, with their whole hearts in the restoration of the National Authority, are fast coming to the conclusion they will find their own surest safety in the proposed Extension. Among these last I have found no one more enlightened or truly patriotic than Col. James H Taylor[13] formerly the holder of more than a hundred slaves.

All seem embarrassed about first steps. I do not entertain the slightest doubt that they would all welcome some simple recommendation from yourself, and would adopt readily any plan which you would suggest. They would receive, without resistance from any & with real joy in many hearts, an order for the enrollment of all loyal citizens without regard to complexion, with a view to reorganization. This would be regarded by all not as an interference but a facility so far as the order should relate to enrollment of whites, and with almost universal acquiescence & with favor by the best citizens, in its whole scope.

Union meetings are being held in various parts of the State.[14] A few words from you will aid them greatly. I am anxious that *you* should have the honor of the lead in this work. It is my deliberate judgment that nothing will so strengthen you with the people or bring so much honor to your name throughout the world as some such short address as I suggested before leaving Washington.[15] Just say to the People "reorganize your state governments; I will aid you by enrollment of the loyal citizens; you will not expect me to discriminate among men equally loyal; once enrolled vote for delegates to a Convention to reform your State Constitution; I will aid you in collecting & declaring these *suffrages*; your Convention & yourselves must do the rest; but you may count on the support of the National Government in all things constitutional expedient." This will terminate all discussion. The disloyal men will feel that the argument is closed & will at once conform themselves to the new order.

Yours faithfully S P Chase

President Johnson.

ALS, DLC-JP.

1. The *Russia*, commanded by Captain A.M. Smith, had been used as an army transport and mail carrier by the South Atlantic Blockade Squadron and had seen action at Fort Fisher. *OR*, Ser. 1, XLVII, Pt. I, 35; Ser. 1, XLII, Pt. II, 594; *OR-Navy*, Ser. 1, XI, 431.

2. William T. Sherman (1820–1891), Grant's most trusted subordinate, had just concluded a triumphant year-long campaign through Georgia and the Carolinas.

3. The *Wayanda* was a revenue-cutter. Sherman, *Memoirs*, II, 369.

4. General Joseph E. Johnston (1807–1891) led the last-ditch Confederate resistance to Sherman's advance through the Carolinas, finally surrendering his army on April 26, 1865.

5. On April 13, 1865, Johnston opened surrender negotiations with Sherman; four days later, in the aftermath of Lincoln's assassination, the two men resumed discussions. Pushing for an agreement which would embrace all remaining Confederate forces in the field, Johnston sought assurances protecting the civil status of the surrendered soldiers. Sherman drafted a set of terms which he believed was consistent with Lincoln's desire for a lenient peace, and, after securing Johnston's signature, transmitted the document to Washington for approval on April 18. The terms went beyond those given by Grant to Lee at Appomattox, including provisions for the convening of state legislatures, a guarantee of political and property rights, and the reestablishment of the Federal court system. Rejecting these proposals, President Johnson sent Grant to Sherman's headquarters to supervise Johnston's capitulation on April 26, on the same basis as the Appomattox agreement. Sherman, *Memoirs*, II, 325–67; Raoul S. Naroll, "Lincoln and the Sherman Peace Fiasco—Another Fable?" *Journal of Southern History*, XX (1954), 459–83.

6. Henry W. Halleck (1815–1872) was army chief of staff after Grant replaced him as general-in-chief in March, 1864. Assuming command at Richmond when news of the rejection of the Sherman-Johnston armistice reached him, he immediately telegraphed Secretary of War Edwin M. Stanton that he had ordered Generals George G. Meade, Philip H. Sheridan, and Horatio G. Wright "to pay no regard to any truce or orders of General Sherman respecting hostilities," and suggested that other Union commanders under Sherman's jurisdiction be instructed to do the same. He hinted that Sherman's ar-

mistice had allowed Jefferson Davis to escape with "six to thirteen million dollars" in gold. Sherman, *Memoirs*, II, 372.

7. Sherman's letter to Grant, dated April 28, charged that Stanton's publication of his correspondence with Johnson had created "very erroneous impressions." After explaining his actions, he lashed out at the secretary of war, whose action "invited the dogs of the press to be let loose upon me." Stanton and others unfamiliar with the South, Sherman suggested, would fail in their attempt at reconstruction: "As an honest man and soldier, I invite them to go back to Nashville and follow my path, for they will see some things and hear some things that may disturb their philosophy." *Ibid.*, 360–62.

8. Godfrey Weitzel (1835–1884), a favorite of Benjamin F. Butler, was in command of the all-black XXV Corps when it entered Richmond on April 3, 1865.

9. On April 12, 1865, the Richmond *Whig*, with Weitzel's approval, published an "Address to the People of Virginia," calling for a meeting of the Virginia legislature for purposes of restoring the Old Dominion to the Union. Lincoln had initially approved an effort on the part of several prominent Virginians to assemble in order to withdraw the state's troops from the Confederate army, but when he discovered that they had seized this opportunity to maintain the legitimacy of the state legislature and had exceeded the scope of his offer, he withdrew his offer, remarking that Appomattox had already withdrawn Virginia's troops from the war effort. Sherman was unaware of Lincoln's decision when he drew up the convention. McPherson, *Reconstruction*, 25–26.

10. Sherman thought "to force the enfranchised negroes, as 'loyal' voters at the South, will produce new riot and war." William T. Sherman to John Sherman, May 8, 1865, W.T. Sherman Papers, LC.

11. John M. Schofield (1831–1906), commander of the Army of the Ohio, had just been named to head the Department of North Carolina.

12. Schofield's General Orders No. 32, dated Raleigh, April 27, reminded the people of the Emancipation Proclamation, that "all persons" before "held as slaves are now free," and that the army's duty was to maintain "the freedom of such persons." Former slave owners should employ freedmen at "reasonable wages," and the freedmen should "remain with their former masters and labor faithfully" as long as they received kind treatment. Otherwise, they should "seek employment elsewhere," but would not be supported in idleness by "congregating" about towns or military camps. *OR*, Ser. 1, XLVII, Pt. III, 331.

13. Planter James H. Taylor (b. c1802), worth some $30,000 in personal property before the war, later took advantage of his contact with Chase to lobby, though unsuccessfully, for a treasury department post. James H. Taylor to Andrew Johnson, July 31, September 4, 1865, and Emma R. Taylor to Johnson, July 28, 1865, Appls. and Recomms., RG56, NA.

14. Meetings throughout North Carolina in the weeks following Johnston's surrender produced resolutions which deplored Lincoln's assassination, requested that Johnson frame measures looking toward a rapid reconstruction, and conceded the collapse of slavery. *American Annual Cyclopaedia and Register* (New York, 1866), 624. For examples, see Wilmington *Herald*, May 13, 1865; Raleigh *Standard*, April 19, 1865.

15. On April 29, Chase had submitted the draft of a speech on reconstruction outlining a process dependent on the participation of "loyal citizens" and the enfranchisement of blacks. *Chase Diaries*, 271–72.

————◄►————

Wilmington, N.C. May 8, 1865

My dear Sir,

General Dodge[1] is about going to Washington, and I beg leave to recommend him to you as a capable officer and a gentleman who seems well informed as to the State of public Sentiment.

I have conversed with many Citizens here and see nothing to change the opinions I have already expressed on the subject of reorganization.

It has been suggested that the easiest move is to let the General Commanding or Military Governor if one be appointed select a sufficient number of loyal persons from the Justices of the Peace composing the Court Quarter sessions of each County to make the enrollment of loyal citizens: and this it seems to me would be judicious[.][2]

It is of the first importance if a Military Governor or Commander of a District forming a State be appointed to have him entirely in harmony with yourself on the whole matter of reorganization. Great difficulties may be avoided by your personal attention to this matter.

All restrictions on trade within the State or outside except upon the importation of munitions of war strictly so called should be abrogated. There is nothing in the law to prevent it. The act of July 13, 1861 which prohibits commercial intercourse except under licence of the President[3] until insurrection shall have ceased leave to you the determination of the question how extensive the intercourse shall be and the right to proclaim when the insurrection is ended.[4] Nothing, at this moment, is more important than to let the people buy what, where, & of whom they will outside of states where war is yet active & sell what & where & to whom they will: arms & ammunition & rebels in arms excepted.

I am just leaving this place & will write more fully as soon as possible.

Yours faithfully S P Chase

President Johnson.

ALS, DLC-JP.

1. George S. Dodge (b. c1839) was chief quartermaster at Wilmington following the fall of Fort Fisher in January, 1865. CSR, RG94, NA.

2. Provisional governor William W. Holden undertook this task in June. Raper, *Holden*, 63.

3. "An Act further to provide for the collection of Duties on Imports, and for other Purposes," approved July 13, 1861, called for the suspension of "all commercial intercourse" between states or parts of states in rebellion and "the rest of the United States" as long as hostilities continued. The President, however, could "license and permit commercial intercourse" with sections in rebellion "in such articles, and for such time, and by such persons, as he, in his discretion, may think most conducive to the public interest; and such intercourse, so far as by him licensed, shall be conducted and carried on only in pursuance of rules and regulations prescribed by the Secretary of the Treasury." *United States Statutes*, XII (1859–63), 255, 257.

4. Johnson had anticipated Chase's suggestion. On April 29, 1865, he had issued a proclamation reopening trade within the "insurrectionary States" east of the Mississippi River, excluding contraband of war. Although Chase conferred with Johnson that day, he made no mention of the order in his diary, and apparently left Washington still unaware of it. On May 9, treasury secretary Hugh McCulloch, with Johnson's approval, published guidelines regulating such trade; the President opened the same region to international trade on May 22. In the following weeks the President issued several more proclamations restoring normal trade relations. McPherson, *Reconstruction*, 7; New York *Herald*, May 11, 23, 1865.

Charleston, May 12, 1865.

My dear Sir,

I wrote you briefly from Wilmington. I hope you have taken an opportunity to confer with General Dodge who bore my letter. I found the other two generals—Hawley[1] who commands the District & Abbot[2] who commands the post—ready in mind & heart to sustain your policy of enfranchisement and reorganization.

The white citizens may be divided into three classes; (1) the old conservatives who opposed secession and are now about and, in some cases, even more opposed to letting the black citizens vote; these would like to see slavery restored:—(2) the acquiescents who rather prefer the old order of things & would rather dislike to see blacks vote but want peace and means of living & revival of business above all things & will take any course the government may desire; this is the largest class:—(3) the progressives who see that Slavery is stone dead & are not sorry; who see too that the blacks made free must be citizens, &, being citizens must be allowed to vote; & who, seeing these things, have made up their minds to conform to the new condition & to lead in it. These are the men of brains and energy; but they are few, & few of the few have been hertofore conspicuous. In the end, however, they will control.

One of the best specimens of the first class I met in Wilmington was Mr. Moore.[3] He is an able lawyer; a good citizen; a good man; thoroughly sincere & truly upright. He was a Whig of the Clay school; opposed secession earnestly & only submitted to it perforce. I promised to convey his views to you & will as well as I can.

They may be stated thus: (1) The best mode of reorganization in North Carolina is to reassemble the Legislature which was lately in session & require each member to take the oath of allegiance to the United States. He thinks nearly every member would take the oath & that this would be the severest humiliation to them & the most impressive lesson to all others. (2) The courts, Supreme, Superior, & Quarter Sessions should be immediately required to resume the exercise of their respective jurisdictions; &, if this cannot be done, that the Courts of Quarter Sessions, composed of the Justices of the Peace of each county should at least be put in action. (3) If the Administration has decided not to recognize the Legislature, elected while the State was in rebellion, then that the white loyal citizens shall be enrolled under order of the military commander by Justices of the Quarter Sessions, selected by him, or by other citizens where loyal Justices cannot be found to act; and that the citizens enrolled should be invited to elect a Convention to revise the Constitution & provide for the election of Governor & Legislature; for the election or appointment of Judges; & for the doing of such other things as may be necessary to restore civil government & national relations. (4) That unrestricted trade except in arms & powder within the state, with other states & with foreign nations should be restored.

His first proposition is of course inadmissable. I think the second equally so, except as to the Courts of Quarter Sessions: perhaps these might well be authorized to resume their functions, each Justice taking the oath; but until complete state restoration their action must necessarily be subject to military supervision. The third seems right except that I would not restrict suffrage to whites. The fourth strikes me as altogether expedient & just.

Nothing needs be said of the second class of citizens—the acquiescents—except that its existence ensures the success of any policy, right & just in itself & enforced with steady vigor, which you may think best to adopt.

The third class includes the men of the future. I met several individuals of it. One of the best specimens at Wilmington was Col. Baker,[4] who was in the rebel service; made prisoner & pardoned by President Lincoln. He seemed to comprehend the new situation & was ready to take an active part in the regeneration of North Carolina on the basis of universal suffrage. He is what you & I would call a young man—say thirty five—active, ready, intelligent, ambitious, of popular manners. Another individual a paroled Colonel from South Carolina was described to me by Mr. Lowell,[5] connected with the detective service of the Treasury Department, who mixed freely with the people without being known to be of our party. They met at the Palmetto Hotel, where few of the northern men go. He declared himself fully satisfied that the Confederacy was gone up; that slavery was gone up with it; that the negroes must now be citizens & voters; &, for his part he was determined not to be behind the times.

This classification will give you with tolerable accuracy, I think, the sentiments of the several classes into which the southern whites may be divided; & will probably satisfy you that there is no course open, if we wish to promote, most efficiently, the interests of all classes, except to give suffrage to all. I see that the New York Herald, which, though rather unreliable as a supporter of anybody or anything, is a very fair barometer of opinion on measures, has come out for general suffrage.[6] It never sustains a cause, which has been unpopular, until it is about to triumph.

At Wilmington, besides many white citizens, a colored deputation called on me. It was composed of four individuals. The spokesman was the minister of the 1st Presbyterian Church (Colored) in Philadelphia,[7] who came down sometime ago at the instance of some benevolent association to look into the condition of the colored people & report upon it. Of the other three one was a carpenter, who many years ago bought himself & wife & two children[.] The whole family was conveyed to a white citizen, whose character was their only security against actual as well as legal slavery. Another also a carpenter had hired his time and had all the wages he could earn over the hire paid to his master. The third was a barber who had also bought himself, & then, like a sensible fellow, married a free woman & had himself conveyed to her. They wanted my advice in their present circumstances; were anxious to know whether or not they were to be allowed to vote, & whether they would be maintained in possession of the lands they had hired. I gave them the best advice I could; to be industrious, economical, orderly & respectful, proving by their conduct their worthiness to be free—as to the right of voting I could not tell whether they would have it immediately or not; but they would certainly have it in time if they showed themselves fit for it: I wd. give it at once if I had the right to decide; but the decision was with you & you would decide according to your own judgment, with the best feeling towards all men of all classes. If they should get it immediately they must not abuse it if they should not they must be patient. As to the lands I said I did not doubt that leases already made for this year would be maintained; but that they could not expect to own the lands without paying for them. They must work hard now; get & save all they could, & await the future hopefully & patiently. They were well satisfied with what I said & I hope it will meet your approval.

I could write a great deal more, but it would do no good. While I am observing, you are doubtless resolving and acting. I am sure you will follow out the great principles you have so often announced & put the weight of your name and authority on the side of justice and right. My most earnest wishes will be satisfied, if you make your administration so beneficent & so illustrious by great acts that the people will be as little willing to spare Andrew Johnson from their *service* as to spare Andrew Jackson. And it will be an exceedingly great pleasure to me if I can in any way promote its complete success.

I shall try to write again from Hilton Head.

With the greatest respect & esteem
Yours truly S. P. Chase

P.S. If you can find time for writing me at New Orleans, where I expect to be in two weeks I shall be glad. I am very desirous to know from yourself, what you think of my observations & suggestions & what you are doing & intending to do.

The President.

ALS, DLC-JP.

1. North Carolina-born Joseph R. Hawley (1826–1905), a prominent Connecticut Republican, later served as governor, congressman, and senator from his adopted state.

2. Gen. Joseph C. Abbott (1825–1881) remained in North Carolina after leaving the army to participate in politics as a Republican, winning election to the U.S. Senate in 1868.

3. Within weeks of his conversation with Chase, Bartholomew F. Moore (1801–1878), prominent unionist and legal authority, conferred with Johnson over reconstruction policy and urged him not to confiscate the holdings of large slaveowners. Raper, *Holden*, 60, 275.

4. Captured at Petersburg in June, 1864, Col. John A. Baker was released from Fort Pulaski upon taking the oath the following March. Reid described him as "a tall, slender

man, of graceful manners, and ardent culture and experience." Some accounts claim that Baker's newfound loyalty did not endear him to his old neighbors, and he soon departed for the West Indies. Robert K. Krick, *Lee's Colonels* (Dayton, Ohio, 1979), 37; Reid, *After the War*, 43; Wilmington *Herald*, May 18, 1865.

5. Mr. Lowell, an Indiana resident who had moved to Kentucky, otherwise unidentified, was recommended by Congressman George W. Julian for his post in an undated letter to then treasury secretary Chase. Application File, Internal Revenue, Treasury Department, RG56, NA.

6. On May 3, 1865, the New York *Herald* urged Johnson: "Give the emancipated negroes of the rebel States, the right to vote along with the whites." This position proved short-lived; on May 24, the *Herald* concluded: "According to the constitution the question of negro suffrage is left to the several states, and there we are content to leave it." New York *Herald*, May 3, 24, 1865.

7. The Reverend Jonathan C. Gibbs (c1827–1874), in North Carolina on missionary work, soon established a freedmen's school there. Moving on to Florida, he joined the Republican party, serving as secretary of state and superintendent of public instruction. Joe M. Richardson, "Jonathan C. Gibbs: Florida's Only Negro Cabinet Member," *Florida Historical Quarterly*, XLII (April, 1964), 363–67.

Hilton Head, May 17, 1865.

My dear Sir,

Since writing my last which I was obliged to bring here & which will go north with this on the Arago,[1] I have been at Charleston, on the Islands in this vicinity and in Savannah.

At Charleston, I saw a number of the most prominent citizens remaining in the town, among them the former Mayor Macbeth,[2] Messrs Williams,[3] a merchant & Phillips & Seymour,[4] lawyers. The same general fact is observable here as elsewhere—the utter absence of all *purpose* if not of all disposition to offer any further resistance to the authority of the Union; and yet a strong desire to retain if possible the political ascendancy in their several states. A few and only a few comprehend & accept the new situation. They would like to reconstitute the state government to suit themselves; but will acquiesce in any plan you think best. Here as elsewhere I endeavored to impress on their minds the disposition of the Government to act with moderation & forbearance & through the people in the matter of reorganization, & I believe I have left, wherever, I have talked with the white citizens a better spirit than I found; though never holding back my own opinions as the necessity of universal suffrage for the best interests of all concerned. Of course, I have been careful to make them understand that the whole question of reorganization is in your hands, & that you will act according to your own best judgment, with a fixed determination to consult the best good of the whole country.

A number of colored people called on me after the white citizens had gone. They were all anxious to know what their future was to be: and I endeavored to counsel them as well as I could. They attach very great importance to the right of voting—more perhaps than to any other except that of personal liberty. Gen. Saxton[5] had arranged for a large meeting & requested me to attend it & I did so in company with General Gillmore.[6] The number in attendance was very large & they were full of the most ardent loyalty. What I said to them may be pretty well gathered from the account in the Charleston Courier,[7] which I enclose herewith. I had no opportunity to see the report until after I had reached Savannah or I should have made it somewhat better. The audience seemed quite as intelligent as a similar gathering in the north. The colored citizens of Charleston are more intelligent than elsewhere. Schools for free blacks have never been prohibited.

General Hatch,[8] who commands the Department, may be fully relied on in any plan of reorganization, and will be able, I doubt not, to secure quiet acquiescence & ultimate cordial good will.

On Saturday Morning I arrived here. General Gillmore arrived soon after & before noon General Saxton had reached Beaufort by a shorter route. There is a populous colored village on this Island, named Mitchell after General Mitchell.[9] The number of inhabitants is about three thousand. They have a church, a minister, & schools. A few cultivate the soil in large & small parcels; most are in government employment; but all are doing well—some very well.

On Sunday I went to Beaufort & thence across Ladies Island to St Helena's to the old Baptist Church to which the planters' families formerly resorted, with their black servants[.]

A large School House has been built since the loyal occupation near the Church & between them under the interlacing branches of three or four enormous live Oaks, was a vast Congregation almost wholly of negroes. Dr. Fuller addressed them admirably.[10] Quite a number of them had been his slaves, & the scene was a most interesting one. I added a short exhortation to industry, temperance, truthfulness, & self improvement. I wish I had time to write or you to read a more particular Description; but it is not possible.

In the afternoon I attended a similar meeting at Beaufort, but here the people were better dressed & a couple of thousand colored soldiers formed part of the audience. Dr. Fuller told them he differed from me as to the right of voting; as he would give it only to those who could read a chapter in the Bible; but said that it was certain they must have the right either with restriction or without it. Was not this something strange to be said in South Carolina, by an Explanter to his Ex Slaves? Generals Gillmore & Saxton & a considerable number of other officers were present at both meetings.

The condition of the fields attracted much attention. Dr. Fuller said he had never seen such thorough cultivation or such promise of fine crops on St Helena[.] And the population seemed happy & thrifty.

A Freedmen's School, Beaufort, South Carolina
Courtesy of The National Archives

On Monday I visited some of the schools, and was much gratified by the extreme anxiety which almost all manifested for education: all ages seem to feel it; the middle aged most.

Savannah—to which place I went night before last, spending yesterday there, was Charleston over again, except that there was no great meeting. A great desire was manifested to have one; but I would not consent; having determined to make no more addresses, fearing I might be taken for a politician or preacher rather than a Chief Justice.[11] There were similar interviews with white & colored citizens; similar expressions of opinion from both classes; & similar schools. I thought I observed, however, among some of the more active white citizens of the middle class, a greater apprehension of restored disloyalism & its ascendancy and a greater desire to be protected against it by the extension of suffrage to the colored citizens.

I find here this morning the New York Herald of the 13th & Mr. Mellen[12] has received the new trade regulations. The Herald refers to your address to Colored ministers but does not contain it.[13] I am very desirous to see it. I hope you gave some intimation of your purpose to Extend the right of suffrage:[14] or that if you did not you soon will. Every body will follow your lead; and I can only repeat my profound conviction that nothing will more exalt your character in the estimation of mankind.

Your order respecting further hospitality to insurgent vessels by foreign nations is to the point & most timely.[15]

Yesterday morning as we were going to Savannah, the steamer conveying Jefferson Davis[16] & his companions came along side, & was made fast to our vessel. Gen Gillmore asked me if I wished to see him; but I said, "No. I would not let any of our party see him. I would not make a show of a fallen enemy." I was dressing, & before I had finished the boats had parted company. As the telegraph operates from Macon to Washington you had doubtless received information of the Capture before we did.[17] The arch leader of the rebellion is now in your hands. I congratulate you on the capture. It makes it impossible for insurrection to revive, & leaves to you only the task of restoring peace by reorganization.

I enclose a paper of practical suggestions, which seem to me worth considering so far as they have not already been considered. They can do no harm if they do no good.

Yours most truly S P Chase

P.S. I enclose an order[18] of General Gillmore, which, I think, will please you.

The President.

Suggestions.

Trade.

The late regulations, in effect, restore the old condition as it existed before rebellion, except as to the export of Cotton & the collection of internal duties: but are unnecessarily complicated through a wish to avoid clashing with the act of Congress. Would it not be best to issue a short order, stating that within certain states—all the states east of the Mississippi—& that part of Arkansas & Texas occupied by National forces, the insurrection has so far ceased as to allow free internal trade & free export & import to & from other states. This would greatly simplify the matter & be in substantial conformity with the legislation of Congress. Nothing in my judgment would contribute more to tranquillity & practical restoration.

Military Matters.

1. The objects of the war is two fold, (1) the suppression of armed insurrection; (2) the restoration of national relations through the reorganization of the state governments. The first is substantially accomplished: the second taxes nerve & brain.

2. As yet the rebels are disarmed only; not reconciled; hardly acquiescent: and there are no state governments to prevent outbreaks. Military supervision, for the present, therefore is indispensable.

3. Should not this military supervision be exercised in a mode as nearly analogous to that of State Government as possible: and to this end would it not be best to make each State a Department & each General commanding a Military Governor, in name as well as in fact; with a distinct declaration that the arrangement is temporary & only auxiliary to reorganization? [19]

4. In the selection of Generals to command in the Several States the greatest care should be used to find men suited to their work; thoroughly loyal to the government and as ready to maintain the rights & promote the welfare of black as of white citizens. Success depends on this.

5. So far as I am able to learn Gen. Schofield in North Carolina may be well trusted with that State or Department.[20] Should circumstances require his presence elsewhere Gen. Cox[21] is admirably suited to the position. This Department is now under General Gillmore. I have met no officer who seems to me so well suited to his work: no one more able or more loyal in all respects or more thoroughly in sympathy with your own views. Should the Department be divided in to State-Departments I should hope that he might be assigned to Georgia, where it seems to me he would be most useful. General Hatch or General Saxton would be excellent for Florida or South Carolina. General Saxton has had so much experience in the latter State that he would be most useful there.[22]

6. Military Commanders being once established in each state reorganization would be easy. An order might at once be made for the Enrollment of loyal white or black Citizens & the mode of enrollment prescribed.

7. Enrollment might be made either by Provost Marshalls, or what would seem to me a better mode by boards of loyal citizens in each county or other convenient place or precinct; who could administer the proper oath and make the necessary examination to be sure of loyalty & issue certificates of enrollment which should be evidence of right to vote.

8. The enrolled citizens should then be invited to vote for delegates to form a new constitution or amend the old: & the new amended constitution should be submitted to them for ratification or rejection. The Convention of Delegates should also provide, in the event of ratification, for the election of Governor & other State officers & of Members of the Legislature & for the election or appointment of Judges & Justices of the Peace, & for the declaration of the results of these elections; & for the entrance upon their respective duties of the persons elected or appointed under the State Constitution.

9. The State Government being thus reconstituted all the political functions of the Military Commander would cease & his duties would be confined to the repression of disorder in aid of the state authorities; & the whole machinery of the National & State Governments would be once more fully restored & in practical operation.

10. This restoration of the late insurgent States to their national relations will be peace.

ALS, DLC-JP.

1. The *Arago*, an ocean steamer, saw service on the Atlantic and Gulf coasts throughout the war. *OR*, Ser. 1, XI, Pt. III, 157; XV, 607–8.

2. Lawyer Charles Macbeth (c1807–fl1866) had been mayor of Charleston during the secession crisis and the war. 1860 Census, S.C., Charleston Dist., 2nd Ward, 41; Charleston city directories (1859–66), *passim*.

3. George W. Williams (1820–1903), a wholesale grocer and banker, had participated in local politics, including a term as city alderman. *Cyclopedia of Eminent and Representative Men of the Carolinas . . .* , I, 362–64.

4. John Phillips (c1815–fl1874) and Robert W. Seymour (c1805–fl1881). The former had served on the state executive council and in the still-convened secession convention (1862). 1870 Census, S.C., Charleston, 3rd Ward, 21; 4th Ward, 219; Charleston city directories (1859–81), *passim*; C. Vann Woodward, ed., *Mary Chesnut's Civil War* (New Haven, Conn., 1981), 455; Yates Snowden, ed., *History of South Carolina* (5 vols., Chicago, 1920), II, 876.

5. Rufus Saxton (1824–1908), a fervent advocate of emancipation, supervised the establishment of black colonies on the Sea Islands. He assisted in raising black troops, carried out the distribution of land under Sherman's Special Field Order No. 15, and served as assistant commissioner of the Freedmen's Bureau for South Carolina, Georgia, and Florida.

6. Quincy Adams Gillmore (1825–1888), chief engineer for the Port Royal expedition in 1861, had commanded the land forces operating against Charleston in 1863. He returned to the South Carolina coast in 1865 to head the Department of the South and oversee the occupation of South Carolina.

7. On May 13, 1865, the Charleston *Courier* carried an account of Chase's speech, in which the chief justice staked out his claim as an advocate of black rights throughout the war effort. Pronouncing himself in favor of black suffrage, "the freeman's weapon in peace," he urged his black audience to "show by your acts that you deserve to be entrusted with suffrage" through hard work and patience, in order to counter claims that blacks were lazy and irresponsible. Reid, *After the War*, 581–86.

8. John P. Hatch (1822–1901), after suffering a serious wound at South Mountain in 1862, was relegated to administrative commands along the Atlantic coast.

9. Ormsby M. Mitchel (1810–1862), who in 1862 approved the famed Andrews train raid in north Georgia, died later that year, only a month after he took charge of the Department of the South. However short his stay, Mitchel had made a favorable impression on local blacks, and the settlement near Hilton Head was dubbed "Mitchelville" in a military order outlining the community's political structure.

10. Whitelaw Reid left a description of the encounter. The former slaves crowded around Fuller, sang, and listened to him as he advised them to work hard to contest racist stereotypes of blacks as lazy and indolent. After the impromptu ceremony, the blacks warmly greeted Fuller, who later noted that he had never seen them "appearing so well or so contented." *Ibid.*, 102–14.

11. Chase seems almost prescient here. On May 24, the New York *Herald*, labeling the chief justice "the great negro-worshipper," assailed him for undertaking a "stumping tour" through the South. Its May 22 account of Chase's speech was critical, describing the audience as "promiscuous." The *Herald* had previously reported that the chief justice had been speculating on a realignment of parties which would enhance his efforts to win the presidency in 1868, suggesting that Chase was "in search of his old friends in the South." New York *Herald*, May 20, 22, 24, 1865.

12. William P. Mellen (c1813–1873), chief treasury agent and steadfast Chase supporter, ostensibly was present on the tour to make recommendations for reopening southern trade.

13. On May 11, 1865, Johnson met with a delegation representing the National Theological Institute for Colored Ministers. For the address, see Washington *National Intelligencer*, May 13, 1865.

14. Far from fulfilling Chase's hope, Johnson said nothing about suffrage. Instead, he deplored what he perceived to be the tendency of many freedmen "to think that with freedom everything they need is to come like manna from heaven" and "to become loafers and depend upon the Government to take care of them." He urged the ministers to correct "one great fact—that four millions of people lived in open and notorious concubinage." Although promising "to do all that I can for the elevation and amelioration of your condition," he also raised the possibility of black colonization "should it be found that the two races cannot get along together." *Ibid.*

15. On May 10, Johnson had issued a proclamation ordering the capture of Confederate cruisers remaining at large and warning other nations that if they continued to receive these cruisers, the United States would close its ports to their vessels and take other measures "toward vindicating the national sovereignty." *OR*, Ser. 3, V, 18; Richardson, *Messages*, VI, 308–9.

16. Jefferson Davis (1808–1889), President of the Confederacy.

17. On the morning of May 10, Federal cavalry under Gen. James H. Wilson finally tracked down Davis and a small entourage outside of Irwinville, Georgia. The president was caught fleeing from his tent, covered by a raincoat and his wife's shawl, his attire becoming a source of controversy as several reports asserted that he had tried to disguise himself in women's clothing. Taken to Macon, Davis was on his way to Fortress Monroe when Chase nearly encountered him. Long, *Civil War Almanac*, 687.

18. On May 14, Gillmore issued General Order No. 63, denying the authority of Andrew G. Magrath (South Carolina), Joseph E. Brown (Georgia), and Abraham K. Allison (Florida) to act as governors of their respective states, and reminding citizens that the blacks were free and "it is the fixed intention of a wise and beneficent Government to protect them in the enjoyment of their freedom and the fruits of their industry." *OR*, Ser. 1, XLVII, Pt. III, 498–99.

19. Johnson's plan, as announced on May 29, did not conform to Chase's proposal, but rather established a provisional civil governor, appointed by the President, to superintend

Friends of the Freedmen I:
Rufus Saxton and Quincy A. Gillmore.
Courtesy of The National Archives

the reconstruction process. Military commanders were directed to "aid and assist" these governors, and were ordered "to abstain from, in any way, hindering, impeding, or discouraging the loyal people from the organization of a State Government." The line of jurisdiction between civil and military authority remained ill-defined, and resulted in some difficulty. See, for example, Carl Schurz to Johnson, August 29, September 1, 1865, infra; Richardson, *Messages*, VI, 312–14.

20. Chase's confidence in Schofield seems not to have been reciprocated. On May 10, the general wrote Grant that he believed that Chase's policy "would . . . lead to disastrous results." He opposed black suffrage as impractical and as promising violence and concluded by commenting "if a policy so opposed to my views as that proposed by Mr. Chase is to be adopted I respectfully suggest that I am not the proper person to carry it out." *OR*, Ser. 1, XLVII, Pt. III, 463.

21. Jacob D. Cox (1828–1900), Ohio Republican, returned to his home state and was elected governor later that year after publicly advocating the establishment of separate black colonies along the Atlantic coast and rejecting black suffrage.

22. Under General Order No. 118, issued June 27, the states referred to in this paragraph came under either the Division of the Atlantic (North and South Carolina) or the Division of the Gulf (Georgia and Florida). Among Chase's suggested candidates as state-department commanders, Schofield remained in North Carolina and Gillmore in South Carolina. Saxton became the assistant commissioner for the Freedmen's Bureau in South Carolina; Hatch would be mustered out; Cox was later ordered to Ohio. *OR*, Ser. 1, XLVII, Pt. III, 667–68, 672.

Fernandina, Fla., May 21, 1865.

My dear Sir,

This is probably the last letter with which I shall trouble you before arriving at New Orleans though I may possibly have another opportunity from Key West.

I believe I have not mentioned the colored community or rather its organization at Hilton Head. Enclosed you will find the order under which it is constituted—its organic Law.[1] General Littlefield[2] tells me that it works very well. The Recorder is fond of calling himself Mayor & the Councilmen style themselves Aldermen. They are all colored; & subject to the supervision of the General. They administer justice in all matters with[in] the scope of the organizing order. One case of partnership as related to me by General Littlefield, was as well, though not so formally decided, as it could have been by the Supreme Court itself— and the case was one of some complexity. It is quite a fair specimen of self government, even by the less intelligent of the blacks, to which class the citizens of "Mitchell" belong.

Nor do I know that I have mentioned the fact that every where through the country the colored citizens are organizing Union Leagues.[3] These associations embrace all the most intelligent. I found them in a greater or less degree of advancement in nearly every place. They must exercise a great influence over the future of the class they represent— and not a little on the character of the States in which they exist. They form a power which no wise statesman will disregard.

At Fernandina (this place) I found that at a public meeting, presided over by Major Sears, Engineer in Charge of Fort Clinch,[4] a vote was taken on the question whether the colored citizens should participate in the election of Mayor &c & it was decided in the affirmative. An election for Mayor, Councilmen & other officers was held accordingly—the blacks & whites voting. When I arrived I was asked to swear in the Mayor elect—Mr. Mot,[5] a French gentleman, of great intelligence & industrial enterprise. Of course I complied, & had the honor of administering the oath of office to the first Mayor of Fernandina under the new regime.[6]

So you see that colored suffrage is practically adopted in Florida—or rather that part of it included in Amelia Island.

I was at Jacksonville day before yesterday. Mr. Yulee[7] called on me. He said he had been appointed, with one or more other gentlemen, by the acting Governor of Florida, Allison,[8] Commissioners to wait on you in reference to reorganization. He was very solicitious to know whether the Acts of Mr. Allison, in making this commission, & in calling the Legislature would be respected at Washington; and seemed a good deal disappointed when Gen. Gillmore showed him the order[9] which I enclosed to you from Hilton Head. He asked if the order was made pursuant to instructions: to which Gen Gillmore replied that he had no express instructions, but had acted on his own judgment in conformity to what he believed to be your policy.

The Great object of Mr. Yulee & those who think & feel as he does is to get the power of the State—or rather to keep that power in the same hands in which it now is; and they especially object to the blacks voting. They declare themselves satisfied that the Union must be restored & that Slavery, as a personal relation, must cease: but earnestly urge that some mode of coercing labor must be adopted in lieu of personal slavery, or that the Southern States will be Africanized and ruined. It is curious to observe, how little they seem to realize that any change in personal or political relations has been wrought by the war.

I was much concerned on seeing a statement that you had been ill in a New York paper.[10] Let me beg you to run no risks of your health.

Faithfully yours S P Chase

President Johnson.

ALS, DLC-JP.

1. The order outlines the political organization, the powers of the "Council of Administration," and the structure of the educational system of Mitchelville. Reid, *After the War*, 89–91.

2. Milton S. Littlefield (1830–1899) had been recruiting black troops along the coast of South Carolina and Florida for two years. He returned south three years later to embark on a colorful career as newspaper editor, railroader, and Republican politico in North Carolina and Florida.

3. Originally designed to foster southern unionism, by 1865 the Union Leagues had expanded their activities as a branch of the Republican party, including efforts to organize, educate, and in some cases, protect black voters in the South. Richard H. Abbott, *The Republican Party and the South, 1855–1877* (Chapel Hill, 1986), 25, 59–65.

4. Alfred F. Sears (*c*1826–*fl*1895) had been stationed at Fort Clinch since 1864. CSR, RG94, NA.

5. French-born Adolphus Mot (*c*1814–*fl*1870) had tutored Chase's children. Moving to Fernandina to grow olives, he served as clerk of the local tax commission and as mayor, later returning to Washington, D.C. 1870 Census, D.C., Washington, 2nd Ward, 257; Columbus city directories (1858–62), *passim*; New York *Times*, July 2, 1865; Jerrell H. Shofner, *Nor Is It Over Yet* (Gainesville, Fla., 1974), 32.

6. Not everybody was so charmed by the ceremony. The New York *World* was furious: "But what a spectacle! A Chief-Justice of this great nation interfering in a petty election in the wilds of Florida to advance his fortunes as a negro-suffrage candidate for the presidency!" New York *World*, May 30, 1865.

7. David L. Yulee (1810–1886), planter, Democratic senator, and a leading advocate of secession, had successfully resisted Confederate efforts to seize his property for the war effort. "He is very anxious about reconstruction," Chase noted to Sumner; "thinks that the whites, without any distinction not made by the old State Constitution, should be entrusted with the work; admits that personal slaveholding is at an end, but wishes to substitute some form of compulsory labor; insists that the South will be Africanized & ruined if this is not done." Chase to Sumner, May 20, 1865, Free Library of Philadelphia.

8. Abraham K. Allison (*c*1813–*fl*1870), president of the Florida state senate in 1865, attempted to serve as acting governor after the death of Governor John Milton. Arrested under Gillmore's May 14 order, he was incarcerated again five years later for obstructing blacks' efforts to vote. *Ibid.*, 18, 214, 230; Ralph Wooster, "The Florida Secession Convention," *Florida Historical Quarterly*, XXXVI (1957–58), 383.

9. See Chase to Johnson, May 17, 1865, n.18.

10. The New York *World* reported on May 13, 1865, that Johnson, "who was quite ill at one time this week, is fully restored to health."

Key West May 23, 1865.

My dear Sir,

We are met here by the agreeable news that the Stonewall has been surrendered to the Spanish Government & this after an offer to surrender on condition that the act should not enure to the United States was made & refused.[1] This news is, I suppose, reliable as it comes from an officer of the Navy who left Havana yesterday. I congratulate you that the rebellion, as an armed power, is as dead at sea as on land: and hope soon to hear that the business of blockaderunning, which seems to be still carried on briskly and profitably between the coast of Texas & Havanna is dead also.

This place is of little political importance. The town contains not more than 3500 inhabitants of all colors and the whole county of Monroe, of which it is Capital, not more than 1500 more. A number of the citizens have always remained loyal; but a larger number, have been either actively or in every thing but active on the side of rebellion. I hear of one striking illustration of the defectiveness of the amnesty system. A man named Tift[2] who has a considerable property here, went into the service of the rebellion—not as a civil or military officer, but as a contractor for various work as founder & smith, & aided very largely— much more largely than many general officers in sustaining those who sought the overturn of the Government. This man, as the law & proclamation now stand may come back and take the oath prescribed by the amnesty proclamation: and be just as active and as hostile as ever; only not resorting to arms, because he is convinced that by arms nothing can be accomplished. Why would it not be well to substitute for the present plan of amnesty, something like this: let rebels, with such exceptions as you see fit to make, be exempted from punishment & restored, wholly or partially, as you may think best, to civil rights on taking some such oath as you prescribed in Tennessee & on satisfying a commission of loyal men to be named in each county that their disposition to resume the character & fulfil the duties of loyal citizens is sincere & thorough. Such a commission could be easily created; and its decisions, summarily made, would be easy & sufficient testimonials of renewed loyalty.[3]

General Newton[4] is absent from this post in Tallahassee or at St Marks for an interview with General McCook.[5] The General is well spoken [of] by the loyal men here in whom all have confidence. He has hesitated how far to go in recognizing the blacks as citizens with the right of suffrage, because uncertain whether he will be sustained by the Government. If I see him before final departure for[sic] Key West I shall take pleasure in saying to him that I have every reason to think that he will be supported in all that he may judiciously do in that direction.

General McCook as I learned at Fernandina has been granting paroles on condition that the prisoner paroled shall conform to the laws in force before February 1861: which seems to me equivalent to a sanction to the old Slaveholding system; though, I presume, it is not intended as such; but rather as a declaration of the nullity of the secession ordinance. But is it wise to make such conditions in paroles.

A more serious complaint was made of General Wilson[6] to the effect that he promised if he did not use military force in compelling persons heretofore slaves of a railroad corporation to return to its service.

It is important to the success of your administration that no *even* apparent support should be given to slavery by generals in command.[7]

I am more & more impressed with the importance of making each State a Department & assigning to the command of each Department a General in full sympathy with your own views. In such a Department, coincident in territory with a State & bearing its name, Military Government could be made very much like State Government, & be very useful in facilitating reorganization.

                                        Yours very faithfully S. P. Chase
P.S. I go from here to Havana, hoping to see Gen. Newton on my return: and thinking it may be useful for me to see him. I begin to be very anxious to get back to the north.
The President.

ALS, DLC-JP.

1. The Confederate ironclad ram, *Stonewall*, built in France and purchased in Denmark, sailed from Europe during the last days of the war under the command of Captain T.J. Page. In mid-May, after refusing to surrender to the Union navy, Page gave the ship to Cuba's captain-general in return for money to pay the crew. Maurice Melton, *The Confederate Ironclads* (New York, 1968), 271–84.

2. Dry goods merchant Asa F. Tift (*c*1812–*fl*1880) had been a member of Florida's secession convention. 1860 Census, Fla., Monroe, Key West, 49; Jefferson B. Browne, *Key West: The Old and the New* (St. Augustine, Fla., 1912), 12, 90, 91, 142.

3. Johnson's May 29, 1865, amnesty proclamation announced administration policy. Tift, who was a wealthy man, had to (and did) make special application to Johnson for amnesty, since he fell under the proclamation's list of persons not covered by the general amnesty. Civil War Amnesty Case Files, Florida, RG94 (M1003), NA.

4. John Newton (1822–1895), a veteran of Gettysburg and the Atlanta campaign, had been installed as commander of the District of West Florida in October, 1864.

5. Edward M. McCook (1833–1909), who had commanded cavalry under Sherman, George H. Thomas, and James H. Wilson, later was minister to Hawaii and territorial governor of Colorado.

6. James H. Wilson (1837–1925), once one of Grant's staff officers, had emerged as an able cavalryman under Sheridan, Sherman, and Thomas, and commanded the forces which captured Jefferson Davis. In truth, Wilson advocated harsh treatment of the defeated South and a period of federal guardianship over the freedmen during the transition from slavery to freedom.

7. "The officers who commanded under Sherman & are now occupying portions of Georgia & Florida are far from sound on the reorganization question," Chase told Sumner. "One, at least, has given aid to the capture of men as slaves within the last few weeks, even to the extent of taking enlisted men from the ranks. I hope the President will lose no time in setting all this right. It is very unfortunate." Chase to Sumner, May 20, 1865, Free Library of Philadelphia.

Harvey M. Watterson:
A Trusted Tennessean

If the President found the lecturing and hectoring of the chief justice unpalatable, far more to his taste were the reassuring reports from his second emissary to the defeated South. Harvey M. Watterson, former Tennessee congressman and long-time friend of the President, made his first foray into the former Confederacy on the heels of Johnson's first proclamations addressing the problems of restoration. The policy had been a month in preparation. The rejection of the agreement between Generals Sherman and Johnston seemingly pointed to the establishment of more rigorous conditions for reconstruction; Johnson's recognition of Lincoln's provisional government in Virginia on May 9, while alarming some Radicals, was seen by many as simply carrying out policies previously established. North Carolina would provide the new administration with its first opportunity to shape a policy for restoring the southern states to the Union. Here, many Radicals believed, Johnson would show where he stood on the issue of black enfranchisement.[1]

With the disposal of the status of Virginia's provisional government, the cabinet immediately turned to the Tar Heel State. Stanton had furnished each cabinet member with a copy of his proposed proclamation outlining the restoration process. The draft elicited little controversy until the discussion turned to the issue of black suffrage. Stanton, Postmaster General William Dennison, and Attorney General James Speed advocated it; Gideon Welles, treasury secretary Hugh McCulloch, and interior secretary John P. Usher opposed it, Welles commenting that such a step represented a "subversion" of the rights of each state to determine the qualifications of its own voters. The question remained unresolved; the President desired to give the matter more thought. At the same time the cabinet, after some deliberation, endorsed Speed's draft of an amnesty proclamation.[2]

Over the next twenty days Johnson worked on drafts of both proclamations. On May 12 Sumner and Benjamin F. Wade assured their radical colleagues that the President would endorse black suffrage. Welles, however, was confident that Johnson "will shape it right." The Tennessean proved worthy of Welles's confidence. Within days word leaked out that he would remand the question of black suffrage to the states. On May 20 he met with a delegation of North Carolinians, among them

1. Benedict, *Compromise of Principle*, 105.
2. *Welles Diary*, II, 301.

Bartholomew F. Moore, who had just encountered Chase at Wilmington. He then consulted with William W. Holden, a Raleigh newspaper editor and politician, who had run for governor on a peace ticket in 1864. Johnson soon decided that he had found in Holden the man to head North Carolina's provisional government.[3]

On May 29 Johnson issued both proclamations. The amnesty proclamation was more strict than those issued by Lincoln during the war, for Johnson excepted from general amnesty not only high ranking civil and military officials, but those who possessed in excess of $20,000 taxable property—a direct blow at the slave oligarchy he despised. Individuals falling under the excepted catagories had to apply to Johnson for pardon, although the President promised that "clemency will be liberally extended." All others were granted "amnesty and pardon, with restoration of all rights of property, except as to slaves," provided they took an oath of future loyalty. The other proclamation, naming Holden provisional governor, instructed him to call a convention to revise the state's constitution. Of key importance was Johnson's delineation of the qualifications of voters electing delegates to the convention: not only did they have to be "loyal to the United States" by meeting the conditions set forth in the amnesty proclamation, but they also had to meet the suffrage qualifications set forth in the state's prewar constitution— which explicitly barred blacks from voting. Chase had been ignored.[4]

In issuing these proclamations, Johnson doubtless knew he was disappointing advocates of black suffrage. Nevertheless, he had never promised to mandate such a measure; rather, he had said that while he did not oppose it, he did not wish to make it an issue of policy—better to leave the initiative where he believed it belonged, with the states. Indeed, he wanted to find out how southerners were responding to his initiatives. Welles and Dennison were already touring the Atlantic seacoast. On the day the proclamations were issued, the cabinet officers traveled the streets of Charleston, and the navy secretary remarked after viewing "the devastation of the city" that "No place has suffered more or deserved to have more." The next day Welles spoke with military authorities at Savannah "on the condition of affairs in Georgia and the South generally." On their return north they visited Wilmington, Richmond, and Fortress Monroe.[5] If Johnson could look forward to a supportive report from Welles, he was probably more skeptical of the prospects promised by Pennsylvania Radical John Covode, dispatched to Louisiana on the day the proclamations were issued. Stanton had instructed him to report on the progress of the state's restored govern-

3. Thomas and Hyman, *Stanton*, 445; *Welles Diary*, II, 305; George F. Milton, *The Age of Hate: Andrew Johnson and the Radicals* (New York, 1930), 186–87; Benedict, *Compromise of Principle*, 106.

4. Richardson, *Messages*, VI, 310–14.

5. *Welles Diary*, II, 310–15; New York *Tribune*, June 12, 1865.

ment and the condition of freedmen working federally-owned plantations. Since many Republicans viewed Louisiana as a test case for reconstruction, Covode's report could damage prospects elsewhere.[6]

What Johnson wanted were the advice and observations of people he trusted and who were personally loyal to him. One of these people was Watterson, a lifelong Democrat who had served with Johnson in the state legislature. He had retired from public office in 1847, editing Democratic newspapers in Nashville and Washington for seven years before returning to his home at Shelbyville. But the friendship formed with Johnson remained strong, and when the senator began to sound out his prospects for the Democratic presidential nomination in 1860, Watterson attended to his interests in Tennessee, helping to secure a delegation pledged to its favorite son. Watterson's efforts to stop secession proved unavailing, and he retired home to wait out the war, watching his son Henry join the ranks of the graycoats.[7]

Johnson saw that Watterson could perform valuable service by undertaking a tour of the South, since the ex-editor had formed connections with various politicians over the years. Certainly Watterson's southern unionist perspective appeared far more compatible with Johnson's opinions than did the advice offered by Chase. Having decided on a policy to pursue, Johnson wanted someone to assess its impact on white southerners, someone who shared his point of view on reunion as well as on "the negro problem." Surely Watterson's attitude toward blacks and slavery was no secret; in the 1865 state constitutional convention he denounced "the everlasting *Nigger*—that dark fountain from which has flowed all our woes" and suggested that compensated emancipation would benefit whites more than blacks—a position Johnson had long advocated. It was no coincidence that Harvey Watterson commenced his journey days after Johnson on May 29 issued his proclamations concerning amnesty and outlining the reconstruction process in North Carolina. Virginia and North Carolina were on the itinerary for this first trek. Perhaps it was also no coincidence that Chase had commenced his May tour by visiting these two states.[8]

From Richmond, Watterson submitted his first report. He found the city quiet and orderly, as if the last four years of conflict had never occurred. The good feeling he attributed to the fine behavior of the occupation forces. Virginians had accepted the verdict at Appomattox and appeared eager to return to the Union on an equal footing with northerners. Slavery was dead; whites were "heartily sick of the peculiar institution." Johnson's policy seemed the perfect set of guidelines for such a people to follow, especially as they already had a provisional

6. Stanton to Covode, May 29, 1865, Lets. Sent, 1865, Dept. of War, RG107, NA.
7. Louisville *Courier Journal*, October 2, 1891; Johnson to Robert Johnson, January 12, 1860, *Johnson Papers*, III, 381.
8. Nashville *Dispatch*, January 14, 1865.

government established. Watterson quickly assured his friend that he was on the right track; Virginians, he said, applauded both his commitment to resist centralization and the North Carolina proclamation.[9]

Watterson's endorsement of the administration of Richmond affairs by Generals Henry W. Halleck and Edward O.C. Ord reflected his belief that one way to conciliate white southerners was to repress the freedmen. They had removed the all-black XXV Corps from the former Confederate capital; within weeks the unit was dispatched to the Texas-Mexico border. A New York *Tribune* reporter, writing on the day of Watterson's first letter, noted the city police, aided by military authorities, were more than zealous in arresting and punishing blacks. One black, accused of assaulting a white, was placed standing in a coffin, his head barely exposed, and the coffin was hung outside a house. Blacks were required to carry passes with them at all times. The same day several Richmond blacks wrote editor Horace Greeley, complaining of "a daily mounted patrol, with their sabers drawn," whose duty seemed to be "the hunting of the colored people," and stated, "our present condition is worse than ever we suffered before. . . . All that is needed to restore Slavery in full is the auction-block as it used to be." A delegation traveled to Washington the following week to lay the problem before the President. Within weeks Halleck and Ord were ordered elsewhere.[10]

Johnson must have eagerly awaited Watterson's account of affairs in North Carolina, the initial laboratory of the President's Reconstruction experiment. Certainly Watterson's first letter must have brought a smile to his face. "No people were ever more thoroughly conquered and subdued," the editor announced. "Point out to them the way that leads to amicable relations with the Government of the United States, and they will be certain to take it." Holden seemed the ideal choice for provisional governor in Watterson's eyes; others, notably newspaper reporter Sidney Andrews, met North Carolinians who offered a different opinion—that the governor "was hated by one class of people and feared by the other." [11]

But, Watterson added, certain conditions contained the possibility of disrupting the growth of reunionist sentiment. Topping the list were the black troops garrisoned at New Bern, commanded by Boston-born Charles J. Paine. Emancipation was a fact that southern whites accepted reluctantly, but many rebelled at the sight of former slaves, now clad in blue, telling them what to do—and with the power to enforce their will. Paine had compounded the problem by suspending General Innis N. Palmer from his command. Palmer, according to Watterson,

9. Watterson to Johnson, June 7, 1865.

10. Bernarr Cresap, *Appomattox Commander: The Story of General E.O.C. Ord* (San Diego, 1981), 220–22; New York *Tribune*, June 12, 15, 1865.

11. Watterson to Johnson, June 20, 29, 1865; Andrews, *The South Since the War*, 174.

was very popular among North Carolina whites; this was undoubtedly due in part to his views on race. "Like yourself, too," Watterson told the President, "he is for a white man's government, and in favor of free white citizens controlling the country." Other obstacles to reunion remained; the behavior of treasury agents had embarrassed the government, and many residents of New Bern wanted to return to their old homes, now occupied by federal officials or their tenants. Prompt action to remove these irritants, Watterson suggested, would foster good feelings.[12]

Other observers were far less sanguine. One reporter argued that "the war has done comparatively little toward emancipating the poor white man from the domination of the wealthy and hitherto controlling class," and listed several cases of violence against blacks. A New York *Times* correspondent, while noting that complaints had been made against the black troops stationed at New Bern, added that the white troops at Raleigh were also ill-disciplined. He added that while "many soldiers of the late rebel army talk of the surrenders, and of the result of the war," he had "yet to hear the first one say that the South was not fairly, effectually and completely whipped."[13]

Watterson did not limit his activities to observation alone. He freely represented himself as Johnson's confidant, assuring anxious southerners that the President would resist radical notions of reconstruction and black suffrage. Discussions about the President "formed a large share of the conversation" in several instances: "Of course I was at home on that subject, and rest assured that I have done it ample justice." Reports of Chase's interviews had filtered back to Raleigh, and many North Carolinians wanted to know if Johnson would yield to the Radicals on this issue. Watterson assured them that the President would "stand firm" against the imposition of black suffrage.[14]

Fearful of reports of yellow fever in Wilmington, Watterson cut short his visit; still, he came away convinced that "All is politically right in North Carolina."[15] Certainly he had worked hard on his twin tasks of advocating Johnson's policy and making recommendations to the President concerning measures to enhance the success of his program, identifying various obstacles to reunion. Johnson had every reason to be satisfied with his old associate, for he, and not Chase, truly represented his policies.

12. Watterson to Johnson, June 20, 1865.
13. New York *Tribune*, June 21, 23, 1865; New York *Times*, July 2, 1865.
14. Watterson to Johnson, July 8, 1865.
15. Watterson to Johnson, June 27, 1865.

Letters

Richmond, Va. June 7th 1865

His Excellency Andrew Johnson
President of the United States
Sir.

I reached Richmond on last Friday,[1] and rest assured that I have not been idle. I proceed at once to give you the result of my labor: The city is as quiet as before the Rebellion. You may walk the streets for days, and not witness one act of disorder or violence. The soldiers are well-behaved—and seemingly as a matter of pride—in preserving order and protecting property. The most respectable and most intelligent citizens openly declare that property, and all personal rights, are as secure now as before the Rebellion. Prominent citizens of Petersburg and Lynchburg do not hesitate to avow that property is as safe in those cities now as before the Rebellion. In neither of those cities is there the least apprehension of disorder or wrong[.][2]

This is owing, doubtless, in some degree, to the high character and decided abilities of the officers[3] selected for command in this, the capital of the State, but, considerably, to the good character of the soldiers, who, having accomplished the patriotic end of their enlistment—the suppression of the Rebellion—are indisposed to revenge or lawlessness.

Almost as a corollary, there has been a marked change of opinion and feeling towards the Northern people. It is generally acknowledged, *and by both sexes*, that where they expected general outrage, they have met with nothing but kindness. With scarcely a dissenting voice the exclamation is—"that these Yankees are not as bad people as we thought them to be[.]"

From external appearances, you can scarcely realize that the city was lately the centre of a great Rebellion.

The people of the City, and of the State generally, accept the result of the Rebellion—success of the Federal arms and failure of the Confederate—as a fact fixed and irreversible. The submission is complete and sincere.[4] There is scarcely an exception in town or country. Further resistance is regarded as utterly hopeless and foolish. Mr Wise[5] made a speech at the Halifax April Court, advising the people to give up the contest, once and forever, to submit themselves cheerfully to the Federal Government and laws, and to go home to work to recuperate their broken fortunes. A distinguished citizen of the State was heard recently to remark—"We are lying down for the wave to wash over us: all we ask is that we will not be allowed to be washed entirely away, and submerged in the great deep forever; and that we ask the most generous treatment the Government can award us". This is the almost universal sentiment. Indeed, considering the acerbity of the late great conflict, and the extent of the Rebel sentiment, the general submission of those in rebellion to the authorities of the Union, may be regarded as one of the most remarkable changes ever known in the history of human opinion. It has been remarked, as an evidence of the general and sincere submission, that since Gen Lee's[6] surrender, there has been no adverse military organization, and that any attempt at guerrilla operations, would meet with general denunciation.

A leading citizen of Lynchburg, after speaking of the occupation of that city by the Federal troops, thus writes:

Fortunately for our city, a more gentlemanly and more humane set of officers, and I may add of soldiers, never occupied an enemy's country. Not one dollar's worth of private property was molested, nor an outrage of the most trivial character perpetrated. We only know they are here by meeting a few occasionally. I hope things may pass off quietly. As far as my information extends, I feel confident that with but few, *very few* exceptions, Virginia will return in good faith to her allegiance to the Federal Government, and that if a kind and conciliatory course be pursued towards the seceded or rebellious states, they will all, with entire good faith and sincerity, resume their membership in the Union of old. Give them a chance, and they will be as loyal as any northern state. The view generally taken is this—that the matter of controversy has been settled by force of arms. upon which they cast their fortunes, and that the issues raised having been decided against them, they ought and must yield the points, and, for the future, make cheerful and unreserved acknowledgement of the supremacy of the Federal Union and its laws[.]

All, indeed, the people seem to want is, restoration of civil government, and a policy that will assure them that they may safely return to their accustomed vocations without fear of molestation[.]

Accordingly, there is no opposition whatever to the restored Government of the State headed by Governor Peirpoint. There is not only no factious opposition to his government, but the best citizens hail with high satisfaction his advent to the capital as foretokening the restoration of civil government, law, order and quiet.[7]

It has been said by the Press that the elections thus far indicate a "general sweep" by the disunionists. It is altogether a mistake. Every member known to be elected is known as a decided friend to the restored Government.[8] In truth, the people are almost universally tired of the War, sigh for peace and civil government; and the President of the United States having recognized the legality of the restored Government,[9] no one is ready to dispute it. The acquiescance is most remarkable.

Under the auspices of Governor Peirpoint, the work of reconstruction will go on, slowly, it may be, but surely, and satisfactorily to nearly the whole people[.]

It can not escape observation that Jefferson Davis has fallen into great disfavor, if not odium.[10] The general idea is that he clung to the Confed-

erate cause long after he knew its fortunes to be desperate, and that he
should have proposed terms of settlement long before Gen Lee's surrender.[11] His administration is regarded as savoring strongly of self-
ishness, and he has little sympathy except with the women, who speak
much of his great piety.

On the subject of slavery, one of the most remarkable revolutions
known in the history of human opinion has unquestionably occurred[.]

The people are not only willing to return to the Union without slavery, but are heartily sick of the peculiar institution. They say it will be
the source of constant disquiet, and thousands have reached the conclusion that for the white man at least Emancipation is the true policy.
Little is said in question of President's[12] Emancipation policy. The prevailing idea is—the thing is done; better let it rest as it is; we shall be
better off with hired than with slave labor[.]

A gentleman of high position in the State and of much ability states
that after traveling through the southside counties—(South of James
River)—the portion of the State having the densest slave population—
he had become satisfied that nine tenths of the slave-holders were not
only willing to be rid of their slaves, but anxious. Many of the farmers
have already made terms with their former slaves, and are paying them
wages as freedmen. All the people ask is some system of management of
the freedmen that will ease them off in the transition from slave to free
labor. Make the negro work, and stand by his contracts, and all, they
say, will be well.

The regret at Mr Lincoln's assassination is universal. The general
impression is that he would have wound up the Rebellion on the best
basis, and that a high generosity to the Southern people would have
marked his measures, and secured a cordial conciliation and stable
reconstruction.

They are looking, with lively interest, to your policy, and the feeling
is one decidedly of hope.

Two points in your administration have already attracted general attention, and elicited unqualified approval: First, your declaration that,
while prominent traitors must be punished, and the Rebellion fully
crushed, nevertheless, the Government of the United States is not to
become a great federal consolodation:[13] second, the programme for reconstruction in North Carolina.[14]

Conservatives of all political denominations in this state fear that, in
the throes of the great troubles that have afflicted us, a centralization
will be inaugurated totally absorbent of state authority. You have given
them much comfort on this point[.]

With respect to the reconstruction programme for North Carolina,
the gratification is general and extreme. In adopting the suffrage qualification existing immediately antecedent to the secession of that state,

great liberality is discovered, and a purpose to refer the matter of negro suffrage to the loyal voters of the states.

Doubtless, before December next, reconstruction will have been fully consummated in Virginia, and this great state restored, on the basis of good will and harmony and interest, to her former position in the great Union of American states.

Such is the information I have been able to gather, and I believe that it can be implicitly relied on.

I shall set out for Wilmington, N.C. within the next two days, highly gratified at the signs of the times in Old Virginia.

Your friend & obt. St
H. M. Watterson

ALS, DLC-JP.

1. June 2.

2. Richmond's blacks would not have endorsed Watterson's pleasant picture. They complained that, despite their loyalty to the Union cause, "our present condition is, in many respects, worse than when we were slaves," and that the military authorities, by insisting that all freedmen carry passes on their travels around the city, had exacerbated the situation. Furthermore, "passes do not in all cases protect us from arrest, abuse, violence and imprisonment"; incarcerated blacks were "hired out . . . for the most insignificant sums." A delegation of blacks presented Johnson with their grievances on June 16. Fields Cook et al. to Johnson, June 16, 1865, Edward McPherson Papers, LC; New York *Herald*, June 17, 1865.

3. Generals Henry W. Halleck and Edward O.C. Ord. Another visitor, however, reported to Pennsylvania Radical Simon Cameron that at the headquarters of Halleck and Ord "real loyalty" was "at a discount." Ord and Halleck were so sympathetic to many former Confederates that within a month Grant transferred them elsewhere, and Gen. Alfred Terry, who was more adamant about protecting the rights and interests of white unionists and blacks, assumed command of the Department of Virginia. J. W. Shaffer to Cameron, July 21, 1865, Cameron Papers, LC; John T. Trowbridge, *The Desolate South, 1865–1866*, Gordon Carroll, ed. (New York, 1956), 97–98.

4. A week later, Radical newspaper reporter Henry Van Ness Boynton gave a different picture. "With the exception of the younger class of hot-headed rebels, the external conduct of all is proper, and shows an outward respect for authority. But underneath this calm, society is seething and boiling, as if a volcano were struggling beneath it. . . . Everything looks as if the South had only laid down the sword and rifle as weapons, and changed the fighting ground to the political arena." Cincinnati *Gazette*, June 17, 1865, quoted in Michael Perman, *Reunion Without Compromise: The South and Reconstruction, 1865–1868* (Cambridge, England, 1973), 22.

5. Henry A. Wise (1806–1876), Virginia governor and mild unionist, had gone with his state and served as a Confederate general.

6. Robert E. Lee (1807–1870), Confederate commander of the Army of Northern Virginia, had surrendered to Grant at Appomattox Court House on April 9, 1865, in part to avoid the transformation of the war into a guerrilla conflict.

7. Within weeks, Pierpont's proposal to reenfranchise former Confederates met with vociferous resistance from Republicans, who claimed that such a step would merely reinstate rebel rule. Ambler, *Pierpont*, 278.

8. On May 25 six counties along the eastern portion of Virginia held elections for the state legislature. Before long northern newspapers reported that disunionists had "swept the state," despite the protests of several Virginians that such was not the case. New York *Tribune*, May 31, June 1, 6, 1865.

9. On May 9 Johnson issued an executive order recognizing the shadow Virginia government established by Lincoln as the provisional government of Virginia, with Pierpont as governor. McPherson, *Reconstruction*, 8–9.

10. A reporter noted the same sentiment when he toured Virginia in August. "From the day I entered Virginia it was a matter of continual astonishment to me to hear the common people denounce the Davis despotism. They were all the more bitter because it had deceived them with lies and false promises so long." Trowbridge, *The Desolate South*, 90.

11. After Lincoln's reelection, Davis apparently had little faith in the prospects for a negotiated peace. Even so, after hearing Francis P. Blair's proposal for reconciliation based on a joint blue-gray invasion of Mexico, he appointed Alexander H. Stephens, John A. Campbell, and R.M.T. Hunter to confer with Lincoln at Hampton Roads, Virginia, in February. The southerners, however, refused to accept Lincoln's twin conditions of reunion and emancipation. Clement Eaton, *Jefferson Davis* (New York, 1977), 259.

12. Abraham Lincoln.

13. When Johnson met with a delegation of Indiana politicians headed by Governor Oliver P. Morton in April, he reminded them "that while I have opposed dissolution and disintegration on one hand, on the other I am equally opposed to consolidation, or the centralization of power in the hands of a few." Speech to Indiana Delegation, April 21, 1865, *Johnson Papers*, VII, 610–15.

14. On May 29, Johnson issued a proclamation outlining the process of reconstruction for North Carolina and appointing William W. Holden provisional governor. In subsequent weeks he issued similar proclamations for six other former Confederate states. McPherson, *Reconstruction*, 11–12.

COPY OF DISPATCH NO 2

Newbern N.C. June 20th 1865

His Excellency Andrew Johnson
President of the U.S.
Sir:

The couplet in regard to the death of the Irishman's pig, might be appropriately employed in describing the downfall of Jeff Davis' Confederacy:

> When it lived, it lived in clover
> When it died, it died all over[1]

I find the same feeling here that universally prevails in Virginia. No people were ever more thoroughly conquered and subdued. Point out to them the way that leads to amicable relations with the Government of the United States, and they will be certain to take it. Those persons to whom you have granted amnesty and pardon are exceedingly thankful, and the few that I have seen of the excepted classes are quite hopeful. All disunion feeling, and every wish to establish a separate Southern Confederacy, have been pulverized by the War. If there be any thing like it in history, it has escaped my observation[.]

Not a great many of the old citizens, I am sorry to be obliged to say, are here; and turn which way you will a majority of the persons you see are negroes. It is estimated that there are of such persons, within a circle of twenty miles round about Newberne, from forty to fifty thousand, and even higher. These have assembled, since the occupation of this re-

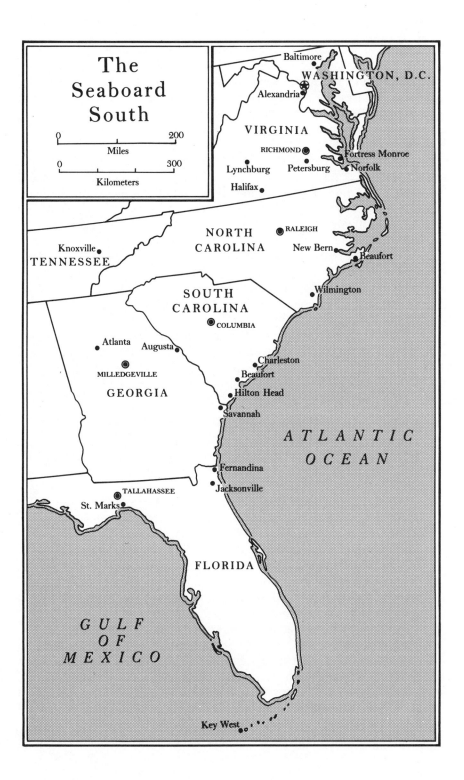

The
Seaboard
South

0   200
Miles

0   300
Kilometers

Baltimore

WASHINGTON, D.C.

Alexandria

VIRGINIA

RICHMOND

Fortress Monroe

Lynchburg   Petersburg   Norfolk

Halifax

NORTH
CAROLINA

RALEIGH

Knoxville

New Bern

TENNESSEE

Beaufort

SOUTH
CAROLINA

Wilmington

COLUMBIA

Atlanta   Augusta

MILLEDGEVILLE

Charleston

Beaufort

GEORGIA

Hilton Head

Savannah

ATLANTIC
OCEAN

Fernandina

TALLAHASSEE

Jacksonville

St. Marks

FLORIDA

GULF
OF
MEXICO

Key West

gion by the Federal forces,[2] from various portions of the State. Many of
them are without labor, and there is no demand sufficient to furnish
them with employment. Some thousands of these negroes have heretofore been *rationed* by the Government, and it is apprehended that
when this support is withdrawn, plunder and robbery will ensue. So
here is work, and plenty of it, for the Superintendent of the Freedmen's
Bureau.[3]

I feel that it is beyond the line of my duty to go into an argument on
any subject. What you want are facts. Well—I give it to you as a fact
that Newberne is now garrisoned by at least three thousand colored
troops under the command of Gen. Payne[4]—a militia man from Boston
at the beginning of the War. I also give it to you as a fact that the citizens of the town are deeply impressed with the belief that they deserve
no such punishment as Gen. Payne and his negro troops.[5] That it is
wholly unnecessary and very bad policy, there can be no question.
Boston, to day, is not more loyal than Newberne[.]

This Gen Payne suspended Gen I. N. Palmer,[6] on the 6th of the
present month.

The "Daily North Carolina Times", the only paper published here,
and loyal to the core, in speaking of Gen. Palmer, on the 16th inst, said:

> The numerous friends of this worthy officer will be pleased to learn that he
> has been promoted to the rank of Major General. We trust that he may long live
> to enjoy the honor and dignity of the position thus confered.
> The General has been long and favorably known in this department as a man
> of kindness and moderation, and the former citizens of this community, those
> who have remained here as well as those who have recently returned to their
> homes, all so far as we have been able to learn, and we have mixed freely among
> them, speak in the highest praise of his sterling qualities and universally mani-
> fest a desire that he shall be permitted to remain with us until our troubles are
> over and civil law fully established.

Whether Gen Palmer desires to remain here I do not know, but the
Times has expressed the wishes of the people, not only here, but of the
whole state; and should he be placed in command of the Department of
North Carolina, there is no officer who would be more acceptable to her
citizens, or who would more faithfully carry out the views of the Government. He is an old army officer, and an honor to his profession. Like
yourself, too, he is for a white man's government, and in favor of free
white citizens controlling this country.

I need not tell you that all the Treasury agents who have lived and
flourished, during the past two years, are not saints.[7] It would be
strange if some of them are not good men, but really it does seem that
such are exceptions to the rule. If the history of their operations in the
Southern states were correctly written out at length, surely they would
never again have the impudence to hold up their heads among honest
men. I had my eye on a pretty bad case in this town (one Peter Lawson
of Lowell)[8] which I intended to report to you, with specifications, but

since I received your Proclamation of the 13th inst,[9] I deem it unnecessary. Peter's "occupation" is now gone, and every honest man in this community is glad of it.

Last, though not least: when Newberne was captured by the Federal forces under Gen Burnside,[10] in March 1862, a large part of the population left their homes and went to the interior. The Military, on its entry, and afterward the Treasury department, took possession of the abandoned property; and all the dwellings, plantations, and houses of business belonging to those who became refugees, are now either held by the military, or are under the control of Treasury agents, have been rented by the year; and the business houses, mills, wharfs, docks &c. are in possession of temporary tenants and inaccessible to the owners.

A large number of the old residents, since the termination of the War, have applied for the restoration of their property. The following letter from Gen Palmer will show what has been done about it:

Newberne N.C. June 20th 1865

Hon. H. M. Watterson Newberne
My dear Sir.

In reply to your request to be informed what action has been taken by me while in command of this District to enable persons to avail themselves of the benefits of the President's amnesty proclamation I will state:

That whenever persons made a respectful application for the restoration of property, I required them to shew that they belonged to neither of the excluded classes, and if they had taken upon themselves all the obligations required, an order was at once issued which would secure to them the title to their property, and the possession of it as soon as it was no longer needed for any public purpose.

All the cases were examined with great care, and nearly all the applicants were persons who had taken no active part in the rebellion, but who had been dragged away from this place at the time of its capture, or who had been frightened away by the order of Gen. Branch[11] who ordered the place to be burned as soon as he saw that it must be captured.

Some seventy of these applications were examined and the order for the restoration in the greater part of these was made on the 3d inst. On the 6th inst. however, I was released from the command of the District by Gen Payne, who brings with him such a large force that he may have found it necessary to retain all the buildings I had proposed to give up immediately.

Newberne in my opinion needs no large force. A few companies *near* the town would I think answer every purpose, but I have no desire to question the propriety of the acts of my superior officers. Were the matter left to me, however, I should consider it sound policy to clear the town of troops and let the people come back and get about their usual avocations[.]

I have understood that but few persons have been able as yet to obtain possession of their property. A good deal of it is in possession of the Treasury agent, and what action is taken by his Department to comply with the President's order I can not say[.]

I am, Sir, Very respectfully
Your Obt. Servant I. N. Palmer
Bvt Maj Genl Vols

I will simply add that, in my humble opinion, the sooner the views of Gen Palmer in regard to Newberne matters are carried out, the better for this people, the better for the United States, and the better for your Administration.[12]

I shall go up to Raleigh to morrow, where I learn that Gov Holden[13] is getting along finely.

Your Friend & obt. Servant

H. M. Watterson

ALS, DLC-JP. This "copy," rather than the original—both found in the Johnson Papers—bears the presidential receipt stamp and was presumably the version seen by the President.

1. A variation on the nursery rhyme about Little Betty Pringle's pig: "When he was alive he lived in clover / But now he's dead and that's all over." Watterson's son Henry used the couplet in a telephone interview concerning the 1918 armistice, claiming that its source was Ben Jonson, who used it as an inscription for the headstone marking the grave of a dead pig. Iona and Peter Opie, eds., *Oxford Dictionary of Nursery Rhymes* (Oxford, 1951), 73; Arthur Krock, ed., *The Editorials of Henry Watterson* (New York, 1923), 426.

2. Federal troops had seized points along the North Carolina coastline in early 1862.

3. General Oliver Otis Howard (1830–1909) had been placed in charge of the Freedmen's Bureau the previous month. Within weeks he found himself in conflict with President Johnson and others over the proper policy to pursue to protect and promote the welfare of the freedmen.

4. Charles J. Paine (1833–1916), who had commanded several black divisions, headed the District of New Bern.

5. Many white southerners resented the presence of blacks, whom they regarded as inferior, clad in blue uniforms and possessing both the authority and the ability to make whites comply with the law. South Carolinian Henry Ravenel, for example, complained of the "gang of diabolical savages sent here with arms in their hands to insult & degrade us. Is this the process by which brotherly love is to be infused through the Southern States?" In New Bern, there had been several clashes between black soldiers and townspeople, resulting in at least one death. At least one paper, however, testified to the good behavior of the black troops in Paine's command. Arney Robinson Childs, ed., *The Private Journal of Henry William Ravenel, 1859–1887* (Columbia, S.C., 1947), 246; New York *Times*, July 2, 1865; Jacksonville (Fla.) *Times*, October 12, 1865.

6. Innis N. Palmer (1824–1900) had been on duty along the North Carolina coast for several years.

7. Although many observers, North and South, complained about the corruption of treasury agents, one recent student of the subject concludes that the great majority were honest men. Robert F. Futrell, Federal Trade with the Confederate States, 1861–1865: A Study of Governmental Policy (Ph.D. dissertation, Vanderbilt University, 1950), 460–62.

8. Peter Lawson of Lowell, Massachusetts, was appointed a purchasing agent by treasury secretary William Pitt Fessenden on February 28, 1865; his duties terminated with Johnson's recent proclamation. *Ibid.*, 425, 453–54.

9. On June 13 Johnson issued a proclamation lifting most restrictions on internal trade east of the Mississippi River. Richardson, *Messages*, VI, 317–18.

10. Ambrose E. Burnside (1824–1881) scored one of his rare military successes in early 1862 when he conducted the Union's invasion of the North Carolina coast.

11. Lawrence O'Bryan Branch (1820–1862), North Carolina politician and editor, contested Burnside's advance on New Bern in 1862.

12. Palmer had made previous inquiries about returning property. In May, Gen. John M. Schofield, in notifying Palmer that property controlled by the Treasury Department could not be reclaimed by the military for purposes other than government use, added, "Army officers cannot settle any question of confiscation. The desire of the commanding general is that officers have as little as possible to do with such matters." Schofield to Palmer, May 16, 1865, Schofield Papers, LC.

13. William W. Holden (1818–1892), prominent prewar Democratic editor, emerged as an open opponent of the Confederate war effort in 1863, highlighting his break by

Friends of the Freedmen II:
Oliver O. Howard and Charles Sumner.
Courtesy of The National Archives

running unsuccessfully for the governorship on a peace platform the following year. Appointed provisional governor by Johnson on May 29, 1865, he failed to gain election that year, but won the office as a Republican three years later.

———◄●►———

Raleigh. N.C. June 27th 1865

Mr President.

Learning that Gen Cox,[1] in the morning, will set out for Washington, I avail myself of the opportunity to send you a line of friendship.

At Richmond, at Newberne, and at Raleigh, I have reason to know that I have done some service to the Administration by my representation of its *head*. I have often said in the right quarter that from two positions the Chases and Sumners[2] would never drive the President: First, that the Southern states are in the Union, and have never been out:[3] second, that the suffrage question belongs to the States alone.[4]

I will send you my report to-morrow, and the next day will leave for Wilmington[.]

All is politically right in North Carolina[.]

Your friend H. M. Watterson

ALS, DLC-JP.

1. Major General Jacob D. Cox.

2. Massachusetts senator Charles Sumner (1811–1874), prominent antislavery politician, advocated enfranchising blacks as essential to the success of reconstruction.

3. As early as February 11, 1862, Sumner had offered a set of resolutions which asserted that seceded states had forfeited their rights as states within the Union and were now territories under the jurisdiction of Congress. Through his "state-suicide" theory he hoped to strike directly at slavery, bypassing the argument that it was protected by state law and concepts of federalism by asserting that these guarantees did not apply to states in the Confederacy. Thaddeus Stevens' "conquered provinces" theory, while based upon somewhat different assumptions, looked toward the same end. McKitrick, *Andrew Johnson and Reconstruction*, 93–115.

4. Sumner and Chase argued that the federal government could demand enfranchisement of freedmen as a condition of readmitting the seceded states. *Ibid.*

———◄●►———

COPY OF DISPATCH NO 3

Raleigh. N.C. June 29th 1865

His Excellency Andrew Johnson
President of the U.S.
Sir:

I had myself but an imperfect idea, when I left Washington, of the extent to which the Southern people were subjugated. I feared that a rebellious spirit still animated the hearts of thousands. Be assured that my visit to Virginia and North Carolina has dispelled all my apprehensions on that point. I have talked with quite a number of gentlemen of every shade of politics, since my advent into this state and city, and they all concur in the sentiment,—that the Rebellion has been ground into unpalpable powder. None can be found so insane as to think of further resistance to the authority of the United States.

North Carolina, like Tennessee, was literally dragged into the Rebellion,[1] and I feel a lively sympathy for the great body of her citizens. The old Secession leaders see that they are politically ruined, and all I have to say to that is—God be praised. Never again, even if inclined, will they be able to mislead their neighbors.

Gov Holden is progressing with the great work before him about as rapidly and as satisfactorily as any mortal man could well do. He is a calm, clear-headed, systematic, laborious gentleman; and I can bear testimony to the kindness and courtesy he displays in his official intercourse with everybody. These admirable traits in his character are fast removing any prejudices that may have been engendered against him by the terrible conflict through which we have just passed.[2] The general idea prevailing here is—and in that idea I fully concur—that you could not have made a better selection for Provisional Governor of North Carolina. I doubt, all things considered, whether you could have made as good. I think he is the very man for the business. In the work of reconstruction, he has already appointed Magistrates in about 55 counties out of 85. These Magistrates, I need not inform you, will organize the counties and re-establish civil law. Out of these he is choosing special Boards, of the best men, to administer the amnesty oath to the people. These Boards, he says, will sift the wheat from the chaff. None but loyal men will be allowed to vote or hold office.[3]

Gov Holden says that on account of the immense area of territory in the Western part of the State, and the want of mails, the work of reorganization can not proceed as rapidly as he desires.[4] He hopes, however, that by the beginning of next year, he will have all the machinery of State government in complete operation.

I take it for granted that the Post Master General[5] will, as soon as he can, give mail facilities to North Carolina. She is greatly in need of them. A mail should be at once established, if possible, to every county town, at least.

Gov Holden says that there are many persons in the western part of the state who ought to be pardoned, but without mails, it will require much time to send their petitions and get answers.

There is much complaint that property belonging to persons who have been restored to their rights by the amnesty proclamation, is still held by Treasury agents. Gov Holden thinks, and so do I, that an order to place such persons in possession would be hailed with gratitude, and would add at once to the prosperity of Newberne, Wilmington, and other towns.[6]

Gov Holden is confident that, within the next four or six weeks, the county police or militia will be organized.[7] He thinks, after that organization is perfected, and I fully concur with him, it will not be necessary to keep many troops in the State.

The appointment of Magistrates or Justices in the counties, about 3,500 in all, and of Mayors and Commissioners of towns, will go far to promote order and obedience to law.[8] This work is nearly accomplished.

You can scarcely have an idea of the present poverty of these people. I mean, specially, their want of ability to raise money. As a humane man I must be permitted to say that, if it be at all possible, let the collection of the Federal tax be suspended for a time.[9] The people *generally* are *not* able to pay it. When they are, I am well assured, they will do it cheerfully.

Hon Kenneth Rayner,[10] with whom we both served in Congress, has just left my room. He read me his petition to you for a special pardon. Notwithstanding its length, I trust that you will find time to read it. It is so true, so sincere, and so manly, that I regard it as a model paper.[11]

I shall set out in the morning for Wilmington,—highly pleased with this my first visit to Raleigh.

Your friend & obt Svt
H. M. Watterson

ALS, DLC-JP. This "copy," rather than the original—both found in the Johnson Papers—bears the presidential receipt stamp and was presumably the version seen by the President.

1. Watterson exaggerates his point. Unlike Tennessee, where the actions of Governor Isham G. Harris obviously aided the secessionist cause in a divided state, North Carolina, reacting to Lincoln's call for troops, chose to secede on May 20, 1861, by a unanimous vote of its secession convention. Resistance to Confederate rule and a sturdy peace movement, however, emerged rather early in North Carolina. Marc W. Kruman, *Parties and Politics in North Carolina, 1836–1865* (Baton Rouge, 1983), 220, 241.

2. Watterson is referring to Holden's efforts to achieve a negotiated peace during the war, capped by his unsuccessful campaign for governor in 1864.

3. Holden included in his definition of loyalty supporters of his 1864 gubernatorial candidacy—many of whom had been advocates of the Confederacy in early times. Obviously the provisional governor's appointment policy was designed to enhance his political future by providing him with a cadre of office-holding adherents. Dan T. Carter, *When the War Was Over: The Failure of Self-Reconstruction in the South, 1865–1867* (Baton Rouge, 1985), 48–49.

4. One Tarheel newspaper commented, "Were the mails in full operation, we believe the work of reconstruction would be easy and speedy." Salisbury *Banner*, June 19, 1865, quoted in Wilmington *Herald*, June 23, 1865.

5. William Dennison (1815–1882), Whig and Republican politician who served as governor of Ohio (1860–62), was appointed postmaster general (1864), resigning in 1866 owing to his dissent from Johnson's Reconstruction policy.

6. Johnson was in the process of developing a policy on property confiscation and restoration during the summer of 1865. Within a month Attorney General James Speed began to halt proceedings for the sale of confiscated land, commencing the restoration process. Benedict, *Compromise of Principle*, 249.

7. In the summer of 1865 Holden attempted to organize county police forces to "maintain order." These organizations usually operated under the supervision of Federal military officers and consisted of Confederate veterans. At Wilmington, the police were employed to subdue black resistance to the reestablishment of white control. Raper, *Holden*, 65; W. McKee Evans, *Ballots and Fence Rails: Reconstruction on the Lower Cape Fear* (Chapel Hill, 1967), 80–81.

8. Holden made provision for the appointment of local judicial officers in his June 12

proclamation outlining his policy. Military authorities, however, retained jurisdiction in cases involving blacks, in part because state law prohibited black testimony against whites. The provisional governor's appeal to Johnson to overturn this decision proved unavailing. Raper, *Holden*, 65–66; Sefton, *Army and Reconstruction*, 37; Holden to Johnson, August 3, 1865, Johnson Papers, LC.

9. Although Johnson's May 29 proclamation establishing North Carolina's provisional government specifically directed the secretary of the treasury to "put in execution the revenue laws of the United States," Secretary McCulloch suspended collection of taxes on June 21; six days later, he ceased levying the 25% tax on cotton. Richardson, *Messages*, VI, 313–14; Raper, *Holden*, 67; New York *Herald*, September 20, 1865; Futrell, *Federal Trade*, 454.

10. Whig lawyer Kenneth Rayner (1808–1884), renowned for his debates with John Quincy Adams over the House of Representatives' "gag rule" forbidding the introduction of antislavery petitions, had advocated secession in North Carolina's secession convention, later recanting his position. In 1866 he demonstrated his fealty to Johnson by writing an unattributed biography of the President.

11. Rayner, mentioning that Watterson had advised him to forward his application for pardon "Just as it was," characterized himself as such "an enthusiastic, ardent, and uncompromising Union-man" that he had been "denounced . . . by fire-eating secessionists *as an* Abolitionist." Assuring Johnson that the "most perfect quiet order and calmness prevail" in North Carolina, he urged the President to suspend the collection of federal property taxes to preserve what remained of the state's economy. Southerners, according to Rayner, looked toward Johnson with "confidence and hope," and he predicted that the President "will very soon rally around him a party (no, I will not say party, but a brotherhood) of honor and patriotic men that will defy all the carpings of the factions, and all the intriguers of vicious political aspirants." Rayner to Johnson, July 8, 1865, Johnson Papers, LC.

COPY OF DISPATCH NO 4

Wilmington, N.C. July 8 1865

His Excellency Andrew Johnson
President of the U.S.
Sir.

It is hardly necessary for me to say to you that, in the estimation of these people, the Rebellion has been utterly annihilated. Many are glad of it. Those who are not, submit about as gracefully as badly whipped men can well do. They say—and I believe them to be sincere—that they have had enough of war to last them the remainder of their days; and if another rebellion takes place—so far as they are concerned—it will have to come from the North[.]

This town, like Newberne, is garrisoned by a brigade of negro troops. This may be for the best, but I do not believe it.[1] I deem it unnecessary to add another word on this subject—having no doubt that you are well informed in regard to all such matters.[2]

The Postmaster,[3] Collector of the Port[4] &c. recently appointed for Wilmington, are all good men. There is some question, however, whether they can take the oath required.[5] Nobody doubts that they are and have been all the while good union men; but like nearly everybody in North Carolina, from 17 to 55 years of age,[6] they may have, in some form or other, been mixed up with the Rebellion[.]

I stayed in Raleigh a week longer than I intended at the date of my dispatch from that city. It being the capital of the state, I had an opportunity of making the acquaintance and talking with gentlemen from nearly every part of the State. I feel that I have pretty thoroughly canvassed North Carolina; and I can say to you with confidence that her future loyalty is as certain as that of any State in the Union. The original Secessionists are surely all dead, or have fled to parts unknown; for I am yet to find the first man who is willing to admit that he belonged to that class of politicians!

Hailing from the President's own State, many have sought my acquaintance. In every instance you formed a large share of the conversation. Of course I was at home on that subject, and rest assured that I have done it ample justice. You know, and I know, what you have done for the Southern people since your inauguration, and I never fail to detail all that—act by act. In the single item of cotton—I mean your abolishment of the enormous tax upon it[7]—you have generously surrendered to the South at least fifty millions of dollars. I say to these people, suppose Chase, or Sumner, or even Hannibal Hamlin[8] were President, think you that the last farthing of this iniquitous tax would not be collected?

All assent to this interrogative proposition, and they at once begin to realize the pleasing fact that they have a friend instead of an enemy in the Presidential Chair[.]

When I meet a gentleman disposed to complain, because the President dont do this, or does do that, I say to him—Sir, if the President were at once to do all you desire, it would be a sad day's work for the South. And why? Because it would array against him an overwhelming majority in both branches of Congress, and thus render him utterly powerless to help the South. No, no, my friend, you had better let the President go on in his own way. He understands perfectly what he is doing, and all will be right in the end. This view of the subject generally satisfies the party[.] He had never thought of it before.

Permit me to assure you that your Administration is growing daily in the confidence of the people of North Carolina. The position that you are now understood to occupy in regard to negro suffrage,[9] is more than any thing else doing the work. I have been sometimes asked if I thought the President would stand firm on this question. Stand firm, I would reply, when was Andrew Johnson ever known to be driven from a political position deliberately taken. I would then give the person a mess of Tennessee politics.

It is clear to my mind that you are to have a war with the friends of Chase, who is evidently a candidate for the next Presidency, and expects to be elected on the issue of negro suffrage. Let it come—the sooner the better for your Administration and the better for the country. You will whip them to death. I will here repeat what I said to you in Washington. These agitators constitute one wing of the concern that brought on the late terrible war. The Southern wing has already been crushed, and the victory will never be complete till the Northern wing is put *hors de combat*. Then and not till then will the country have repose[.]

I am very anxious to get out of this place, for it is very sickly. There is a fever raging here and it is said to have become an epidemic.[10] If I can not get a government transport for Savanah within the next two days, I will be forced to go back to Fortress Monroe for one. In that event I think I will run up to Washington[.] You may wish to change my programme[.]

Your friend & obt. Svt

H. M. Watterson

ALS, DLC-JP. No "original" version found in Johnson Papers.

1. In June the Wilmington *Herald* praised the behavior of black troops, noting that "the city has been remarkably quiet, the street fights and disturbances so common a week ago having entirely ceased." Within two weeks, however, while the paper reported that "the negro troops, as a body, have behaved even better than the white troops that preceded them," it concluded, "the trouble is that the discipline of these troops is not as thorough as it should be. . . . If it is the desire and the purpose of the government to harmonize and conciliate these southern communities the black troops had better be withdrawn and whites substituted." This editorial was inspired by stories of the murder of a white merchant by a black soldier; four days later the merchant, alive, well, and unharmed, denied that any incident took place. Wilmington *Herald*, June 12, 23, 27, 1865.

2. Within weeks several townspeople, including municipal officials, petitioned Johnson to remove the black troops. "Inspired by a sincere sentiment of loyalty" and "anxious to promote harmony and conciliation," the petitioners declared that they "cheerfully accept the abolition of slavery as a fixed and unalterable fact," and pledged to treat the freedmen "with all the consideration to which their altered condition entitles them." While accepting the necessity for martial law as a temporary expedient, the townspeople suggested "that the presence of *colored troops* in our midst is not calculated to allay public anxiety and to produce that harmony and cheerful submission to the laws which your Excellency . . . is so anxious to preserve." Such reservations were not based "solely upon the fact that they are of a different and inferior race; but because they are a fruitful source of discontent, and demoralization to the civilians of their own race in our midst, and of irritation, and dissatisfaction to the whites." At the same time it was rumored that black troops were drilling freedmen in the use of small arms—but a northern reporter concluded that these reports were generated by "the continuous fault-finding and evil prophesying of this detestable clique of unsubdued traitors." John Dawson et al. to Johnson, [August] 1865, Johnson Papers, LC; New York *Times*, August 2, 1865.

3. William M. Poisson (b. *c*1839), a man of "unblemished character, fine business attainments, and universally acceptable," was appointed postmaster. 1860 Census, N.C., New Hanover, Wilmington, 96; Wilmington *Herald*, July 3, 1865; Appointments, Vol. 1, 273, Johnson Papers, Series 6B, LC.

4. Parker Quince (b. *c*1797) was appointed August 7; originally it was rumored that he would become surveyor of customs. *Ibid.*, 283; New York *World*, June 23, 1865; 1860 Census, N.C., New Hanover, Masonboro Sound, 188.

5. The ironclad oath, demanded of all federal officeholders, required the individual to pledge past as well as future loyalty to the United States. Much to the disgust of Charles Sumner and other Radical Republicans, treasury secretary Hugh McCulloch, unable to staff government posts with individuals who could subscribe to such an oath, appointed former Confederates to federal positions. Benedict, *Compromise of Principle*, 249.

6. In part a reference to the Confederate Conscription Act of 1864, which expanded the eligible age of draftees to include adult white males between 17 and 50. Resistance to the draft was widespread in North Carolina. Emory M. Thomas, *The Confederate Nation* (New York, 1979), 260–61.

7. Johnson's June 13 proclamation on commercial intercourse terminated "all restrictions upon internal, domestic, and coastwise intercourse and trade, and upon the removal of products of States heretofore declared in insurrection," including regulations passed by Congress the preceding July 2 instructing treasury agents to pay no more than seventy-five percent of the New York market value for cotton grown in the Confederacy. McCulloch's June 27 circular implemented this decision. Richardson, *Messages*, VI, 317–18; Futrell, Federal Trade, 381, 454.

8. Former congressman and senator Hannibal Hamlin (1809–1891) had been Lincoln's first vice president. He returned to the Senate in 1869 and later served as minister to Spain.

9. Johnson's North Carolina proclamation had made it clear that he would not impose black suffrage on the ex-Confederate states; rather, each state would still determine its own suffrage qualifications.

10. Watterson may have exaggerated the seriousness of conditions. A week and a half earlier the local paper termed rumors of a yellow fever epidemic "a causeless panic"; a week later, it would claim, "The health of the city of Wilmington for the two or three weeks past has been in every respect as good as ever known here previously at this season of the year." Wilmington *Herald*, June 27, July 14, 1865.

Carl Schurz:
Rebuffed Radical

Johnson's proclamations of May 29th stunned many Radicals. The North Carolina proclamation appeared to snuff out any chance to impose black suffrage by allowing southern whites to establish their own voting qualifications. Judged by its terms alone, the amnesty proclamation potentially could deny Confederate civil and military leaders a role in the reconstruction process; but in practice Johnson seemed almost too willing to grant pardons to all but a few. Certainly this was a surprise to those who recalled the President's pledge to make treason odious. One of the most astonished was Carl Schurz, the German-born Republican politico who had just completed a less than glorious military career.

Schurz's Radical credentials were solid. Fleeing Germany after the collapse of the 1848 revolution, he finally settled in Wisconsin, where he carried his commitment for democracy into the emerging Republican party. His ethnic background proved attractive to party leaders, who hoped to use him to woo German immigrant voters; Schurz parlayed this perception to achieve political prominence. He worked hard to elect Lincoln in 1860, and was rewarded with the mission to Spain. But diplomacy bored him, especially when a war promised fame and glory; in 1862 he returned to America, and soon he was wearing a brigadier's shoulder straps. A good performance at Second Bull Run was soon overshadowed by serious setbacks at Chancellorsville and Gettysburg, when troops under his command gave way in the face of Confederate assaults. A promotion to major general was recognition of his political value, not his military ability, as the Lincoln administration sought to win over German immigrants to the war effort. On leave at the beginning of 1864, he sought a new command, enlisting military governor Andrew Johnson in his quest, but neither Grant, Sherman, nor George H. Thomas wanted him. At last he found a home as chief of staff to Henry W. Slocum's Army of Georgia during the last month of the war.[1]

If Schurz proved less than adept with the sword, he remained indefatigable with the pen. Lincoln had asked him to write whenever he wished to forward suggestions, and the new general had barely reached his new command when he took advantage of the invitation, commenc-

1. For Schurz's life, see Hans L. Trefousse, *Carl Schurz: A Biography* (Knoxville, Tenn., 1982) and Claude M. Fuess, *Carl Schurz, Reformer (1829–1906)* (New York, 1932).

ing a correspondence that was often strained and sometimes sharp. He so earnestly urged Lincoln to advance more vigorously the cause of emancipation that at times he pierced the normally thick skin of the President. Stung by Schurz's smug suggestion that he might not appreciate the horrors of war brought on by generals who "were not foursquare for emancipation," Lincoln replied that "there are men who have 'heart in it' that think that you are performing your part as poorly as you think I am performing mine."[2] Nevertheless, Schurz believed he had been instrumental in guiding the President on the path toward black freedom; doubtless he thought he would continue to advise the railsplitter during Reconstruction.

Lincoln's death was not necessarily a disaster to Schurz's ambition, for he believed his previous contact with "Andie Johnson" would prove invaluable. Always more than willing to offer unsolicited advice, Schurz made sure to visit the new President within weeks of the assassination. "So far he seems all right," he wrote his wife; "there are no longer any traces of bad habits, and the hints he gives in regard to policy permit us to hope from him on the whole an energetic and at the same time discreet use of his executive powers." To Charles Sumner, with whom he had formed a close friendship, he relayed his confidence that Johnson's "objects . . . are all [that] the most progressive friends of human liberty can desire." However, Schurz continued, it was Johnson's policy, "and in many respects a correct one, to bring about these results practically without making them the subject of popular discussion in the shape of an openly announced program."[3]

Like Lincoln, Johnson had concluded his conversation with Schurz by suggesting that he write "whenever I had anything worthy of consideration to suggest." In Schurz's mind this seemingly harmless invitation was transformed into a request to offer advice, and he made haste to avail himself of the opportunity, conferring with the President by pen and in person about the trial of Lincoln's assassins, the prosecution of Jefferson Davis, and the proper policy to pursue toward Mexico. The general concluded that such exchanges showed "that I am in a good way to acquire here a personal influence which, in certain contingencies, may prove of great significance."[4]

Johnson did sound Schurz out on his proposed plan for reconstruction on May 26, showing him a draft of his proclamation outlining the process for North Carolina. The President "seemed uncertain and perplexed"; Schurz was upset, believing that Johnson was acting too hast-

2. Trefousse, *Schurz*, 126.

3. Schurz to Margarethe Schurz, May 4, 1865, Schafer, *Intimate Letters*, 335; Schurz to Charles Sumner, May 9, 1865, Bancroft, *Schurz Correspondence*, I, 255 (brackets in source).

4. Schurz to Johnson, May 13, 1865, Johnson Papers, LC; Schurz to Margarethe Schurz, May 19, 21, 1865, Schafer, *Intimate Letters*, 336–37.

ily. Among the changes he proposed was the elimination of the limited suffrage provisions, presumably so blacks could vote. The President "listened so attentively that I was almost sure he would heed my advice." Schurz suggested that Johnson might need more information on southern conditions; maybe the President could dispatch "some sensible and reliable person" to supervise the implementation of the policy by military commanders, especially as Schurz had earlier expressed his skepticism at their ability to "be sufficiently on their guard against the machinations of the old leaders."[5]

According to Schurz, Johnson was "exceedingly" pleased by the suggestion, "and he even went so far as to ask me, whether I would return to Washington at his bidding to aid him in the matter." Schurz was so eager to accept that he offered to stay at the capital to await the summons to duty, but Johnson failed to respond, and the general journeyed back to his home in Bethlehem, Pennsylvania. There he read with raised eyebrows Johnson's two May 29 proclamations outlining amnesty policy and the process of restoring civil government to North Carolina. Schurz had come away from his talks with Johnson concerned that the President might in fact be too harsh on the South, and the nation "would have to pass through a disgraceful period of 'bloody assizes'" before proceeding with reconstruction. Now Schurz feared that quite the reverse was true.[6]

The general swung into action with an alacrity he had rarely displayed on the battlefield. He advised Sumner to hurry down to Washington to hold Johnson to his previous intentions: "The President's opinions are quite unsettled on the most vital points." Perhaps the new chief executive, removed from his familiar surroundings of Tennessee, had lost some of the "combativeness" which had characterized his career there: "I fear he has not that clearness of purpose and firmness of character he was supposed to have." Then Schurz took up the case with the President via letter. Emphasizing that the North Carolina proclamation "has . . . been generally interpreted as a declaration of policy . . . adverse to the introduction of negro suffrage," he warned that black enfranchisement could spark a controversy between Congress and the President, turning a "difference of opinion" into "direct opposition." To avoid such a misunderstanding, Schurz forwarded one suggestion. South Carolina's elective franchise had been defined by a property qualification, including ownership of slaves. Obviously events had rendered this clause useless. Why not, in the absence of any viable guidelines, allow all loyal inhabitants "without distinction" to elect delegates to the state's constitutional convention? Even Democrats would accept this;

5. Schurz to Sumner, May 9, June 5, 1865, Bancroft, *Schurz Correspondence*, I, 254, 258–59; Schurz to Margarethe Schurz, May 26, 1865, Schafer, *Intimate Letters*, 337.

6. Schurz to Sumner, June 5, 1865, Bancroft, *Schurz Correspondence*, I, 259; Schurz, *Reminiscences*, III, 150.

after all, this was *South* Carolina, hotbed of secession. Like Chase, Schurz based the argument for black suffrage not on race, but on fealty to the Union cause.[7]

Schurz's proposal appeared to be a skillful maneuver flanking Johnson's constitutional concerns. As he pointed out, the Constitution never contemplated the appointment of provisional governors or a presidential directive for the convening of a state constitutional convention. If this idea rankled the President's sensitivities, he must have frowned upon reading Schurz's declaration that his proposal "will be far more *democratic* than the policy you have adopted with regard to North Carolina." Certainly, someone who gloried in his plebeian status did not want a lecture on democracy from a German immigrant. And, if that was not worrisome enough, the general also was contemplating an elaboration of his ideas through the press in the form of letters addressed to Johnson![8]

The President responded to Schurz's discourse by inviting him to Washington once more. As the general traveled to the capital, he stopped off at the home of Dr. Heinrich Tiedemann, an old friend. For entertainment, the Tiedemann family held a seance; their visitor, intrigued by the idea, asked to talk to Abraham Lincoln. Years later Schurz claimed that the spirit of the martyr President not only spoke to him, but "told" him that Johnson was planning to ask him to undertake a tour of the South. Since this idea had been discussed before, it was not such an astounding prediction. Nevertheless, it proved accurate. The President "complained of being unable to procure reliable information, and, consequently, being always obliged to act in the dark." It would be up to Schurz to enlighten him.[9]

In the absence of any explanation from Johnson, we are left to speculate why he asked Schurz to undertake such an assignment. The general believed that the President, regarding his North Carolina plan as "merely experimental," wanted information on conditions in the Deep South. Of the prospects for reconstruction there the Tennessean appeared "very doubtful and even anxious" whether restoration "could be done with safety to the Union men and to the emancipated slaves." Schurz recalled later that Johnson "appeared to me like a man who had taken some important step under pressure, against his own inclination, and who was troubled about himself." Perhaps. But just prior to Schurz's visit Johnson had issued a proclamation similar in form to the one on North Carolina launching the reconstruction process in Missis-

7. Schurz to Sumner, June 5, 1865, Bancroft, *Schurz Correspondence*, I, 259; Schurz to Johnson, June 6, 1865, Johnson Papers, LC.
   8. *Ibid.*
   9. Schurz to Henry Meyer, June 15, 1865, Schafer, *Intimate Letters*, 338; Schurz, *Reminiscences*, III, 154–55; Schurz to Margarethe Schurz, June 16, 1865, Bancroft, *Schurz Correspondence*, I, 264.

Carl Schurz.
Courtesy of The Library of Congress

sippi; two days after he spoke with Schurz he repeated the action for Georgia and Texas, and within weeks did the same for Alabama and South Carolina, concluding with Florida on July 13. These do not seem to be the actions of a troubled man.[10]

If Schurz's explanation appears somewhat unsatisfactory, other answers—such as Hans Trefousse's suggestion that Johnson wanted "to mollify him or to get rid of him"—reduce the general to a nuisance, blinded by his own self-esteem. While certainly Schurz's ego did cloud his perspective, this interpretation says little for Johnson's political sagacity, since he was authorizing someone to act as his representative who dissented in many particulars from his policy. Surely Johnson knew that Schurz questioned the wisdom of his proposals; indeed, the general had reminded him of their differing attitudes several times. Schurz later recalled that Johnson did not seem deterred by this, flattering him with "assurances of his confidence in my character and judgment."[11]

Perhaps part of the problem was that the two men did not quite agree on the purpose of Schurz's mission. Schurz had suggested that the President should appoint someone "to supervise and aid the political action of our military commanders in the South," believing "it would be an excellent arrangement for keeping the Government well informed of what is expected of them, for facilitating business generally and for preventing a great many mistakes which otherwise are very likely to be made." In short, he had outlined a liaison function, an idea which proved attractive to the President. After his visit with Johnson, however, Schurz wrote a friend that the purpose of the mission was "to study the conditions and make reports and recommendations to him as to the policy that should be pursued," which he hoped would be presented as a report to Congress "so shaped as to play a distinctive role in this weighty business." This went beyond the purpose of conveying information; he envisioned himself as a policy maker, whereas Johnson wanted him to help implement and report on a policy already decided upon. The confusion would prove crucial.[12]

Schurz compounded the problem in searching for a means to derive income. Out of the army, he needed some means of support; in fact, he was reluctant to embark on the trip. Secretary of War Stanton urged the general to accept Johnson's offer. The President, claimed Stanton, "was set upon by all sorts of influences, and that what he needed most, was to learn the truth." He also pointed out that if Schurz declined, the President could later claim that Radicals had refused to inform him on

10. Schurz, *Reminiscences*, III, 157–58.

11. *Ibid.*, 158–59; Trefousse, *Schurz*, 153.

12. Schurz to Johnson, June 6, 1865, Johnson Papers, LC; Schurz to Frederick Althaus, June 25, 1865, Schafer, *Intimate Letters*, 341–42.

the true state of affairs at the South. Even if the general's report failed to influence Johnson, it would be made public, assuring him of some input. Chief Justice Chase, just back from his own trip, seconded Stanton. Schurz later said that he was impressed that neither man "made the slightest suggestion as to what they expected me to report"; however, Schurz's radicalism was well known, obviating the need to prompt him. But the problem of money remained. Schurz unsuccessfully sought to withdraw his resignation from the army; then he discovered that a trip South would add to his life insurance premium.[13]

Charles Sumner came to the rescue, although the type of aid he offered ultimately undermined Schurz's credibility with Johnson. To Chase, the senator had relayed his opinion that "the President has lately shown a disposition to treat what he has done as an experiment." If the chief justice's mission had failed, perhaps another observer could plead the Radical cause with more success, and Sumner would make sure that the opportunity would not be lost. He offered to obtain funds to pay the extra premium, procured a secretary, and proposed that the general could offset expenses by writing reports of his impressions for northern papers. Since Sumner from the outset conceived of Schurz's trip as a boon to the Radical cause, he saw no inconsistency between the general's obligation to Johnson and his advocacy of other policies in the public print. Unfortunately, neither did Schurz nor Secretary Stanton, who apparently approved the idea. There is no evidence to suggest that Johnson was aware of these plans; certainly Schurz was aware that he was in an ambiguous position, for he asked Sumner to ensure that his dispatches remained unattributed: "You will easily divine the reason." Arrangements were made with the Boston *Advertiser* to publish the reports.[14]

As Schurz prepared to journey south, he wrote several letters which reveal that he already thought he knew what he would find. "The Union must be reconstructed upon the basis of the results of the great social revolution brought about during the War in the South," he told a fellow German. Southern whites, however, were "thoroughly hostile to the tendencies of this revolution," especially the implications of a free labor system and race relations. A rapid restoration would soon leave the federal government powerless to intervene. Prompt action was required to ensure that southerners would not attempt to repeal the results of the war in the future. In the meantime, he advised Johnson "not to have any elections held in the Southern States previous to the meeting of Congress." Sumner reminded him to emphasize that southerners

13. Schurz, *Reminiscences*, III, 158.

14. Sumner to Chase, June 25, 1865, Chase Papers, LC; Sumner to Schurz, June 22, July 11, 1865, Bancroft, *Schurz Correspondence*, I, 265, 267; Schurz to Sumner, August 2, 1865, Schurz Papers, LC.

had to extend "complete justice to the negro. Preach this doctrine—talk it wherever you go."[15]

Schurz left New York on July 12, headed for South Carolina. With him were Captain Louis H. Orleman, 119th New York Volunteers, assigned by Stanton as his secretary; a Mr. Yerrington, dispatched by Sumner to assist Schurz in gathering information; and the Marquis de Chambrun, French diplomat and a crony of Sumner. On the steamer he encountered an ex-rebel officer returning home from a prisoner of war camp. Before the war the rebel had been a planter south of Savannah; now he wondered how he was going to get his former slaves to work for him. Making contracts was out of the question because free blacks "won't work when they are not obliged to." Even the President "knows that niggers must be made to work somehow." To Schurz's suggestion that the man work his own farm, he replied: "I never did a day's work in my life." The general concluded that southern whites, convinced that free labor would not work, were contemplating how "to impose as many duties upon, and grant as few rights to, the negro as possible."[16]

Once in South Carolina, Schurz visited Beaufort, Hilton Head, and Charleston, straying from the coast once to venture to Columbia. He found that his wife's fears for his safety were unfounded: "It is not more peaceful in any quarter of the world." At Beaufort he found confirmation for his free labor beliefs in a conversation with a Massachusetts man who was leasing a plantation and contracting black laborers. "A sensible, practical yankee brought up under the influences of free labor society, is better calculated to solve the great labor problem in the South in a practical manner" than an ex-slaveholder, "whose every step will be guided by his former prejudices." From Charleston his newspaper report reiterated the need for "Northern capital and Northern enterprise" to assist the rebuilding of the South, even if it was against both the "old prejudices" and "ridiculous old delusions" of many southerners.[17]

Cheered by the prospects for reconstruction offered on the coast, Schurz traveled via rail to Orangeburg in sweltering heat, and then mounted a mule and set out toward Columbia. Here it seemed apparent to him that, without the presence of the Freedmen's Bureau, blacks would be laboring in conditions not all that far removed from slavery. Planters described their former slaves as so "demoralized" that they were of no account regardless of their status, and would only work under compulsion. To them, the only benefit of abolition was the severing of the planter's obligation to take care of his slaves. With such little

15. Schurz to Frederick Althaus, June 25, 1865, Schafer, *Intimate Letters*, 341; Schurz to Sumner, July 3, 1865, Bancroft, *Schurz Correspondence*, I, 266–67; Sumner to Schurz, July 11, 1865, *ibid.*, 267.

16. Joseph H. Mahaffey, ed., "Carl Schurz's Letters from the South," *Georgia Historical Quarterly*, XXV (September, 1951), 227–28.

17. *Ibid.*, 230; Schurz to Margarethe Schurz, July 26, 1865, Schafer, *Intimate Letters*, 343.

faith in free labor, planters engaged in a self-fulfilling prophesy by subverting the system's chances for success. The general appeared more understanding when he described the behavior of the freedmen. Admitting that blacks wandered from their plantations and stood up to their former masters, he preferred to note their restraint in throwing off the chains of slavery. Given the instability inherent in the changing situation, he advised that federal troops remain "to prevent explosions."[18]

In his efforts to learn as much as possible, Schurz spent his days speaking with "everybody that I could reach." However, his main source of information proved to be army officers and prominent citizens. Several officers presented their views in writing, sometimes as responses to a series of questions, and Schurz forwarded these statements with his reports to Johnson, adding that the writers "are entirely foreign to political partizanship" and did not possess "extreme views" on "questions involving the negro race." Having gathered his information, he sat down at night to compose his reports and newspaper pieces.[19]

The general finished his first report to Johnson on July 28, concluding that efforts to hurry along reconstruction in South Carolina were premature: Whites "have no clear conception yet of the true nature of their situation and of the problem they have to solve. Nor is this surprising; for their whole social organization has been upset by a single, sudden, stunning blow." Privately he was even more harsh. "I have come to the firm conviction that the policy of the government is the worst that could be hit upon," he confided to his wife. In fact, Johnson's policy only served to make "the confusion . . . worse confounded."[20]

Schurz's experiences in Georgia only confirmed his prejudices. "The convictions with which I came here are becoming strengthened every day," he told Sumner. Many whites barely concealed their hostility toward northerners; attitudes were worse toward the freedmen. One Georgia planter told Schurz of his dismay at discovering that a black girl refused to be whipped. In his eyes this seemed to prove that "this is an intolerable state of things." In Atlanta whites shot blacks without hesitation at any sign of resistance to forced labor. Schurz visited one black wounded in the stomach; the victim died within hours. While the general praised provisional governor James Johnson as "the kind of man we need," he came away from the state convinced "that things are very far from being ripe yet for the restoration of civil government." He reached the same conclusions after touring Alabama.[21]

According to Schurz, white women could be especially fierce in dis-

18. Mahaffey, "Letters," 238, 240–43.

19. Schurz, *Reminiscences*, III, 161–62; Schurz to Johnson, July 28, 1865.

20. *Ibid.*; Schurz to Margarethe Schurz, July 26, 30, 1865, Schafer, *Intimate Letters*, 344–45.

21. Schurz to Sumner, August 2, 1865, Bancroft, *Schurz Correspondence*, I, 267–68; Mahaffey, "Letters," 252; Schurz, *Reminiscences*, III, 173; Schurz to Johnson, August 20, 1865.

playing their sentiments. He attributed this to the "general tendency of feminine nature to let the emotional impulse interfere with the cool and sober consideration of circumstances and interests." In part this was due to the climate, he continued: "the warmer sun enhances the vivacity of temperament," making southern women "peculiarly charming in friendly intercourse, but also peculiarly vehement in a conflict." Northern officers were often the targets of a woman's wrath, a sign that reconciliation was far off.[22]

At Augusta, Schurz was greeted "in the pleasantest manner" by Major General James B. Steedman, commanding the Department of Georgia. The commander provided Schurz with a statement which appeared to support charges of an unrepentant South; however, two days after Schurz mailed off his report Steedman shared his thoughts about his visitor with the President. In contrast to his statement to Schurz stressing the need for a continued military presence, the district commander assured Johnson that "everything is moving satisfactorily towards the complete restoration of this state." Of Schurz, Steedman commented that he "made thorough and impartial enquiry as to the condition of affairs," but added, "he is opposed to your policy, and regards your effort to restore the revolted states as premature, if not an absolute blunder." This was important information in the President's possession. Convinced that Schurz was out to subvert his policy, he could treat the general's reports as biased and exaggerated.[23]

Arriving in Mississippi, Schurz quickly found himself involved in a controversy between provisional governor William L. Sharkey and Schurz's old commander, General Slocum, now heading the Department of Mississippi. Responding to reports of robbery and disorder in the countryside west of Jackson, the governor, already dissatisfied with Slocum's administration of affairs, issued a proclamation on August 19 calling on each county to raise two militia companies. Obviously these companies would be dominated by Confederate veterans; indeed, Sharkey encouraged them to enlist, citing their previous military experience as a decided advantage. In explaining his action to Johnson, the governor charged that the Freedmen's Bureau, under the direction of Colonel Samuel Thomas, "is badly managed here"; blacks "are bold in their threats and the people are afraid."[24]

Military commanders were furious with the proclamation. Major General Peter J. Osterhaus, surprised by reports of county meetings to organize militia companies, reminded Sharkey that such actions were not allowed under martial law unless supervised by federal authorities. The governor curtly replied that he had authorized such action, due to

22. Schurz, *Reminiscences*, III, 181.
23. Schurz to Margarethe Schurz, August 9, 1865, Schafer, *Intimate Letters*, 346; Steedman to Johnson, August 15, 1865, Johnson Papers, LC.
24. Sharkey to Johnson, August 20, 1865, *ibid.*

the military's inability to protect citizens: "I beg to remind you that for twelve of fifteen consecutive nights, passengers traveling in the stages between here and Vicksburg have been robbed, and these things have occurred within twelve or fifteen miles of your own headquarters." He added that Johnson had already approved of such measures in advance.[25]

Slocum intervened on Osterhaus' behalf, in part because his subordinate suspected that unreconstructed whites had provoked the very incidents on the stage road that furnished them with an opportunity to reestablish the militia. On August 24, he issued an order nullifying Sharkey's proclamation and reaffirming the role of the federal military as the primary law enforcement agency. This action appeared to be in line with administration policy, for on the same day Johnson wired Sharkey advising the governor to stop organizing the militia. But the governor pressed his case. To Johnson he raised the spectre of a black revolt at Christmas, an increasingly familiar prediction, and reminded the President of his promise to allow him to organize the militia.[26]

At this point Schurz entered the fray. On August 29 he telegraphed Johnson in support of Slocum's position, calling it "the only one by which public order & security can be maintained," adding that organizing the militia "would have been a fatal step." In a more lengthy letter he praised Slocum's administration, asserting that Mississippi "is more perfectly garrisoned" than any other state that he had observed. About Sharkey he was a bit more circumspect, hinting that while well-meaning, the governor was easily influenced by his advisers, "a set of old secessionists" and former Confederate officers. To Stanton, Schurz was more blunt: decisive action in support of Slocum "would at once put a stop to all the vagaries on the part of Provisional Governors."[27]

Sharkey's telegrams had persuaded Johnson to uphold the governor's proclamation, reversing his previous inclination. Already suspicious of Schurz's motives, he seized the opportunity to put the general in his place. On August 30, he informed Schurz that he had decided to sustain Sharkey, in part because southerners "must be trusted with their government." Indulging himself in some overblown oratory, Johnson insisted that his decision affirmed his desire to restore "the original design of the Government . . . administered upon the principles of the Great Chart of Freedom handed down to the people by the founders of the Republic." Schurz's mission, according to Johnson, "was to aid as far as practicable in carrying out the policy" just outlined.[28]

Schurz read Johnson's lecture at Baton Rouge. He quickly responded,

25. Osterhaus to Sharkey, August 21, 1865, and Sharkey to Osterhaus, August 22, 1865, *Schurz Report,* 104.
26. Dept. of Miss., G.O. #22 (August 24, 1865), *ibid.,* 62–63; Johnson to Sharkey, August 24, 1865, and Sharkey to Johnson, August 26, 1865, Johnson Papers, LC.
27. Schurz to Johnson, August 29, 1865, *ibid.*; Schurz to Stanton, August 29, 1865, Stanton Papers, LC.
28. Johnson to Schurz, August 30, 1865, Johnson Papers, LC.

defending Slocum's action on behalf of "the safety of the Union people and freedmen as well as the honor of the govt." Then he turned to Johnson's definition of his mission's purpose. "According to your own words I understand your policy to be Experimental," he asserted. "I understand it to be the object of my mission to observe and report to you and to make suggestions[.]" Having brought their varying perspectives into the open, Schurz requested Johnson to explain his reasoning behind his decision to support Sharkey. No explanation ever arrived; Johnson now knew that Schurz was a lost cause.[29]

Bitter at Johnson's decision, Schurz confided to his wife that the President's action was "the most irresponsible trick so far enacted in Washington." He had tried to stop such folly, but feared his efforts would go for naught. "If the President persists in pursuing a false course," the general continued, "he must not be surprised if, later, I bring into the field against him all the artillery I am assembling now." Still, he held out the hope that Johnson might still use him "for the investigation of one or another specific matter." This was merely an exercise in self-delusion: the tone of Johnson's last telegram suggested that Schurz's usefulness was at an end.[30]

"I have found all of my preconceived opinions verified most fully, no, more than that," Schurz had written his wife from Jackson, Mississippi. "If I can only make my main report, I shall open the eyes of the people of the North." Unfortunately for the general, word of his attitude had already made its way to Johnson. Even before the Sharkey-Slocum incident, reports appeared in several northern papers that Schurz's behavior "does not meet the approval of the President," in part because of his submission of reports to northern newspapers. If Schurz wished anonymity, he was quickly disappointed, for by early August most northern papers had identified him as the author of the *Advertiser* letters. Frederick Tiedemann, a former aide to Schurz, compounded the problem by admitting the charge, stripping his superior of any remaining secrecy. Schurz first saw such reports in the September 5 issue of the New Orleans *Times*.[31]

Embarrassed, the general immediately wrote Johnson in an effort to clear his name. In the process he revealed that he thought he had done nothing wrong. He pointed out that Stanton had authorized the transmission of the newspaper reports, and added that he needed the fees derived from them to offset expenses. The announcement had damaged his credibility among southerners, impairing his ability to gather infor-

29. Schurz to Johnson, September 1, 1865.

30. Schurz to Margarethe Schurz, September 2, 1865, Schafer, *Intimate Letters*, 349–50.

31. Schurz to Margarethe Schurz, August 27, 1865, Bancroft, *Schurz Correspondence*, I, 268–69; New York *Times*, August 2, September 3, 1865; Chicago *Tribune*, August 11, 1865; New Orleans *Times*, September 5, 1865.

mation. Moreover, Schurz asserted that "the paragraph has the appearance of coming from an authoritative source." Most likely it did: Johnson was very skillful at planting newspaper stories. The Radical Cincinnati *Gazette* came to Schurz's support. "He takes exactly the view of matters in the Southern States that every honest, thinking man who is a friend of the Union . . . is compelled to take."[32]

Unwilling to accept the fact that Johnson no longer heeded his advice, Schurz continued to relay observations and opinions. In Louisiana he found the unionists excluded from the administration of the wily J. Madison Wells. To make sure that Johnson could not accuse him of simply serving as the mouthpiece of Louisiana Radicals, the general assembled the testimony of moderate and conservative unionists protesting the Wells regime. Schurz concluded that the only way to bolster the unionist cause was to replace Wells.[33]

Louisiana conservatives moved quickly to discredit Schurz's objectivity. New Orleans mayor Hugh Kennedy, Wells's staunchest supporter, reported that Schurz allowed himself to be "monopolized" by Radicals, who manipulated him "to advance their schemes." Two days later the mayor came away from a discussion with the immigrant investigator convinced that his perspective was shaped by impractical theories of equality. "The General seems much indoctrinated with New England fancies," he told Johnson, "and not to be indisposed to putting the South in pupillage for Eastern experimenting." Schurz's notions of black education were but one sign that he was not aware "that a country lately in the throes of revolution is not exactly in the mood for academical discussions."[34]

Kennedy knew that Johnson would be receptive to such opinions, since he too was aware of the newspaper report of Johnson's displeasure with his observer. He complained that most investigators dispatched by the government "are of the radical & anti-state reorganizing class." Local Radicals "immediately fraternize with them, full charge them with every species of misrepresentation, feast & drink them ostentatiously, & finally, it is said, make a joint concoction in the form of a report to the Secretary of War, and another of a different type for the President's information." The mayor had done his homework well when it came to confirming Johnson's prejudices; having already sworn his allegiance to the new administration, he sought to cement his position by echoing the charges which had appeared in the papers several days before.[35]

Thomas Cottman, one of the leaders of the conservative faction, was

32. Schurz to Johnson, September 5, 1865; Cincinnati *Gazette*, September 6, 1865.
33. Schurz to Johnson, September 4[8], 1865.
34. Hugh Kennedy to Johnson, September 10, 12, 1865, Johnson Papers, LC.
35. *Ibid.*

even more explicit in his denunciation of Schurz. "The natural instincts of an Austrian would be to exercise his influence through Lager Beer Saloons," he sneered, "but common sense would suggest other than the enemies of State & Federal Government for associates." Like Kennedy, Cottman complained to Johnson that the general spent all his time among radical adherents, defining "radical" as opposition to Wells. To assure that Johnson viewed the situation correctly, Kennedy and Cottman went to Washington and conferred with the President.[36]

Schurz traveled across southern Mississippi and Alabama, then explored the Red River Valley, but his findings merely echoed previous reports. The three months he had promised Johnson had passed; he began to make his way back to Washington. Stanton told him to see Johnson; the President greeted his envoy "with civility, indeed, but with demonstrative coldness." Several days later, after reading yet another report that he had fallen into disfavor with the chief executive, the general demanded an explanation. "I examine my conduct in vain to discover anything that could have been personally offensive to the President," he told the war secretary. To Sumner, Schurz expressed his disbelief at Johnson's behavior, even though he was preparing a report designed to condemn the Tennessean's policy.[37]

Back in Bethlehem, Schurz worked long hours to compose his report. He planned to ask the President to allow it to be published, fulfilling a previously expressed hope that it "can perhaps be so shaped as to play a distinctive role in this weighty business." Aware that it was "somewhat doubtful" that Johnson would accede, he suggested to Sumner that Congress call on him to present the report. "The President is not at all favorable to me on account of my report," Schurz told the Massachusetts senator. "He wanted to use me as the official support of his policy and he is now angry that the results of the journey are a hinderance to him." Schurz failed to add that he had assumed all along that if Johnson was merely made aware of conditions in the South (as seen by a Radical), he would scrap his policy in favor of an overhaul of southern society. The general had turned a fact-finding mission into a fault-finding mission, discrediting himself in Johnson's eyes.[38]

What emerged from weeks of writing was a carefully crafted and masterful statement of his contention that Johnson's "experiment" had failed. While admitting that he possessed "preconceived notions," Schurz claimed that he would not have accepted the mission if he was not prepared "to abandon or modify" them, "as my perception of facts and circumstances might command." Southerners, he concluded, were

36. Cottman to Johnson, September 9, 1865, *ibid.*; Trefousse, *Schurz*, 157.

37. Schurz to Stanton, October 17, 1865, and to Sumner, October 17, 1865, Bancroft, *Schurz Correspondence*, I, 272–76.

38. Schurz to Frederick Althaus, June 25, 1865, and to Margarethe Schurz, December 5, 1865, Schafer, *Intimate Letters*, 341–42, 354.

"so despondent" after Appomattox "that if readmission at some future time under whatever conditions had been promised, it would have been looked upon as a favor." But Johnson's proclamations, far from taking advantage of this "fearful expectancy," replaced the "worst apprehensions" with "new hopes." Now "the success of the experiment depends upon the spirit and attitude of those" who, at one time or another, supported the Confederacy. While most southerners readily accepted "the results of the war," Schurz added that they expected the immediate restoration of their civil and political rights, and defined the results of the war so narrowly as to preclude extensive changes in their society. While many professional and business men were making sincere efforts "to accommodate themselves to the new order of things," most politicians, he felt, were prepared "to make any ostensible concession that will not prevent them from arranging things to suit their taste" as soon as they regained "absolute control of their home concerns." Too, "incorrigibles," mostly young men, continued to "persecute Union men and negroes whenever they can do so with impunity, insist clamorously upon their 'rights,' and are extremely impatient of the presence of the federal soldiers." These three groups vied for the control of the "multitude of people who have not definite ideas" and "whose intellects are weak, but whose prejudices and impulses are strong."[39]

Schurz rejected the rationale behind Johnson's amnesty policy, asserting that past experience had shown that such policies "have never insured the stability of a government, and never improved the morals of a people." Indeed, white southerners still abused northern visitors and army officers, signs that the "reliable kind of loyalty which springs from the heart" had not returned. The situation of southerners who remained loyal throughout the war "was of a precarious nature," and was sure to worsen once troops were withdrawn; what passed for unionism now was proof that one had opposed secession, regardless of subsequent service for the Confederacy. This was in pointed contrast to Tennessee, where Schurz reminded Johnson that voters had selected unyielding unionists to office. Unless loyalty was rewarded, he added, unionists would find themselves ostracized, not praised, for the stand they took, and would withdraw from further involvement in public affairs. "Treason does, under existing circumstances, not appear odious in the south," he concluded; while it might be understandable that loyalty would take time to develop, he doubted the wisdom of constructing policy based on the anticipation of its emergence.

Nor were the majority of white southerners prepared for the advent of blacks working within a free labor system. White southerners, consulting their prejudices, looked for evidence in "the disorders neces-

---

39. Schurz to Johnson, [November, 1865], *Schurz Report*, 2–46. All remaining quotations are from this report.

sarily growing out of the transition state" to support their assertion that blacks would not work without compulsion. As a result, not only did southern landowners seek to preserve the discipline characteristic of slavery, but blacks found themselves victims of white violence, perpetrated by leading citizens as well as by poor whites. Although Schurz admitted that the majority of white southerners did not engage in such practices, they were unwilling to stop those who did. Nor did southerners accept the fact that blacks had not only lost their white masters but had become their own masters—they were still supposed to work for whites. Perhaps the clearest manifestation of the need to "control" the freedmen was found in the ordinances adopted by several Louisiana municipalities, restricting black physical and economic mobility. Most whites rejected the idea of public education, a measure Schurz deemed essential in securing true freedom for blacks.

While admitting that some white characterizations of black behavior were not "made without some show of reason," Schurz concluded that "the negro generally works well where he is decently treated and well compensated," suggesting that many problems were due to the planters' inexperience with managing free laborers. He dismissed charges of vagrancy and wandering about by pointing out that most blacks, having variously reunited families, fled to the cities for protection, or tested their freedom by walking about, had now settled down in one place. Once more the upheaval accompanying emancipation was seized upon by whites as exemplifying typical black behavior and not seen for the unique situation it was. While some blacks undoubtedly behaved insufferably toward whites, most charges of insolence were rooted in the failure of blacks to display the deference, even subserviency, expected of them by whites. Simply put, whites had yet to accept black freedom, and, unless they did so, the result of continued friction might well be the "war of races" predicted by many. Alleged fears of insurrection and disorder had already justified the formation of state militia units; the existence and behavior of such organizations might produce the very evils they were intended to suppress.

The problem with southern society, according to Schurz, was that it was undergoing a social revolution that had been arrested in midcourse by Johnson's lenient policy of reconciliation. The only way to restore stability was to construct it anew "so as to bring it in harmony with the rest of American society." The majority of southern whites were not prepared to be entrusted with this task; the federal government had to oversee, indeed guide, the course of revolution. Not only must the Freedmen's Bureau be continued, but troops had to remain in the South, and restoration of civil authority had to be delayed until a more stable environment had been created by federal authority. "For the future of the republic," he warned, "it is far less important that this business of reconstruction be done quickly than it be well done." To create this stable environment as well as to complete the revolution, blacks should be enfranchised before a state could be fully restored to the Union. He concluded by advising Johnson to recommend that Congress continue to investigate southern conditions before deciding whether to seat southerners elected to Congress. Patently Schurz hoped that the members of that body would concur in his assessment of the temper of the South and its people; certainly the President had not been converted to his views by his letters and their voluminous enclosures.

Letters

Hilton Head S.C. July 28th[1] 1865

To his Excellency Andrew Johnson,
President of the United States.
Sir,

In obedience to your request I visited the State of South Carolina "for the purpose of observing and reporting upon matters affecting the public interest that might come under my notice,"[2] and now beg leave to submit the following report:

The opportunities of observation I enjoyed were ample, thanks to the kindness of Maj- Genl. Gillmore and his subordinate commanders who gave me every accomodation in their power. The information I am going to lay before you, is derived partly from personal observations, partly from conversations with the military and civil officers of the United States in this Department, as well as a considerable number of prominent and intelligent individuals, citizens of this State who may be presumed to be well acquainted with the condition of things and whose views and opinions undoubtedly represent those of large numbers of their fellow citizens. I visited Hilton Head and Beaufort, spent several days in Charleston, and went into the interior of the State as far as Columbia. While moving about I had a great many occasional meetings with people belonging to the humbler classes of society.

The observations made by Genl. Gillmore at our first interview appeared to me so important, that I requested him, and afterwards several other military and civil officers of the government, to give me their views in writing. Their replies are herewith submitted to you.[3] They may be considered of great value inasmuch as they proceed from men who have excellent opportunities for observation, and who—this may be said of the military officers at least—are entirely foreign to political partizanship. As to questions involving the negro race they are by no means men of extreme views. My own conclusions I have formed exclusively upon what I saw and heard myself. It would be impossible for me to give you a detailed account of the large number of conversations I have had as they were carried on without restraint and in an off hand manner. You did not expect me to take any formal testimony, and the manner in which you gave me your verbal instructions authorized me to believe, that you would accept my statements with the confidence due to the word of a man who has a conscientious appreciation of the trust reposed in him. The people of this State with regard to their attitude towards the Government of the United States, may be divided into two classes:

1.) those who in the course of the war have come into direct contact with our forces, and

2.) those who have not.

I wish to be understood as speaking neither here nor in what follows of the consistent Union men of South Carolina, whose number among the whites is so insignificant as to make their influence hardly felt.

The intelligent part of the first class are ready, as they express it, to "acknowledge and submit to the results of the war." In almost all the conversations I have had, this was their standing admission, and almost uniformly in the same words: "The war has decided that there shall be no secession and that the slaves are emancipated. We cannot be expected to give up our principles and convictions of right, but we submit to the result and want to be reinstated in the enjoyment of our rights." Most of them are by no means willing to acknowledge the constitutionality of coercion and of the Emancipation Proclamation. It is generally a submission to overpowering force. In some of their drafts of contracts with freedmen[4] which I had occasion to examine, they speak of the latter as "freed by the act of the military forces of the United States."—(It is proper to add that our military commanders recognize no contract containing such expressions.)[5]

In those parts of the state which have not been touched by the war and were not held for some time under military control, the people adhere not only to their former opinions, but to a certain extent also to their former practices. The following is an extract from a report addressed by Brig. Genl. Fessenden[6] commanding one of the Districts of this Department, to Maj. Gen. Gillmore, dated at Winnsboro' July 19th, 65:

The spirit of the people, especially in those districts not subjected to the salutary influence of Genl. Shermans army, is that of concealed, and in some instances, of open hostility, though there are some who strive with honorable good faith to promote a thorough reconciliation between the Government and their people. A spirit of bitterness and persecution manifests itself towards the negro. They are shot and abused outside the immediate protection of our forces by men who announce their determination of taking the law into their own hands in defiance of our authority. To protect the negro and punish these still rebellious individuals, it will be necessary to have this country pretty thickly settled with soldiers.——

Among the papers accompanying this report you will find a letter addressed to me by Brev. Brig. Gen. Bennet[7] describing the spirit prevailing in another district, a spirit only a shade different from that referred to by Genl. Fessenden. In some localities the planters were but lately endeavoring to hold the negro in a state of slavery until the arrival of our troops put an end to it. One of the subdistrict commanders told me that he knew some planters within the limits of his command who had made contracts with their former slaves, for the avowed purpose of keeping them together on their plantations, so that they might more easily reduce them to their former condition when, upon the restoration of the civil power, the "unconstitutional" Emancipation Proclamation would be set aside.

I have no doubt, however, that people will gradually modify their ideas as the lines of our military occupation are extended. Seeing and feeling the necessity of submission to the Government of the United States, I think a large majority are ready to "return to their allegiance" *as far as the mere restoration of the political machinery of the Government is concerned*, especially as this restoration would place their internal affairs again under their immediate control. Although they do not mean to abandon their "principles and convictions of right," there is no attempt at open resistance to our troops, and it is probable that all those that are permitted to vote, will avail themselves with alacrity of any opportunity to resume the control of their home affairs and to elect Senators and representatives to Congress.

But as to their willingness to carry out the spirit of the Emancipation Proclamation the case stands differently. I believe, indeed, that in a short time all the isolated attempts to keep the negro in a condition of slavery will be abandoned. I believe also, that the more intelligent recognize the impossibility of restoring slavery in its old form at some future time—not as though they did not desire it, but because they think that the "demoralization" of the negroes renders it impossible. But my experience here convinces me that they are as little as ever inclined to put in the place of slavery a bona fide system of free labor. In almost every conversation I had with former slave owners I encountered the emphatic assumption *that the negro will not work without compulsion*. This view of the case seems to be universally entertained and deeply rooted. If they mean what they say, they are convinced that the negro cannot be made a free laborer. Or if they say it without meaning it, they show that they do not want him to become a free laborer. The organization of a free labor system upon the assumption that the laborer will not work unless compelled to do so, is an evident absurdity. By what I have heard and seen I am driven to the conclusion that the free labor experiment is in a large majority of cases not undertaken in good faith, which will necessarily lead to the most serious complications unless the sentiments of the dominant class be changed by experience.[8]

It is true, the contract system is being tried under the supervision of our military commanders and the agents of the Freedmen's Bureau, and it will in a short time probably be introduced all over the State. Under more favorable circumstances its success might have a beneficial influence, but, as things are at present, it can hardly be expected to work very successfully this year. The reasons are these: In the first place, everything is in a transition state. The laborers have not yet arrived at a clear idea of the rights and duties their new condition devolves upon them, and the employers are everywhere inclined to govern their conduct with regard to their laborers by the traditions of the old system;

and secondly, most of the contracts were and are being made in the very midst of the agricultural labor season. And now, wherever anything goes wrong, wherever an irregularity occurs, it is charged against the free labor system; it is used as a practical argument in support of the theory that the negro will not work without severe compulsion. While I have heard a few more enlightened persons in Charleston speak of the general conduct of the colored population with satisfaction, nay, with admiration,[9] there is no end to the complaints raised in the country. Some cases were brought to my notice where plantations, the owners of which complained loudest of the laziness of their former slaves, were kept by the negroes in far better order than any in the neighborhood. These complaints are in many instances undoubtedly well founded, but hardly anybody seems inclined to make due allowance to the confusion necessarily attending such a state of transition, while almost everybody seems to be ready to accept any delinquency on the part of a negro as full proof of the impracticability of the free labor system with the colored population.

Such is at present the state of the popular mind, as far as the whites are concerned; and if under present circumstances they are called upon, to change their political constitution and to make laws for the organization of their labor system, it is greatly to be apprehended that their action will be governed, not by the spirit of the Emancipation Proclamation, but by an experience which in fact is none, or rather is completely overshadowed by their traditional impressions and prejudices. I would invite your attention to the opinions expressed by Genl. Gillmore upon this point; the conclusions I have formed upon my own experience, coincide entirely with the views submitted by him.[10]

It is true, the confusion of ideas at present prevailing here, is to a certain extent natural; but it being natural, the people in their present state of mind cannot safely be called upon to incorporate the ideas they now entertain in fundamental laws to serve as a basis for the future development of their social organization. It is my firm conviction that the result of any independent legislative action by the people of this State under present circumstances would be, not indeed, the restoration of slavery in its old form, but an attempt to introduce a new sort of compulsory labor whatever name it may assume;—What such an attempt might lead to, it is hazardous to predict; I see great reasons for fearing that it would result in open collisions between the two races, which, in their turn, cannot fail to bring great calamities upon the whites and calamities still greater upon the blacks.

It is therefore my decided opinion, conscientiously formed, that the calling of a state convention in South Carolina is premature.[11] The people are not yet in a fit condition to legislate. They have no clear conception yet of the true nature of their situation and of the problem they have to solve. Nor is this surprising; for their whole social organization has been upset by a single, sudden, stunning blow. The change is so tremendous that they require time to survey it in all its length and breadth.

I would therefore most earnestly advise you to postpone the calling of a convention til a more propitious period. Even a comparatively short delay may have a very beneficial effect, while nothing can be gained by precipitation. People will have time to think and to inquire into the exigencies of their condition a little more deliberately and dispassionately. The former slave owner will gradually familiarize himself with the idea that the free labor experiment *must* succeed, and the freedman will soon learn to take a sober and sensible view of his freedom. There are at present a good many people in the remote corners of this state who actually do not yet clearly understand what has happened,—it will require some time to reestablish the railroads and other internal communications necessary to facilitate the interchange of opinions and to bring the people under the influence of the public sentiment of the country. The hope excited among the disloyal element by the reconstruction policy of the Administration [12] and the interpretation they put upon it, will subside and leave them less confident and exacting. New men will have time to spring up and to render the influence of the old leaders less absolute. Northern immigration will soon begin to flow in and to establish itself under the protection of the military, and its influence will be quickly felt. Daylight will gradually reach the poor whites whose only political impulses at present seem to consist in a stupid hatred of the negro and subserviency to their old leaders.

In times like these changes operate themselves rapidly, and by giving them a little time, grave mistakes may be avoided which, if once committed, it will be extremely difficult to redress. As you told me once yourself, it is of the highest importance that the thing be started rightly; then let it not be started at a time when a wrong start is almost inevitable. I do not think that delay is the only thing that will prevent great evils; but I do think that those evils are all likely to be thrust upon us by precipitate action. I will admit that the early restoration of civil authority in these parts would be desirable in some respects, especially as far as the settlement of questions concerning property are concerned,— and I shall submit some suggestions with regard to this matter at the close of this report. But whatever advantages the early restoration of civil power would bring with it as far as private interests are concerned, they are insignificant compared with the great dangers to which it would expose us.

It must not be supposed that the reestablishment of the civil government in this State would render the presence and active interference of the military forces of the United States unnecessary. On the contrary, the latter would become more necessary than ever. Our military power is looked upon by both whites and blacks as their protector, by the whites because they think that as long as our forces are here, the blacks will abstain from excesses; and by the blacks, because they look upon our officers and soldiers, and upon them alone, as their natural friends, and consider themselves safe as long as they are here. I asked one of the most intelligent gentlemen I found here, Mr. James B. Campbell,[13] what they would do, if the Government should withdraw the troops; he replied; "We would entreat you to send them back to us immediately." Mr. Spratt[14] of Charleston, who some time before the war was an advocate of the reopening of the slave trade, replied to the same question very pointedly: "We want your troops to remain here until we can reorganize the militia force of South Carolina to keep the negroes down." I received the same answers as often as I asked the question. The military officers of the United States are in fact the only tribunal to which under present circumstances differences between whites and blacks can be submitted with equal satisfaction to both parties, and I am certain, the decisions of no other tribunal would be so readily acquiesced in. Let the civil government be now restored, and the negro will distrust every South Carolinian in authority as his natural enemy. This distrust may wear off in the course of time as things become more firmly settled, but, at present, every experiment in the way of the exercise of civil authority is likely to lead to collisions, *and everybody here feels the danger*. Nor is the distrust on the part of the colored people unfounded; for it is well known to our military commanders here, that, but for their interference, hardly any fair contract would have been made between planters and freedmen. And even now attempts are made at some places to hold the freedmen by force on the plantations, and at others to eject them by force. Scenes of violence are not unfrequent, and the presence of the military will be necessary for a considerable time, to prevent their becoming general.

The continuance of the military authority may be called an evil.[15] But, in my opinion, the evil will be far greater if the civil power be restored and the military power be every day obliged to override it. If it is desirable that military rule should cease as soon as possible, it is still more desirable that the civil authority be not reestablished until it can be maintained and respected. I would entreat you not to build any hopes upon the restriction of suffrage to those who have given no other evidence of their loyalty than by taking the oath of allegiance. In the first place while the restriction may perhaps, to a certain extent, be enforced in such places as Charleston, where there is some Union element, it is almost certain to be completely disregarded in the country where there is nobody to watch the operation; and secondly, those who by taking the oath acquire the right of voting, hardly differ in their way of thinking as to the material points from those who do not. I repeat, after having looked over the whole field, and forming my conclusions upon my observations honestly and conscientiously, I feel in duty bound to express the opinion, that the steps done towards the restoration of civil government in this State at this time are premature and fraught with serious dangers and will lead to the gravest complications; that the safety of the people demands a continuation of the military rule until the dominant class has in good faith accommodated itself to the results of the war or other means are found for the peaceable maintenance of individual rights; and finally, that, even if at present the civil power be restored, it will in all probability soon be found necessary again to overrule it by the military power and to suspend its operation. The first means that would suggest itself to obviate these difficulties, is to arrest the movement now in progress and to put it off to a more favorable period. This measure itself will do much to bring the people of this State to a just appreciation of the conditions they have to comply with.

Permit me now to offer some suggestions concerning matters of minor importance.

1.) There is considerable anxiety felt here as to property liable to confiscation. The uncertainty which prevails, impedes the transfer and improvement of real estate. It is important that in all cases in which the Government intends to apply the confiscation act,[16] it should be done as soon as possible so that all doubts be removed as to title.[17] It is noticed that many persons from the north who want to acquire property here for purposes of business, find themselves obliged to give up or change their plans on account of this difficulty.

2.) Gen. Gillmore tells me that he is frequently called upon by planters for information regarding the status of their plantations located upon or near the Sea-islands, and whether they have been sold by the tax-commissioners or not. As the Tax-Commissioners have gone north with the records of their operations, he suggests that one of the commissioners at least or a clerk with the records be sent back to Beaufort at once so that the necessary information can be furnished. It would probably be best to have the whole commission here at this important period, as many people are coming in to pay their direct taxes.[18]

3.) It is important that the Freedmen's Bureau send without delay agents to every county (Parish, District) in this State. The post-commanders have so far done the business of the Freedmen's Department, but not being in direct communication with the head of the Bureau, their action cannot be expected to coincide in all cases with his views. They are, however, now furnished with all of Genl. Howards orders by the commander of the Department. In case the Freedmen's Department has not officers enough at its disposal, it would perhaps be best to make the post-commanders ex officio agents of the Bureau.[19]

4.) A large force of teachers should be sent into the interior of this State to commence their operations as soon as the crops are in, in October or November. Nothing has been done in this line except on the seabord. They should be sensible and discreet persons, to give the negroes a correct idea of the rights and duties connected with their present condition.[20] I look upon this as a very important matter.

5.) Considerable interest is felt at Charleston in the case of Mr. Wagner,[21] a large business operator. He is excluded from the benefit of the Amnesty-Proclamation by the $20,000 clause. All persons I became acquainted with in Charleston, the best Union people included, seem to concur in the belief, that his pardon and restoration to the possession of his property would be a public benefit, and the opinion I formed of him upon personal acquaintance, leads me to think that it would be a favor well bestowed. His petition for pardon will be presented to you by Mr. James B. Campbell.[22]

6.) I deem it of very great importance that the federal offices should be filed with *real* union men wherever any such can be found. This is especially important with regard to the office of U. S. District Attorney, and I would respectfully suggest, that, if no suitable person can be found here, one be sent here from elsewhere.[23] I have heard of no individual here that could be recommended for that position.

I just learn through Gen. Gillmore who has received telegraphic despatches to that effect, that Gov. Perry[24] has issued a proclamation calling upon all civil officers in this State to resume their functions.[25] If the report proves true and the governor tries to carry out his intentions to their full extent, it is not unlikely that the necessity of interference on the part of the military power will soon become apparent.

To day I shall go to Savannah and from there into the interior of Georgia.

I am, Mr. President, very truly and respectfully
Your obedient servant C. Schurz.

P.S. I have had no opportunity to see Gov. Perry who but two or three days ago returned to the State, and can now no longer delay my departure.

I enclose letters addressed to me[26] by Maj. Genl. Gillmore,[27] by Brev. Maj. Genl. Hatch,[28] Brev. Brig. Genl. Bennet, Dr. Mackey[29] and Mr. Sawyer of Charleston.[30] I would especially invite attention to the letter of Genl. Gillmore.

ALS, DLC-JP.

1. A copy of this letter in the Carl Schurz Papers, Library of Congress, is dated July 27.

2. From Secretary Stanton's letter of instruction. Stanton to Schurz, July 7, 1865, Schurz Papers, LC.

3. Schurz made a practice of enclosing statements, clippings, and other material when transmitting his reports to Johnson. Most statements were either reproduced in *Sen. Ex. Doc.* No. 2, 39 Cong., 1 Sess. (hereafter cited as *Schurz Report*), which contains Schurz's account of conditions in the South, along with Grant's report of his tour later that year, or are in the Johnson Papers, LC.

4. During the late spring and summer of 1865 military commanders and Freedmen's Bureau agents encouraged black laborers and white landowners to agree to written contracts in an effort to restore social stability, commence economic recovery, and foster the acceptance of the free labor ethos. Gen. Rufus Saxton proposed a model contract granting a laborer living quarters, rations, medical care, fuel, and a portion of the crop in exchange for his work. As Schurz reports in the ensuing pages of this letter, the system stumbled in 1865; white landowners offered far less than what Saxton had suggested and attempted to impose a system which maintained some of the advantages of slavery as a form of labor control; blacks were reluctant to enter into agreements, persisting in the belief that the federal government would undertake a program of land redistribution and give every black family forty acres and a mule; spring planting commenced far behind schedule. Martin Abbott, *The Freedmen's Bureau in South Carolina, 1865–1872* (Chapel Hill, 1967), 66–71; Donald G. Nieman, *To Set the Law in Motion*, 61–66.

5. On June 24, Hatch had instructed his subordinates not to recognize contracts which contained "such expressions," since implicit in such phrases was a challenge to the permanence of emancipation. New York *Herald*, July 6, 1863.

6. James D. Fessenden (1833–1882), son of Maine senator William Pitt Fessenden, was assigned to Gen. David Hunter's staff in 1862, and took part in the training of black troops, an action countermanded by Lincoln. Seeing service along the coast of South Carolina and in the Chattanooga, Atlanta, and Shenandoah Valley campaigns, he was mustered out in 1866.

7. William T. Bennett (b. *c*1837) of Michigan, commissioned captain, 1st U.S.C.T. in 1863, had by the end of the war attained a colonelcy, commanding the 33rd U.S.C.T. and was brevetted brigadier. At the time of Schurz's visit he headed the 1st Sub-District, Military District of Charleston. Returning from a trip through the interior, Bennett criticized both white planters and black workers for inhibiting the emergence of a free labor system. Planters, who held tight to the prerogatives and prejudices of slaveowning, were not the proper men to supervise black labor. Blacks exhibited "a general spirit of idleness amounting to vagabondism." CSR, RG94, NA; Bennett to Schurz, July 25, 1865, Johnson Papers, LC.

8. In contrast, a New York *Herald* correspondent described how former slaveholders, with "good grace, and, I might almost say, cheerfulness," accepted the end of slavery. While planters held fast to the perception of slaves as "lazy, filthy, treacherous and ungrateful," they now had the opportunity to shed themselves of the responsibility to care for elderly, infirm, and other "superfluous negroes," allowing them "to choose and retain only the likeliest field hands." New York *Herald*, July 19, 1865.

9. This observation should not be surprising, for white aristocrats had befriended Charleston's free blacks, who in exchange for accepting paternalism achieved economic and social security. Both white laborers and upcountry planters resented the alliance and sought to restrict if not eliminate the status of free blacks. Michael P. Johnson and James L. Roark, eds., *No Chariot Let Down: Charleston's Free People of Color on the Eve of the Civil War* (Chapel Hill, 1984), 7–15.

10. The Charleston *Courier*, on the day after Schurz's arrival in the city, presented a different view, denying reports "relating to the harsh treatment of the colored people by the whites of South Carolina. . . . The new system of labor inaugurated is working admirably." Charleston *Courier*, July 17, 1865.

11. On June 30, when appointing Benjamin F. Perry provisional governor, Johnson had instructed him to convene a convention to amend South Carolina's constitution in accordance with the President's policy. Three weeks later Perry announced that the election for delegates would be held September 4 and the convention would assemble September 13. Richardson, *Messages*, VI, 326–28; McPherson, *Reconstruction*, 22.

12. The question of southern reaction to Johnson's reconstruction policy, as embodied in the Amnesty and North Carolina proclamations of May 29, 1865, has sparked vigorous debate. Radical journalist Whitelaw Reid argued that prior to these proclamations, southern whites were prepared to accept any terms. After they absorbed the impact of Johnson's policy, Reid observed that they "now began to talk of their rights, and to argue constitutional points; as if traitors had rights, or treason were entitled to constitutional protection." A correspondent for the conservative New York *Herald* concurred, writing of "a radical, sickly, deathly change" in public opinion. Once southerners "considered that they had forfeited all their rights under the constitution. . . . Now they do not plead for

mercy, but demand their rights." Historians critical of Johnson's policy as too lenient echo these assertions of southern submissiveness and malleability; however, Michael Perman has argued that southerners were not passively compliant, but defiantly optimistic, prior to the issuance of the May 29 proclamations, which merely allowed the open manifestation of these sentiments. Reid, *After the War*, 294–97; Eric McKitrick, *Andrew Johnson and Reconstruction* (Chicago, 1960), 198–213; Perman, *Reunion Without Compromise*, 18–25; New York *Herald*, July 30, 1865.

13. Charleston lawyer James B. Campbell (*c*1809–*fl*1880) served as a delegate to the National Union Convention (1866) and was elected to the U.S. Senate that year, although denied his seat. Yates Snowden, ed., *History of South Carolina* (5 vols., Chicago, 1920), II, 880–93; 1860 Census, S.C., Charleston Dist., 4th Ward, 117; Charleston city directories (1874–1880), *passim*.

14. Fire-eating editor Leonidas W. Spratt (1818–1903) in 1853 had advocated the reopening of the African slave trade, reasoning that, regardless of the result of his specific proposal, the debate would spark southerners to defend slavery on its merits. A good states rights Democrat, he had protested against the Confederacy's prohibition of the slave trade. Ronald T. Takaki, *A Pro-Slavery Crusade: The Agitation to Reopen the African Slave Trade* (New York, 1971), 1, 14, 19, 239.

15. In fact, Schurz, in his effort to convince the President of the continued need for a military presence, made no mention of recent clashes between soldiers and citizens in Charleston. On July 12 General Bennett established a curfew for Charleston and upbraided his men for discourteous and insolent behavior. The following day he instructed all citizens to turn in their firearms and other weapons. New York *Herald*, July 19, 1865.

16. In July, 1862, Congress enacted legislation authorizing the President to seize Confederate private property and providing for its confiscation through judicial proceedings. After the war Radical Republicans hoped to achieve land redistribution through enforcing this legislation.

17. Johnson's May 29, 1865, amnesty proclamation looked toward restoring the property rights of most white southerners. The status of confiscated land, however, hung in abeyance for several months. On June 2, Johnson ordered the Treasury Department to turn over "all abandoned lands and property contemplated" by the Freedmen's Bureau bill to the Bureau. In July, Attorney General Speed informed Freedmen's Bureau head Gen. Oliver O. Howard that he could dispense land already confiscated. Liberally construing Speed's advice, Howard prepared Circular No. 13 on July 28, directing bureau representatives to commence the redistribution of land under their control. Johnson put a halt to this on August 16, ordering the restoration of land to all pardoned Confederates. Howard countered with a second circular letter, September 4, which made restoration contingent on his approval, and preserved land rented to freedmen or under confiscation proceedings for the Bureau's use. The President quickly quashed this effort, ordering Howard to conform to administration policy. On September 12, with Johnson's approval, Howard reluctantly issued Circular No. 15, revoking the previous circular letters and establishing a restoration policy which ensured the return of most of the land to pardoned Confederates. McPherson, *Reconstruction*, 12–13; Nieman, *To Set the Law in Motion*, 49–53.

18. Land seized under the terms of the direct tax legislation passed in 1862 was to be sold by federal tax commissioners in 1863 and 1864. White investors, not black laborers, purchased the majority of the land available. During 1865 and 1866, more land was sold, most going to freedmen. Land not actually sold to third parties was restored by Johnson to prewar owners. Willie Lee Rose, *Rehearsal for Reconstruction: The Port Royal Experiment* (New York, 1964), 200–14, 272–96; Joel Williamson, *After Slavery: The Negro in South Carolina During Reconstruction* (Chapel Hill, 1965), 86.

19. Ulysses S. Grant made a similar suggestion in his report to Johnson in December. By the end of 1866, General Howard reported that "Whenever practicable military commanders of states have been appointed assistant commissioners." Earlier, on August 26, 1865, Grant had moved to remedy the shortage of officers caused by demobilization by permitting assistant commissioners to retain as agents officers of mustered out regiments until department commanders assigned replacements. *Ibid.*, 13; Report of the Commissioner of BRFAL, *House Ex. Doc.* No. 1, 39 Cong., 2 Sess., 1.

20. It would be well into 1866 before the freedmen's education movement had spread from its toehold along Union-occupied territory into the upland South. By June, Thomas

G. Wright, working in western South Carolina with the American Freedmen's Union Commission, reported 24 teachers stationed in the area, 10 from the North. At the same time Reuben Tomlinson, superintendent of education in South Carolina for the Freedmen's Bureau, reported that 54 schools staffed by 130 teachers were educating 8,000 blacks under his auspices. Ronald E. Butchart, *Northern Schools, Southern Blacks, and Reconstruction: Freedmen's Education, 1862–1875* (Westport, Conn., 1980), 128; Abbott, *Freedmen's Bureau in South Carolina*, 85–86.

21. Merchant Theodore D. Wagner (1819–1880) had taken Lincoln's December amnesty oath. John A. May and Joan R. Faunt, *South Carolina Secedes* (Columbia, S.C., 1960), 221; Civil War Amnesty Case Files (1865–67), S.C., RG94, NA.

22. Campbell did so, and Wagner was pardoned August 8. *Ibid.*

23. The position of U.S. district attorney remained vacant through September, 1865. Northern-born David T. Corbin, who would become a leading Republican, held the post as of September 30, 1867. *U.S. Official Register* (1865), 295; (1867), 318.

24. Staunch unionist, Democratic editor, and state legislator, Benjamin F. Perry (1805–1886) resisted secession until it was an accomplished fact. Appointed provisional governor of South Carolina in June, he was subsequently elected U.S. senator, but failed to be seated in December. A delegate to the 1866 National Union convention, Perry later opposed congressional reconstruction.

25. On July 20 Perry instructed "all civil officers in South Carolina who were in office when the civil government of the State was suspended, in May last" to "resume the duties of their offices" upon taking the oath of allegiance. The governor claimed that not only did Johnson approve his proclamation, but that the document was prepared in the presence of the President. Ultimately Johnson sustained Perry over the protests of military authorities, despite his original reservation that his appointee had acted hastily. New York *Herald*, August 7, 9, 21, 1865; New York *Times*, October 27, 1865; Benjamin F. Perry, *Reminiscences of Public Men* (Philadelphia, 1883), 37.

26. Schurz requested many of the people he spoke with to compose written responses to several questions: was Union sentiment strong enough to entrust white southerners with self-government; were whites willing to accept emancipation and its consequences and accord blacks a "satisfactory social status"; would a delay in the restoration process assist in engendering loyalty to the nation; was the use of free labor working out? Frederick A. Sawyer to Schurz, July 20, 1865, Johnson Papers, LC.

27. Gillmore doubted that South Carolina's whites possessed a strong sense of loyalty to the United States; they "accept the condition which has been imposed upon them, simply because there is no alternative." Still preferring slavery as the best means of controlling black labor, they would miss no opportunity to restrict blacks' freedom. He counseled delaying the restoration process, fearing that "not only *hasty* and *ignorant* but *excessive* legislation" and the withdrawal of the military would "augment" current problems. Gillmore to Schurz, July 27, 1865, *Schurz Report*, 47–49.

28. Hatch thought that white southerners could not be trusted with self-rule; the old leaders "cannot see that a new order of things exists." Speculating that they would pass legislation "which shall virtually re-establish slavery," he recommended that more time pass before restoration of civil government. Hatch to Schurz, July 24, 1865, *ibid.*, 49–50.

29. Albert G. Mackey (1807–1881), long-time Charleston physician and a staunch unionist, traveled north in 1865 to lecture on southern postwar attitudes and was rewarded for his loyalty with the collectorship of the port of Charleston. He presided over the 1868 constitutional convention, but lost his bid for a U.S. Senate seat. Responding to Schurz's inquiry, he observed that most South Carolina whites were still secessionists, who "seem with their loyalty to have lost their modesty." Prejudice, he reported, was still deeply rooted in the white mind, so what might seem "satisfactory" to whites might not seem so to blacks. "Time of course would work wonders," but he questioned the practicality of delaying restoration. *DAB*, XII, 98–99; Francis B. Simkins and Robert H. Woody, *South Carolina During Reconstruction* (Gloucester, Mass., 1966 [1932]), 30–31, 94–95, 120; Mackey to Schurz, July 23, 1865, Johnson Papers, LC.

30. Massachusetts-born educator Frederick A. Sawyer (1822–1891) went to South Carolina in 1859 to head the normal school program and was stranded after the outbreak of hostilities, finally returning north in 1864. The next year he was again in Charleston, where he was appointed collector of internal revenue. In 1868 he won election to the U.S.

Senate as a Republican. In his observations to Schurz, Sawyer adopted a fairly conservative stand, remarking, "In many cases the best friend of the negro in his new relation will be found to be his former master." Counseling that delaying readmission "has its dangers as well as its advantages," Sawyer concluded: "In no State has the submission to the power of the Union been more unreserved and complete than this." Simkins and Woody, *South Carolina During Reconstruction*, 31, 120–21, 467n; Sawyer to Schurz, July 20, 1865, Johnson Papers, LC.

———————

Macon Ga. August 13th[1] 1865

To his Excellency Andrew Johnson
President of the United States.
Sir,

After having spent a few days at Savannah I traversed the State of Georgia by way of Augusta and Atlanta, stopping at the principal points, visited Milledgeville day before yesterday and then returned to this place. To-morrow I intend to leave for Alabama by way of Columbus. I have had frequent conversations with the most prominent men of the State, with a large number of planters and people belonging to other classes of society. The information I gathered in this manner together with my own ocular observations enable me to give an opinion on the condition of affairs in this State, which, I think, may be taken as reliable.

Almost all I have said with regard to South Carolina, the spirit and temper of the people, their intentions and aspirations, the relations between freedmen and planters etc. will, with equal force, apply to the people of Georgia. I have the honor to enclose a statement of the views entertained by Maj. Genl. Steedman[2] concerning the present state of affairs in Georgia, as expressed to me in conversation.[3] His views agree in every particular with my own observations, and it is hardly necessary that I should more elaborately go over the same ground.

I may, however, mention some facts tending to elucidate some of the points touched by Genl. Steedman.

The newspapers, North and South, have had much to say about certain enthusiastic Union meetings in this State, giving evidence of a spirit of returning loyalty. Facts have come to my knowledge which will enable you to estimate the true value of these things. The papers had glowing descriptions of the enthusiasm displayed by the citizens of Savannah at a meeting called to listen to Gov. Johnson[4] immediately after his return from Washington. I was informed by eye witnesses some of whom had been managers of the affair, among others by Gov. Johnson himself, that that meeting was by no means, as the papers reported, composed of the leading and substantial citizens of that place. Gov. Johnson did by no means meet with an enthusiastic reception on their part. But few of them were present, and those few sat there in gloomy silence, and all the applauding that was done, and all the enthusiasm that was shown, proceeded from the Northern men and Army officers present on the occasion. The editor of the Savannah Republican[5] wrote a truthful account of the matter, but was requested by the Mayor of Savannah, Dr. Arnold,[6] to substitute another one because a true statement of the actual facts of the case might create unpleasant feelings. The editor agreed to do so, and thus the meeting at Savannah went before the country as an enthusiastic Union demonstration on the part of the people of Georgia. Several other meetings that occurred in this State, were of a similar character.

I will not go into details as to the street and hotel talk especially of young men which I had frequent opportunities to overhear, and which in most cases equalled in point of bitterness anything we were accustomed to read in Southern newspapers during the palmiest days of the rebellion.

The most unsatisfactory state of things I found in and around Atlanta. The planters in that region, or at the least the most reckless and restless spirits among them, seem to have combined to keep the negroes in their former state of subjection, and to kill those that refused to submit.[7] While I was there, several negroes came into town with bullet- or buckshot-wounds in their bodies, giving evidence of the treatment they had received. In the very streets of Atlanta, freedmen were attacked and maltreated by whites without the least provocation, almost every day. During my sojourn there one negro was stabbed dead, and three were poisoned, one of whom died. I saw the victims and examined the cases myself. Only in a few instances the perpetrators were caught and arrested. I enclose a report on these cases furnished me by the provost marshal of the place.[8] The commander of the Subdistrict Brev. Brig. Genl. Salm,[9] who had been but a short time in command and was doing all he could to put an end to this state of things, informed me that only a few miles from the city a gang of guerrillas was prowling about, and that a small detachment he had sent out to serve an order upon a planter, had been driven back by an armed band of over twenty men headed by an officer in rebel uniform. From the company of infantry he had sent out to scour that neighborhood, no report had been received at the time of my departure.

The post commander at Madison, Major Kummer 69th N.Y. Vol.[10] reported to me, that a small guard he had placed over a lot of cotton about seven miles from that place, had several times been attacked by armed bands, and had been obliged to defend themselves by a regular musketry fire.

The post commander at Griffin, Capt. Feldstein 68th N.Y. Vol.,[11] informed me that he had received the most alarming reports about the outrages committed by planters upon negroes in that region, and an old Union man living in that place, assured me, that, in case our troops were withdrawn, he would have to leave, as his life would not be safe.

Brig. Genl. Croxton,[12] commanding at Macon, informs me that in the Southwestern District of the State things look somewhat better, except the country around Columbus where the shooting of negroes by whites is not unfrequent.— Outrages like these could be prevented, or at least repressed and punished with greater facility, were not at most places the garrisons too weak to do more than the necessary guard duty.[13] One of two things ought to be done: either there ought to be little garrisons under intelligent officers distributed all over the State so as to be able to move to any point where the presence of the military may be required, in a few hours, or the country ought to be regularly patrolled, which, however, cannot well be done by infantry, and there is at present no adequate cavalry force at the disposal of the Department Commander. Genl. Wilson[14] informs me that the 4th U.S. Cavalry will soon be ordered to report to Genl. Steedman. This will go far to supply the deficiency; but that regiment has only eleven officers present, and under present circumstances when troops are employed for such a variety of purposes, the presence of officers with their commands is more necessary than ever, especially when those commands are to be distributed or to move about in little detachments to restore and maintain peace and order over a vast extent of country.

I have mentioned the above occurrences for the purpose of showing that a great many things are happening here which give unmistakeable evidence of a bad spirit on the part of the inhabitants. I may add that Northern people who have settled down in business in the different towns of this State, are quite generally complaining of the demonstrations of unfriendly feeling with which they are received and the many annoyances to which they are exposed.

Gov. Johnson, with whom I had a full exchange of views and who is, I am happy to say, of all the Georgians I have seen yet, the most earnest and thorough going friend of the national cause,—excepting, perhaps, Mr. Joshua Hill,[15] late member of Congress, who, to judge from the views he expressed to me, is equally devoted and sincere—is by no means satisfied with the present condition of things. He expresses serious apprehensions as to the fitness of the people of Georgia to legislate upon the problems before them with a just appreciation of the objects to be attained as long as they permit themselves to be governed by their old prejudices. He is not at all confident that they will come up to the requirements of the situation. While he deems it probable that they will, in revising their constitution, recognize the abolition of slavery in Georgia, he entertains great doubt as to their being prepared to vote for the "Constitutional Amendment." He fears that the rejection of the "Constitutional Amendment" by the people of Kentucky[16] will have a very bad effect upon the people of Georgia and prevent a healthy development of public opinion, and I am afraid, he is but too well justified in that apprehension. The Governor is in favor of placing the negro upon an equal footing with the whites before the law, as far as his standing in the Courts of Justice etc. is concerned, and permits no opportunity to pass by unimproved, to urge these matters upon the attention of the people. But he is by no means sanguine as to the result.

In the above I have given you the dark side of the picture. I must not omit to say that I met with a great many planters who sincerely condemned the outrages committed upon negroes and seemed disposed to take the free labor experiment in hand with an earnest desire to succeed. At Savannah I had a little meeting of planters who all seemed to be animated with this spirit. The more enlightened of them even went so far as to recognize the necessity of considerable changes in their code of laws. But almost none of them had succeeded in separating in their minds the idea of compulsion from negro labor, and all I have heard and seen convinces me, that if the slightest hope or prospect of a return to something like the old system were held out to them, they would grasp at it with eagerness. The truth is, that but few people in this State have arrived at a correct understanding of their situation; that their minds are given to all sorts of speculations as to the manner, not in which free labor can be organized and made profitable to both employer and laborer, but in which the introduction of true free labor can be avoided, and that a complete restoration of civil government cannot be effected with safety to the results of the war until the thoughts of the people, and especially the leaders are turned into a different channel. I have made every possible effort to induce some of the more advanced minds to take a bold stand on these questions, to discuss them openly and without prevarication and to make the people understand what will be required of them. To the honor of Gov. Johnson be it said, he has so far shown himself the boldest and most earnest man in the State. Aside from him, I have prevailed on Judge Lochrane [17] of this city to take bolder ground in a speech he is going to deliver in a few days at Atlanta,[18] and I have no doubt he will produce a good effect. The movement once started it will roll on, and, if vigorously prosecuted, its result can hardly be doubtful. But it will require time. I said in my letter from Hilton Head, that I considered all haste in this matter dangerous inasmuch as the people of this region are not sufficiently advanced yet to legislate intelligently upon the subject,—and all I have seen and heard so far confirms me in that opinion. *I find that those are most clamorous for the immediate restoration of civil government in these States, who can least be trusted.* There is no enemy of the national cause in this region who is not anxious that the "people" resume at once absolute control of their affairs, that the "Yankee soldiers" be withdrawn and that the State militia be reorganized, while men who are most sincerely in sympathy with the national Government desire, not so much that these things be done at once, but that they be done when the foundations of a healthy development are firmly laid and are beyond the danger of being broken up

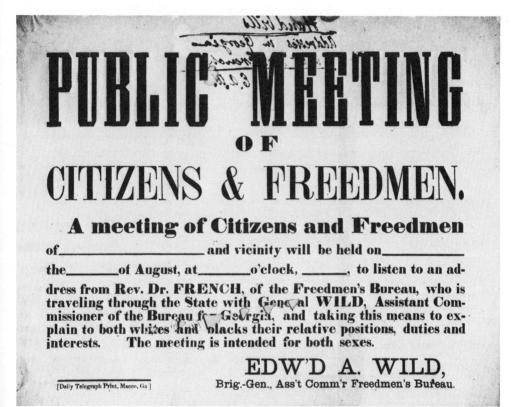

PUBLIC MEETING

OF

CITIZENS & FREEDMEN.

A meeting of Citizens and Freedmen

of_____ and vicinity will be held on_____

the_____of August, at_____o'clock, _____, to listen to an address from Rev. Dr. FRENCH, of the Freedmen's Bureau, who is traveling through the State with General WILD, Assistant Commissioner of the Bureau for Georgia, and taking this means to explain to both whites and blacks their relative positions, duties and interests.   The meeting is intended for both sexes.

EDW'D A. WILD,

Brig.-Gen., Ass't Comm'r Freedmen's Bureau.

[Daily Telegraph Print, Macon, Ga.]

General Wild Comes to Visit: A Broadside, 1865.
Courtesy of The Smithsonian Institution

again by a reaction. I am more than ever of the opinion that we can gain all by moving on slowly and deliberately, and that on the other hand we shall prepare for these States a future full of danger, disorder and confusion if we withdraw the control of the General Government before the objects are secured which under existing circumstances cannot be secured but by the interposition of the National authority. The people, left free to regulate their own concerns, are certainly inclined to day to throw obstacles in the way of their future progress, which, if things be judiciously managed, they will, a year hence, no longer think of.

Permit me now to bring some matters to your notice which require the immediate attention of the Government.

1.) It is absolutely necessary that the Freedmen's Department should, in this State, receive a more efficient organization. Aside from the districts under the immediate control of the agencies established at Savannah and Augusta, I did not find a single district in this State properly attended to. Planters who want to make contracts with the freedmen on their plantations, did not know where to go to have their contracts approved, and military commanders who, in the absence of regular agents of the Freedmen's Bureau, took the matter into their own hands, had no orders or instructions to guide their actions. Gen. Steedman has now issued an order directing the provost marshals stationed all over the State, one to every four counties, to attend to this business;[19] he would have made a similar arrangement long ago, had he not understood, that Genl. Wilde[20] was sent here for the purpose of setting the machinery of the Freedmen's Department in motion.

As to Genl. Wilde I would respectfully call your attention to the opinion expressed about him by Genl. Steedman in the enclosed statement of his views.[21] I am sorry to say, there seems to be but one opinion as to Genl. Wilde's fitness for his position. Genl. Gillmore speaks of him in the same terms.[22] I have not succeeded in effecting a meeting with Gen. Wilde and am therefore not able to give his side of the story. But if he was sent here to organize anything, he has certainly failed. All I can learn of him is that he is travelling about with Dr. French,[23] a chaplain, holding meetings and making speeches to the negroes. I understand that at several points these speeches have had an excellent effect. On the whole, I conclude from what I hear about it, that his activity in this line is doing good, especially in this State.[24]

But the time is approaching when agents ought to be stationed all over the State to superintend the making of contracts for next year. This is a matter of extra ordinary importance, and, perhaps, of some difficulty. The impression has got abroad among the negroes that something very important is going to happen about Christmas. A great many of them firmly believe that the Government will divide among them the lands belonging to their former masters. Hence they quite generally refuse to enter into any arrangements with the planters extending beyond that time. It is feared that serious disturbances will take place about Christmas, unless measures be taken by the Government to disabuse the negroes of that delusion.[25] Hence the necessity of having agents stationed among them all over the State as soon as possible. Such agents must either be sent here by the Freedmen's Bureau, or the provost marshals and post-commanders must be recognized as exofficio agents in the absence of regularly appointed ones.[26]

The former is certainly preferable. If an officer is to attend to the affairs of the freedmen as they ought to be attended to, it will require all his time and will leave him not a minute for other business. I would suggest that men be selected who are or have been in the military service; they will cooperate better with the military machinery, and, besides, a man with a military uniform on will have more influence with the negroes than a civilian. The negroes want to be sure that he who assumes to transact their business, is a "real Yankee." The agents might be taken from the number of Assistant Adjutant Generals or Quartermasters or Commissaries not yet mustered out.

It is essential that the sympathies of such agents should be strongly and sincerely with the freedmen, but it is also essential that they be men of good solid sense and that their enthusiasm be not too strong for their judgment.

If the Government should prefer to entrust the provost marshals and local commanders with the administration of the freedmen's affairs, all the orders and instructions issued by the Freedmen's Bureau should be forwarded to them through Department Headquarters as soon as possible.

It ought to be taken into consideration that but few if any field- and line-officers can be spared from their organizations, as the nature of the duties they have to perform requires their presence with their commands. If, therefore, the Government cannot send as many agents of the Freedmen's Bureau as are required for the subagencies, it ought to send at all events as many as possible.

2.) I mentioned above that the 4th U.S. Cavalry which, as I am informed is to pass under the control of the Department Commander, has but eleven officers present, its whole strength present for duty being about 700 men. The duties which this regiment will have to perform, render it very desirable, if not absolutely necessary, that all the officers belonging to it should be ordered to rejoin it without delay.

3.) One of the greatest inconveniences under which the people are laboring, is the want of all postal accommodations. Proper mail arrangements would greatly facilitate the dissemination of newspapers and documents, the interchange of ideas between the people North and South, and thus materially contribute to a beneficial development of public opinion in this region. Besides, it is a matter of great importance for the business community.

4.) Gov. Johnson has commenced to reorganize the Courts of Justice in this State. I consider it necessary, and the Governors opinion coincides with mine, that all cases arising between whites and blacks as well as all cases in which the government of the United States is concerned, should for the present be excluded from these courts.[27] Gov. Johnson is also in favor of the admission of the testimony of colored persons. I would respectfully suggest that the Government establish these points as a general rule to govern the action of Courts of Justice at present in operation in the States lately in rebellion.[28]

I am, Sir, very truly and respectfully
Your obedient servant C. Schurz

P.S. I enclose the following documents: 1.) Statement of views expressed by Maj. Genl. Steedman. 2.) Letter from Capt. Ketchum, Agent of the Freedmen's Bureau at Savannah.[29] 3.) Report of the Provost Marshal at Atlanta. 4.) Letter from Brig. Genl. Croxton, Comdg Columbus District Ga.[30] 5.) Report of a conversation with Mr. Wm. King of Savannah.[31] Mr. King is the gentleman who was sent as a messenger by Genl. Sherman to Gov. Brown after the capture of Atlanta. He is a Union man, and his views are the most liberal that I have heard expressed by any of the planters I have come in contact with.

C.S.

ALS, DLC-JP.
1. A copy of this letter in the Schurz Papers, Library of Congress, is dated August 12.
2. Prewar Douglas Democrat James B. Steedman (1817–1883), commanding the Department of Georgia, served with the Army of the Cumberland and formed a close relationship with then military governor Johnson. Steedman believed that in Johnson "the loyal people of the South have a friend and supporter who will never make peace on any terms that will enable the traitors of the revolted States to take possession of State governments to the exclusion of the loyal." Steedman to Johnson, April 15, 1865, Johnson Papers, LC.
3. Steedman observed that white Georgians "are submissive but not loyal," and if restored to power they would "escape from the legitimate results of the war." Planters "have absolutely no conception of what free labor is"; whites in general refused to recognize the rights of blacks. He urged that the military continue to adjudicate clashes between blacks and whites and, given the attitudes of white Georgians, questioned the advisability of the rapid restoration of civil authority. *Schurz Report*, 52–53.
4. James Johnson (1811–1891), who served one term in Congress (1851–53) as a member of the Georgia Union party, was appointed provisional governor in June, 1865. Later he became customs collector at Savannah (1866), was a Grant elector in '68 and '72, and served as judge, Georgia superior court (1869–75). I.W. Avery, *History of the State of Georgia From 1850 to 1881* (New York, 1881), 502.
5. John E. Hayes, who had served as correspondent of the New York *Tribune*, took over the offices of the Savannah *Republican* on December 26, 1864, and edited the paper for four years. T. Conn Bryan, *Confederate Georgia* (Athens, Ga., 1953), 206; J. Cutler Andrews, *The North Reports the Civil War* (Pittsburgh, 1955), 511–13.
6. Richard D. Arnold (1808–1876), Savannah physician since 1832, was a leading force in Savannah politics, first as editor of the Savannah *Georgian*, then as alderman, and finally as mayor for six terms, including the last years of the Civil War. Richard H. Shryock, ed., *Letters of Richard D. Arnold, M.D., 1808–1876* (New York, 1970 [1929]), 7–9.
7. Schurz elaborated on this point in one of his Boston *Advertiser* dispatches, reporting

that "a considerable number" of violent incidents "have happened and are still frequently occurring. The planters have organized themselves into bands, and are protecting each other in the enjoyment of their 'inalienable rights' as slave-owners." Boston *Advertiser*, August 19, 1865.

8. Capt. Edward Johnson, 68th N.Y. Inf., provided Schurz with a list of "Altercations between Whites and Negro's," containing a description of seven cases transpiring over a sixteen-day period where whites were charged with "Assaulting Negro's on street without any cause injuring them considerably." Elaborating in great detail on the nature of the wounds, Johnson commented that the assaults, "but a few of the instances coming to my knowledge weekly," were "done . . . when the negro has no protector. . . . In nearly every case the guilty parties are spirited away. In some parts of the country their seems to be such a bitter hatred towards the negro that nothing but life seems to appease them." He added that he refused to approve labor contracts unless the black laborer was present. Report of Capt. Edward Johnson, August 10, 1865, Johnson Papers, LC.

9. Prussian prince and soldier of fortune Felix Salm-Salm (1828–1870) emigrated to the United States in 1861, believing that his experience as a cavalryman would aid in the suppression of the slaveholders' rebellion. Brevetted brigadier, he later joined Maximilian's forces in Mexico, and subsequently served as major in the Prussian army, dying at the battle of Gravelotte in the Franco-Prussian War.

10. Arnold Kummer (*c*1839–*fl*1891) rose from private to major, 68th New York Inf., by 1864. He was wounded and captured at Second Bull Run, and suffered a serious wound at Gettysburg. CSR, RG94, NA.

11. Theodore Feldstein (b. *c*1835) served three months in the 1st Conn. Inf., then joined the 68th New York Inf. as a first sergeant in 1861. By 1863 he had advanced to the rank of captain. *Ibid.*

12. Cavalry commander John T. Croxton (1836–1874), a veteran of the Army of the Cumberland, headed the District of Southwest Georgia until he resigned in December, 1865.

13. In September, 1865, there were 15,779 federal troops stationed in Georgia. Sefton, *Army and Reconstruction*, 261.

14. James H. Wilson.

15. Successively a Whig, Know-Nothing, and Constitutional Unionist, prewar congressman Joshua Hill (1812–1891) opposed secession. During the war he participated in an effort to have Georgia negotiate a separate peace. In 1868 he was elected to the U.S. Senate. William J. Northen, ed., *Men of Mark in Georgia* (7 vols., Spartanburg, S.C., 1974 [1907–12]), III, 71–76.

16. The state legislature's earlier (February) rejection of the Thirteenth Amendment, by votes of 13–21 in the Senate and 29–57 in the House, had within the past week been confirmed by the return of a Conservative majority to the legislature, after a campaign in which ratification of the amendment was a major issue. The amendment would be once again rejected in the forthcoming November session. McPherson, *Great Rebellion*, 598; E. Merton Coulter, *The Civil War and Reconstruction in Kentucky* (Gloucester, Mass., 1966[1926]), 278–84.

17. Irish immigrant and lawyer Osborne A. Lochrane (1829–1887), a member of the state supreme court during the war, later supported congressional reconstruction and was appointed judge of the Atlanta circuit and of the Georgia supreme court. Northen, *Men of Mark in Georgia*, III, 203–6.

18. Lochrane proved unable to speak; instead, on August 16, 1865, he wrote the editor of the Atlanta *Intelligencer* that "Georgia must rise from failure and disaster to life and industry" by facing the consequences of the war. He urged white Georgians to grant blacks full civil rights in order to prevent a northern backlash which might result in the imposition of black suffrage. "We must teach the freedman his duty, as well as proclaim his rights, his responsibilities must be made known to him; and the follies which have entered his brain with his new-found freedom must be driven out." Atlanta *Intelligencer*, August 17, 1865.

19. On August 7, Steedman issued Circular No. 2, directing provost marshals to adjudicate all disputes over wages, debts, and contracts between freedmen and whites (as well as between freedmen), and establishing guidelines to assist the provost marshal in reaching a judgment. Augusta *Constitutionalist*, August 10, 1865.

20. Edward A. Wild (1825–1891), after assisting Massachusetts governor John A.

Andrew's efforts to raise black regiments, was promoted brigadier in 1863 and headed a brigade of black troops along the Carolina coast and at Petersburg.

21. Steedman castigated Wild as "entirely unfit for the discharge of the duties incumbent upon him," possessing "very little judgment" and displaying "much vigor where it is not wanted." Nor was he alone in questioning Wild's abilities. At the onset of the Petersburg campaign Gen. William F. Smith reported to Grant's chief of staff that Wild was "entirely unfitted for command." *Schurz Report*, 52; John Y. Simon, ed., *The Papers of Ulysses S. Grant* (14 vols., Carbondale, Ill., 1967–), XI, 119n.

22. Wild's recent behavior justified both his surname and complaints about his judgment. Entering Washington, Georgia, the last week of July, he strung several men up by the thumbs to extract confessions about a bank robbery. In early August he ejected Mrs. Robert Toombs from her home to make room for a black school and a headquarters site. His evident enthusiasm for his work made him anathema to local residents, one of whom characterized him as "one of those close, secret, cold-blooded villains," who was "reveling in power and wickedness." Within days Steedman revoked Wild's confiscation of the Toombs residence and arrested Wild. Grant and Howard vied for the honor of relieving him from duty. Eliza F. Andrews, *The War-time Journal of a Georgia Girl, 1861–1865* (New York, 1908), 344–60; William Y. Thompson, *Robert Toombs of Georgia* (Baton Rouge, 1966), 220; Grant to Stanton, August 30, 1865, Stanton Papers, LC; Howard to John A. Rawlins, September 4, 1865, BRFAL, Letters Sent, RG105 (M742), NA; Atlanta *Intelligencer*, August 8, 1865.

23. Methodist minister Mansfield French (1810–1876), a close friend of Chief Justice Chase, was associated with philanthropic efforts on behalf of the Port Royal experiment. After the war, with his hopes of winning election to the U.S. Senate from South Carolina thwarted in 1868, he returned north in 1872. Rose, *Rehearsal for Reconstruction*, 26–27, 393–94.

24. The Atlanta *Intelligencer* on August 5, reporting on a meeting conducted by Wild and French, characterized the latter's remarks as filled with "much good advice, and we hope it may have a beneficial effect on the freed population in our midst." Eliza Andrews, describing French as a "whang-nosed fanatic," offered a different perspective. "The negroes have been corrupted by the teachings of such wretches as this French and Wild," she confided to her diary. Andrews, *Journal*, 344, 360.

25. Early in September, French reported to Steedman that many Georgia whites had a "fearful apprehension that the freedmen have a deep laid plot for an insurrection and slaughter," which would be triggered by the Christmas holidays. This unfounded rumor, which reemerged in many a southern community through the fall of 1865, was doubtless sparked by speculation among blacks that the federal government would undertake a massive program of land redistribution which would reward each black family with "forty acres and a mule" as a Christmas gift. On November 11, Gen. Oliver O. Howard, head of the Freedmen's Bureau, instructed his agents to inform blacks that there would be "no division of lands, that nothing is going to happen at Christmas. . . . Insurrection will lead to nothing but . . . destruction." Dan T. Carter, "The Anatomy of Fear: The Christmas Day Insurrection Scare of 1865," *Journal of Southern History*, XLII (August, 1976), 345–64.

26. See Schurz to Johnson, July 28, 1865, n.19.

27. While the President failed to respond to Schurz's suggestion, several generals acted on their own to protect blacks and federal personnel from civil actions. On January 12, 1866, Grant issued General Orders No. 3, directing military commanders stationed in the South to protect from prosecution all U.S. military personnel and loyal citizens for acts done in compliance with federal authority. He also instructed his subordinates to protect from prosecution freedmen "charged with offenses for which white persons are not prosecuted or punished in the same manner and degree." This order expanded the protection offered U.S. military personnel from civil prosecution under the Habeas Corpus Act of 1863. McPherson, *Reconstruction*, 122–23; Sefton, *Army and Reconstruction*, 66–67; Nieman, *To Set the Law in Motion*, 85.

28. On December 15, 1865, the Georgia state legislature voted to let freedmen testify in cases involving blacks only. Within a year, in Clark v. State of Georgia (35 Georgia 175), the state supreme court declared that blacks could testify in all cases. McPherson, *Reconstruction*, 32–33; Mildred C. Thompson, *Reconstruction in Georgia: Economic, Social, Political, 1865–1872* (Savannah, 1972 [1915]), 336.

29. Alexander Phoenix Ketchum (1839–1905), detached from duty with the 128th U.S.C.T. to work in the Freedmen's Bureau, served on the staffs of Generals Saxton and O.O. Howard before resigning in 1867 with the brevet rank of colonel. Ketchum reported that planters still believed in the superiority of slave labor to free labor, and that "the rebel spirit is as bitter as ever." CSR, RG94, NA; Ketchum to Schurz, August 1, 1865, *Schurz Report*, 105.

30. Croxton concluded that whites submitted to Union rule by necessity: "There are no loyal people in Georgia, except the negroes." Believing that Georgia's whites would draft legislation which would "reduce the freedmen to a condition worse than slavery," he urged that the Freedmen's Bureau be staffed with "men of energy and business capacity." Croxton to Schurz, August 14, 1865, *ibid.*, 53.

31. Cotton merchant and insurance agent William King (1804–1884) was selected by Gen. William T. Sherman as an envoy in Sherman's unsuccessful attempt to secure Georgia's withdrawal from the Confederacy in exchange for the good conduct of Sherman's troops. In his conversation with Schurz, King offered the opinion that blacks would not work "unless compelled to." He rejected the contract system as a failure, preferring that the freedman "be held in the position of a ward." He urged the retention of Union troops in the region to protect unionists and to intercede in racial disputes. Robert Manson Myers, ed., *The Children of Pride: A True Story of Georgia and the Civil War* (New Haven, 1972), 1585–86; *Schurz Report*, 83–84.

Montgomery Ala. August 21st 1865

To his Excellency Andrew Johnson
President of the United States.
Sir,

At Columbus Ga. I met Genl. Wilde, Assistant Commissioner of the Freedmen's Bureau whose movements in the State of Georgia I had occasion to notice in my letter of the 13th inst. He gave as a reason for his failure in effecting a more efficient organization of the Freedmen's Department in that State, that the military commanders to whom he applied for details of officers, did not furnish them.[1] This is undoubtedly correct, but in my former letters I mentioned already the difficulties under which military commanders are laboring. Permit me to repeat that I consider it very desirable, that agents of the Freedmen's Bureau should be sent from Washington, as many and as soon as possible. Even if officers could be detached in sufficient numbers from their respective organizations, they will, in most cases, serve only a short time, as their regiments are liable to be mustered out. In the Freedmen's Department a certain stability is necessary; agents become efficient only after having acquired some experience, and frequent changes cannot but seriously disturb the working of the machinery. This stability can be attained only by the appointment of men who can remain at their posts without being liable to be removed except for reasons connected with their position in the Bureau.[2]

You are probably advised of the imporant order issued by Brig. Gen. W. Swayne,[3] Assistant Commissioner of the Freedmen's Bureau, on the 4th inst.[4] Governor Parsons[5] has published a circular letter concerning the same matter, "to the Judges and Magistrates of the State of Alabama," of which I enclose a copy.[6] Both Governor Parsons and Genl. Swayne are very sanguine of the success of the experiment. I confess that it appears very doubtful to me, whether the setting aside of the old laws will prevail upon the Judges, Magistrates and other civil officers, to drop their old prejudices. Experience will have to show whether Alabama juries at the present time are prepared to find a white man who killed a negro, guilty of murder, or another, who whipped a negro, guilty of assault and battery.

I have inquired about cases that had arisen between whites and negroes and the manner in which they were treated by the civil authorities. I received the following information from Genl. Swayne:

No trials were had yet of such cases by state or county courts. But the alacrity of a sheriff was tested in one instance.

1st case, in Montgomery County. About Aug. 1st, a negro was shot dead by a white man. A warrant was issued immediately to arrest the party. The sheriff was ordered to proceed at once, but he delayed action about 30 hours. The guilty party had time to escape and disappeared.

2d case, in Lowndes County. About August 8th a negro was shot by a white man. Gen. Swayne applied to the Governor for instructions. The Governor consented to have the arrest of the guilty party effected by the military, and the arrest was successfully effected without delay.

I enclose a report addressed by Capt. Poillon,[7] Agent of the Freedmen's Department, to Gen. Swayne, and desire to invite your particular attention to it. It gives a horrible picture of the condition of things in the counties therein mentioned. Gen. Swayne informs me that some affidavits corroborating the statements contained in the report have already been received by him, and that he has ordered the whole evidence to be sent up. He tells me also, that as far as his information goes, murders of blacks by whites are occurring at the rate of about one per day. He receives reports however only from those districts in the State where agents of the Bureau are stationed.

I hear rumors of murders and other atrocities, more or less authenticated, from all sides. Although I should be happy to see the machinery of civil government in working operation as soon as possible, consistently with the general interests of the people, I doubt very much whether such a state of things can be reached and regulated by the ordinary courts under present circumstances.

I understand that in this State most of the troops are concentrated at certain points where there is no necessity for any concentration of forces. If the troops were so distributed as to be within reach of every county in the State, I am sure most of these outrages could easily be prevented. The mere presence of troops would deter many people from attempting anything of the kind. The presence of a Judge or magistrate will have no such effect, nor is it likely that civil officers will show much alacrity in bringing such occurrences to the notice of the military authorities. I have no doubt, a great many things have happened, of which we never were and never shall be informed unless the occupation be made more perfect.

I would, therefore, respectfully suggest, that the Commanders of Departments be ordered to make such disposition of their troops as will enable them to keep themselves informed of what is going on in any part of their commands, and to reach any locality at least with a little force in one or two days. I understand there are troops enough in this Department to answer this purpose, and there is no necessity for an imposing display of forces anywhere.[8]

Aside from the outrages committed upon negroes there is an amount of stealing going on among the whites which is quite appalling. Everybody that wants something seems to be helping himself to it. On the same newspaper slip which contains the Governors letter to the Magistrates and Judges, you will also find a proclamation referring to this subject.[9] This state of things is likely to grow worse unless vigorously counteracted; in many districts in this State the corn-crop is a complete failure owing to an unusually severe drought. There will necessarily be much destitution, and unless sufficient measures be taken to repress the lawless spirit of numerous classes of people, the consequences may become very serious.

As to the tendency of the popular spirit with regard to future political action I have so far gathered in this State less information than I had in South Carolina and Georgia. I have seen and conversed with a number of people of different standing in society, and have found no marked difference between the feelings and views of citizens of Alabama and those of citizens of Georgia and South Carolina. Only in this city a more enlightened and liberal spirit seems to prevail among those most likely to have given thought and consideration to the problems that are to be solved. Governor Parsons feels as sanguine with regard to the elections for the State Convention as he does with regard to the success of the judicial experiment. He confidently predicts that the Convention will be composed of the best and most liberal minded men in the State;[10] that the members will be elected not on party issues but on their own individual merit as to intelligence and character; that the Constitutional Amendment will be adopted; that the negro will be permitted to give testimony in the Courts of Justice; that his right to hold and to convey property will be recognized, and that, perhaps, the admission of the negro to the exercise of the elective franchise will be referred to the action of the Legislature. I am not prepared to say that the expectations entertained by the Governor are unfounded, nor do I, from what I have seen, feel inclined to entertain them myself. In strange contrast to these predictions stands the attitude of a majority of the papers published in this State which lose no opportunity to attack or sneer at the acts of the General Government, especially those concerning the freedmen, in stranger contrast still the many revolting outrages perpetrated upon colored people in different parts of the State, and even under the shadow of the State Capitol. I will however, at present, confine myself to a mere statement of the Governors opinion. The question will very soon decide itself.

I beg leave to submit the following suggestions:

1.) My observations lead me to believe that the new system of labor would work more successfully if the negroes could be transferred from the plantations upon which they were formerly held as slaves, to others where they could at once enter into their new relation with their employer as free laborers. This new relation would establish itself more naturally and easily if no other individual relation had ever existed between the employer and the laborer. I communicated this idea to Gov. Johnson of Georgia, and it struck him as founded upon a sound theory. I have discussed the same matter with several planters here and at other places, and their opinions on the subject almost uniformly coincided with me. I know well, an attempt to introduce this system generally and at one time, would result in great confusion, set the whole negro population wandering and relieve the planters of the duty to keep the aged and children on their plantations, an obligation now imposed upon them by the government. But I beg leave to suggest that the agents of the Freedmen's Bureau be instructed to favor such changes wherever they can be effected without serious inconvenience.

2.) If the Government concludes to permit Gen. Swayne's General order No 7 to go into effect it will be absolutely necessary to watch the proceedings of the Courts in cases between whites and freedmen with the closest attention. Unless this is done it will be impossible for the military authorities to keep well informed of the treatment negroes receive, and to ascertain any "evident denial of justice." I would therefore suggest that the following regulation be ordered:

a.) In every case arising between a white man and a negro an agent of the Freedmen's Bureau must be admitted as the next friend of the negro.

b.) The proceedings in every such case including the testimony shall be sent with in a certain specified time to the Assistant Commissioner of the Freedmen's Bureau in the Department, and by him to the Headquarters of the Freedmen's Bureau at Washington.

c.) The agents of the Freedmen's Bureau are ordered to report every case of outrage committed by a white man upon a negro in which no judicial proceedings were had, to the Headquarters of the Bureau at Washington.

Unless such regulations be adopted,[11] it will be impossible for the authorities to form a clear opinion of the working of the system adopted by Gen. Swayne and to give the freedmen that measure of protection without which he will be absolutely at the mercy of those who seem determined to persecute him in the most fiendish manner. I have communicated these suggestions to Gen. Swayne and he promises to endeavor to agree with the Governor upon regulations incorporating them. But it would be well for the Freedmen's Bureau to issue general orders to that effect.

3.) I hear from several responsible sources that there is much cotton-stealing going on on the part of Government agents and parties acting in concert with them[.] Gov. Parsons tells me that he has written you on the subject.[12] I would suggest that some reliable detectives be sent to this State to investigate these matters. Gov. Parsons desires that they report to him.

4.) I learn that a petition has gone up to you for the pardon of Dr. Andrews[13] who was sentenced to ten years imprisonment for killing a negro. I wish to state, that but recently two negroes were hung here for killing a white man, but that no white man has yet in this State been punished for killing a negro, except Dr. Andrews; I wish to state further that Dr. Andrews is at the present moment at large, walking about in this city. I do not desire to enlarge upon the merits of his case, but I feel compelled to say, that unless the severest punishments known to the laws be visited upon white men killing negroes the Southern States will soon be a vast slaughter pen for the black race. The report of Capt. Poillon, when I first read it, seemed to me extravagant. I then visited the hospitals of this city and found out upon the best possible evidence that a similar state of things exists here. I have the honor to enclose two lists of cases treated in two of the hospitals, and certified to by the Surgeons.[14] Several attempts to kill occurred while I was here, and if such things can happen in broad daylight under the very eyes of the State Government and of the military forces of the United States, what may happen where there is no such check upon the brutal instincts of the masses? It seems to me that in such matters lenity is out of place. I have heard of some instances in which provost-marshals were but too ready to release persons who had committed such outrages, on parole. I would suggest, that Department Commanders be ordered not to permit the release of any murderer under any circumstances.—

I intended to proceed from here to Mobile, but learning that the State Convention of Mississippi is now in session, I shall go there by way of Selma and Meridian. Finding the leading men of the State together, I expect to gather more information there than I might obtain at any other place. I intend to visit subsequently the State of Louisiana and the Southern part of Alabama.

Very truly and respectfully
Your obedient servant C. Schurz

ALS, DLC-JP.

1. Wild made the same complaint in two letters to General Saxton. Nieman, *To Set the Law in Motion*, 13.

2. A New York *Herald* reporter in Georgia at the time asserted that "certain abuses of a very grave nature have grown up in the administration here of the affairs of the Freedmen's Bureau." New York *Herald*, August 6, 1865.

3. Wager Swayne (1834–1902), son of Supreme Court Justice Noah Swayne, received the Medal of Honor for his actions at the battle of Corinth and participated in the Atlanta campaign and Sherman's marches through Georgia and South Carolina. In 1865 Gen. Howard appointed him to direct the operations of the Freedmen's Bureau in Alabama; Johnson removed him two years later.

4. Issued August 4, Swayne's General Order No. 7 made all judicial officers, magistrates, and sheriffs Bureau agents for the administration of cases involving blacks and directed them to recognize no distinction according to color in applying state law. If civil authorities refused to comply, martial law would be declared over the area in question. Fleming, *Reconstruction in Alabama*, 428; New York *Times*, September 6, 1865.

5. Originally a Whig, Lewis E. Parsons (1817–1895) journeyed into Democratic ranks in the 1850's via the Know Nothing movement, and won election to Congress in 1859. On June 21, 1865, President Johnson appointed him provisional governor for Alabama. Elected U.S. senator later in the year, he was denied his seat; during the next years he battled against the ratification of the Fourteenth Amendment and the 1867 state constitution before jumping to the Republican party.

6. Parsons' order directed civil officials to comply with Swayne's General Order No. 7. New York *Times*, September 6, 1865.

7. On July 29, 1865, Captain William A. Poillon (b. *c*1818), 68th U.S.C.T. and assistant superintendent of freedmen, reported to General Swayne on a series of violent incidents resulting in the deaths of blacks. In all, he listed seventeen specific incidents. Blacks were beaten, hung, burned to death, shot, and mutilated: "*Murder with his ghastly train stalks abroad at noonday and revels in undisputed carnage*, while the bewildered and terrified freedmen know not what to do," he concluded. Violence served to coerce blacks to work, he argued, "by every device an inhuman ingenuity can devise." *Schurz Report*, 73–74.

8. Some 18,057 troops were stationed in Alabama at the time Schurz wrote. Sefton, *Army and Reconstruction*, 261.

9. On August 19 Parsons issued a proclamation outlining the process whereby Alabamians would take the loyalty oath prescribed by Johnson. He added, "Crimes of all kinds appear to be alarmingly on the increase, but especially cotton stealing and horse stealing. . . . Fellow-citizens, all this must be stopped." New York *Times*, September 3, 1865.

10. Of the delegates elected to the state constitutional convention, 45 had been Whigs/Constitutional Unionists; 24 had supported Breckenridge in 1860; 30 had cast their ballot for Douglas. Some 18 of them had favored immediate secession, while of the 11 who had attended the 1861 secession convention, 10 had voted for secession. Walter Fleming estimated that about 63 delegates were "conservatives," with the rest being "north Alabama anti-Confederates." Fleming, *Reconstruction in Alabama*, 358–59.

11. In Alabama, Freedmen's Bureau agents sometimes dispatched troops to arrest whites who had committed crimes against blacks when civil authorities failed to act, and removed cases from civil to military courts when they suspected that civil authorities would not secure fair trials. Nieman, *To Set the Law in Motion*, 26.

12. Not found.

13. In May, planter James T. Andrew (b. 1827) was convicted by a military court of the murder of Thomas Waller, "a free colored citizen," despite Andrew's contention that he had shot Waller to prevent him from stealing a neighbor's horse. Parsons forwarded to Johnson the petition of several Montgomery citizens seeking Andrew's release, citing his "kind treatment of Negroes" and "infirm health" in support of their request. The President referred these documents to Judge Advocate General Joseph Holt, who not only advised Johnson not to intervene but dismissed Andrew's defense, pointing out that the neighbor had reported the loss of two mules, not horses, and that Andrew had no proof that Waller had stolen anything. Characterizing the shooting as "a ruthless, brutal murder," Holt stated: "This case evidently belongs to a numerous and revolting class of crimes . . . being perpetrated upon the (slave) colored population of the South by their late traitorous and exasperated masters." He went on to argue that the federal government should protect blacks from white violence "because this long down-trodden, but now

emancipated, race have the strongest claims upon the national gratitude, growing out of their loyalty in the midst of the traitorous white population by which they were surrounded, and out of the courage and faithfulness with which they have laid down their lives on so many battle-fields in defence of the Union." This impassioned plea proved unavailing; on October 26, 1865, Johnson ordered Andrew's release. 1850 Census, Ala., Montgomery, 1st Dist., 151; 1860 Census, Ala., Montgomery, 2nd Dist., Ramal P.O., 44; Holt to Johnson, August 31, 1865, JAGO Letterbook, Vol. 12, 556–57, and October 12, 1865, JAGO Letterbook, Vol. 20, 6, RG153, NA; Andrew to Johnson, August 14, 1865, Amnesty Papers, RG94 (M1003), NA; General Court Martial Orders No. 592, October 26, 1865.

14. Schurz enclosed two reports from Montgomery hospitals. J.M. Phipps, acting staff surgeon, in charge of the post hospital listed eleven cases of blacks "killed or maimed" by whites. Several blacks were shot or clubbed to death; others had parts of their heads (ears, chin, scalp) severed. J.E. Harvey, assistant surgeon, 58th Illinois, reported from the Freedmen's Hospital on three cases of blacks shot by whites. *Schurz Report*, 70–71.

Vicksburg Aug 29 '65

His Excy The President of the U. S.

Gen Slocum[1] has issued an order prohibiting the organization of the militia in this state— The organization of the militia would have been a fatal step[.][2] All I see & learn in the state convinces me that the course followed by Gen Slocum is the only one by which public order & security can be maintained; Today I shall forward by mail Gen Slocums order[3] with a full statement in the case[.][4]

Carl Schurz Maj Gen

Tel, DNA-RG107, Tels. Recd., President, Vol. 4 (1865–66).

1. Henry W. Slocum (1827–1894) held various commands in the Army of the Potomac and participated in the Atlanta campaign and the March to the Sea. After heading occupation forces in Mississippi for several months, he returned to New York in 1865 to reenter state politics as a Democrat, heading the fall ticket as candidate for secretary of state.

2. Responding to reports of lawlessness and disorder among both whites and blacks, Mississippi's provisional governor, William L. Sharkey, on August 19, called on each county to organize two militia companies to act as a police force, explaining to Johnson that mismanagement by Freedmen's Bureau agents was fostering black unruliness, and requesting Johnson to lift martial law. The President advised Sharkey to refrain from organizing militia companies for the time being and to rely on Slocum's troops. The governor replied on August 25 that the President's proposal "will leave us in a helpless condition," claimed that Slocum's force was inadequate, and that the black troops did "more harm than good." Three days later he added that he had heard rumors of a black uprising at Christmas. Meanwhile, Gen. Peter J. Osterhaus, commanding troops in the northern part of the state, protested Sharkey's action. William C. Harris, *Presidential Reconstruction in Mississippi* (Baton Rouge, 1967), 71–74; Sefton, *Army and Reconstruction*, 27–28.

3. Slocum's General Orders No. 22 of August 24 revoked Sharkey's proclamation, promising to arrest anyone who organized militia, and established procedures for the employment of troops to preserve order. *Schurz Report*, 62–63.

4. Schurz informed Secretary Stanton of the dispute the same day. He endorsed Slocum's order, and hoped that Johnson would "approve this order publicly and emphatically" to "put a stop to all vagaries on the part of Provisional Governors." He added, "So-

ciety is in a frightful state of demoralization, and the civil authorities present a lamentable picture of impotence and imbecility. Take the military away and a brutal, savage mob will rule the whole concern." Schurz to Stanton, August 29, 1865, Stanton Papers, LC.

Vicksburg, Miss. Aug. 29th 1865.
To his Excellency Andrew Johnson,
President of the United States.
Sir,

In my report from Montgomery Ala. I laid before you the information I had gathered so far about the condition of things in Alabama. Since then I visited Selma and Demopolis. What I saw and learned there confirmed me in the opinion, that the civil authorities as far as they are or can be reestablished under present circumstances, are entirely incapable of restoring anything like public order and security. The demoralization of the people is frightful to behold in its manifestations. Murder, assault with intent to kill, theft and robbery are matters of every day occurrence. The people seem to have lost all conception of the rights of property. Travellers are frequently attacked on the public highways, cotton is stolen in enormous quantities, horses and mules are run off whenever they are not watched with the utmost care, and the perpetrators are almost never arrested and punished. Some cases of that kind happened almost under my own eyes while I was at Selma. I enclose a report furnished to me by the Provost Marshal at Selma,[1] to which I beg leave to invite your particular attention.

At Demopolis I received information very much to the same effect, only that murders did not occur so frequently; the Assistant Superintendent of Freedmen at that place, Capt. A. C. Haptonstall,[2] knew only of two bodies of negroes and one of a white soldier that had been thrown into the Black Warrior River and floated down, all three bodies with marks of violence upon them. As to theft and robbery as well as negro-whipping the same practices prevail, as far as I have been able to ascertain, all over the State.

I beg leave to repeat what I said in my former reports: It is absolutely indispensable that the country should be garrisoned with troops as thickly as possible. There ought to be a company at least in every county. I have not seen Maj. Genl. Woods,[3] comdg the Department of Alabama, so as to converse with him about the matter; I intend to go to Mobile from New. Orleans. I understand, however, that he does nothing with regard to the maintenance of order in the State without being called upon by the civil authorities. The result is apparent. It seems to me, Gov. Parsons, in undertaking to maintain order in the State by the machinery of the civil government, has undertaken a thing which he cannot carry through, and which, I have abundant reason to believe, a good many of his subordinate civil officers are not disposed to carry through. Governor Parson's own proclamation, of which I sent you a copy in my last, furnishes sufficient evidence of this fact. The Governor himself feels it, although he may not be willing openly to acknowledge it.

In my letter dated Montgomery Aug. 20th[4] I stated that there was an abundance of troops in the State for all practical purposes, but since then I have learned that a considerable number of regiments is going to be mustered out.[5] This may change the aspect of things. I would suggest that the Commanders of Departments be ordered to furnish the War Department an estimate of the number of troops necessary for garrisoning every county in their respective States and for keeping at the principal points a force adequate to any emergency that is likely to arise. In my opinion [it] is unsafe to deplete these States too rapidly. We may need more troops three months hence than we do now.

From Demopolis I went to Meridian and Jackson Miss. I regret to say that I did not succeed in reaching Jackson previous to the adjournment of the Convention. The action of that body is before you. It may be worth while to give you a glimpse of its secret history.[6] In the Committee which was charged with recommending to the Convention some action to be taken with regard to the Ordinance of Secession, two propositions were taken into consideration: one to declare the Ordinance of Secession "repealed", thus, by implication, declaring the ordinance of secession a lawful act that might be done or undone by the people at pleasure;—and another to declare the Ordinance of Secession "null and void". The two propositions were discussed distinctly upon the issue of the legality or illegality of secession. The vote in the committee stood seven in favor of "repealing", and seven in favor of declaring the Secession Ordinance "null and void". The Chairman of the Committee, Mr. Amos R. Johnson,[7] gave his casting vote in favor of declaring it "null and void" stating as his reason, that the State would not be readmitted if they did adopt another policy. In the Convention he delivered the following opinion: "If we do this, the President and the Copperhead party will be with us to defeat the Black Republicans."[8]

Although the Convention had adjourned when I arrived at Jackson I still found some of its most influential members there, and from my conversations with them and with some gentlemen who had closely watched the proceedings of the Convention, I formed the opinion, that the conviction that the rejection of the Secession doctrine and the abolition of slavery in the State were indispensable to secure readmission, was the principal if not the only thing which secured the adoption of these two measures. You will have noticed that the Congressional Amendment to the Constitution was not adopted; the main reason urged against its adoption was that the second section of the Amendment was hostile to State rights.[9]

It is evident that the action of the Convention with regard to the abolition of slavery is very incomplete in itself, and must necessarily be amplified by laws to be passed by the Legislature to be worth anything. As to the prospective action of the Legislature I abstain from expressing any opinion; that body will soon make a record for itself.

One important thing, however, I must not omit to state. Most of the members of the Convention were elected on their general merits as to intelligence and character without a full canvass of their opinions on distinct issues; there were but two or three among them that we would call thorough going Union men.[10] Acting upon motives of policy which they appreciated but which the people did not appreciate, they did not dare to submit their action to the people for ratification. A motion to that effect was at once smothered in the Convention and not taken up again.[11] Some of them explained this by saying, that they wanted to avoid all further agitation of the subject, but others confessed openly that they knew they did not represent the people.

My observations lead me to believe that this is the truth. The people of the State of Mississippi feel with regard to the main problems before them, especially the negro question, as the people of Alabama Georgia and South Carolina do. There is no difference worth mentioning. Some of the more enlightened men are gradually acquiring a more accurate idea of the things that will be required of them, and thus, obeying the impulse from abroad, show a certain progressive spirit. But so far they have not been able to modify or control the brutal instincts of the masses; nor have they shown much courage in boldly facing them. A member of the convention said to a friend of mine: "We dare not say to our people what I now tell you, but we may gradually bring them up to it if we get a chance. Just as soon as the Legislature meets we will try to give the negro the right to give evidence before the Courts etc. But we dare not now come before the people with that sentiment." If gentlemen like this member succeed again in smuggling themselves into the Legislature, the action of that body will be, if not quite satisfactory, at least to a certain extent progressive. But if the people succeed in securing a true representation, we must look for bad results.

There is far less disorder in this State than in Alabama. In[I] enclose a list of capital offences that came to the notice of the Commander of the northern District of Mississippi, Genl. Osterhaus.[12] From the two other Districts I have received no reports yet. Most of the cases on the list happened before the military occupation of the State was completed. At the present moment this State is more perfectly garrisoned than any of those that I have visited.[13] The consequence is that order is more efficiently preserved, and that crime, even where it could not be prevented, is at least at once traced up and the offenders punished. There is a garrison in every county, and the machinery is in very fine working order. The promptness with which, whenever any crime is committed, the arrest of the perpetrators is effected, shows that the thing can be done if only those whose business it is, are honestly disposed to do it. In Alabama, where the matter is left to the sheriffs, hardly one offender in twenty is caught and brought to justice.

I enclose a letter addressed to me by Maj. Genl. Osterhaus, giving an account of the condition of things in his command.[14]

I wish to call your particular attention to what he says about the four murders recently committed in Attala county. That county had been the theatre of gross outrages when the military occupation was effected; the garrison was successful in restoring tranquillity and order. About two weeks ago the regiment to which the garrison belonged, was mustered out, and no sooner was the garrison withdrawn when four murders happened in quick succession, two of white Union men and two of negroes. This fact proves, that a bad spirit was prevailing there, that the garrison succeeded in checking it, and that the withdrawal of the garrison was the signal for a fresh installment of murderous outbreaks. There is evidence at the same time of the spirit of the people and of the efficiency and the necessity of the garrison system.

You have been informed of Gov. Sharkey's[15] attempt to reorganize the militia of the State, calling especially upon the young men who had distinguished themselves for gallantry in the rebel service, to take up arms. I have the honor to enclose Gen'l. Osterhaus' correspondence with Gov. Sharkey[16] and with Department Headquarters[17] about this matter; I enclose also Genl. Slocum's Genl. Order No. 22[18] having reference to the same subject. These documents contain so full an account of this whole business that I have but little to add.

I have made Gov. Sharkey's acquaintance and have come to the conclusion that he is a good, clever old gentleman, and probably a first class lawyer, but not in the least calculated for the discharge of duties so delicate and so responsible as those pertaining to his present position. He is continually surrounded by a set of old secessionists whom he considers it his duty to conciliate. These men are naturally very anxious to have our forces withdrawn from the State, so as to have it all their own way; and they being anxious, Gov. Sharkey is anxious also. In order to have the U. S. forces withdrawn it was considered advisable that the militia be organized. As a reason for ordering the organization of the militia some outrages committed between Jackson and Big Black are seized hold of, probably perpetrated by some of the same men who are very eager to see the militia organized. Gen. Osterhaus has since arrested some of them, and all the indications point that way.[19] It would seem that, before venturing upon a step of such importance, Gov. Sharkey ought to have felt it his duty to consult with Gen. Slocum, the Commander of the Department, or at least with Gen. Osterhaus, the Commander of the District who had his office in the same building with the

Dramatis Personae of the Mississippi Militia Controversy:
Peter J. Osterhaus, William L. Sharkey, and Henry W. Slocum.
Courtesy of The National Archives

Governor and is in daily communication with him. But the Governor did not give the least intimation of his design and suddenly issued his ⟨own⟩ proclamation, a proclamation calling upon rebel soldiers to take matters into their hands because the Union troops had proved inefficient.

It would be wrong to suppose, however, that Gov. Sharkey is entirely unaware of the difficulties surrounding him; he admits that all the outrages that are committed, are perpetrated upon negroes and Union men; and he said to me in the presence of Genl. Osterhaus that, if the Union troops were withdrawn, the life of no Northern men in Mississippi would be safe. At the same time he is anxious to have the Union troops make room for his militia and told me, he expected to see our forces withdrawn in a very few weeks. Gen. Slocum's order, aside from repelling the insult thrown into the face of the U. S. forces in this Department by the Governors proclamation, is eminently calculated to restore order and prevent the perpetration of crime in every District of the State. While the organization of the returned rebel soldiers as a State militia would have been the terror of the Union men and negroes, Genl. Slocums policy as set forth in his order, can hardly fail to make Mississippi the quietest State in the South, and I have no doubt it would have a most excellent effect if the same policy were applied to Alabama and Georgia. As to Alabama especially I see no other remedy.

If it was your policy to place the Governments of the States lately in rebellion into the hands of the Union element of those States, I am sorry to say that this policy has been most completely disregarded in Mississippi. Leaving the union sentiments of Gov. Sharkey out of discussion, I have not been able to learn of a single thorough Union man in this State having been placed in office. But the contrary has been the case. One of the best and most consistent Union men in this State is Judge Houghton.[20] He was one of the Probate Judges. While all the other Judges in the State were reinstated in their functions—I can not hear of a single exception,—Judge Houghton was dropped and in his place Gov. Sharkey appointed Mr. A. B. Smedes,[21] the President of the rebel vigilance committee, whose principal business consisted in dragooning Union men into obedience or running them out of the State. Thus, a Union man was virtually removed from office to make room for one of the most active and odious disloyalists. Gov. Sharkey was applied to by some prominent Union men of Vicksburg to correct this apparent mistake; but it turned out that Gov. Sharkey did not consider it a mistake. He replied that Judge Houghton was incompetent, while Judge Houghton had been elected by the people to the Probate Judgeship for three successive terms. This would seem to speak for his fitness.

The Secretary of State[22] appointed by Gov. Sharkey as well as one of the Governors two Aids were rebel officers, and it seems generally that if any discrimination is made, it is made in favor of men of rebel antecedents. In his recommendations for appointments to federal offices the

Governor seems to have been equally unfortunate. I understand that upon his recommendation Mr. Richard Barnett[23] was appointed postmaster at this place. The same Mr. Barnett was sent out of our lines by Gen. Dana[24] as one of the most prominent and notorious disloyalists of this city, and the members of his family made themselves so obnoxious by their ostentatious manifestations of hatred to the Union, that they were sent out of our lines by Gen. McPherson.[25]— I understand also that on the Governors recommendation Col. Jones Hamilton[26] was appointed United States Marshal for the Southern District. I am informed here by persons who have every opportunity of knowing, and whose statements are considered trustworthy at Department Headquarters, that Col. Hamilton served during the war as a Provost Marshal, a conscripting officer and an officer of the Cotton Bureau on the rebel side. If such men received federal appointments it was not because there were no true Union men in this State,—for I have seen here a sufficient number of gentlemen of unflinching loyalty, good intelligence and respectable standing in society—but because the Governor chose to recommend rebels in preference to Union men.

I presume it is the desire of the Administration to build up a Union party in the Southern States; but I apprehend this object cannot be attained if the power and patronage connected with federal offices are placed into the hands of late rebels to the discouragement of the true Union element. I have discussed this matter with Gen. Slocum, and the experience he has had in this Department leads him to be decidedly of the same opinion.

By what I have said I do not mean to impeach Gov. Sharkeys loyalty. I consider him a good, honest, but very weak man who permits himself to be moulded as to his views and policy by those who take hold of him with the greatest energy and assiduity. I do not see in him the right man in the right place. If the Government should choose to let him remain where he is until a Governor is regularly elected, I would respectfully suggest that he be advised to confine himself strictly within the sphere of duties assigned to him in the proclamation by which he was appointed.[27]

While writing this report I was called upon by several Union men of this city, who informed me that they would find themselves obliged to sell out what interests they have here, and to leave the place if Genl. Slocum's order concerning the militia should not be sustained by the Government. I find this feeling to be quite general among the Union people and especially among those who came from the North to invest money and do business here. It seems to me very essential that Genl. Slocums order should be openly approved by the President and the Secretary of War. It would reassure the Union men and the colored people and show the unruly spirits in this region that the Government will not permit them to disturb the public peace with impunity.

I understand the Government has been memorialized for the withdrawal of the colored troops from this State principally on the ground that their presence is very obnoxious to the people. I have been very careful in forming an opinion as to the policy of garrisoning these States with colored soldiers, and the information I have gathered, leads me to the following conclusions:

There is one complaint brought against them which has some foundation in fact. Colored soldiers doing duty in the country are sometimes found to put queer notions into the heads of negroes working on the plantations; and their camps are apt to be a point of attraction for colored women. These complaints I heard urged especially in South Carolina. But these difficulties are easily overcome by keeping the soldiers in a strict state of discipline or, in particularly bad cases, by taking the obnoxious individuals out and placing them on duty in the larger depots. I understand, this remedy has worked well in South Carolina; in this State I heard no such complaints at all.

On the other hand I hear complaints from all quarters that white soldiers garrisoning the country, in a great many instances combine with the white population against the blacks and sometimes aid the former in inflicting cruel punishments on the latter.[28] A good many cases of this description have come to my notice. But this is not all. I am reliably informed that much of the cotton stealing going on all over the country especially in Alabama, is effected not only with the passive connivance, but by the active aid and cooperation of white soldiers. The reports that have come to me, leave no doubt in my mind as to the truthfulness of this statement. Finally, white soldiers are generally tired of serving; they say that the war is over, that they were enlisted for the war, and that they want to go home. Their discipline is in a majority of cases rather lax, and they perform their duties with less spirit than the exigencies of their situation require.

The discipline of the black troops, on the contrary, is uniformly as good as their officers want to have it. They perform their duties with pride and a strict observance of their instructions. I have not heard of a single instance, nor even of a suspicion, that a colored soldier connived at any dishonest practices such as cotton stealing etc. In this State I have not heard a single officer complain of their conduct. Gen. Osterhaus who at present has none but colored troops in his District, tells me that he never saw any better behaved troops, and that, if the choice between a white and a black regiment was offered him for such duties as they have at present to perform, he would without hesitation choose the blacks.

That their presence is somewhat distasteful to former slaveowners, I have no reason to doubt, especially to those who like to whip a negro but do not like to pay him wages. But it seems to me, the garrisoning of this country with colored troops is apt to produce one important moral result. When discussing with men of liberal views the many atrocities perpetrated in the country, they almost uniformly tell me, apologizingly: "You see, it is so difficult for our people to realize that the negro is a free man." If this true—and no doubt it is—if the main cause of the horrible outrages committed almost daily, is the not-realizing on the part of the Southern people that the negro is a free man, there is no better remedy than to make the fact as evident as possible to all concerned. And there is nothing that will make it more evident than the bodily presence of a negro with a musket on his shoulder.

For these reasons it is my deliberate opinion that the negro troops now garrisoning the country ought not only not to be withdrawn, but that they are the best troops that can be put here for the duties now to be performed.

I am informed that Mr. William Porterfield[29] of this city is an applicant for one of the most lucrative mail contracts in this part of the country, and that he has received encouraging assurances from the employees of the Post-office Department at Washington. Mr. Porterfield bases his claims upon a protection paper he received from Gen. Grant intended to cover his property. I learn from *the most reliable sources* that he is one of the most disreputable characters in this part of the country in every respect. He was several times indicted for felonies and the official records of the cases can be found in this city. Mr. G. L. Little,[30] Treasury agent in this city, took up a copy of them together with other documents concerning Mr. Porterfield to Washington. Aside from his general character he has been one of the worst rebels in this place. If such a man received any favors at the hands of the Government, and if power is placed in the hands of such characters, the Union men have certainly a right to feel themselves aggrieved.

I would respectfully suggest that as to federal appointments in this State, Gen. Slocum be consulted. He has better means of information than anybody else.

Very truly and respectfully
Your obedt servant C. Schurz.

Enclosures: No, 1. Letter of Maj. Houston, Prov. Mar. at Selma.
             No. 2. Letter of Gen. Osterhaus to C. Schurz
             No 3. List of capital offenses committed in Northern
                      District of Mississippi
             No 4. Letters addressed by Gen. Osterhaus to
                    Department
             No. 5 Headquarters.
             No. 6. Maj. Genl. Osterhaus to Gov. Sharkey
             No. 7. Gov. Sharkey to Maj. Genl. Osterhaus.
             No. 8. Genl. Slocums Genl. Order No. 22.
             No. 9. Gov. Sharkey to Col. Yorke
             No. 10. Lt. Col. Yorke to Genl. Davidson.

I would invite special attention to No. 9 and 10., two letters bearing upon the militia question.[31]

C. S.

ALS, DLC-JP.
1. Major John P. Houston (b. c1833), 5th Minn. Inf., administered the amnesty oath to ex-Confederates as provost marshal in Selma, Alabama. He informed Schurz of twelve cases of blacks murdered by whites, and detailed the difficulty of bringing the accused to trial and securing a conviction; the dozen incidents were "but a small part of those that have actually been perpetrated." He concluded that "crime is rampant; that life is insecure as well as property; that the country is filled with desperadoes and banditti who rob and plunder on every side, and that the country is emphatically in a condition of anarchy." CSR, RG94, NA; Houston to Schurz, August 22, 1865, *Schurz Report*, 71–72.
2. Abram C. Haptonstall (b. c1843) had risen from private to captain, 47th Ill. Inf. CSR, RG94, NA.
3. Charles R. Woods (1827–1885) headed a division in the XV Corps during the Atlanta campaign, the March to the Sea, and the march through the Carolinas, rising to major general. After his service as head of the Department of Alabama, he remained in the regular army until 1874.
4. Actually August 21.
5. By January, 1866, only 7,832 soldiers remained in Alabama as compared to the 18,057 stationed there in September, 1865. Sefton, *Army and Reconstruction*, 261.
6. The actions of the convention were hardly secret. An account of the debate over the secession ordinance appeared in the September 6 New York *Times*.
7. Amos R. Johnston (1810–1879), Whig lawyer from Jackson and editor of the Jackson *Standard*, had advocated Mississippi's return to the Union after the fall of Vicksburg. In 1868 he presided over the state constitutional convention; during the next eight years he left the conservative wing of the Republican party for the Democrats.
8. Schurz had confused Johnston's August 22 speech on the repeal of the secession ordinance with the judge's comments three days earlier on abolishing slavery, in which he advised his fellow delegates that failure to abolish slavery might arm Radicals with the ammunition needed to impose black suffrage. "I hold that we are bound . . . to come up boldly and promptly to the support of the President of the United States, and the conservative party, against the power and influence of the Northern radicals. All that party in the North called the Copperheads are with us on this question; and even from the ranks of the Black Republicans, there springs up many conservative patriots, armed for the coming struggle on this great question." The New York *Independent* quoted a similar statement from Johnston on abolishing slavery: "If we put a proviso to our amendment, it will discourage the President, who is our friend, and the great conservative party in the North. Our failure then will be inevitable. If we act wisely, we shall be joined by what is called the 'Copperhead party,' and even by many of the 'Black Republicans.'" New York *Independent*, September 7, 1865; *Journal of the Proceedings and Debates in the Constitutional Convention . . . of the State of Mississippi, August, 1865* (Jackson, Miss., 1865), 89–90.
9. Section Two of the Thirteenth Amendment stated: "Congress shall have power to enforce this article by appropriate legislation." Republicans argued that this clause authorized them to pass further legislation defining the postwar status of the freedmen; Democrats (and Johnson) resisted this expansion of national power, arguing that the Thirteenth Amendment ended slavery, nothing more. Harold M. Hyman and William M. Wiecek, *Equal Justice Under Law: Constitutional Development, 1835–1875* (New York, 1982), 390.
10. On August 14, 1865, ninety-nine Mississippians assembled at Jackson as delegates to the constitutional convention. Former Whigs heavily outnumbered Democrats, since most state Democratic leaders either declined to run or were barred by Johnson's amnesty provisions from holding office until pardoned. Of the seven delegates who had also attended the secession convention of 1861, six had cast their votes against secession. W. Magruder Drake, "The Mississippi Reconstruction Convention of 1865," *Journal of Mississippi History*, XXI (October, 1959), 233–34.
11. Before the convention adjourned on August 24, it concurred in a committee report

that popular ratification of its handiwork was "not practical or expedient . . . under existing circumstances." In testimony before the Joint Committee of Reconstruction, Sharkey offered a different rationale for this action, suggesting that he "was so well satisfied with the temper, disposition, and wish of the people, that I did not think it necessary to submit the amended constitution to them at all." *Ibid.*, 250–51; Harris, *Presidential Reconstruction in Mississippi*, 57.

12. Prussian-born immigrant Peter J. Osterhaus (1823–1917) led a division at Vicksburg and Chattanooga and fought in the Atlanta and North Carolina campaigns as a major general. On September 28 he received "a list of crimes and assaults against freedmen"; Col. R.S. Donaldson, acting assistant commissioner, Freedmen's Bureau, concluded that the reports "indicate that cruelty is frequently practiced." *Schurz Report*, 105.

13. Some 13,873 soldiers were stationed in Mississippi in September, 1865. Sefton, *Army and Reconstruction*, 261.

14. Osterhaus reported that in the wake of defeat crime became commonplace, as whites stole cotton and mistreated blacks and unionists until the arrival of troops. He feared that the withdrawal of troops would inaugurate a renewal of disorder, rendering the region "intolerable." In his opinion, white southerners "hardly realize the great social change brought about by the war," especially in their blueprints for black labor; only with the institution of free labor could "a feeling of contentment and loyalty replace the now prevalent bitterness and recriminations." Osterhaus to Schurz, August 27, 1865, *Schurz Report*, 59–61.

15. Whig lawyer, legislator, and judge William L. Sharkey (1798–1873) presided over the Nashville Convention of 1850. His unionism both irritated Confederate authorities and commended him to Johnson as a suitable choice for provisional governor in 1865. Chosen U.S. senator in October, he was not seated; during the next two years he participated in the National Union movement and unsuccessfully sought an injunction against the Military Reconstruction Act in *Mississippi v. Johnson* (U.S., 1867).

16. On August 21 Osterhaus, having seen newspaper notices concerning the organization of militia companies in Hinds and Madison counties, called them to the attention of Governor Sharkey. The general explained that while Mississippi was occupied by federal troops operating under martial law, "no military organizations can be tolerated which are not under the control of the United States officers." He added that in his opinion the troops stationed in the area were sufficient to preserve the peace, "provided the civil authorities will co-operate sincerely with the military commanders." Sharkey responded by informing the general of the August 19 proclamation authorizing the raising of militia and cited several instances of robbery on the stageline between Jackson and Vicksburg as justification for his action. He commented that he had secured President Johnson's approval of this step in advance during an interview at Washington. Osterhaus to Sharkey, August 21, 1865, and Sharkey to Osterhaus, August 22, 1865, *ibid*, 104.

17. On August 21 Osterhaus wrote headquarters for instructions, enclosing his letter to Sharkey and copies of a notice calling for the formation of militia companies in Madison and Hinds counties. The next day he received a copy of Sharkey's proclamation and informed headquarters that he questioned both its wisdom and rationale. Osterhaus to J. Warren Miller, August 21, 22, 1865, *ibid*, 102, 103.

18. See Schurz to Johnson, August 29, 1865, n.3.

19. In his August 22 report to headquarters, Osterhaus reported the arrest of the stage robbers, pointing out that their targets were federal employees, a Massachusetts schoolmaster, and "some darkies." He reasoned that the robbers were actually "guerillas . . . waging a war against the 'invaders,'" and that their actions were desired to provoke Sharkey's proclamation: "there is no doubt on my mind that the young men 'who steal the dispatches from our messengers' will become good members of the intended militia." *Ibid.*, 103.

20. Outspoken unionist L.S. Houghton (b. *c*1816) had written Lincoln in 1863 about an early restoration of Mississippi. Houghton to Lincoln, August 29, 1863, Lincoln Papers, LC.

21. Legislator and lawyer Abraham K. Smedes (*c*1820–1872) was appointed probate judge on June 26. Lynda L. Crist to editors, January 27, 1986.

22. James R. Yerger, Mississippi's secretary of state, was a CSA lieutenant on the staff of Gen. Samuel G. French.

23. Barnett served as postmaster until 1869. *U.S. Official Register* (1869), 499.

24. Napoleon J.T. Dana (1822–1905) saw action with the Army of the Potomac, held several administrative posts, and headed the Department of Mississippi.

25. Assigned to Grant's staff in 1862, James Birdseye McPherson (1828–1864) impressed Grant so much that before the year was out he was commanding a corps as a major general. His performance during the Vicksburg campaign was rewarded when he rose to command the Army of the Tennessee in the Atlanta campaign. On July 22, 1864, McPherson was killed during the battle of Atlanta.

26. Jones S. Hamilton (b. 1832) was adjutant general of Mississippi (1862–63). His name does not appear on the list of U.S. marshals in the *U.S. Official Register*.

27. The boundaries between civil and military authority were ill-defined in 1865, leading to clashes such as the Sharkey-Slocum incident. Neither Johnson, Stanton, nor Grant issued any detailed directives, leaving both local military commanders and civil officials to their own devices. Johnson's June 13 proclamation setting reconstruction into motion in Mississippi instructed Sharkey to convene a constitutional convention and gave him "authority to exercise . . . all the powers necessary and proper" to assist the restoration process. The President ordered the military authorities to "aid and assist the said provisional governor" in his actions. Richardson, *Messages*, 314–16.

28. For example, Schurz arrived at Charleston in the aftermath of a clash between the 165th New York, a Zouave regiment, and black troops, growing out of a dispute between the Zouaves and some black stallkeepers at the market. Within weeks members of the Zouave regiment were charged with mutiny. New York *Times*, July 24, 1865; New York *Herald*, July 26, 1865.

29. William Porterfield (*c*1802–1865), born in Ireland, settled in Vicksburg in the late 1830's and became a prosperous businessman. According to local rumor, his second wife, Julia Lyons, was the daughter of Joseph Davis, the brother of the Confederate president. During the war, Porterfield had been ordered outside Union lines for expressing the hope that yellow fever would ravage bluecoat ranks. Bowing to Mrs. Grant's entreaties, General Grant rescinded the order and advised Porterfield to watch his tongue in the future. James T. McIntosh, ed., *The Papers of Jefferson Davis* (5 vols. to date, 1971–), II, 64n; John Y. Simon, ed., *The Personal Memoirs of Julia Dent Grant* (New York, 1975), 122, 143n.

30. George L. Little.

31. On August 18 Sharkey notified Lieut. Col. P. Jones York, commanding at Port Gibson, that York's August 10 order disbanding a police guard ran contrary to the governor's instructions: "I had express authority from the President himself to organize the militia if I thought it necessary to keep order. . . . I . . . hope you will revoke your order." Eight days later York explained the reasons for his order to Maj. Gen. John W. Davidson, describing the disloyalty, rash behavior, and itchy trigger fingers of the local police. *Schurz Report*, 76–77.

New Orleans Sept 1 1865.

Andrew Johnson. Prest.

Your despatch reached me this morning off Baton Rouge.[1] Genl Slocums order prohibiting militia organization was out before I saw him[.] when I urged its approval by the Government I had no responsibility of my own in the matter but I consider his action judicious and well timed[.] first reason in some localities county patrols had been already organized[.] they had to be suppressed on account of their open hostility to Union men & freed people[.] organizing the militia at the present time will be putting arms & power into the hands of the persecutors of Union men & negroes. A number of Union men at Vicksburg declared to me that if Gen Slocums policy was discountinanced they would no longer feel safe and at once prepare for leaving the state[.]

I stopped at Natchez yesterday & received information to the same effect[.] second reason the governor. Prepared to organize the militia avowedly for the reason that the inhabitants refused to assist our military in the suppression of crime and the call was addressed Expressly to the young men who had distinguished themselves for Gallantry in the rebel service[.] no general having the honor of his govt. at heart could hesitate to stop such insulting procedures. Third reason. The State is still under martial law and ought to be. The Existence of armed bodies not under the Control of the military commander is incompatable with that state of things and will at once and Continually lead to collisions which otherwise Can be avoided— It is certainly desirable to reduce expenses and to withdraw the troops as soon as circumstances will permit but it is my solemn Conviction that circumstances do not yet permit it— In nothing but our troops can the union men and freed people find protection. and safety at present. If you were here to see for yourself you would at once come to the same Conclusion. The Elements called upon to form the militia are Just those that Commit Crime but do not suppress it. In my opinion the safety of the Union people and freedmen as well as the honor of the govt. demand that Genl slocum be openly sustained and that Governor sharkey be censured for his proclamation[.][2] according to your own words I understand your policy to be Experimental. I understand it to be the object of my mission to observe and report to you and to make suggestions[.] I Confined myself strictly to this & did not interfere, practically in any way. I Endeavored to aid you by giving you reliable information firmly believing that It could not be the policy of the Govt. to withdraw its protection from the Union people and freedmen before their rights and safety are sufficiently secured. I Entreat you not to disapprove Genl Slocums Conduct[.] my report from Vicksburg will give you a clear View of the case. I intend to Visit Mobile from here. and then to return to Washn. stopping at New Orleans & vicksburg. I would thank you for an indication of your policy Concerning the mississippi Militia case. Despatches will reach me here—

Carl Schurz

Tel, DLC-JP; DNA-RG107, Tels. Recd. by Pres., Vol. 4 (1865), 268–72.

1. On August 30, 1865, Johnson telegraphed Schurz, "I presume Gen Slocum will issue no order interfering with Governor Sharkey . . . without first consulting the Government, giving the reasons for such proposed interference[.]" The President went on to assert that southerners "must be trusted with their government, and if trusted my opinion is they will act in good faith and restore their former Constitutional relations with all the States composing the Union." After citing George Washington's characterization of state militia as "the Army of the Constitution," Johnson stated that his objective was to restore "the original design of the Government . . . administered upon the principles of the Great Chart of Freedom handed down to the people by the founders of the Republic." He pointedly reminded Schurz that his "mission to the South was to aid as far as practicable in carrying out the policy" outlined by Johnson. Johnson to Schurz, August 30, 1865, Johnson Papers, LC.

2. To Schurz's surprise, Johnson sustained Sharkey, sending the governor a copy of

his August 30 telegram to Schurz, giving Sharkey permission to publish it, and instructing Slocum to revoke General Order No. 22; Slocum did so two days later. Johnson to Sharkey, August 30, 1865, Governor's Papers, Ser. E, Mississippi Dept. of Archives & History; Sharkey to Johnson, August 31, 1865, Tels. Recd., President, RG107, NA; Johnson to Sharkey, September 2, 1865, Johnson Papers, LC; Thomas Eckert to Slocum, September 2, 1865, *American Annual Cyclopaedia* (1865), 584; General Orders No. 23, Department of Mississippi, September 4, 1865, *ibid.*

———— ••• ————

New Orleans. Sept 2. 1865.

Andrew. Johnson—Prest.

Maj Genl Canby[1] authorizes me to state that the organization of Local militia companies was tried in his dept. but that he found himself obliged to disband them again because they indulged in the gratification of private vengeance & worked generally against the policy of the Govt. Genl Sheridan[2] issued an order in Texas Embracing the identical point contained in Gen Slocums order.[3]

Carl Schurz

Tel, DLC-JP; DNA-RG107, Tels. Recd. by Pres., Vol. 4 (1865–1866), 267.
    1. As commander of the Military Division of West Mississippi, Edward R.S. Canby (1817–1873) accepted the surrenders of Gens. Richard Taylor and E. Kirby Smith. Anxious to restore civil rule to Louisiana, he nevertheless grew exasperated with the belligerence of white southerners: "They appear to think that all the concessions should be on the part of the Government." Canby to W.T. Sherman, October 5, 1865, W.T. Sherman Papers, LC.
    2. One of Grant's favorite generals, hard fighting Philip H. Sheridan (1831–1888) had by Appomattox emerged as one of the top Union generals. After the war Grant sent him to the Texas-Mexico border to encourage the French to withdraw their support of Maximilian. Sheridan played a central and controversial role in Reconstruction in Louisiana and Texas (1865–67, 1875) and was removed by Johnson over Grant's protests in 1867.
    3. On June 30 Sheridan issued General Order No. 5, announcing the end of de facto resistance in Texas, and took this occasion to have it "distinctly understood that no homeguards or armed bands for self-protection will be permitted in the State," judging federal forces "competent to protect individuals and their property." Lets. Recd., 1865, RG108, NA.

———— ••• ————

New Orleans Sept 3d 1865

Hon A. Johnson President of U.S.

If it is contemplated to change the government of Louisana into a provisional Government & to appoint Govr Welles[1] Provisional Gov'r I would request that action be suspended until my report is rec'd.[2] I have important communications to make[.] Answer[.][3]

Carl Shurz

Tel, DLC-JP2.
    1. Louisiana planter and unionist James Madison Wells (1808–1899), elected lieutenant governor in the Union provisional government in 1864, became governor the following March upon the resignation of incumbent Michael Hahn. Although angering

Radicals by appointing former Confederates to office, he won election as governor supported by Louisiana Democrats. During the next several years he managed to offend both Democrats and Republicans, as he drifted back to Republican ranks. Sheridan removed him in May, 1867, calling him "a political trickster and a dishonest man [whose] conduct has been as sinuous as the mark left in the dust by the movement of a snake." In 1876 Wells presided over Louisiana's Returning Board, a center of controversy in the disputed presidential election that year. Taylor, *Louisiana Reconstructed*, 140.

2. Both Wells and his opponents were willing to see Johnson reestablish a provisional government. Wells, assuming that he would be appointed provisional governor, believed that he would then be immune from military interference in running Louisiana. The governor's opponents sought Wells's ouster through the appointment of someone else as provisional governor. By September, it appeared obvious that if Johnson did reinstate the provisional government, he would select Wells to head it.

3. Johnson never replied.

New. Orleans Sept. 4th[1] 1865.

To his Excellency Andrew Johnson,
President of the United States.
Sir,

In my telegraphic repy to your despatch of Aug. 30th concerning Gen. Slocum's order prohibiting the organization of the State Militia in Mississippi, I omitted to touch a few points a short discussion of which will serve to elucidate some features of the conflict of authority in Mississippi. I found it to be generally the opinion of our military commanders that the Provisional Governors had no authority beyond that which was defined in the proclamations appointing them, i.e. to make the necessary preparations for calling a Convention, and that if any power beyond that was exercised, the military had a right to interfere if they deemed it necessary, unless the Provisional Governor could show special instructions from the President.[2] The organization of any State-troops, I am confident, would have been stopped by any of our military commanders that I have seen, unless based upon such special authority. It is quite natural for commanding officers to entertain such ideas, as there is nothing to guide them and to define the authority of the Provisional Governors, except the Presidents proclamations. This would seem to be sufficient, aside from other circumstances, to account for Genl. Slocums issuing his order without previously applying to the War Department for instructions.

Permit me to refer to one sentence in your despatch of Aug. 30th which seems to have sprung from an erroneous impression. "If there was any danger from an organization of the citizens for the purposes indicated, the military are there to detect and suppress on the first appearance any move insurrectionary in its character." There is no danger of their indulging in any insurrectionary movement under the rebel flag or in any way resembling a general rebellion; they are not likely to attack our troops in large bodies or to make a pronunciamento against the

Government of the United States. But in all cases that have come to my knowledge, where "county patrols" or other militia organizations were permitted, they indulged in the gratification of private vengeance, persecuted helpless Union people and freedmen and endeavored to keep the plantation negroes in a state of virtual slavery. In my letter from Vicksburg I enclosed a report from Lt. Col. Yorke to Genl. Davidson, and Gen. Canby is having some reports copied for me which I will forward to you, and which show this to have been actually the case. These facts led to the necessity of disbanding them. If our military force is very much reduced in these States, it will be impossible to watch things closely in the interior of the country. The parties that perpetrate such outrages will certainly not report them, and things which by the close garrisoning of the country can easily be prevented, will, when the garrisons are removed or thinned out, in many instances escape the notice of our military authorities, and the civil authorities, of which the militia organizations would form part, would hardly show any alacrity in punishing them. Such at least is the experience of all those who are in a position constantly to observe, and it will in all probability continue to be so, until the sentiments of the people shall have undergone a very material change. Now, outrages committed upon Union people and negroes and the overriding of the spirit of the Emancipation Proclamation may, perhaps, technically not be called "insurrectionary movements", but in point of fact they are nothing else. It is a continuation of the war, not against the armed defenders of the Government, but against its unarmed friends.

In another part of the despatch you say: "The people must be trusted with their own government; and, if trusted, my opinion is they will act in good faith."— That eventually the people must be trusted with their own government, is certainly true. With their *own* government strictly speaking, they might, perhaps, be trusted now. But the question is, can they under existing circumstances be trusted with governing other people? Can those who during the war were our sworn enemies, be now already trusted with governing those who were and are our sworn friends? For it must be considered, that the colored people as well as the small number of faithful Union-men are perfectly helpless in the hands of those who but recently were the open enemies of the Union. My experience is, and it can be shown by volumes of testimony, that the time has not come yet when we can, without violating our moral obligations, leave our friends white and black without the most vigilant protection. I beg you most earnestly, not to construe what I say as if I were opposed to the early restoration of civil government on any other ground than that which I state to you. It is my solemn conviction that the time is not yet when the government can be turned over to these people without most seriously endangering the interests, nay the lives of those to whom the nation owes protection. Where the troops are not scattered all over the country, as for instance in Alabama, the people are "trusted with their own government." There they have their civil tribunals and sheriffs and police. But they are governing themselves, and they are governing especially the negroes in a horrible manner. As evidence I can point to the documents, among which is Gov. Parson's own proclamation, which I sent you from Montgomery. Believe me, I am not exaggerating this matter, and I am not disposed to do so. I should be very glad to see our military establishment, and, with it, the expenses of the government reduced to the lowest possible figure. But it is the truth that every step the Government does in weakening our military forces here and in placing power into the hands of the people, is received as an encouragement by the worst and most mischievous elements of the population. Southern delegations that go to Washington and paint the condition of things in these States in the rosiest colors, do certainly not state facts as they are. They may be perfectly honest in speaking of their own loyal disposition and good intentions. But their ruling desire being to resume the control of their home affairs, they do not care to make the government acquainted with the principal difficulties of the case. In many cases they are, perhaps, themselves not aware of what is going on. I am sure I am not overestimating the importance and significance of the things I observe. It is a stubborn fact that our truest friends are threatened and persecuted and that the negro is denied his freedom wherever the population has a chance to act upon its own impulses without being immediately checked. This condition of things may change when the new system of labor is once in general and promising operation, and when it is generally felt that the labor of the colored people is indispensable to the prosperity of the Southern country. But at present it is not so, and until it is so we can not afford to withdraw or even relax our protective vigilance. I am in favor of encouraging the desire of self-government wherever it can be done without at the same time encouraging the vindictive spirit and the bad passions of the masses. We shall undoubtedly succeed in passing over this period of transition without serious convulsions, if we move on slowly; but every precipitate concession is taken an undue advantage of and brings on immediate danger of disturbance. The determination of the Government to hold its protecting hand over those who are at present the wards of the nation, must make itself felt to be effective, and it is for this reason that I am so warmly defending Genl. Slocums policy in Mississippi. The struggle against the results of the war is by no means at an end.

Once more referring to your despatch I wish to say, that I have been careful not to interfere in any way with the policy or measures adopted by the Provisional Governors. As I already said in my telegraphic reply, Genl. Slocums order was already out when I saw him—although I am free to confess, had I been in his place, I would have done the same thing under the same circumstances and with the same information in my possession.— I have confined myself strictly to what I considered my office. Whenever I got hold of an intelligent man who as I thought could exercise a beneficial influence upon his neighbors, I have used my best endeavors to encourage him in using that influence in the right direction, and I may flatter myself, I have made a good many converts to sound principles. I have endeavored to remove prejudices and to calm down unreasonable apprehensions. My traces may be found some day. If this, aside from my giving reliable information to you, may be called aiding your policy, I am conscious of having aided it to the best of my ability. I shall certainly not deny that my sympathies are with loyalty and freedom against open or disguised disloyalty and oppression, and of these sympathies I never made a secret.

I will now proceed to a discussion of Louisiana affairs. I requested you in my telegraphic despatch of Sept. 3d, if it was contemplated to transform the State government of Louisiana into a Provisional Government, to suspend action until you received my report. My reason for this request was the following: I found it stated in the organ of Gov. Wells and Mayor Kennedy,[3] that Gov. Wells was expecting his commission as Provisional Governor of this State, which commission, it was asserted, was already made out. Dr. Cottman[4] was going round here telling people that Gov. Wells would have that appointment as soon as he signified his willingness to accept it. These statements being made so publicly and confidently, it was reasonable to suppose that there was some foundation for them.

Shortly after my arrival here I had conversations with some of the most prominent men of this city, which convinced me that you would hesitate to do so important a step if you were acquainted with all the circumstances connected with the case. Therefore I telegraphed my request to you. Since then I have seen a large number of people from the interior of the State as well as the city, and am now able to give you a clear account of the state of things here.

The transformation of the State Government of Louisiana into a Provisional Government would involve the setting aside of the Constitution of 1864, and if Gov. Wells be made Provisional Governor, it will entrust him with the preparations necessary for the election of a convention and the making of a new Constitution. Having the vast machinery of the State Government with all its power and patronage in his hand— there are over two thousand civil officers in Louisiana, all selected and appointed by him—he will have a very great, perhaps a decisive influence upon the result of the operation. The Constitution at present in force is perhaps the most liberal so far adopted by any Southern State. Still, it may be wise to set it aside by appointing a Provisional Government, if a still better Constitution and a better government can be obtained. This will depend in a large measure upon the manner in which the Governor uses his influence through the large number of his appointees.

There is a larger proportion of real Union men in Louisiana than in any of the States I have visited. It is perhaps as large as that in Tennessee. But my investigations force the conclusion upon my mind, that the Union element is almost completely excluded from the State Government. I have no doubt, from what I learn here, that the Union people of the State would soon become strong enough to obtain the control of affairs by securing a considerable majority in the elections, were the influence of the State Government used in their favor instead of being thrown almost exclusively in favor of the ⟨rebel⟩ disloyal and pro-slavery element. But I think I am safe in saying that the latter is the case. This assertion may stand in strange contrast with the representations made by Gov. Wells and Mayor Kennedy and their political agent Dr. Cottman, but after having investigated things on the spot, I am satisfied of its correctness. I am not here representing the views and grievances of the radical wing of the Union party. I have gone from the most radical to the most conservative, stopping at that line which separates Unionism from decided rebel- and proslavery-sympathies, and I find that the condemnation of the course of Gov. Wells is unanimous. I might submit to you multitudes of statements about this matter; I will confine myself to a few letters addressed to myself by the representative men of the State. I enclose a letter from Hon. R. King Cutler,[5] U.S. Senator elect. Mr. Cutler is by no means a "radical"; on the contrary, he is a man of decidedly conservative principles, not a professional politician, and was elected to the U.S. Senate on his general merits. I enclose also his "Address to the citizens of Louisiana" published but a short time ago. It shows him to be a man of moderate views whose sympathies are rather against the "radicals." But in his condemnation of Gov. Wells administration he is even more emphatic than the rest.

I enclose also a letter addressed to me by Gov. Michael Hahn,[6] U.S. Senator elect. You will remember that Gov. Hahn, although a shade less conservative than Mr. Cutler, was opposed by the party calling itself "radical" at the first gubernatorial election. In his letter he expresses his opinion about the administration of Gov. Wells with less emphasis than in conversation, probably restrained by a feeling of delicacy.

The letter written by Hon. S. Wrotnowski,[7] Sec. of State, elected on the same ticket with Gov. Hahn, explains itself.

I enclose also a letter addressed to me by Mr. T.P. May,[8] U.S. Treasurer, a wealthy planter and formerly a large slaveowner.

It is hardly necessary that I should invite your attention to the views expressed by Genl. Banks[9] in his letter.[10] Genl. Canby also gave me his opinion in writing,[11] and, I am sure, nobody will class him with any "radical faction."

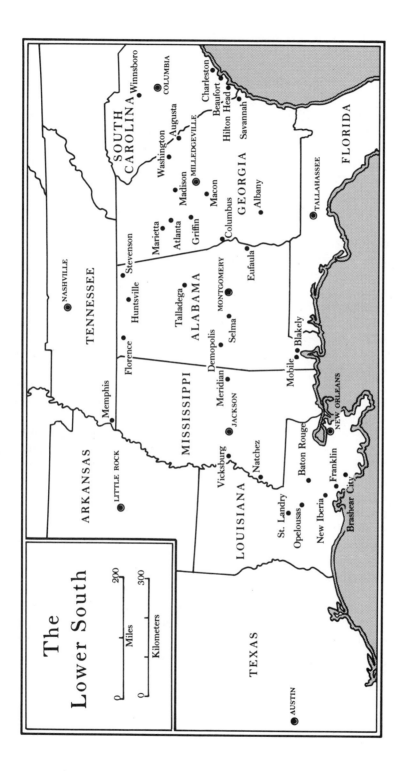

The
Lower South

Miles

Kilometers

0   200

0   300

AUSTIN

TEXAS

ARKANSAS

LITTLE ROCK

LOUISIANA

St. Landry
Opelousas
New Iberia
Franklin
Brashear City
Natchez
Vicksburg
Baton Rouge

MISSISSIPPI

Memphis

JACKSON
Meridian

TENNESSEE

NASHVILLE

Florence
Huntsville
Stevenson
Talladega
Demopolis
Selma
MONTGOMERY

ALABAMA

Mobile
Blakely

NEW ORLEANS

Marietta
Atlanta
Griffin
Columbus
Eufaula

Madison
Macon
Albany

GEORGIA

Washington
MILLEDGEVILLE

Augusta

SOUTH
CAROLINA

Winnsboro
COLUMBIA

Charleston
Beaufort
Hilton Head
Savannah

FLORIDA

TALLAHASSEE

I might have accumulated an endless mass of testimony concerning the unsatisfactory conduct of affairs in this State, had I not thought that the voices of the two U.S. Senators elect, of two Major Generals one of whom has been, and one of whom is now in command of this Department, as well as of other prominent citizens holding important public positions would be sufficient. To send you the opinions of "radical" leaders, such as Mr. Durant[12] and Mr. Flanders[13] I deemed unnecessary. Their dissatisfaction with the present State-Administration is, of course, still greater. I add only an extract from an official report of Mr. Conway,[14] Asst. Commissioner of the Freedman's Bureau, to show how the appointment of disloyal and pro-slavery men affects the situation of the freedmen in this State.[15]

I have a complete list of all of Gov. Wells' appointments made with a statement of the antecedents of the appointees. But as this list comprizes over 2,000 names, its preparation will require some time. I shall forward it as soon as it is ready, to give you a complete view of the changes introduced by Gov. Wells.[16] These changes are of the most sweeping kind, and the policy followed by Gov. Wells in the State, is faithfully carried out by Mayor Kennedy in the city. If ever so many removals had been made for the purpose of filling the places with other and, perhaps, better Union men, there would have been less ground for complaint. But to see good Union men ousted to make room for rebel officers just returned from the army, and to see thus the power and influence of official position placed into the hands of the enemies of the Government, cannot but create a feeling of disgust and despondency among those who have been always the Governments friends. You, Mr. President, as Military Governor of Tennessee, adopted the policy of placing power only into the hands of reliable loyalists. You succeeded in keeping the State in loyal hands. Just the opposite of your policy is carried out here, and just the opposite must be the result. The true Union men, seeing themselves unsupported by the Government, feel like giving up. They feel like the conquered people, and men who stood by the rebellion until the hour of its final downfall, act like conquerors, which in a certain sense they are. The former look sad and the latter chuckle.

The Union party consisted in a large proportion of the poor people. In some of the parishes that were under our control for some time, men belonging to that class were by Gov. Wells' predecessor put into office. I am assured that they had all to give way to the leading planters, and that all the positions of influence are again occupied by the aristocracy.

Even the judiciary was not spared. I will not enumerate cases but give a representative example. Gov. Wells removed E. Heistand,[17] Judge of the lst District Court of New-Orleans, a thorough Union man and in every way a worthy citizen. In his place he put E. Abell[18] who in his first charge to the Grand Jury took occasion to denounce the Freedmans Bureau, to advocate its abolition and to reflect upon emancipation generally. As a member of the Convention of 64, he alone made a minority report against emancipation,[19] (Debates Conv. page 97). he refused to sign the Constitution, as I am informed on account of its acknowledging emancipation, and in a speech on a resolution endorsing the nominations of the Baltimore Convention, he indulged in the following language: "I was born close to Mr. Lincoln, though perhaps some of you did'nt know it, and consider him a very honest old man. I can't say exactly whether I shall vote for him or not. I think that when elected he was a sound lawyer and a right good railsplitter. If we have him for president and a tailor for vice-president I think that when we get them in the White House, we shall have a fine family. It seems to me it will be like a man's going into a jewellers shop, knowing nothing about the business, and undertaking to mend a watch—he will spoil the whole concern. I rather think I shall not vote for the resolution". (Debates of Conv. page 576.)— I enclose his charge to the Grand Jury.[20] And there are hundreds of appointments far more obnoxious than this. The Secretary of State in his letter informs us that he has been obliged to hand commissions to rebel officers still wearing their uniforms.

Gov. Wells has thus shown in what direction he would use the influence and power connected with his position, if as Provisional Governor he were authorized to give the State a new start.

Permit me here to touch upon an error which, in my opinion, it is dangerous to fall into in times like these. Gov. Wells and men who act like him, are very apt to say, that the disloyalists can all be made loyal, if we only give them some encouragement. And what is the encouragement they want? They want to have it all their own way; they want exclusive power. If we had given them that encouragement in 1860 and 61, they would perhaps not have risen in rebellion. And if we consent to give them that kind of encouragement now, there are many who will ask the question, whether it would not have saved us much trouble if we had done so five years ago. Gov. Wells does so encourage them, does put power into their hands to the almost absolute exclusion of true Union men, and the immediate result is that they threaten to drive out the Yankees and their friends at the next opportunity. You can hear that threat at every street corner.

If it is contemplated to give the State a new start, Gov. Wells is according to my conviction not the man to superintend the operation. But if another man, a good Union man, be appointed Provisional Governor, the change would be likely to produce very favorable results.

In the first place, the State might be rid of a bad and demoralizing administration. The Union people would regain their confidence in themselves and in the national Government. By a judicious use of the Government patronage a strong loyal party might be built up, which by lending a willing hand to the Government, would very materially facilitate the transition from slave-labor- to free-labor-society. This, I firmly believe, can be made a loyal State in the Northern acceptation of the word, if only the Union party is properly sustained by the Government.

And secondly, if this course be adopted, there is, I am assured, no danger that the Constitution be changed for the worse—a danger which would really exist with Gov. Wells as chief manager. On the contrary, there is a possibility that its good features [will] be still further developed.

I deem, therefore, the transformation of the State Government with a good Union man at its head, an advisable measure, while with Gov. Wells, I would consider it a very dangerous, nay a fatal step.

It has suggested itself to me, that the Government might not be inclined to do such a step without considering Gov. Wells' claims as present incumbent. But there is another man whose claims are superior to his. That is Gov. Hahn. The latter was elected Governor by the people. He resigned the Governorship when he was elected U.S. Senator. If the State Government be made a Provisional Government, the acts done by the Legislature under that State Government are thereby set aside, and Gov. Hahn has lost not only his Governorship but loses his U.S. Senatorship also. It would seem, therefore, that, if the change is made and personal claims are taken into consideration, Gov. Hahn's title to the Prov. Governorship is better than Gov. Wells'.

With Gov. Hahn I am well enough acquainted—I have had several conversations with him—to know that he is a man of ability; of thoroughly loyal principles and progressive political views which, however, are by no means extreme. He is not counted among the "radicals" of this city. His political record is, as far as I have been able to ascertain, unobjectionable. Although there are divisions in the Union party, as there were when Gov. Hahn was first elected, I believe he would command the support of the whole Union element, because he would be an immense improvement upon Gov. Wells. Genl. Canby is of the opinion that the Government ought to send a Provisional Governor here from some other State, a man who has never been mixed up with Louisiana politics; and I think myself, this would in many respects be best. But as this would run against the general policy of the Government, the reappointment of the man who was originally elected Governor by the people and only gave up his post to accept the U.S. Senatorship, would appear to me the most natural thing. Besides, he does not appear to be a man of strong passions and resentments and would, I believe, abstain from making the transition from one regime to another harsh and violent.

On the whole it is my conscientious opinion, that Gov. Hahns appointment to the Provisional Governorship—or, if the Government is inclined to act without regard to personal claims, the appointment of some other reliable Union man,—would be the best thing that can be done for this State. In fact, I believe it is the only thing that can save this State from the grasp of the disloyal element. The Union-men feel confident that, if properly supported by the Government, they can carry the State in a general election, while, if things continue as they are now, they feel powerless and despondent. And it is natural. When affairs are in as unsettled a condition as here, people are always apt to flock to the strong side. At present it is believed here—and it is even the general opinion among Union men,—that Gov. Wells, Mayor Kennedy and Dr. Cottman have more influence in Washington than the whole Union element of Louisiana combined, and that it is in vain to oppose their policy whatever it may be—and the persons mentioned, through their friends, are not backward in fostering the impression. To day their partisans are proclaiming on the street, that if Gen. Canby does not stop interfering with them, they are going to have him removed, just as they had Gen. Banks removed;[21] and notorious disloyalists are boasting of their power. Let the tables be turned, let the true sympathies of the national Government make themselves practically felt, and the opposite result will be easily attainable. Louisiana can be made the leader of the free labor movement in the South, and it would certainly be worth while to have a firm and reliable Union State at the mouth of the Mississippi.

The Constitution of the State, Art. 154, provides as follows: "As soon as a general election can be held under this constitution in every parish of the State, the Governor shall, by proclamation, or in case of his failure to act, the legislature shall, by resolution, declare the fact and order an election to be held on a day fixed in said proclamation or resolution, and within sixty days from the date thereof, for governor, lieut. Governor, Secretary of State etc."—

The Governor has so far failed to order an election, although every parish in the State has been under our control since the first week of June. It is rumored that he does not intend to do so, and this rumor seems to be well founded.[22] On the 3d inst. the "Southern Star", the newly established organ of Gov. Wells and Mayor Kennedy, had an article which clearly indicated that Gov Wells is in daily expectation of his appointment to the Provisional Governorship and that the election prescribed by the constitution will, for the present, not be ordered. The day fixed by the Constitution for regular elections is the first Monday in November, and as the Governor has to order the election sixty days previous to the day on which it is to be held, his proclamation ought to be out before the 7th inst if he desires the election to be held at all. If his proclamation is not issued the duty will devolve upon the legislature to order the election by resolution. The old legislature, elected when only a portion of the State was under the control of the Government, holds over in part only, namely one half of the Senate. Art. 7 of the Constitution provides that "Representatives shall be chosen on the first Monday in November every two years;—The term of office of the first General Assembly shall expire as though its members had been elected on the first Monday in November 1863."—This would terminate the existence of the "House of Representatives" on the first Monday in January 1866, so that, if no election be held this year, there will be no Legislature to "order by resolution" an election according to the Constitution if the Governor fails to order it by proclamation. This failure will therefore avoid the provisions of the constitution and produce very serious complications. The Governor himself as well as the other members of the State Government will have no constitutional existence beyond that day, and affairs will have to be regulated by some power outside of the State authorities.

I would have called upon the Governor to obtain his views upon this matter, but he has left the city and, as the papers state, intends to spend some time at his home in Rapides Parish on Red River. The Secretary of State had no orders left with him to issue a proclamation in the Governor's name.

It seems, therefore, if it is the intention of the National Government to appoint a Provisional Governor for this State, that the moment when the constitutional government of this State is on the point of coming to a stand still, or rather when the measures absolutely necessary for the continuance of its Constitutional existence fail to be taken, would be the most propitious for doing so. If the Governor neglects to order an election as provided by the Constitution, he prolongs his authority and power by a sort of coup d'etat and the most natural solution of this difficulty would indeed seem to be the appointment of a Prov. Gov. in his place.

In [I] enclose copies of two Ordinances passed by Police Boards[23] appointed by Gov. Wells, showing the spirit in which the Governors appointees act. As soon as the town of Opelouses had passed that Ordinance the contagion spread over the neighborhood, and several other towns made similar attempts. The military authorities put a stop to it. I enclose also copies of commissions[24] issued by Gov. Wells to certain parties as agents of the State of Louisiana to collect and ship to Gov. Wells certain quantities of cotton alleged to have been purchased by rebel governor Allen[25] in his official capacity. Gen. Canby is of opinion that this cotton belonged to a ⟨the Confederate Government⟩ State in insurrection and is now the property of the United States, and of this opinion he informed Gov. Wells.[26] The Secretary of State, who furnished me the copies herewith forwarded, tells me that the commissions have not been revoked to this day.

Very respectfully Your obt servt C. Schurz.

Enclosures:

1. Letter of Hon. R. King Cutler.
2. Letter of Gov. M. Hahn.

3. Letter of Maj. Gen. Banks
4. Letter of Maj. Gen. Canby with documents.
5. Letter of Hon. S. Wrotnoski
6. Letter of T. P. May.
7. Report of T. W. Conway.
8. Address of Hon. R. King Cutler.
9 & 10. Ordinances passed by Police Boards
11. Commissions of Cotton agents.
12. Judge Abells charge to Grand Jury.

ALS, DLC-JP.

1. Although dated September 4, this letter was not sent until the 8th, due to the late submission of several letters. "My report from here is on its way— It was delayed by circumstances which I could not control— I request again that action with regard to Louisiana be suspended until it is received— I am going to Mobile today & shall return to this City next week— Despatches will find me here[.]" Schurz to Johnson, September 8, 1865, Johnson Papers, Ser. 2, LC.

2. The delineation of the division of authority between army commanders and civil officials proved difficult to define in 1865. While Johnson's proclamations ordering the formation of provisional governments instructed military authorities "to aid and assist" the provisional governor and "to abstain from, in any way, hindering, impeding, or discouraging the loyal people" in their effort to reorganize state governments, Slocum and his subordinates were in possession of a subsequent telegram from Secretary Seward reaffirming Johnson's belief in the primacy of military authority. "The government of the State will be provisional only until the civil authorities shall be restored, with the approval of Congress," Seward stated. "Meanwhile military authority cannot be withdrawn." Seward to Sharkey, July 24, 1865, *Sen. Ex. Doc.* No. 26, 39 Cong., 1 Sess., 60.

3. Irish immigrant and secessionist sympathizer Hugh Kennedy (1810–1888) owned and edited the New Orleans *True Delta* during the war. In 1865 Wells appointed him mayor of New Orleans; General Banks removed him, but Wells, with Johnson's support, restored him to office.

4. Veterinarian and sugar planter Thomas E.H. Cottman (b. c1810), a delegate to the 1861 secession convention, had been involved in the Etheridge conspiracy of 1863 to wrest control of the House of Representatives from Republican hands. He now sought the reconstruction of Louisiana on the most conservative terms possible. McCrary, *Lincoln and Reconstruction*, 99, 178–79; Tunnell, *Crucible of Reconstruction*, 220.

5. Unionist lawyer R. King Cutler (b. 1822), elected to the Senate in 1864, was never seated. In 1866 he was one of the guiding spirits in the convening of a unionist meeting in New Orleans which sparked the July 30, 1866, riot. Cutler confided to Schurz that Wells was "a traitor to the union cause," surrounding himself with "original, rampant, fire eating rebels," including Kennedy and Cottman. The governor and his supporters, Cutler charged, "are managing by any and all means, (some as foul as Hell itself)" to restore power to ex-Confederates. Like Wells, Cutler favored the appointment of a provisional governor; unlike Wells, he advocated such a step as a means of removing Wells from power. Cutler to Schurz, September 5, 1865, Johnson Papers, LC; Tunnell, *Crucible of Reconstruction*, 224.

6. German immigrant Michael Hahn (1830–1886), was elected governor of unionist Louisiana in 1864 in line with Lincoln's plan of reconstruction. Elevated to the Senate in 1865, he was not seated, and returned to New Orleans to participate in politics as a Republican. In his letter to Schurz, Hahn charged that Wells had "falsified all his pledges to the Union people," appointing ex-Confederates and proslavery advocates to office, and in several instances had removed elected officials in pursuit of his ends. He reiterated his belief (an accurate one) that Wells was anxious to be appointed provisional governor to increase his power. Hahn to Schurz, September 6, 1865, Johnson Papers, LC.

7. Stanislas Wrotnowski (b. 1803), Polish immigrant, owned a cattle farm and a sugar refinery in 1860. Baton Rouge registrar for the election of delegates to the 1864 convention, he won election as secretary of state, using his position to resist Wells's policy in

1865. Wrotnowski wrote that most of the governor's appointees "are Fresh From the late so called 'confederate army', or were strong sympathyzers of the rebellion," some still wearing their uniforms. Wells's action "has discouraged and mortified all the Union men to such an extent as to demoralize them." Tunnell, *Crucible of Reconstruction*, 223; McCrary, *Lincoln and Reconstruction*, 196, 199; Wrotnowski to Schurz, September 7, 1865, Johnson Papers, LC.

8. Louisiana sugar planter Thomas P. May (b. *c*1842), who saw brief service as a Confederate cavalryman in 1861, two years later emancipated his slaves and reestablished his plantation on a free labor basis. After the war he edited the New Orleans *Times* and served as United States treasurer in New Orleans. On September 6 he offered Schurz his opinion that "We are here involved in an apparently hopeless chaos," adding that Wells's appointments created "an *unanimous* feeling of disgust and disapproval" among unionists. Reid, *After the War*, 228; Tunnell, *Crucible of Reconstruction*, 22; May to Schurz, September 6, 1865, Johnson Papers, LC.

9. Prewar congressman and Massachusetts governor Nathaniel P. Banks (1816–1894), despite a mediocre military career, played a major role in wartime attempts at reconstruction in Louisiana, resigning his commission when Canby overrode his removal of Kennedy as mayor of New Orleans.

10. Banks advised the President to remove Wells and Kennedy owing to their policy of arbitrarily removing elected officials and their appointment of Confederate sympathizers to several posts. Banks to Johnson, September 8, 1865, Johnson Papers, LC.

11. Canby noted the resurgence of pro-Confederate sympathy in the state and mentioned his distrust of Wells's advisers and appointees. Canby to Schurz, September 8, 1865, *Schurz Report*, 56–57.

12. Prewar Democrat Thomas J. Durant (1817–1882) worked hard for the reorganization of Louisiana's government under federal protection, and, after turning down Lincoln's offer of the military governorship, served as attorney general in order to supervise voter registration. Opposed to the 1864 state constitution, he left the state in disgust after the New Orleans riot of 1866. Joseph G. Tregle, Jr., "Thomas J. Durant, Utopian Socialism, and the Failure of Presidential Reconstruction in Louisiana," *Journal of Southern History*, XLV (November, 1979), 485–512.

13. Republican Benjamin F. Flanders (1816–1896) was appointed city treasurer by Butler in 1862; at the end of the year he served a short stint in Congress. In the 1864 gubernatorial election he lost to Hahn; three years later Sheridan appointed him governor in place of Wells. He also served as mayor of New Orleans (1870–72) and as assistant U.S. treasurer (1873–82) while an active member of the Republican party.

14. Minister and North Carolina unionist Thomas W. Conway, appointed head of the Bureau of Free Labor in Louisiana in 1863, was named assistant commissioner of the Freedmen's Bureau for Louisiana two years later. By September, 1865, his efforts on behalf of black education had angered many white Louisianians, who secured his removal. News of this action reached New Orleans the first week of October. He remained in Louisiana as an active Republican. McFeely, *Yankee Stepfather*, 168–75.

15. Protesting Wells's "wholesale appointment" of Confederate sympathizers, Conway concluded: "if the freedmen were left to the mercy of the people who formerly owned them as slaves, we might with one count of the fingers of our hands number the years which the race would spend with us." Conway to Canby, [April 30, 1865], extract, Johnson Papers, LC.

16. Not found.

17. Ezra Heistand (b. *c*1817) practiced law in New Orleans after his removal. 1850 Census, La., Jefferson, 2nd Ward, Lafayette, 296; New Orleans city directories (1855–73), *passim*.

18. Edmund Abell (b. *c*1811) was the leading defender of slavery at the 1864 constitutional convention. Wells named him district judge in 1865, but two years later Sheridan removed him for his failure to prosecute New Orleans rioters and his resistance to military reconstruction. *Ibid.*, 57, 96, 107, 224; Joseph G. Dawson, III, *Army Generals and Reconstruction: Louisiana, 1862–1877* (Baton Rouge, 1982), 47.

19. Abell had warned his fellow convention delegates about the dangers of emancipation, including disease and death for blacks and competition for jobs between blacks and poor whites. Taylor, *Louisiana Reconstructed*, 46.

20. On August 7, Abell, complaining that New Orleans blacks were "crowded together in filthy and unwholesome dens, illy provided for, inviting disease and epidemic," charged that the Freedmen's Bureau, "the nursery of discontent and the school of vagrancy," was "at war with the best interests of the colored people and the destruction of the producing interests of the state," and called for its removal. Jackson (Miss.) *Clarion*, August 23, 1865.

21. After lobbying in Washington on behalf of Louisiana's readmission during the winter of 1864–65, Banks returned to New Orleans in April, 1865. Displeased that Wells had ejected from office many Hahn supporters, Banks countermanded the governor's orders and replaced Mayor Kennedy with an army captain. Wells and Kennedy successfully appealed to Johnson for support; within a month Banks was stripped of his position under the pretense of reorganizing departments. Fred H. Harrington, *Fighting Politician: Major General N. P. Banks* (Philadelphia, 1948), 164–68.

22. Some two weeks later, on September 21, Wells ordered an election to take place November 6. Taylor, *Louisiana Reconstructed*, 71.

23. These ordinances from Opelousas and St. Landry Parish, restricting the movement, actions, and economic transactions of blacks, appear in *Schurz Report*, 92–94.

24. Not found.

25. In 1863 Gen. Henry W. Allen (1820–1866) was elected Confederate governor of Louisiana; after the Confederacy's collapse he fled to Mexico. Even so, several extremists still had the audacity to enter his name in the 1865 gubernatorial race, and Allen polled 5,497 of the 27,808 votes cast.

26. Treasury agent George S. Denison later contradicted Canby's impression that the cotton was U.S. property, because it was never actually delivered to Confederate authorities, and remanded the cotton to Wells's agent, William M. Polk. Denison to McCulloch, November 18, 1865, James A. Padgett, ed., "Some Letters of George Stanton Denison, 1854–1866," *Louisiana Historical Quarterly*, XXIII (October, 1940), 1229–31.

Private   New Orleans Sept. 5th 1865.

To his Exc'y Andrew Johnson
President of the United States.
Dear Sir,

The enclosed paragraph[1] is clipped from one of to-day's New Orleans papers. I cannot deny that it was a painful surprise to me. You remember that I did not seek the mission on which I am at present employed. I accepted it thinking that I could render the country some service. The paragraph has the appearance of coming from one of the Government offices. The charge that I reported the information I gathered, to newspapers and not to you, is certainly unjust. You must have received my elaborate reports from every State I visited, and I am conscious of having done everything I could, to inform myself well, and to bring to your notice whatever I thought could be of interest and service to the government.

That I have written some letters to newspapers is true;[2] but in those letters I gave nothing that ought to have been kept secret. I think there could be no harm in my publishing incidents, anecdotes and observations that were apt to entertain a newspaper reader, but in most cases not calculated to form part of an official report. Nor did I authorize any newspaper to mention my name in connection with those letters; on the contrary, I forbade it, and I regret to see that it has been done against my express directions.[3]

The principal reason why I wrote those letters is well known to the Secretary of War,[4] for I previously informed him of it. The compensation I receive from the Government is insufficient to cover the expenses incidental to my travels, aside from transportation and subsistence, and to provide for the wants of my family at the same time. I have no independent income; when I left the service I had but little laid up, and I am obliged to depend upon the yield of my labors. In order to go South according to your desire, I had to give up all other engagements. If my suggestion to cancel my resignation,[5] had been accepted for the time being, I should have been above the necessity of doing something for the support of my family while travelling. But that suggestion not being accepted, I saw myself obliged, either to decline going, which, after your having selected me for this business, would have been inconsistent with my notions of duty, or to do something to make my going financially possible—especially as a trip so far South involved the payment of a considerable extra premium upon my life insurance.[6] I informed the Secretary of War of all these circumstances.

And now to find myself abused in the newspapers for endeavoring to keep honestly above water while trying to serve the country; to see myself publicly threatened with a recall because I am obliged to make up with my own labor for the insufficiency of the compensation I receive from the Government, this, I must confess, is rather hard. It is a thing to which I ought not to be subjected, and I feel, unless you do indeed think that I have neglected my duty in some way which I at present fail to comprehend, I am justly entitled to some reparation before the public. It is exceedingly annoying to me to be preceded where ever I go, by a public announcement that the President does not approve of my conduct; and when I go home, to find the opinion spread abroad that I was *recalled* for violating my trust. If it was indeed deemed improper for me to write letters to news papers, the Secretary of War might have told me so at the start, for I informed him of my being obliged to resort to it. He probably has my letter still in his possession.

I repeat, the paragraph has the appearance of coming from an authoritative source, and I leave it to you to decide whether I am not entitled to some manifestation on the part of the Government that will clear me of these damaging imputations and set me right before the public. There is no selfish motive in the world that would have induced me to accept this mission; there was neither pleasure, nor gain, nor advancement in it. If I do not claim any praise for having accepted it under such circumstances, I certainly ought not to be left under the cloud of unjust censure. This mission will terminate my official connection with the government; I should be sorry if the parting were darkened by any unpleasant incidents. I feel confident however, if I leave it to your sense of justice to give me that reparation which I consider to be honestly due me, you will not permit me to suffer in standing and reputation.

Very truly yours
C. Schurz.

ALS, DLC-JP.

1. The New Orleans *Times* had reprinted an item headlined, "Gen. Carl Shurz to be Recalled," with the dateline of Washington, D.C., August 22, which asserted that Schurz's tour activities were not approved by Johnson and predicted that Schurz "will be recalled soon." The article claimed that the general's chief transgression was his writing reports for northern newspapers, instead of reporting directly to Johnson through the War Department. The piece had also appeared in the Philadelphia *Inquirer* of August 28, prompting a response from Schurz's former staff officer, Fritz Tiedemann, who claimed that Schurz's letters to both the New York *Times*, which denied that the general was writing articles for the paper, and the Boston *Journal* went through the War Department. New York *Times*, September 3, 1865; New Orleans *Times*, September 5, 1865.

2. Schurz had written five letters for publication in the Boston *Advertiser* under the name "Observer," having arranged their placement through Charles Sumner. These letters are reprinted in Joseph H. Mahaffey, ed., "Carl Schurz's Letters from the South," *Georgia Historical Quarterly*, XXXV (1951), 222–57.

3. Writing from Savannah a month earlier, Schurz had warned Sumner: "I do not wish it known I am writing for the *Advertiser*. You will easily divine the reason." However, several northern papers, reprinting the *Advertiser* pieces in early August, identified Schurz as the author. Schurz told abolitionist George Stearns that he had written solely for the *Advertiser*, but would cease submitting articles due to the paper's lapse in revealing his identity. He asked Stearns to secure another paper to publish his efforts, noting, "I am collecting material that will enable me to spread out a picture before the people which will open their eyes." New York *Times*, August 2, 1865; Chicago *Tribune*, August 11, 1865; Schurz to Stearns, August 29, 1865 and Schurz to Sumner, August 2, 1865, Schurz Papers, LC.

4. Jacksonian Democrat, antislavery politician, and attorney general under Buchanan, Edwin M. Stanton (1814–1869) succeeded Simon Cameron as Lincoln's secretary of war (1862) and remained in the cabinet when Johnson became President. His support of congressional reconstruction brought him into conflict with Johnson; the President's repeated attempts to remove him brought on the impeachment crisis in 1868.

5. Schurz had arrived in Washington during the first week of May, 1865, anxious to resign from the army: "I am now impatient to withdraw from soldiering and begin a regulated activity in which there is a future." He resigned May 6 only to regret this decision. Schurz to Mrs. Schurz, May 1, 4, 1865, Schaffer, *Intimate Letters*, 335; William F. Amann, ed., *Personnel of the Civil War* (2 vols., New York, 1961), II, 10.

6. Charles Sumner had made arrangements with several Bostonians to pay the extra premium on Schurz's insurance policy. Sumner to Schurz, June 22, 1865, Schurz Papers, LC.

New Orleans La. Sept. 15th 1865.

To his Excellency Andrew Johnson
President of the United States.

Sir,

I have just returned from Mobile and desire to submit a few observations on the condition of things in Alabama. The elections for the Convention have taken place and the character of the men elected as far as I have been able to ascertain, seems to bear out the predictions of Gov. Parsons.[1] There was no canvass preceding the election, except upon personal grounds, and, as a general thing, the most respectable persons seem to have been chosen.[2] I learn however that the vote was very light;[3] I have requested Gen. Woods to furnish me an extract from the reports of the officers sent into the different counties to administer the amnesty oath, stating the number of oaths taken. This will give an estimate as to the number of persons that have taken part in the election. I shall forward it as soon as it reaches me.[4]

I have the honor to submit to you a statement dictated to me and signed by Maj Genl. Chas. R. Woods, commanding the Department of Alabama.[5] Every item it contains is fully borne out by information I have received from a variety of sources. Gen. Woods showed himself exceedingly careful in his statements, being unwilling to have anything go from him over his own name that has not come to him in an official form. The state of things he describes as existing in Washington County Ala. he ⟨supposes⟩ believes to exist in a great many other localities from which no official reports have—and, indeed, could not have—reached him, as only his military subordinates, and not the civil authorities, furnish him information.

I would invite your special attention to the last paragraph in Gen. Wood's report. I have noticed similar things at a good many other places. Rumors are spread about impending negro insurrections evidently for no other purpose than to serve as a pretext for annoying police regulations concerning the colored people. I have seen instances of this in every State I have visited, and in no case could the least evidence of any such intention on the part of the negroes be furnished. The negroes certainly do not think of any such thing as long as they consider themselves protected by our troops. While I was at Mobile, Gen. Woods received a petition signed by a considerable number of citizens, appealing to him in the most extravagant language to keep the negroes down, and stating that every night armed bands of negroes were roaming through the streets making it unsafe for white people to show themselves, and that a certain negro preacher was, in his church, calling upon the negroes to dip their hands in the blood of the whites.[6] An investigation was at once instituted and it turned out that both statements were entirely unfounded. The preacher is known as a very good hearted and well-educated man entirely incapable of making such bloodthirsty appeals, and as to the armed bands, the patrols sent out during the night reported that they had found a few negroes on the streets who at once went home when told to do so,— but not the least symptom of an insurrectionary spirit was discovered.— In every case that has come to my notice, investigations led exactly to the same conclusions.— I mention this matter merely to caution you against similar reports that may from time to time come to you.[7] The rumors are undoubtedly spread in most instances, for purposes of a mischievous character. As long as our troops are here, they pass over harmlessly. But where the colored people are without protection in the hands of the bad elements of society, such things must inevitably lead to acts of violence and aggression.

I had a conversation with Col. John Forsyth,[8] Mayor of Mobile, late U.S. Minister to Mexico. He admitted that the presence of our troops was still necessary, although he seemed to share the common Southern prejudice against our black soldiers.

Genl. Woods governs himself strictly by what he conceives to be the desire of the Government. He abstains carefully from every interference with civil affairs and acts only when called upon by the Governor or other civil authorities. The deplorable condition of things in Alabama, a description of which I have already given in my report from Montgomery, seems to render it very desirable that a little more latitude should be allowed to the military. If the civil authority in that State was re-established for the purpose of protecting their lives, the liberty and the property of the citizens and of administering the laws, the failure could hardly be more complete. Such a state of anarchy, such impotency of the constituted authorities would in any Northern State cause the organization of "vigilance Committees" whose action is but another form of martial law. In Alabama matters might be regulated by a simple application of the latter, and, indeed, it seems to become more necessary every day. I asked Gen. Woods whether he thought that the organization of a State-militia force would be calculated to remedy the evil. He replied, that in his opinion it would not, and he thought Gov. Parsons had too much sense to recommend it.[9]

I enclose a statement written by Capt. Poillon,[10] Asst. Superintendent of Freedmen etc. at Mobile, and one dictated to me by Genl. Thomas Kilby Smith,[11] who having just been relieved of the command of the Southern District of Alabama, is on his way home. I would respectfully invite your special attention to both these papers. I will confess that the statement of Capt. Poillon seemed to me exaggerated, although the Captain himself makes the impression of a coolheaded and truthful man. I therefore read it to Gen. Kilby Smith who not only vouched for Capt. Poillons truthfulness on the strength of intimate personal acquaintance with him, but assured me, that he himself of his own experience knew most of Capt. Poillons statements and observations to be correct and founded on fact. Capt. Poillon also gave me a number of affidavits corroborating his report on the murders committed in four counties of Southern Alabama, which I shall forward for your information as soon as they can be copied. The report referred to is the one I sent you from Montgomery.

The two papers signed by Col. Robinson[12] and Hon. F. W. Kellogg[13] respectively bear partly upon the admission of negro testimony in the courts of justice. It appears that Genl. Swayne's order turning over the cases arising between whites and blacks to the civil tribunals if the judges and magistrates pledge themselves to admit the testimony of colored persons, is quite generally carried out in the cities and towns, but is a dead letter in a great many counties in the interior. Capt. Poillon says the same of the whole district under his charge except the city of Mobile. This leaves the freedmen in the interior without protection, and the interior of the country is just where they want it most. I notice that several newspapers express the opinion that the general acceptance of this plan would render the existence of the Freedmen's Bureau unnecessary. This is by no means the case. Not only is it indispensable that the interests of the freedmen should be attended to by the agents of the Bureau in the Courts of Justice, inasmuch as without this protection the testimony of the freedmen would in a great many cases be arbitrarily overridden, although accepted as a matter of form, but also to transact the business of the freedmen outside of the courts, as the making of contracts etc. To answer these objects the organization of the Freedmens Bureau in Alabama is still very insufficient, there being no agents in a great many places where they ought to be. I draw this conclusion from the reports coming into Mobile from different parts of the State. In fact I have found only two States in which the organization of the Freedmen's Bureau closely approaches what it ought to be; those States are Mississippi and Louisiana. In South Carolina it was, when I was there, in process of completion and may, by this time, be in efficient working order.

It appears also, from what I could learn at Mobile, that one of my most important suggestions, made in my report from Montgomery, has been left unheeded. It was that, if Gen. Swayne's plan to turn over all cases arising between whites and blacks to the civil tribunals, be adopted, an agent of the Freedmen's Bureau should be ex officio present at the trials as the best friend of the freedmen, and that a complete report of the proceedings in every case of that description, inclusive of the testimony, be sent up to the Headquarters of the Freedmen's Bureau in the State. Unless such precautions are taken, the freedmen will not only labor under very great disadvantages, owing to the inveterate prejudices of the people, but the appointed protector of the freedmen, the Bureau, will hardly ever be informed of any injustice that is done, and thus remain without reliable information as to the working of the system. This is, in my opinion, absolutely necessary to secure anything like fair dealing.

I had a conversation about this point with Mayor Forsyth in Mobile, and when I asked him, whether he thought that there was a jury in Alabama that would find a white man guilty of assault and battery for having whipped a negro, he did not conceal his doubts. I refer to the opinion of Hon. F. W. Kellogg upon that matter; it agrees exactly with the conclusions I have formed from my conversations with Southern men. Mayor Forsyth frankly admitted the influence of Southern prejudice. I would, therefore, repeat my recommendation that the Freedmen's

Bureau be ordered to issue a regulation about this matter embodying the suggestions contained in my Montgomery report.

Col. Robinsons statement, that he found "a general disposition among the planters to set the colored people who had cultivated their crops during the summer, adrift as soon as the crops could be secured," is corroborated by a great many reports that I have received occasionally from other parts of the country, not only in Alabama but in all the States I have visited. It shows how necessary it is to have agents of the Bureau in the interior of the country, to prevent the confusion and suffering which inevitably would ensue if such a disposition were carried into execution.

I beg leave to call attention to Mr. Kelloggs statement "that persons excluded from the amnesty by the $20,000 clause are shipping their cotton to Liverpool, and invest their means there." It is reasonable to suppose that this is the case not only at Mobile but at other maritime places.

Permit me now to return to Louisiana affairs. I am sorry to say the Governor [14] has not yet returned from Red River and consequently I have had no opportunity to see him. No proclamation ordering a general election for State officers, legislature and congress has as yet been issued. The day on which it ought to have been issued in compliance with the constitution was the 7th inst. The Governor is expected back every day, and I may still be able to see him.

I had, however, a long conversation with Mayor Kennedy who is generally looked upon as the Governors confidential and most influential adviser. In reply to my questions concerning the prospective action of the Governor, he said that the Governor would probably order an election; but he expressed himself in a manner which convinced me that he did not want to commit himself on the subject. He spoke with great contempt of the Constitution of 1864 [15] as an instrument which had been gotten up in so irregular a manner as to have no legitimate existence and no binding force. He is evidently disposed to set it aside. The conversation turning upon the Congressional Amendment concerning slavery, he told me frankly and emphatically that he would go for the first section but was *decidedly against the second section of it*. [16] If this avowal can be taken as an expression of the sentiments of Gov. Wells, it is of very great significance. The legislature elected under the Constitution of 1864 ratified the constitutional amendment *entire*. If the Government of Louisiana is transformed into a Provisional Government, then, as the papers in the interest of Gov. Wells and Mayor Kennedy declare, setting aside the Constitution of 64 and all the legislative acts passed under that constitution, the ratification of the constitutional amendment by the State legislature would be thrown overboard also, and the influence of Mayor Kennedy and those he represents would be thrown against a reenactment of that ratification. What I learn here leads me to believe, that this is one of the principal desires of the Wells-Kennedy party. In Georgia, Alabama and Mississippi I noticed that all those who may be supposed to be the natural enemies of the constitutional amendment, use its second section as the main pretext and declaim against it to cover their hostility to the whole. Mayor Kennedy's expressions convince me that the chiefs of the State-Administration-party in Louisiana have adopted the same policy. Everything I hear and see at this place strengthens my conviction, that, while the appointment of a thoroughly loyal man who is in full sympathy with the results of the war, would be the best thing that could be done for this State, the continuation in power of the present Governor and the entrusting him with the management of the preparations for a new convention would be the worst. I honestly believe, upon the information I have gathered, we can make Louisiana a firm and reliable Union—and free labor—State, if the policy recommended in my last, or something similar, be adopted; but the State will certainly fall under the control of a disloyal and pro-slavery element if things are permitted to go on as they do now.

I wish to bring an occurrence to your notice which, perhaps, has already been or may be submitted to you by other parties. It is characteristic of the manner in which things are managed here and of the spirit and tendency of those in power.— When Gen. Shepley [17] was Military Governor of this State he appointed a school board to reorganize the public schools of New Orleans. A Corps of loyal teachers was selected and the schools put in operation. I have taken pains to ascertain from men who took an interest in the manner, how the new organization worked; and I find that only one complaint was raised, and that only by a particular class of people. The schools, as I indicated above, were organized upon a *loyal* basis and with a view to educate *loyal* citizens. The national airs and patriotic songs were frequently sung by the children and the doctrines taught were such as to impregnate the youthful minds of the scholars with loyal sentiments towards their country. This feature of the public schools was distasteful to that class of people whose own feelings did not run in the same channel. Mayor Kennedy, by no warrant of law that I can learn of, appointed a new school board for the purpose of effecting a change. The composition of the new schoolboard was such as to induce Gen. Canby to suspend its functions until he could inquire into the loyalty of its members, he having received information to the effect that a majority of the board had been active participants in the rebellion. [18]

I enclose two papers bearing upon this subject, one a copy of a letter sent to Genl. Canby from Mr. C. Black, [19] and the other a copy of the report of the officer charged by Genl. Canby with the investigation. [20] These papers agreeing on all important points, show the character of the new schoolboard. But as no evidence was elicited proving the members incapable of holding office, Genl. Canby considered himself obliged to remove the prohibition, and the schoolboard will now assume its functions.

I enclose also a newspaper slip cut out from the New-Orleans Times of the 12th inst.[21] It is a justification of the Mayor's conduct in this matter, and I would invite you to read it. Although trying to cover over the whole proceeding with the smoothest and blandest language, its substance can be expressed in two sentences: "The schools of New-Orleans are demonstratively loyal institutions; for this reason they have become unpopular with some of our citizens, and they must be brought under the control of the latter so as to make them cease to be obnoxious in that particular." For this purpose a board of rebel sympathizers is appointed.

It is worthy of note that the candidate of the new board for Superintendent of Public Schools, a Mr. Rogers,[22] was Superintendent of a District before the occupation of the city by our forces; that in his schools he introuced the singing of rebel songs, that he went into the rebel Army when the city was taken by our forces, and now immediately after his return is to be made Superintendent of all the schools for the distinct purpose of abolishing the nuisance of loyal songs. This is the way in which the reaction is carried on by those now in power here.

I beg leave to invite your particular attention to a statement ⟨contained⟩ in Mr. Blacks letter concerning the existence of a secret society whose object it is "to remove from office and employment of every kind all persons who remained at their homes and were loyal to the U. S. Government, and to replace them with returned soldiers from the C. S. Army." Genl. Canby authorizes me to say that he has good reasons for believing and does believe, that this organization exists. He has taken steps to investigate the matter by means of detectives and expects soon to be able to expose it.— If such an organization really does exist, it may be concluded from appearances that it has great influence with the State- and City-Administrations.

I would respectfully suggest that, unless it is the intention of the Government to effect a general change in the Administration of this State, Genl. Canby be authorized to put a stop to these proceedings with regard to the public schools of this city. The mayor is not in his place by virtue of a popular election; he was put there by the military authority, although I understand, he claims in his correspondence with Genl. Canby to have been appointed by the President of the United States. However that may be, the same power that has made him can unmake him, it can certainly undo or modify his acts, especially those for which there is no warrant to be found neither in the laws of this State nor in the charter of this city. Such an act was the appointment of this schoolboard, the purpose of which is apparent. Whatever can be done consistently with your general policy to keep the education of the growing generation under the influence of loyal sentiments, ought certainly not to be neglected. It is needless for me to repeat that in my humble opinion a thoroughgoing change in the Administration of this State would be the best means to remedy all these growing evils.

I desire also to bring to your notice how the judicial appointments of Gov. Wells begin to tell upon the situation of the colored people of this State. The enclosed newspaperslip taken from the "Southern Star" of Sept. 9th[23] gives an account of the ground upon which in one of the Courts the inadmissibility of negro testimony was argued and the manner in which it was ruled out by Judge Eastin,[24] one of the appointees of Gov. Wells. The report is worth reading and highly instructive as to the sentiments which are gaining new strength in a part of the community and will continue to gain strength in the same measure as they are sustained by the authorities. Comment upon the report is unnecessary.

I enclose an ordinance passed by the Mayor and common council of the town of Franklin concerning the "discipline of colored persons."[25] It is almost a literal copy of the ordinances passed at Opelousas and Landry.[26] The rejection of the testimony of free persons of color by a Court and the provisions of these ordinances, which, as I have been informed, would have been adopted by a good many more common councils and police boards, had they not, on their first appearance, been overruled by the military authorities,[27] give a fair indication of the spirit and the purposes of a class of men which has again been placed in positions of power and influence by those who at present govern the State of Louisiana. It is my opinion, they would not have gone so far had they not been encouraged so much, and, I have no doubt, they will go still farther if they are permitted to believe that they can do so with impunity. The attempts of the police boards of Opelousas, Landry and the common council of Franklin were checked by the prompt interference of the military authorities. But they have gone sufficiently far to prove, what we may expect if the military check be withdrawn *and such men remain in power*. It may be said that the Governor of the State is not responsible for their action; but they are the creatures of the Governor; he placed them in position, and he failed to fill their places with better men after they had shown what spirit governed them and what use they would make of their power. My conviction grows stronger every day that a majority of the white people of the States I have visited and a very large proportion even of those who at present endeavor to propitiate you with rosy representations and fair promises, will, as soon as they have resumed control of their own affairs unchecked by federal interference, at once attempt to reduce the colored race to a state of virtual slavery and study, not how to build up and develop a true system of free labor, but how to avoid it. I see the premonitory symptoms of this, clear and unmistakeable, wherever any latitude of action is allowed them. It is for the Government to weigh its moral obligations in this matter, and to consider the measures by which such dire results can be prevented. I would respectfully entreat you not to attach too little importance to the expressions of views I forward to you from military and civil officers of the Government stationed in these States. I give them to you in every case in their own language. For the most part I trust only to my own observations. But I consider it my duty to submit to you the opinions of men whom I believe to be competent and conscientious observers, and whose experience here has been longer and whose means of obtaining information in certain localities more extensive than mine. I give my own estimate of them frankly whenever I think them liable to the charge of exaggeration or incorrectness. As to the documents I send you to day, I beg leave to urge upon your special attention the statements signed by Maj. Genl. Woods, & Brig. Genl. Kilby Smith, and the papers relating to the schoolboard of New Orleans. They are fully confirmed by observations of my own and give, in my opinion, a reliable indication of the state of popular feeling and the prospective action of the constituted authorities in this region.

I have abstained for some time from giving a particular account of the affairs and conduct of the freedmen. I am on the point of making a trip into the interior of this State for the purpose of examining personally into this matter. I expect to be thus engaged four or five days and shall then go up the river into the State of Mississippi again.

If after the arrival of this report at Washington you should see fit to give me any advice or instructions *by telegraph*, despatches will reach me through the headquarters of Gen. Slocum at Vicksburg. If not, I shall, in accordance with the written instructions I received from the Secretary of War, which confined my mission to the States of South Carolina, Georgia, Alabama, Mississippi and Louisiana, consider my office performed, especially as the three months which, when accepting the mission, I told you I could afford to devote to this ⟨mission⟩ business, will be nearly over when I shall have completed my investigation in Louisiana and Mississippi.

> I am, Sir, very truly and respectfully
> Your obedient servant C. Schurz.

Enclosures: No. 1. Statement of Bvt. Maj. Genl. Woods.
             No. 2.   "   "   " Capt. Poillon, Asst. Supt. Freedmen.
             No. 3.   "   "   Col. Geo. D. Robinson 97th U.S.C.I.
             No. 4.   "   "   Hon. F. W. Kellogg, Coll. Int. Rev. Mobile.
             No. 5. Statement of Brig. Genl. Thomas Kilby Smith.
             No. 6. Article of "New Orleans Times" on the schoolboard.
             No. 7. Report on rejection of colored testimony by Judge Eastin.

> No. 8. Ordinances passed at the town of Franklin, La.
> No. 9. Statement of Mr. C. Black about loyalty of
>   schoolboard.
> No. 10. Report of Maj. Lowell Prov. Mar. Gen. con-
>   cerning the same.

ALS, DLC-JP.

1. See Schurz to Johnson, August 20, 1865.

2. *Ibid.*, n. 7.

3. Together, the three candidates for governor—Robert M. Patton, Michael J. Bulger, and William R. Smith—polled 44,870 votes. While some 56,000 Alabamians participated in the elections for delegates to the constitutional convention, the 1860 presidential contest saw 89,579 turn out to vote. Fleming, *Reconstruction in Alabama*, 373.

4. Not found.

5. Woods, asserting that he intervened in civil affairs only at Parson's request and that local authorities seemed "unable or unwilling" to enforce the law in the absence of troops, described at some length the depredations of the "lawless element" out in the rural counties. He had taken steps to halt the stealing of cotton, government property, and mistreatment of blacks. The general had given a warning to the Mobile *Daily News*, which, "for the purpose of keeping up an excitement," had published "sensational articles about impending Negro insurrections," without any foundation in fact. Woods to Schurz, September 9, 1865, *Schurz Report*, 61–62.

6. Not found.

7. See Schurz to Johnson, August 13, 1865, n. 20. Johnson had written General Steedman concerning the possibility of a black insurrection and had asked him to "keep a vigilant watch upon this subject." Johnson to Steedman, August 23, 1865, Johnson Papers, LC.

8. Democratic editor and diplomat John Forsyth (1812–1877) was elected mayor of Mobile in 1860. Appointed mayor once more in 1865 by federal military authorities, he resigned the following year, although he remained politically active as an opponent of congressional reconstruction and as a state legislator. William Garrett, *Reminiscences of Public Men in Alabama* (Spartanburg, S.C., 1975[1872]), 731; Long, *Civil War Almanac*, 42.

9. Woods' prediction proved wrong. On September 24, 1865, Parsons submitted a questionnaire to convention delegates concerning the need for a state militia. By mid-1866, there were 2,624 men enrolled—2,496 in counties where the majority of the population was black. Carter, *When the War Was Over*, 220.

10. Poillon reported that in Mobile "prejudice and a vindictive hatred to color is universal," with whites refusing to accept emancipation and its consequences. White hostility was further spurred by newspaper reports of black uprisings: "this is utterly without foundation." According to Poillon, the freedmen, despite their suffering, wanted to work, but prejudice colored white perceptions: if blacks "are ragged and dirty, they are spurned as outcasts; if genteel and respectable, they are insulted as presumptive; if intelligent, they are incendiary, and their humble worship of God is construed as a designing plot to rise against the citizens who oppress them." Poillon to Schurz, September 9, 1865, *Schurz Report*, 72–73.

11. Thomas Kilby Smith (1820–1887) served on Grant's staff, commanded a brigade in Sherman's XV Corps at Vicksburg, and participated in Banks's Red River fiasco before retiring from active field service because of ill health. His statement, submitted to Schurz on September 14, detailed his belief in the continued disloyalty of white Alabamians. He described assaults on black women, threats of violence against military authorities, and promises to destroy black schools and churches. Mobile's blacks, according to Smith, "are, as a general thing, orderly, quiet, industrious, and well dressed, with an earnest desire to learn and to fit themselves for their new status," but whites refused to accept them as freed people. Characterizing the administration of civil law as "a farce," with law enforcement officials often "engaged in the perpetration of the very crime they are sent forth to prohibit or punish," he concluded that the situation required the continued presence of troops. *Schurz Report*, 57–59.

12. Col. George D. Robinson, 97th U.S. Inf., reported on September 9 that black laborers were ousted as soon as the crops were in, and that civil officials refused to assume the duties of a Freedmen's Bureau agent, thereby defeating a policy set forth by General Swayne. *Schurz Report*, 82–83; for Swayne's policy, see Schurz to Johnson, August 20, 1865, n. 2.

13. Francis W. Kellogg, collector of internal revenue at Mobile, submitted a statement to Schurz on September 9, observing that whites did not accept the fact of emancipation and would reject efforts to allow blacks to testify in court. The statement, although signed by Kellogg, is in Schurz's handwriting. Johnson Papers, LC.

14. James Madison Wells.

15. In 1864 Louisiana unionists drew up a new constitution which abolished slavery, established public education, provided for the appointment of judges by the governor, and instituted an income tax and wage and hour regulations for workers. Critics questioned its legitimacy, pointing out that less than twenty percent of the electorate had participated. Taylor, *Louisiana Reconstructed*, 44–52.

16. See Schurz to Johnson, August 29, 1865, n. 6.

17. Participating in the capture of New Orleans, George F. Shepley (1819–1878) was named military governor of Louisiana, serving for two years. After the installation of the Union government in 1864, he joined the staff of the XXV Corps outside Richmond, and held the position of military governor of Richmond from April to June, 1865, when he resigned.

18. Canby suspended the board on September 6, 1865. Kennedy to Johnson, September 7, 1865, Johnson Papers, LC.

19. Black enclosed a list of people who, he claimed, had formed a secret society "to drive out of this state every poor person who does not avow his adherence to the cause of Southern independence and a return to slavery." Undated statement, Johnson Papers, Ser. 18, LC.

20. On September 12, Maj. Charles W. Lowell, 80th U.S.C.T. and provost marshal general, reported to Canby on the loyalty of Kennedy's schoolboard appointees. He found that many of them had advocated southern independence and had supported the Confederate war effort through financial contribution, though few had actually donned gray uniforms. *Schurz Report*, 67.

21. The editorial claimed that the quality of education was declining due to the injection of "political perplexities" into the classroom. With "loyalty" as a new subject following the federal occupation of 1862, children were bombarded with songs and ceremonies, which made them "exceedingly revengeful and unchildlike." Kennedy's recent appointment of a new schoolboard was seen as an effort to restore the schools to "what they were originally intended to be—mere educational institutions." *Ibid.*, 67–68; New Orleans *Times*, September 12, 1865.

22. Before the war, according to Major Lowell, William O. Rogers' "conduct . . . was imbued with extreme bitterness and hate towards the United States." As superintendent he had made school children sing "The Bonnie Blue Flag" and other Confederate songs, and had substituted "C.S." for "U.S." in history texts. Lowell to Canby, September 12, 1865, *Schurz Report*, 67.

23. Clipping not found. On September 6 Kennedy had informed Johnson that the *Southern Star*, "the first out & out, uncompromising Johnson democratic organ in the country," had commenced publication. Johnson Papers, LC.

24. Not identified.

25. Passed July 28, 1865, this ordinance regulated the movements, economic activity, and residency of freedmen, and prohibited public meetings or speaking without prior permission of the mayor. *Schurz Report*, 95–96.

26. These ordinances, resembling the Franklin ordinance, are reproduced in *ibid.*, 92–94.

27. On August 10 assistant commissioner Conway ordered the Franklin ordinance ignored. *Ibid.*, 96.

————◄•►————

New. Orleans, La. Sept. 23d 1865.

To his Excellency Andrew Johnson
President of the United States.

Sir,

I returned from my trip into the interior of this State on the 20th after having penetrated as far as New Iberia on the Teche river. I would have gone farther and visited the Red River country also had I not been sick with fever for some time.[1] The state of my health obliges me to withdraw from the influences of this climate as soon as possible, and I shall leave for Natchez Miss. this evening. The information I gathered on my trip up the Teche as well as a considerable quantity of other material that I have had no time yet to arrange, I shall incorporate in a general report to be submitted to you after my return.[2]

On the 21st inst Gov. Wells issued his proclamation ordering a general election in this State, with the exception of Parish officers, to take place on the 6th of November. I am informed by several prominent gentlemen here, among others by Mr. A. P. Field,[3] President of the Central Committee of the so-called "Conservative Union Party", and personal friend of the Governor, that it cost them an effort to prevent him from setting aside the Constitution of 64 and calling a new Convention on the basis of the Constitution of 52.[4] This latter course, or rather the simple election of a legislature on the basis of the Constitution of 52, thus quietly smothering the "Free-State-Constitution of 64, was openly advocated by the Democratic Party in their manifesto drawn up by Mr. Rozier,[5] and the Governor finds in that party his warmest endorsers and most zealous adherents. Finally however, he was prevailed upon by the "Conservative Union"—men to order the election in pursuance of the Constitution of 64, and that instrument, as the Governor told me this morning, is to form henceforward the basis of all official action.— I send you a copy of the Governors proclamation as published in the official city paper. You will not fail to notice how singularly it is worded.[6]

I am informed that the returning rebels, pardoned and unpardoned, and not a small number of persons that are not qualified to vote, are crowding to the registry to have their names placed upon the list of voters. Several gentlemen belonging to the "Conservative Union-Party", among whom the above mentioned President of their Central Committee, Mr. Field, who are suddenly becoming alarmed, requested me yesterday to call Gen. Canby's attention to this fact and to induce him to put a stop to it. Gentlemen who so far went with the State-Administration and are, at least some of them, still inclined to support it, are all at once becoming fearful lest the "rebels" have it all their own way to the total exclusion of even the mildest type of those that do not go in with them. The reorganized "Democracy" who seem to be in full communion with the returned Confederates, is looming up in great strength. The Democratic manifesto above referred to, aside from advocating the return to the Constitution of 52, is openly out [in] favor of setting aside all constitutional provisions against slavery and of leaving this subject to be disposed of by the legislature.

Even if the Governors intentions are much better than many suppose they are, he will find it very difficult to control the element which he has contributed to render powerful again. In many parts of the country that element seems to have already undisputed sway, and in the city it is no doubt continually gaining in strength.

Mayor Kennedy's newly appointed school board, of which I wrote in my last, has already brought forth its first fruit. As soon as, after the removal of Genl. Canby's prohibition, it went to work, it proceeded at once to elect Mr. Rodgers,[7] the recently returned rebel officer, superintendent of public schools. He is the same man who as district superintendent had introduced in his schools the singing of rebel songs, and who as soon as the city was occupied by our forces in 62, left and joined the rebel army. He is now at the head of the whole educational establishment of the city. Union men predict that now the United States flag will have to come down from the school buildings, where it has floated since Gen. Butler[8] took possession; that in those buildings the national airs will cease to be heard, that the Union teachers hitherto employed will have to look for other situations, and that the doctrines taught and the sympathies fostered will be more in accordance with the tastes of those to whose sensibilities demonstrative loyalty was offensive and for whose benefit Mayor Kennedy saw fit to make the change. I shall not remain here to verify the prediction, but from what I observe I am inclined to consider the apprehension not unfounded. It might be well a few weeks hence to inquire about further developments.

If only the city government were in good Union hands some time before and at the election, it might present a strong barrier against the threatening inroads of the "rebel" element. I think I am safe in saying that in Mr. Kennedy's hands its influence is more apt to be felt in the opposite direction.

Very truly and respectfully
Your obedient servant C. Schurz.

ALS, DLC-JP.

1. Schurz began a draft of this letter the previous day, which included an extended description of his activities. "I went through Lafourche and Terrebonne Parishes and up the Teche river as high as New Iberia, one of the most fertile planting districts of Louisiana. With the exception of the country immediately opposite the city of New Orleans and parts of Lafourche and Terrebonne there is but very little land under cultivation. At Brashear City, at Franklin and New Iberia and throughout the surrounding districts the condition of things is deplorable. The white population, planters as well as poor people, are complaining, growling, moping, but nobody seems to be raising a hand. All those that I saw, without any exception, are singing the same song: their fencing was destroyed by

the armies; their mules and cattle are gone; they have no agricultural implements; they have no cane to plant, they have no money and they are in debt—and, finally, "they cannot make the nigger work unless they are permitted to use means of compulsion." Some of these complaints are undoubtedly well founded, but nobody seems to be making even an effort *to try*. From the negroes I received a corresponding story;—they would like to go to work, but they had no land and no implements, and the planters did not try to employ them; if anybody would employ them they would be glad to work for any wages etc. etc. On all my travels in the Southern States I have not found any people so completely spiritless and helpless as the sugar planters of the most fertile district of Louisiana. As to their future there is but one idea that governs them: they must be permitted "to control their labor" as they style it, and they believe they can and will do it as soon as they are permitted to make and enforce their own laws.—

The country is comparatively quiet, there are some cases of stealing mostly confined to provisions and the like, but nothing on as large a scale as I found it in Alabama. I heard of some small French farmers at some distance from the river who were said to be at work and doing comparatively well, but I did not see any of them.

I intended to visit the Red river country also, but the state of my health obliges me to get out of the influences of this climate as soon as possible. I learn, however, that things there are in the same state." Draft, Schurz Papers, LC.

2. Schurz's final report made no special mention of his activities and observations during this period.

3. New Orleans lawyer Alexander P. Field claimed election to Congress in 1863 and took part in Emerson Etheridge's attempt to create a Democratic majority in the House through manipulation of names on the roll of representatives. He was elected to Congress again in 1864; however, while in Washington to claim his seat, he became intoxicated and assaulted Pennsylvania congressman William D. Kelley, a Radical Republican. Congress investigated the incident; although the Committee on Elections upheld Field's credentials, his actions had discredited Louisiana's reconstructed government, and he was never seated. McCrary, *Lincoln and Reconstruction*, 178–80, 269, 298; *House Reports* Nos. 10 and 16, 38 Cong., 2 Sess.

4. A comparison of Louisiana's 1852 and 1864 constitutions reveals significant differences in the appointment and removal of judges, the determination of representation, and the role of the state in the economic and social life of Louisianians. The 1852 document provided for an elected judiciary and allocated representation by total population (with a clause limiting the number of senators from a parish, designed to limit the clout of New Orleans); the 1864 constitution created a judiciary appointed by the governor, based representation on qualified voters, increased the limit on senators from a parish, and included clauses regulating wages and hours, funding public education, and providing for the possible enfranchisement of free blacks. Of course, it also abolished slavery, which was protected in the 1852 constitution. In short, the later document increased the influence of New Orleans, with its sizable black and white unionist population, at the expense of planters. Conservatives disputed the legitimacy of the new constitution, insisting that the 1852 document remained in force. Taylor, *Louisiana Reconstructed*, 50–51, 72.

5. John Rozier (b. 1817), Missouri native and New Orleans lawyer, was a member of Louisiana's secession convention of 1861. Cooperating with Union occupation forces, he advocated a conservative basis for Louisiana's reconstruction and unsuccessfully ran for state attorney general in 1864. *Ibid.*, 13, 43; McCrary, *Lincoln and Reconstruction*, 63, 174; Tunnell, *Crucible of Reconstruction*, 233.

6. Wells's proclamation, issued September 21, 1865, struck an uneasy compromise between the constitutions of 1852 and 1864. Although he based his call for an election upon the latter document, he claimed that the election "would be conducted in accordance with law, which is the same as under the constitution of 1852," giving rise to Schurz's comment. *Appleton's Annual Cyclopaedia* (1865), 511; John R. Ficklen, *History of Reconstruction in Louisiana* (Baltimore, 1910), 106–7 and n.

7. William O. Rogers.

8. Prewar Democratic politician Benjamin F. Butler (1818–1893) was commissioned major general by Lincoln in a bid to attract Democratic support for the war. His generalship in the field was marked by ineptitude; his administration of occupied areas, notably New Orleans, won him notoriety and contempt, trying the patience of Lincoln and Grant

until his removal in 1865. After the war he won election to Congress and was a leading advocate of Radical Reconstruction, black rights, and Johnson's impeachment.

Natchez Miss. Sept. 26th 65.

To his Excellency Andrew Johnson
President of the United States.
Sir,

Immediately before my departure from New Orleans Gen. Canby received a telegraphic communication from Gen. Woods commanding Department of Alabama, stating that attempts were being made in that State to induce negroes, under various pretences, to go on board of vessels lying near to coast inlets, and to run them off to Cuba or Brazil for the purpose of selling them as slaves. It was stated that employers who brought their negroes on board, received $300 a head. The report came originally from Gen. Swayne, Asst. Commissioner of the Freedmens Bureau in Alabama, and, as I understand, Gen. Swayne as well as Genl. Woods believed it to be well founded. I am also informed that measures were at once taken by the military authorities to prevent the execution of such nefarious designs. Strict secrecy was to be observed with regard to this business in order to insure the arrest of the guilty parties.[1]

Similar rumors reached me from the State of Georgia, but they seemed to me so little substantiated that, at first, I did not place any faith in them. As it appears, however, that such things are being attempted in Alabama, the same may be true of Georgia, and I would respectfully suggest that the attention of the military commanders in the seaboard States be directed to this matter in such a manner, if possible, as not to interfere by premature publication with the researches now going on in Alabama.[2]

In the State of Mississippi no attempt has been made, as far as I can learn, to organize the militia. I am informed that some of the best men of the State have advised Gov. Sharkey not to venture upon so dangerous an experiment at present.

I shall stop a few days at Vicksburg and neighborhood for the purpose of making some further inquiries into the condition of things in this State, and then return to Washington by way of St. Louis. After my return I expect to lay before you a general report touching points to which it was impossible for me to do justice in my dispatches.

I am, Sir, very respectfully
Your obt servt C. Schurz.

ALS, DLC-JP.
1. Reports had reached military authorities in Alabama and Louisiana that freedmen were being enticed to travel to the Gulf coast to cut lumber for three dollars per day by

whites wearing blue uniforms. Once on the coast, the freedmen were kidnapped and sold to buyers in Cuba and Brazil. On September 25, Woods notified Schurz, "I have some information that the President ought to know and I can only reach him through you." William A. Kobbe to Swayne, September 15, and Poillon to Swayne, September 19, 1865, Asst. Commissioner, Ala., Lets. Recd., RG105, NA; Woods to Canby, September 15, to William D. Whipple, September 20, and to Schurz, September 25, 1865, Dept. of Ala., Lets. Sent, RG393, NA.

2. On January 9, 1866, in response to accounts detailing the smuggling of blacks to Cuba and Brazil via Florida and Alabama, Charles Sumner pushed for the framing of a bill (S.132) to prevent such kidnappings, which passed the Senate (February 15) and the House (May 21). *Cong. Globe*, 39 Cong., 1 Sess., 146, 852, 1178, 2727.

Harvey M. Watterson:
Reassurance and Support

Andrew Johnson could not but be disturbed by the publicity surrounding Carl Schurz's southern excursion—especially the news that the former general, while passing himself off as his representative, made clear his disagreement with the administration's southern policy. Undoubtedly the decision to send him south had been a mistake. Johnson felt that he needed the assessment of someone more in line with his own sentiments, someone who shared his attitudes, and someone whom he trusted to check, even counter, Schurz's observations, and give him reliable information. Once again Harvey Watterson seemed an ideal candidate; he proved only too willing to comply, and left Nashville for a second excursion in September, with stops in Alabama, Mississippi, Louisiana, and Georgia—states just visited by Schurz.

In Montgomery, Watterson circulated among the members of Alabama's constitutional convention, reporting their "cheerful acquiescence" in defeat: "Among the intelligent classes no grumblers are to be found." Johnson's appointees, notably provisional governor Lewis Parsons, were doing their part to encourage a rapid restoration. Even newspaper editors, who had once printed "the most vulgar epithets" about Andrew Johnson, were now praising the President. All signs pointed to a South "undivided" in its support of the chief executive. Even so, obstacles remained in the way of perfect peace. Watterson repeatedly complained about treasury agents and military officers who were seizing privately-owned bales and pocketing extra money. "A rogue is a rogue, and never respected your rights nor mine. . . . Some of these official cotton scamps have been arrested and exposed. Years of hard labor in the penitentiary should be their fate." Most importantly, such corruption produced "demoralization and discontent," inhibiting a smooth reconciliation. From Mobile, Watterson detailed the "game of open and shut," and copied paragraphs from newspapers looking for relief from "this cotton business."[1]

Watterson did not restrict his reporting to the President. His son Henry had recently become an editor for the Nashville *Republican Banner*, a pro-administration sheet. Soon columns initialed "H.M.W." began to appear. Of the Alabama convention delegates the elder Watterson noted "a determination on the part of nine-tenths . . . to do whatever the President advises. He is everywhere sustained with enthusiasm."

1. Watterson to Johnson, September 26, October 3, 1865.

Repeating his earlier concerns about the inability of most southerners to satisfy the requirements of the ironclad oath, a prerequisite for holding office, Watterson also advised Alabamians to nominate for Congress only men "either with a good record or no record at all."[2]

From Alabama he moved west to Mississippi and Louisiana. In both states he praised the behavior of southern whites and complimented the governors. Contrary to the declarations of Radical demagogues, he found Mississippi's residents "more loyal to the National Government than they have been for the last twenty years." As an example he cited newly-elected governor Benjamin G. Humphreys, whom he portrayed as a staunch unionist "swept" away by the "storm" of secession, but who nevertheless was "universally popular" with his soldiers. Watterson now judged Humphreys "as loyal as any man in the state." No doubt he sought to reassure the President of Humphreys' loyalty in anticipation of northern reaction upon hearing that barely six months after Appomattox an ex-Confederate brigadier was to head the state of Mississippi—if he could secure a pardon from Johnson. In contrast to Schurz, who relayed to the President his reservations about Louisiana governor J. Madison Wells, Watterson called Wells's nomination for another term "a deserved tribute to his integrity as a man and to his efficiency as a public officer."[3]

The reporter came down hard on the Freedmen's Bureau in both states. In contrast to General Wager Swayne, stationed in Alabama, whom Watterson praised as "a man of integrity and brains," in Mississippi the Bureau was headed by Colonel Samuel Thomas, "a young man" who "has much to learn—especially on the subject of negroes." Sagely donning the robes of age, Watterson attributed Thomas's actions to youthful inexperience rather than to a sincere effort to protect blacks. Obviously southerners (like Watterson and Johnson), not idealistic Yankees (like Ohioan Thomas), knew the true character of the ex-slave. Watterson saw no need to confer with Thomas, and it never entered his head to ask the freedmen their opinion of the situation. Rather, he relayed to Johnson the opinion that the sources of greatest annoyance to white Mississippians were "*negro troops and the Freedmen's Bureau.*" In that connection, he commended Johnson for supporting provisional governor William Sharkey's call for the formation of state militia despite the protests of his generals: "I rejoice that you have sustained him, gloriously sustained him, in his noble efforts to give repose to his state, and strength to the cause of the Union." The ex-editor also assailed the Freedmen's Bureau in Louisiana for "intermeddling," charging that its officers demoralized blacks, "filled them with prejudices and ill feeling against their former owners and present

2. Nashville *Republican Banner*, October 1, 1865.
3. Watterson to Johnson, October 7, 14, 20, 1865.

proprietors." Implicit was the notion that harmony had once existed between master and slave, disrupted only by war and the introduction of outside agitators.[4]

Watterson's final stop was Georgia. He arrived just in time to observe the state constitutional convention. In his mind it had come none too soon, for he relayed General James B. Steedman's comment that there was no further need for troops to maintain order. Watterson also had kind words for General Davis Tillson, a Johnson favorite, who headed the Freedmen's Bureau in Georgia. In fact, everything seemed wonderful in Georgia—Watterson applauded the administration of provisional governor James Johnson, whose "sincere desire" to carry out the President's policy proved that he was "a true friend . . . beyond controversy." Watterson also enclosed a letter from unionist Herschel V. Johnson urging the President to declare senators and representatives elected to Congress by southerners entitled to their seats if the aspirants were "*constitutionally* qualified," an obvious ploy to circumvent loyalty oath legislation. Such a proclamation, according to the former governor, would corner the northern radicals. Either they would be forced to seat the southerners or take upon themselves "the odium of perpetuating a disunion."[5]

Given these endorsements of the President's policy, Watterson decided to return to Washington via Nashville. In his final letters he sought to reassure his friend that his plan was proving a success. Indeed, "a mighty revolution has been wrought in the minds and hearts of the Southern people." Once "afraid" that Johnson "would treat them with vindictiveness," white southerners now supported him wholeheartedly. That the South "will stand by him is just as certain as that God made Moses." Of course, Watterson echoed the sentiment: "I believe, for the first time in my life, that he who strengthens the President strengthens the Government." In short, ex-Confederates were eager "to renew in good faith their former relations," and anyone who claimed the contrary "either knows not what he is talking about, or he has some selfish purpose to accomplish by wilful misrepresentation."[6]

At Nashville, Watterson told a reporter that he was "highly gratified with what he has heard and seen." Praising white southerners for doing "whatever was in their power" to achieve complete restoration, he asserted that they accepted "the result of the war in good faith" and were "rather pleased that 'the peculiar institution' has been crushed out." All that remained was to rebuild the economy; some blacks, who "have not learned what freedom means," had been misled "by men who have

4. *Ibid.* The October 16 New York *World*, reporting Watterson's departure from New Orleans, commented: "It is understood that his opinion of the Freedmen's Bureau is that it is an unnecessary burden to the government."
5. Watterson to Johnson, October 30, 1865.
6. Watterson to Johnson, October 20, 30, 1865.

sought to promote their own interests at the expense of those of the negroes." The reporter was delighted: "How different a liberal, unprejudiced man sees men and thinks from the man who carries his prejudices to such an extent that he can see nothing good in the Southern people." He concluded that the President "now has the views of a gentleman in whose judgment he has entire confidence, and these views exactly coincide with his own."[7]

Henry Watterson once asserted that his father's "judgment was nearly infallible, based upon large experience, and robust common sense."[8] On his tour, however, Harvey Watterson showed that his picture of conditions at the South was only as good as his sources and his own conservative prejudices. He never stopped to ask blacks about their treatment, but preferred to announce in a newspaper column his considered opinion that the "irrepressible nigger hereabouts has either to work or starve."[9] Nor did he confer with army officers unless they had already demonstrated their support of the President's program. In truth, Watterson did not simply observe the state of the South. Rather, he was looking for signs that Johnson's policy was proving a success. By telling the President that white southerners were falling into line behind him, Watterson countered the impression of a recalcitrant South reflected in the unwillingness of several state constitutional conventions to comply with the requirements set down in his proclamations. Perhaps this stiffened Johnson's resolve by convincing him that regardless of the mutterings of some leaders, "the people" were behind him.

One reason that southerners made haste to speak approvingly of Johnson's course was that Watterson made no secret of his intimacy with the President. The newspaperman was all too willing to recall the days when he and Johnson were allies in the Tennessee Democracy, and papers freely commented that he was "a personal and political friend of President Johnson."[10] Some southerners maintained contact with him in order to discern Johnson's intentions. One Georgian, knowing that Watterson was not only "the personal and political friend" of the President but "Sincerely devoted to the maintenance of his administration," later sought his outlook on politics.[11] It is noteworthy that Watterson never reported to Johnson any conversation which contained severe criticism of the President. Many southerners sought to find out more about Johnson through Watterson, and the editor was only too willing to oblige.

In contrast to his tour of Virginia and North Carolina, where he had

7. Nashville *Dispatch* interview, reprinted in the Montgomery *Advertiser*, November 16, 1865, and the Milledgeville *Federal Union*, November 21, 1865.

8. Louisville *Courier-Journal*, October 2, 1891.

9. Nashville *Republican Banner*, October 22, 1865.

10. New Orleans *Picayune*, October 13, 1865.

gone virtually unnoticed, newspapers reported on Watterson's presence, in part because many southerners were dissatisfied with unfavorable reports of conditions in the defeated region. The Louisville *Journal* commended him as "a man of intelligence," adding, "we are gratified to hear him say that, wherever he had been, he found the people anxious for the restoration of civil authority, and that he found none of that bad spirit which a certain class of correspondents seem to take a delight in representing." Surely the Tennessean "will truly represent the disposition of the Southern people." At New Orleans, the conservative *Picayune* judged him "highly competent to present facts such as the President needs, uncolored and unperverted—just, fair and impartial," as opposed to "the one-sided, partial, and very inaccurate reports," rooted in reporters "coming hither with theories and partizan prejudices"—an implicit reference to Schurz.[12]

Certainly Watterson advocated a rapid restoration and rejected efforts to revolutionize the southern social order. "Nothing would tend more to cement the broken Union than the exercise of clemency on the part of the Executive towards our prominent men," he suggested in one newspaper piece.[13] Like Johnson, Watterson, too, was "for a white man's government, and in favor of free white citizens controlling the country." In pursuit of this goal, he assailed the efforts of black troops and Freedmen's Bureau agents to support the ex-slave and to redress grievances. In pushing for a return to normal conditions he lobbied for the ejection of treasury agents, who in disrupting business increased friction between North and South.

In recognition of Watterson's concern about southern cotton, Johnson dispatched him south once more in January, 1866, in the company of Assistant Secretary of the Treasury William E. Chandler. Both Chandler and Watterson agreed that the cotton agents should be withdrawn as soon as possible, although Chandler offered a somewhat different perspective on southern behavior. "The people of the South are bitter, ugly, and out of sorts," he wrote, although he added that they "only ask to be allowed the privilege of grumbling, swearing and threatening a little." Chandler thought this was to be expected, adding that he could not "concur in any representation that matters here are radically bad— they are only superficially so."[14] Watterson wrote no additional letters reviewing the situation, confining himself to two short dispatches concerning the cotton business. In fact, one wonders if his presence did not

11. Iverson L. Harris to Watterson, December 29, 1865, Johnson Papers, LC.
12. Louisville *Journal*, reprinted in the Augusta *Constitution*, October 1, 1865; New Orleans *Picayune*, October 13, 1865.
13. Nashville *Republican Banner*, October 22, 1865.
14. Chandler to [?], January 14, 1866, enclosed in Hugh McCulloch to Johnson, January 20, 1866, Johnson Papers, LC.

represent a conflict of interest, as he was also working for a law firm representing claims against the Treasury Department.[15] In any case, it is doubtful that further correspondence would have revealed any disagreement between Watterson and Johnson, for, as Chandler commented on his return, "I notice that nearly everyone who goes South, whether Radical or Conservative, comes back confirmed in his previous opinions."[16] To this truism Watterson was certainly no exception.

15. Watterson to Johnson, January 29, 1866; Harris to Watterson, December 29, 1865, Johnson Papers, LC.
16. Chandler to O. P. Hubbard, March 5, 1866, William E. Chandler Papers, New Hampshire Historical Society.

Letters

Montgomery, Ala Sept. 26, 1865

His Excellency Andrew Johnson
President of the U.S.
Sir.

I have been in Montgomery seven days—have formed the acquaintance personally of all the men of mind in the Constitutional Convention
now in session, as well as many leading citizens of the City and State.
The sentiment of cheerful acquiescence in the result of the War is universal. No man fit to be out of a lunatic assylum thinks of any further
resistance by arms to the authorities of the Union. The Convention has
already wiped out slavery and declared the secession ordinance of '61
null and void. There is no doubt but it will soon pass an ordinance repudiating the debt contracted by the State for War purposes.[1] Everything will be done that they believe to be indispensable to the resumption
of old relations with the Federal Government. All are willing to lend a
helping hand in the work of restoration[.]

Among the intelligent classes no grumblers are to be found. It is
truly a sublime spectacle to witness the cheerfulness of men who have
been reduced from affluence to poverty. A more admirable and philo-
sophic spirit has never been exhibited by any people on earth. Instead of
mourning or cursing over their misfortunes, they have resolved to make
amends, as speedily as possible, for the errors of the past, and recuperate, if it can be done, their broken fortunes.

The time was that the colored troops were giving a good deal of annoyance to the citizens of Montgomery.[2] That time has passed. There
are but few here now, and of them I hear no complaint.

With the Freedmen's Bureau, it being a new thing under the sun, it
can hardly be expected that the people will become reconciled in a day.
I understand that its operations, at first, created much dissatisfaction,
but under the late orders from Washington[3] and their faithful execution
by Gen Swayne, who is altogether a gentleman and eminently qualified
for his new position, it is but seldom that any murmurs are heard upon
the subject. I apprehend but little trouble in any quarter, as it respects
the freedmen, where the Assistant Commissioner is a man of integrity
and brains. Fortunately for the people of South Alabama Gen Swayne
possesses both.

There has been much complaint, and justly, too, I have no doubt, of
civil and military cotton thieves. A rogue is a rogue, and never respected your rights nor mine. Gen Davies[4] has recently issued a strin-
gent order in regard to the seizure of cotton, and since then there have

been no further depredations.[5] Some of these official cotton scamps have been arrested and exposed. Years of hard labor in the Penitentiary should be their fate.

The gentlemen appointed by you to civil positions, so far as I can learn, are discharging their respective duties with fidelity and satisfaction to the public.

Against Gov Parsons I have never heard a whisper of discontent. He is a man of sense—and when I say this I intend to pay him a high compliment. Just and kind to all, he is universally esteemed.[6] You were fortunate in your selection of a Provisional Governor for the state of Alabama.

You are well aware of the fact, doubtless, that, during the whole four years of war, nearly the entire Press of the South were down on Andrew Johnson. The keenest as well as the most vulgar epithets were applied to him—all of which were swallowed by the people with a relish. What a change has come over their minds within the past few months. From Nashville to Montgomery I have heard nothing but compliments of President Johnson. The confidence they repose in his unbending fidelity to the Constitution and to the whole country, serves to buoy up their spirits and make them forget the calamities that have befallen them. That an undivided South and every conservative man in the North, will ere long be rallying around and sustaining the National Administration, I will not permit myself to question. Surely, surely, things are rapidly drifting in that direction, and I rejoice to know it.

I shall leave for Jackson, Mi, to-morrow, and will return by way of Mobile to Georgia.

Your friend & obedient servant
H. M. Watterson

ALS, DLC-JP.

1. Two days later Governor Parsons informed the President that the convention had that day repudiated the war debt by a 60–19 vote. Parsons to Johnson, September 28, 1865, Johnson Papers, LC.

2. In July the New York *World* printed a report from Montgomery, deploring the behavior of Andrew J. Smith's XVI Corps. "Montgomery is the worst governed city we have met," it declared. "A perfect saturnalia of debauchery and misrule seems to have set in." No black troops, however, were singled out for especial criticism, nor do the records suggest that black regiments were stationed there, although an inspection of black regiments stationed elsewhere in the state reported evidence of their poor discipline and training. Department commander Gen. Charles R. Woods requested his superior to replace the elements of the XVI Corps in Montgomery with "troops that can be depended on: the task of keeping every thing quiet would be very much simplified." New York *World*, July 20, 1865; Woods to W.D. Whipple, September 20, 1865, Dept. of Ala., Lets. Sent, RG393, NA; Post Returns, Montgomery, August 1, 1865, RG94, NA; E. Grosskopff to A. Von Schrader, November 1, 1865, Dept. of Ala., Lets. Recd., RG393, NA.

3. Probably a reference to General Howard's September 12 order, explicitly approved by Johnson, which virtually halted confiscation proceedings. Swayne had also moved to regulate labor contract arrangements, an issue of great concern to planters. Nieman, *To Set the Law in Motion*, 53; Fleming, *Reconstruction in Alabama*, 435–36.

4. Henry E. Davies (1836–1894), who entered the war as captain, 5th N.Y. Inf.

(Duryée's Zouaves), in 1861, saw service in the Army of the Potomac, rising to the rank of major general. After Appomattox he headed the Middle District of Alabama until his resignation in January, 1866. An observer reported to Grant's headquarters that prior to Davies's arrival in Montgomery "the troops were in a confused state, and in some cases inclined to be mutinous." James H. Hardie to John A. Rawlins, December 28, 1865, Dept. of Ala., Lets. Recd., RG393, NA.

5. On September 4, department headquarters ordered military commissions to try civilians accused of stealing government cotton. Five days later Woods complained that civil authorities had proven unable to stop such thievery, with armed bands seizing cotton with impunity. When several cotton agents were brought to trial and convicted, the President sustained the actions of the military commissions. Statement of Charles R. Woods, September 9, 1865, *Schurz Report*, 61; Fleming, *Reconstruction in Alabama*, 413–14.

6. Watterson's desire to flatter the President led him to exaggerate the state's euphoria over Parsons' appointment. Die-hard unionists in north Alabama did not praise Johnson's choice for provisional governor, claiming that Parsons' involvement in the Confederate war effort cast doubt upon his loyalty to the Union. *Ibid.*, 346–47, 352.

DISPATCH NO 6

Mobile, Ala. Oct 3 1865

His Excellency Andrew Johnson
President of the U.S.
Sir.

In my opinion there never was in Alabama such unanimity on any question as there is on the question that the civil strife has ended and that the result is a *finality*. I have neither seen nor heard of a man in the State who regards it in any other light or who looks to any thing but how he can best ⟨promote⟩ put his house in order under and in conformity with the condition of affairs. Every one considers it his first and highest interest to get the State in the Union, as the proper and only means of preserving liberty, and his hope is to accomplish it by heartily supporting and co-operating with the Executive; and the more so, because all know and feel that in the present state of affairs they enjoy practically neither liberty nor protection of the law of the rights of property.

I am satisfied that one of the chief sources of demoralization, among the people, arises from the conduct of subordinate Treasury agents in respect to Government cotton. The Government is defrauded, the people demoralized and made to feel that they are wronged.

The frauds are accomplished by a simple process. A *proper man for the matter* is sent out to collect Government cotton. He goes with the planter's obligation to the Confederate Government, which obligation has been turned over to the U.S. and takes the cotton, employing if necessary military force. When he gets it, the cotton is shipped to a *private consignee*, sold as private cotton and the proceeds divided among *all* concerned. Papers are held for showing to the Government that this cotton really was not Government cotton but was sold in fact by the

Confederate Government to individuals before the surrender—and the Government never learns what has become of it. The planter never heard of any transfer—no owner calls on him for the cotton—he delivers it as Government cotton, (sometimes is paid *in a spirit of liberality* a small sum per pound not to quarrel)—when got, it is no longer *Government* cotton but is passed through the treasury agency here as private cotton—pays its dues as such and is sold &c. Now if Mr A or B is pertinacious and sues the individual who has thus passed his cotton through, and seizes the cotton by legal process, it suddenly becomes Government cotton and a military order is invoked to take it from the warehouse where it is in custody of law and restore it to the Government agent as *Government cotton*. If it passes quietly it is not Government but *individual* cotton: if sued for, it becomes Government cotton and is taken as such.

These facts I have gathered from sources that leave not a shadow of doubt on my mind as to their truth[.]

It is easy to see what a game of open and shut this is; and that the demoralization and discontent produced among the people far transcends any benefit that will accrue to the Government from the cotton it will receive[.]

It is also easy to see how agents so armed to take what ever they may choose to claim, will have their avarice inflamed to regulate their demands only by their desires. I believe the Government is now suffering more from these abuses in Alabama than can be counted or computed in money.

The advent into this state at the present time of the U.S. Treasury agent for the First Special Agency[1] is most opportune. In reference to his movements the Selma *Free Press* says:

> The presence in our midst of Gen. Joseph. R. Dillon, supervising special agent of the Treasury for this state, should be welcomed by the people as the harbinger of better times. His publications touching the delivery of Government cotton, are conceived in excellent taste, and evince a spirit of liberality to the planters which we have no doubt will be met by them in a similar spirit, and greatly redound to the interest of both Government and people. The citizens of this state have been much annoyed and harrassed by people claiming to be Treasury agents. It will be seen by Gen Dillon's orders that the occupations of all such are "gone"! and that the Government has in[it]iated a fresh point of departure in the cotton business, not only in its own interest, but especially in that, of good feeling among our people[.]

I clip a paragraph from an article on the same subject in the Mobile Register, edited by Hon John Forsyth, present Mayor of the City:

> President Johnson has had his eye on this cotton business, and has seen its enormities of wholesale speculation, vexation to the people and consequent widespread demoralization, and is determined to correct it so far as so enormous an evil can be reached. Mr Dillon's instructions are imbued with the spirit of these ideas, and it is hoped that he will be met fairly and squarely by all who hold cotton claimed by the Government. Under his administration private rights will be strictly respected[.][2]

I shall leave to-morrow for Jackson, Mi.

Your friend & obt servant H. M. Watterson

ALS, DLC-JP.

1. Joseph R. Dillin (c1832–1889) was appointed special agent and acting surveyor of customs in Nashville in 1863.

2. Many white Alabamians later charged that Dillin, far from halting the plague of profiteering, participated in questionable practices. Fleming, *Reconstruction in Alabama*, 301–2.

DISPATCH NO 7

Jackson. Mi. Oct 7th 1865

His Excellency Andrew Johnson
President of the U.S.
Sir.

(No fair-minded man, who is acquainted with the true state of popular sentiment in the South, can read the late speeches of Thadeus Stephens,[1] Charles Sumner, and Benjamin. F. Butler, and not feel supreme disgust for those chronic agitators and would be assassins of Southern character. If they have uttered a word of truth, it seems to have been done to gild a falsehood and thereby make it pass as genuine coin.)[2] Right in the face of their declarations to the contrary I will venture to say, that Mississippi and all the States that joined the Rebellion, are at the present time more loyal to the National Government than they have been for the last twenty years. Threats of breaking up the Union are no longer heard—thoughts of setting up a Southern Confederacy are no longer entertained. The Southern people have seen the *elephant*,[3] and they want to see him no more. They are like a fighting fellow at Nashville, some years ago, who, passing down the street, heard a *row* in a grocery. Pricking up his ears he said—"Boys, do you hear that? There's a fight—I'll take *stock in that*". Whereupon he *pitched in*, but in the course of a few minutes he came *rushing out* with sundry *brickbats* following him! He ran off some fifty paces and cried out—"Boys, by George, that stock wont pay!" So it is with the Southern people who took "stock" in the Great Rebellion. Instead of its yielding the promised and expected dividend, they find that the investment has nearly ruined them; and they are all anxious to make a treaty of perpetual amity with their offended Government— Mississippi was the second state to adopt an Ordinance of Secession. She is now second to none in her sincere desire to renew former relations with the Federal Union. She may make mistakes in selecting men to fill certain offices, but be assured that they are not committed in hostility to the authorities of the Nation. Far— very far from it. I understand that Gen. Humphreys,[4] the Governor elect, was one of the most conservative men in the State—almost the counterpart in conservatism of Gov. Sharkey—that he fought the heresy of Secession as long as any man in Mississippi was permitted to fight it. But, alas! when the storm came, it swept him along with all his neighbors and friends. Being elected the Captain of a military company, he accepted the position, and was afterwards made a Brigadier General. Being universally popular with the men under his command, and with all the Mississippians in the Confederate army, it is not strange that they were found to be his fast friends in the recent contest for Governor—a position that he never sought, as I learn, and never desired. He and his supporters, it is agreed on all hands, are now as loyal as any men in the State, or elsewhere—his triumph means nothing inimical to the Government of the United States. It simply means that he has more friends than the other gentlemen who were in the field for Gubernatorial honors. The universal hope is that his election will give no offence at Washington, for none was intended. So says Gov Sharkey—So says Judge Fisher—[5] so says Judge Yerger,[6] and so say all.

The Congressmen elect, Gov Sharkey assures me, never belonged to the secession school. They are known in the State as conservative men—union men, if you please—but whether they can all take the severe oath enacted by Congress in '62, is doubtful.[7] The truth is, that it is difficult, very difficult indeed, to find Congressional timber, in any of these cotton states, which can stand the *test*. What is to be done about it, God knows, for I am sure I do not.

I have been informed that Col. Thomas,[8] the Assistant Commissioner of the Freedmen's Bureau for Mississippi is a young man entirely disposed to discharge his duties honestly. The misfortune is that he has much to learn—especially on the subject of negroes. Ask any man that you may chance to meet in the road or in the streets what are giving the people of Mississippi the greatest annoyance and he will tell you— *negro troops and the Freedmen's Bureau*. Gov Sharkey informs me that he has written to you freely and fully on both subjects;[9] and such I know to be your confidence in his judgment and honesty of purpose, that I deem it unnecessary to say any thing more in regard to these matters. Nor do I deem it at all necessary to drop any opinion of my own in relation to his peculiar fitness for the work you were pleased to assign him. It is sufficient for me to say I rejoice that you have sustained him, gloriously sustained him, in his noble efforts to give repose to his state, and strength to the cause of the Union. Permit me to remark that your endorsement of his militia call,[10] electrified the whole South. From that day to this, I have met with no man who has not a kind word to say of President Johnson. Long life to him, is the fervent prayer of all.

Your friend & obt. S'vt H. M. Watterson

ALS, DLC-JP.

1. Although favoring a protective tariff and a greenback currency, Republican congressman Thaddeus Stevens (1792–1868) is most remembered for his relentless ad-

vocacy of a stern approach to Reconstruction and for his role in Johnson's impeachment.

2. At Lancaster, Pa., on September 6, Stevens had advocated a severe approach to reconstruction, including confiscation and land redistribution, under congressional supervision. Eight days later, at the Massachusetts Republican convention at Worcester, Sumner charged that "the rebel spirit still prevails," and that Congress, not the President, had "plenary powers" over the whole subject of reconstruction, including black suffrage. At the same meeting, Butler expressed his reservations about Johnson's lenient approach and called for the punishment of Rebel leaders and the enfranchisement of blacks. Current, *Old Thad Stevens*, 214–16; Donald, *Sumner and the Rights of Man*, 226–28; Trefousse, *Ben Butler*, 181–82.

3. To confront a crisis, sometimes for the first time, or to undergo an ordeal. The term was most often used in describing the experience of westward trekkers or green troop undergoing fire for the first time. Mary McD. Gordon, ed., *Overland to California with the Pioneer Line: The Gold Rush Diary of Bernard J. Reid* (Stanford, 1983), 31n; Bell I. Wiley, *The Life of Billy Yank: The Common Soldier of the Union* (New York, 1952), 69.

4. Prewar Whig planter and Confederate general Benjamin G. Humphreys (1808–1882) was elected governor in 1865. At the time of his election, he had yet to secure a pardon from President Johnson; three days later, on October 5, the President granted it. Reelected in 1868, he was turned out of office by Military Governor Adelbert Ames. See Humphreys to Johnson, October 26, 1865, Johnson Papers, LC; Harris, *Presidential Reconstruction in Mississippi*, 116.

5. Lawyer, judge, and Whig politician Ephraim S. Fisher (1815–1876) sat on the High Court of Errors and Appeals before the war. His participation in the war effort was limited to a short tenure as colonel of the home guard in 1864. Proposed by the 1865 constitutional convention for the governorship, he lost to Humphreys in the fall election.

6. Either J. Shall Yerger or his brother William. J. Shall Yerger (1816–1867), a Whig lawyer and unionist, had resisted secession at the 1861 convention. Elected president of the constitutional convention in 1865, by the end of the year he was a circuit judge. William Yerger (c1804–fl1873), also a Whig, unionist, and lawyer, had served on the High Court of Errors and Appeals (1851–53). He met with Johnson in 1865 to discuss Mississippi's fate; he advised southerners to accept the terms offered them, including extending the vote to blacks, in 1865 and 1867.

7. Although the electees (James T. Harrison, Absalom M. West, Richard A. Pinson, Arthur E. Reynolds, and Ephraim G. Peyton) had all opposed secession in 1860, Congress refused to seat them when it convened in December, 1865. Harris, *Presidential Reconstruction in Mississippi*, 114–15. On the impact of the ironclad oath, see Watterson to Johnson, July 8, 1865, n. 5.

8. In 1863 Samuel Thomas (1840–1903) was placed in charge of the freedmen around Vicksburg and supervised the Davis Bend experiment. His actions as assistant commissioner of the Freedmen's Bureau in Mississippi in 1865 irritated many whites, including Jefferson Davis' brother Joseph. Their complaints to Johnson helped bring about his transfer to Washington in 1866; he resigned at the end of the year. See Janet S. Hermann, *The Pursuit of a Dream* (New York, 1981), 45–91.

9. In late August, Sharkey had complained to Johnson that "the presence of negro soldiers is not always a protection," since the black garrisons attracted freedmen "in great numbers" who "are idle and guilty of many petty crimes." The widespread impression among white southerners "that the north will be content with nothing but the humiliation & degradation of the south," he suggested, arose "to some extent from the management of the freed mens beareau here." Sharkey to Johnson, August 28, 1865, Johnson Papers, LC.

10. A reference to Johnson's sustaining Sharkey's proposal to raise state militia over the objections of Gen. Henry W. Slocum and Carl Schurz. See Schurz to Johnson, August 29, September 1, 2, and 4, 1865.

New Orleans, La. Oct 14th 1865

His Excellency Andrew Johnson
President of the U.S.
Sir.

What I have said of Virginia, North Carolina, Alabama, and Mississippi loyalty, is true of Louisiana, and need not be repeated. Like causes have produced like results in all the Southern states.

The endorsement of Governor Wells by both the late State Conventions [1] is a deserved tribute to his integrity as a man and to his efficiency as a public officer. He has had to meet many difficult questions and encounter some factious opposition. But in all such cases he sternly discharged his duty and let consequences take care of themselves. The people properly appreciate his services, and have resolved to retain them four years longer.

The principal obstacles to the restoration of order, industry and prosperity of Louisiana, have arisen from the intermeddling of the agents of the Freedmen's Bureau, who have encouraged the negroes to leave the plantations, and have filled them with prejudices and ill feeling against their former owners and present proprietors. [2]

The agents of the Bureau by assuming exclusive jurisdiction of all complaints made by or against the freedman, have deprived the citizens of all the benefits of civil trial. [3] They are subjected to arrest by negro guards on all complaints of negroes; and on the trial have no opportunity of summoning witnesses—execution issues immediately—property is seized and judgment satisfied without any regard to the processes or rights accorded by the laws to all citizens. These trials are conducted by irresponsible subalterns of the Bureau, and are a mockery of all law and justice[.]

The same Bureau has imposed a tax upon all property holders for the education of the Freedman—and, if said tax is not paid after notice, in five days, property is seized to satisfy the claim. [4]

There is no necessity for any such intermediary tribunal in Louisiana, as the laws admit and receive the testimony of freedmen, and give them all and the same civil rights possessed by white freemen. [5]

The administration of the Freedmen's Bureau in Louisiana, has been productive of incalcuable evils to both whites and blacks. According to New Orleans Price Current, the production of the sugar region occupied by them has been reduced from 380,547 hogsheads in 1861 to 6,668 in 1864—from four hundred thousand bales of cotton to ten thousand. [6]

The mortality among the negroes in [the] charge of the Bureau, was never equalled by the ravages of the most terrible epidemics; The Rev Mr Conway in his final report [7] omits a statement of this mortality, but the evidence exists that it has reached a quarter of the negroes who have been gathered on his "home colonies."[8] These "home colonies" have been an enormous expense and burden to the Government and the people. If the sum charged to the Government is not so great, it is because the deficiency has been made up by taxes and confiscation of the people, which have been carried on in the most merciless and desolating manner. These "colonies," besides being the seat of disease and demoralization, have been used, as depots for goods and produce, to trade and speculate on the neighboring planters and to smuggle into the Confederate lines. Large fortunes have been made by government officials, who, under pretext of supplying these "colonies" with subsistence, have carried on large trades in the country.

All Mr Conway's assertions of the prejudice and hostility to the negroes on the part of the whites are untrue—the product of his imagination, his fanaticism, or his malice.[9] The greatest injury which has been done the negroes, has been done by his success in inculcating this idea into their minds and keeping alive their hostility and ill feeling against the whites.

There are five negro regiments in the city, whose presence is a constant source of annoyance to the people and of encouragement of the negroes to acts of insolence.

Mr Conway has been the prominent leader of a party composed almost exclusively of Federal officers in this city, who have passed resolutions and published inflammatory addresses to the negroes to disregard the municipal law and the police regulations, in forcing themselves into cars appropriated to the white people, when there is abundant accommodation in cars allotted to the negroes, which are in every respect equal in accommodation, to those assigned to the whites.[10]

The military still claim and exercise a supervision and interference in civil and judicial affairs which they no where else exercise. In the most ordinary transactions between individuals, and in all affairs of the City administration, this interference is constant and vexatious. The General Commanding[11] is an honest and in the main just man, but his views of the right, duty and policy of military interference in civil matters, are absurd and extravagant to a degree.[12]

The people of this city are loyal and peaceful. The administration of Justice and of the civil law is in the hands of men, who were originally union men,—who were not involved in the Confederate movements,[13] and who can be safely trusted with all the powers needful to secure law, justice, peace, and order.

The pardons and amnesty extended by the President to many persons, are entirely disregarded by certain officers. The Provost Marshalls are now proceeding to strike from the registry of voters the names of persons who were pardoned and admitted to the "exercise of all their civil rights" by the Executive Proclamation for alledged antecedent acts.[14]

Such is my report from New Orleans. I have obtained the facts given from Gov Wells and a score of other gentlemen equally entitled to credit.

I shall set out for Georgia in a few hours[.]

Your friend & Obt. Svt
H. M. Watterson

ALS, DLC-JP.
1. Early October conventions, called by the Conservative Union and Democratic parties, endorsed Wells's reelection. McCrary, *Lincoln and Reconstruction*, 335–36.

2. In July, Freedmen's Bureau Assistant Commissioner Thomas W. Conway directed his subordinates to inform blacks that, while they had to work, "they will in all cases enter into free and voluntary contracts with employers of their own choice. . . . Officers carrying out this order must, in all cases, give the freedmen to understand that they are entirely free to work where and for whom they please, and at the same time that a life of idleness will not be encouraged or allowed." This reversed previous policies which forced blacks to remain on plantations; Watterson's conclusion echoed Governor Wells's complaint in July that Conway's order would "utterly demoralize the negroes . . . to say nothing of the dangerous and revengeful spirit that idleness, and want may engender in the breasts of the negroes toward the whites." New Orleans *Tribune*, July 18, 1865; Wells to Johnson, July 29, 1865, Johnson Papers, LC.

3. Conway, in July, had removed cases involving blacks accused of violating vagrancy statutes from the civil courts; by September he had established Bureau-operated courts in areas where civil courts continued to discriminate against blacks. Howard A. White, *The Freedmen's Bureau in Louisiana* (Baton Rouge, 1970), 135–36.

4. In reality, Freedmen's Bureau agents had merely intensified efforts to collect a tax to fund public education levied by Gen. Nathaniel P. Banks in 1864. These efforts proved frustrating; in October, 1865, Johnson compounded the problem by directing that collection of the tax be suspended. *Ibid.*, 167–76; William F. Messner, "Black Education in Louisiana, 1863–1865," *Civil War History*, XXII (March, 1976), 48–49; James S. Fullerton to Johnson, October 29, 1865, Johnson Papers, LC.

5. Carl Schurz and other observers pointed out that local ordinances passed in the summer of 1865 had patently restricted the civil rights of Louisiana blacks. As might be expected, Commissioner Conway also questioned the fairness of civil officials in administering the law. Schurz to Johnson, September 4, 1865; White, *Freedmen's Bureau*, 136.

6. Watterson's inference—that the actions of the Freedmen's Bureau were responsible for the drop in production levels—is fallacious. The impact of war, in terms of physical destruction, disruption, and the loss of capital, was far more responsible for the decline. Too, 1861 represented a boom year in sugar production, which had averaged 250,000 hogsheads yearly through the 1850's. Taylor, *Louisiana Reconstructed*, 364–80.

7. Conway's 1865 report on black labor conditions in Louisiana was intended to promote the free labor wage system established by General Banks. McFeely, *Yankee Stepfather*, 170–75; C. Peter Ripley, *Slaves and Freedmen in Civil War Louisiana* (Baton Rouge, 1976), 85–86.

8. Several plantations were established by Louisiana's Bureau of Negro Labor to provide for old and infirm blacks. Conway's report did mention "the apparently large number of sick," but reminded readers "that the main object . . . of these colonies . . . was to provide a place of refuge and a *home* for the aged and helpless freedman thrown on the Bureau for support." *Ibid.*, 54; McFeely, *Yankee Stepfather*, 174.

9. Watterson's statement is more a revelation of his own prejudices than a statement of fact.

10. New Orleans street cars were segregated, with cars for black use marked with a black star. In August, 1865, in response to black protests, General Canby ordered a halt to the practice of segregation. Within weeks U.S. Provost Judge Benedict overruled Canby on the grounds that the directive infringed upon the rights of private corporations. In contrast to Watterson's comment that "abundant accommodation" was available to blacks, complaints appeared in New Orleans papers that whites, unable to find a seat on cars reserved for them, often crowded into "star cars," ejecting black passengers. Roger

A. Fischer, *The Segregation Struggle in Louisiana, 1862–77* (Urbana, Ill., 1974), 31–32.

11. Gen. E.R.S. Canby. The New Orleans correspondent of the New York *World* reported that he "is the most popular man ever sent here by the government. He is universally admired and respected, and our citizens are satisfied he will do all in his power to advance the interests of Louisiana." New York *World*, September 4, 1865.

12. In contrast, Canby, who found his position distasteful and frustrating, told Schurz the previous month that he had "abstained from any interference with questions of civil or local state administration, except when it was necessary to protect the freedmen in their newly acquired rights, and to prevent the local courts from assuming jurisdiction in cases where . . . [it] belongs inclusively to the United States courts or United States authorities." Four months earlier he had assured Wells of his desire "to divest myself as soon as possible of all questions of civil administration." A conservative New Orleans paper praised the general: "In his present position Gen. Canby is the shield and protection of our people, instead of an oppressor and tyrant." Canby to Schurz, September 8, 1865 and Canby to Wells, June 19, 1865, *Schurz Report*, 55, 56; New Orleans *Picayune*, October 7, 1865.

13. Other testimony casts doubt on the validity of this assertion. Conway told the Joint Committee on Reconstruction that he had appointed as judges, mayors, and other officials, men still wearing Confederate uniforms; Police Chief John Burke reported that Wells had instructed him to hire Confederate veterans. Wells's supporters themselves indirectly gave the lie to Watterson's claim when they defended the governor's appointment policy on the grounds that not enough qualified unionists existed to fill these positions. Albert Voorhies, Wells's running mate in the fall election, and Robert C. Wickliffe, Democratic congressional nominee, were also ex-Confederates. Walter M. Lowrey, "The Political Career of James Madison Wells," *Louisiana Historical Quarterly*, 31 (October, 1948), 1040; McCrary, *Lincoln and Reconstruction*, 336.

14. On September 1, Canby ordered his provost marshal general to furnish registrars with the names of all residents who, after registering as loyal voters during the war, fled Union-occupied Louisiana to avoid the draft or "evaded the duties and obligations of citizenship." The next month found provost marshals busily inspecting registration books "with a view to strike from the rolls" Louisianans "charged with acts of disloyalty antecedent to the President's amnesty proclamation, and of these who in 1862 registered themselves enemies of the United States." Johnson overruled Canby. New York *Tribune*, September 18, 1865; Montgomery *Advertiser*, October 19, 26, 1865; New York *World*, October 16, 1865; New Orleans *Picayune*, October 15, 17, 22, 1865.

DISPATCH NO 9

Columbus, Ga. Oct 20th 1865

His Excellency Andrew Johnson
President of the U.S.
Sir.

I am working my way round to Milledgeville, where the Constitutional Convention of Georgia will meet on the 25th instant. Being able to ascertain nothing in Columbus that it is important for the President to know, I have concluded to devote this letter to matters and things generally[.]

While I was in New-Orleans I received information that induced me to think that Gov Hamilton[1] of Texas is *not* exactly the right man in the right place. My informants represented that he is odious to a large majority of his people and not at all disposed to conciliate them by acts of simple justice.[2] If this is true you doubtless know it; if it be not, I shall regret that I mentioned the subject.

I think it probable that I have talked with as many intelligent gentlemen, since I left Nashville—a little more than a month ago—as any other man would have done in the same length of time. I am not mistaken in the fact that a mighty revolution has been wrought in the minds and hearts of the Southern people in reference to the President. They were afraid that he would treat them with vindictiveness. Instead of that, he is all kindness. He says in words—and his acts attest their sincerity—"I entertain no personal resentments, enmities, or animosities to any living soul South of Mason's and Dixon's line, however much he may have differed from me in principle". A noble sentiment—worthy of the head of a great nation. It sent a thrill of admiration for its author through the entire South. There may be and doubtless are some scurvy fellows who still cherish malignant feelings, but there is not a sufficient number of them to make mile-posts on the main highways. No Southern State will elect a Senator or Representative to Congress, who is known to be opposed to the developed policy of the National Administration. It is now universally believed in the South that the grand idea in the President's mind is to restore her, on constitutional and just principles, to her old re[l]ations in the Union. That she will stand by him is just as certain as that God made Moses. I need not tell you that I have done all I could to strengthen and give consistency to this confidence. I believe, for the first time in my life, that he who strengthens the President strengthens the Government. So deeply imbedded in my mind is this opinion, that were I your personal enemy instead of your personal friend—if I know my self—my course would be precisely the same.

In reply to the question whether I think the South will be admitted into the next Congress, I always say;—"That depends upon the strength of the National Administration in that body and the character of the material she elects"—not forgetting to impress on my interrogator the importance of sending men who can take the prescribed oath.[3] I sometimes tread on the toes of an aspirant, but I cant help that. It is best that he should know the truth in time not to put himself in a position where the Congressional door may be slammed in his face.

Our old friend Gov. Fitzpatrick,[4] whom I regard as an honest man, and whom I was glad you pardoned, told me in Montgomery, that his friends wanted to elect him to the Senate of the United States, but he did not desire the position. I thought I could clearly see that he was mistaken as to his wishes on the subject. *I have no idea that he would decline the honor, if tendered*. It does seem to me that his withdrawal from that body in '61, after fully endorsing the speech of his colleague,[5] would make his re-admission in '65 somewhat difficult. I think it would be best for him not to make the attempt. This is a time when no Southern man should suffer his political aspirations to become a stumbling block in the way of a speedy return to old Federal relations.

I had quite a talk with Judge Iverson[6] this morning. You know that the mercury in his disunion thermometer stood for many years before the war at least ninety degrees above zero. It indicated intense heat. Now it stands at least ninety degrees below zero—indicating intense cold. In other words, he sees and feels the result of the great mistake he and his political associates made, and his face is now turned in the opposite direction. Like everybody else he speaks kindly of the President.

I shall leave in the morning for Macon, where I will stay two or three days, and then go over to Milledgeville[.]

Your friend & Obt. Svt
H. M. Watterson

ALS, DLC-JP.

1. Lawyer, state legislator, and congressman Andrew J. Hamilton (1815–1875) fled to Washington, D.C., in 1861, and the following year was appointed brigadier general and military governor of Texas. Continued by Johnson as provisional governor, he failed of election in his own right in 1866. Appointed associate justice of the state supreme court, he was unsuccessful in another bid for the governor's chair in 1869.

2. Hamilton's August 25 announcement outlining voter registration for the state's constitutional convention did not allow all who had taken the amnesty oath to vote in the upcoming elections, a decision contrary to Johnson's desires. Texas Democrats, objecting to the exclusion of many former rebels, immediately moved to assure the President of the readiness of the Lone Star State for a rapid reconstruction, causing Johnson to wonder about Hamilton's charges of continuing Texan disloyalty. Carl H. Moneyhan, *Republicanism in Reconstruction Texas* (Austin, Texas, 1980), 25–37.

3. The ironclad oath.

4. Prewar Democratic governor and senator Benjamin Fitzpatrick (1802–1869) returned to public life to preside over the 1865 state constitutional convention.

5. When Fitzpatrick resigned his Senate seat in January, 1861, he concurred in the angry charges of his fellow Alabamian, Clement C. Clay, Jr., that unconstitutional and unfriendly acts by Republicans and the northern people had prompted Alabama's secession, statements which in tone differed markedly from Jefferson Davis' gracious farewell speech. Washington *National Intelligencer*, January 22, 1861; New York *Times*, January 22, 1861.

6. Alfred Iverson (1798–1873), prewar state legislator, judge, congressman, and U.S. senator, resigned his seat after Georgia seceded to practice law and manage a plantation.

DISPATCH NO 10

Milledgeville, Ga Oct 30th 1865

His Excellency Andrew Johnson
President of the U.S.
Sir.

History records no such a spectacle as is now exhibited in the Southern states. After a four year's war, which was inaugurated for the purpose of cutting loose from the Government established by their fathers,

Governing Generals:
James B. Steedman and Charles R. Woods.
Courtesy of The National Archives

the Southern people have suddenly laid down their arms and given un-
mistakable evidence of a determination to renew in good faith their former relations. From the Potomac to the Rio Grande, if a hostile foot
treads the soil, it is that of an enemy to civil society—the thief and ma-
rauder. The voice of every good man, within the eleven states lately in
rebellion, is raised in behalf of peace and re-union under the Stars and
Stripes. This fact is manifest to all, whether citizens or soldiers, who
desire to know and proclaim the truth. The man who gainsays it, either
knows not what he is talking about, or he has some selfish purpose to
accomplish by wilful misrepresentation.

Gen. Steadman has been here, and he authorized me to say to the
President, either in person or by letter, that, in his judgment, the necessity for military rule in Georgia has passed and so soon as civil government is re-established in the State the troops ought to be withdrawn.
By the by, the General has shown himself to be a good officer and a just
man. His open, frank, and honorable conduct, has secured the confidence of the people, and he will carry with him on his withdrawal from
Georgia their sincere wishes for his future prosperity.

Gen Tillson,[1] the Assistant Commissioner of the Freedmen's Bureau
for Georgia, is here. I have had with him several conversations that
were interesting to me; and the other night he delivered a public address in the Capitol.[2] His facts were true, his advice excellent, and his
sentiments sound. I endorse every word that he uttered, and will add,
that I was delighted with the kind, conciliatory and gentlemanly manner in which he communicated his views. I have reason to know that
they fell pleasantly on the ears of the entire audience, and have no doubt
that they will do much good. He is a gentleman of fine intelligence—
frank, honest, and just. In him the Georgians have drawn a prize, and
they are not insensible of the fact.[3]

Gov James Johnson, I need not tell you, is a clear-headed, amiable
gentleman. A more faithful public officer can be found nowhere. His
sincere desire has been and is, I have no doubt, to carry out the policy of
the National Administration. That he is a true friend to that Administration, is beyond controversy.

In a conversation I had with Governor Herschel. V. Johnson,[4] he requested me to deliver several messages to the President. I asked him to
reduce them to writing. He has done so, and here is his letter:

Milledgeville Ga October 28th 1865

Hon H. M. Watterson Milledgeville
Dear Sir.

After the States shall have organized their governments on the basis indicated by the President, I would be pleased, if he would publish a Proclamation
to the effect that they are entitled to representation in Congress, provided they
should elect Senators and Representatives *constitutionally* qualified to hold
seats in the two respective branches. I believe I but utter the universal wish and
expectation that he will do so. It would not only delight the Southern States,

but, in my judgment, it would be a stroke of masterly policy. For being *constitutionally* qualified, no party in the North can be sustained who will advocate their rejection.

Such a proclamation will present the issue distinctly, in advance of the assembling of Congress, whether the Union can be fully restored upon *Constitutional* grounds. This involves two distinct advantages. First, it will elicit the popular will, in time to produce a salutary effect upon the members of Congress from the Northern and Western States and thus devellope the strength of the Conservative element in those states. Secondly. The radicals, who intend to make war on the President, will have to accept the issue thus tendered, of restoration and reconstruction upon the basis of the Constitution and force them to take the initiative in the warfare. The rejection of Southern members and senators, on the basis of the *Constitutional* qualifications, is revolutionary in its tendency and must bring upon its authors, the odium of perpetuating a disunion, which they have fought nearly five years to prevent. They, in a word, become the disunion party. I might elaborate these views, but it is needless; your own mind will readily fill up the picture, of which I have but sketched the outlines.

Our Convention is a dignified and intelligent body. It is composed of the best material in the State. It is animated by patriotic purposes and will finally entitle itself to the congratulations of the President. The President need entertain no apprehension, as to the good faith of our people.

The Treasury Department is taking steps to collect internal revenue. This will destroy our people, if the valuation of property according to the assessment of 1860 is adhered to. It ought to be remembered that the tax-paying capacity of our people is exhausted. Property is not actually worth one fourth of the valuation of 1860. The people are without money and they have nothing to sell. I beg you to appeal to the President in our behalf, on this subject. Ask him, for the sake of justice, to cause the valuation of 1860 to be abandoned and to assess the tax according to its present value. We may *possibly* be able to pay on this basis—but the basis of 1860 will ruin thousands, the large majority of whom are widows and orphans and men who are and always have been, men of small means. If the President could know, as we know, the destitution of the people, I feel sure his great heart would be moved in our behalf.

Clothed with as much power of patronage as is the President, I have no doubt of his ability, by legitimate means, to induce the Clerk of the H.R, in calling the role of states, to call the late seceding States. This is of *vast* importance in the work of restoration. For it puts all on an equality before the House is organized and gives all an opportunity to vote for Speaker. In such a condition of things the Southern States would have great power for good.

You may say to the President, with the most perfect confidence, that he can withdraw military power from Georgia, as soon as he pleases. All is safe. Our Legislature will do justice and give ample protection to the freedman. The people are loyal and will, in good faith, maintain the peace, adhere to the Union and obey the laws and Constitution.

Speaking of the subject of taxation above, I should have said that it is impossible to procure the services of competent officers to assess and collect who can take the test oath. It should be modified or waived[.]

Very respectfully   Your Obt
Herschel V. Johnson[5]

It was my purpose to visit Augusta and Savanah—but having seen Generals Steadman and Tillson, as well as several of the most intelligent citizens of those cities, whose reports are all favorable, I deem it unnecessary to extend my mission any further.

I expect to set out for Washington to-morrow, by way of Macon, Atlanta, and Nashville. It is my purpose to stop in the latter city about a week. In the mean time should I learn any thing worth communicating, you shall again hear from me[.]

Your friend & obt Svt

H. M. Watterson

ALS, DLC-JP.

1. Davis Tillson (1830–1895), an artilleryman who commanded a brigade defending Knoxville, supervised Bureau operations in Tennessee and Georgia until his muster out at the end of 1866.

2. On October 25, as the Georgia constitutional convention embarked on its deliberations, Tillson asked Governor James Johnson to approve the employment of county officers as Bureau agents. Aware that such a policy would lessen the impact of military rule, the governor agreed, and Tillson appeared before the delegates to gain their support. They went one step further in approving Tillson's policy, allowing him to name any citizen as an agent. Andrews, *The South Since the War*, 258–59; Alan Conway, *The Reconstruction of Georgia* (Minneapolis, 1966), 77.

3. Most white Georgians applauded Tillson's tenure, since he devoted much energy to compelling blacks to make and observe contracts; they regretted his departure from the Bureau. He, in turn, so identified with planter interests that upon his retirement he became for a short time a Georgia planter. Edmund L. Drago, *Black Politicians and Reconstruction in Georgia* (Baton Rouge, 1982), 114–15.

4. Prewar Democratic senator, judge, and governor Herschel V. Johnson (1812–1880), Stephen A. Douglas' running mate in 1860, attended the 1861 secession convention, and was a member of the Confederate Senate. Presiding over the 1865 state constitutional convention, he was elected to the U.S. Senate in 1866 but was never seated.

5. The President did not heed the Georgian's suggestion to influence Edward McPherson, clerk of the House of Representatives, with the aim of including southern representatives on the roll of the House. As expected, McPherson omitted their names when he called roll on December 4. In his first annual message, Johnson appeared to acquiesce, acknowledging the right of each house of Congress to determine the qualifications of its members.

Benjamin C. Truman:
The Correspondent as Confidant

While Watterson's letters could privately reassure the President that Schurz's findings were the product of a wrong-headed, prejudiced mind, Johnson was justifiably concerned about the impact of the former general's newspaper columns upon the northern public's perception of the success of his policy. Nor was Schurz the only questioning voice appearing in the northern press. In August, Whitelaw Reid's dispatches describing Chase's May journey began appearing in the Cincinnati *Gazette*, prompting one southern paper to comment, "no one could read them all and live." Johnson publicly assured a delegation of southerners on September 11, just over a week after his controversy with Schurz over the Mississippi militia, that he "did not believe the sensation letterwriters and editors, who were endeavoring to create the impression that there exists in the South disaffection and dissatisfaction."[1]

Southern newspapers had already protested against the treatment of their region in the northern press. "It would be very gratifying to the southern people," noted the Wilmington *Herald*, "if the northern newspaper conductors would send into this country some impartial, ingenuous writers, who would do us justice." Another journal deplored "the short-sighted or malicious policy of seizing upon isolated instances of violence and crime in the Southern States—especially if the negro is in any way a victim—and commenting upon them to the prejudice of the returning loyalty and sense of justice of the Southern people." A third paper chastised "irresponsible scribblers" who, "by misrepresenting, insulting, and slandering the Southern people through the Northern press," were spreading "false and scandalous libels." Even several northern journals echoed these complaints. The Springfield *Republican*, reprinting a Memphis paper's protest over newspaper accounts, regretted the "deliberate misrepresentation of the conduct of the people of the South."[2]

What Johnson needed was someone to issue reports countering these impressions. He turned to Benjamin C. Truman, a New York *Times* war correspondent who had served as Johnson's private secretary during the war, to give him another perspective more in line with his own

1. Montgomery *Advertiser*, August 24, 1865; New York *World*, September 12, 1865.
2. Wilmington *Herald*, August 17, 1865; Jackson *Clarion*, August 23, 1865; Columbus (Georgia) *Sun and Times*, October 25, 1865; Springfield *Republican*, August 10, 11, 1865.

prejudices. Some three years before, the twenty-seven-year old Truman had traveled west to Tennessee as a war correspondent for John W. Forney's Philadelphia *Press* and Washington *Morning Chronicle*; later he also filed dispatches for the New York *Times*. In Nashville the reporter edited the Nashville *Press* for several months in 1863 while befriending Johnson, then military governor. Johnson appointed Truman as his private secretary, sending him to Washington several times to look after the Tennessean's interests. The correspondent evidently saw no conflict between his employment by Johnson and his obligations as a reporter; he also served as a volunteer aide on the staff of several generals, and helped raise a black regiment, while establishing a reputation as a capable reporter.[3]

In introducing Truman to President Lincoln in 1862, Johnson had called him "a gentleman of intelligence and character," and asserted, "Whatsoever statement he may make can be implicitly relied upon." Moreover, Truman had taken great pains to assure Johnson of his personal loyalty in the past, reminding the governor of his "high personal regard." Certainly the President wanted someone he could trust to describe conditions in the South, and, if Truman was a bit of a sycophant, at least he would not write in the lecturing tone which all too often characterized Schurz's missives. And, unlike Schurz and Chase, Truman seemed only too happy to serve Johnson's cause.[4]

These qualities, however endearing they may have been in Johnson's eyes, nevertheless augured poorly for Truman's capacity as an observer. While the reporter made it clear in his opening letter that he would not "deceive" the President "by misrepresenting the real feeling of the people," he preferred to view himself as an advocate of Johnson's policy. As a result, he hobnobbed with influential southern whites, including "nearly all of the leading politicians," generals, and editors, while virtually ignoring white unionists and blacks. Wherever he went he made sure to tell people of his connection to Johnson, often exploiting it in "telling rebel editors what to write" and "telling delegates what was required."[5]

In truth, Truman did not envision himself as a passive observer of southern conditions. Rather, he took it upon himself to address what he perceived as one of the major obstacles to Johnson's success, the role of

3. Newspaper correspondents freely blurred the distinction between the press and government authorities, assuming government positions while maintaining their press activity. Sylvanus Cadwallader of the Chicago *Times* and the New York *Herald* often held semi-official status on Ulysses S. Grant's staff. Several papers explicitly linked Truman's mission to Johnson's dissatisfaction with Schurz; see the Cincinnati *Gazette*, September 14, 1865.

4. Johnson to Lincoln, November 8, 1862, in Nashville *Press*, June 27, 1863; Truman to Johnson, November 12, 1863, *Johnson Papers*, VI, 468–71.

5. Truman to Johnson, October 13, 1865, and March 24, 1866.

southern opinion makers, notably newspaper editors, in shaping public opinion on both sides of the Mason-Dixon line. If southern journals had a just cause of complaint in the characterization of southern conditions in northern journals, many of them were also guilty, in the words of the New York *Herald*, of "getting a little wild again."[6] To Truman, southern newspapermen were doing their readers a double disservice in keeping alive the passions of the late conflict by misleading both northerners and southerners about each other's intentions. In the absence of much direct communication, Americans had to rely on newspapers to discover what was going on elsewhere. Most northern newspapers made haste to reprint excerpts from southern newspapers in their search for information. Fire-eating editorials from southern papers simply convinced northern readers that the South did indeed intend to rise again when the time was right. At the same time, such editorials could serve only to increase the resentment of white southerners for the Yankee invader, fostering further hostility. In such circumstances, Johnson's quest for a conservative settlement would encounter great difficulty.

Truman's observations in the first two states he visited, Alabama and Georgia, underscored the problem. While he told Johnson that "there is little or no spontaneous loyalty or love for the United States Government" in Alabama, he noted that whites admitted their defeat and were willing to comply with the President's policy. Original secessionists and veterans alike were foremost among Johnson's supporters. Truman, however, had little positive to say about the "reticence of pulpit orators" or the "non-committal effusions of half-starved editors." He was furious at Bishop Richard Wilmer's refusal to include the President's name in prayers during Episcopal services, calling Wilmer and his ministers "old salaried hypocrites" who would pray for anyone "if they only get well paid for it." Truman finally got Robert McKee, editor of the Selma *Times*, "to understand that it was unwise to be lauding you in one column continually, and slandering everybody else connected with the Government in another." But his most severe criticism was reserved for famed secessionist John Forsyth, who had returned to editing after the war. Truman told the fire-eater "that he was deceiving the people south and enraging the people north" by his editorials, "doing untold injury to the cause."[7]

Some of Truman's dispatches to the New York *Times* seemed to be little more than paraphrases of his letters to the President, as a comparison of Truman's first letter to Johnson and a report on Alabama which appeared in the October 31 edition of the *Times* reveals. As in his letter to Johnson, Truman seemed most concerned with the impact of southern behavior on northern minds. He chastised "the blood-and-

6. New York *Herald*, July 7, 1865.
7. Truman to Johnson, October 13, 1865.

thunder crowd" in the South, claiming that most of its members had remained at home during the war. Ministers who failed to foster reconciliation by including the President in their prayers were denounced as "gander-legged mutton-heads." In contrast, he praised former Confederates as those "most inclined to do right" in securing a lasting peace. In calling attention to Truman's report, the *Times* claimed that the "great value . . . of the pictures given in our correspondence, lies in the fact of their being free from any bias which might attach, on one hand, to a sectional prejudice for the white residents of the South, or on the other, to a cheap and easy patronage of the colored race."[8]

In Georgia, Truman focused his fire on the members of the state's constitutional convention for hesitating to repudiate the Confederate war debt. He began his letter describing the convention's behavior by suggesting that it would have been "better had it never met." Despite Johnson's own warnings that the debt had to be repudiated, delegates continued to search for some way to guarantee payment of some war-related debts. Truman assisted opponents of such measures, feeding them information for use as evidence in speeches. When the convention adjourned, Truman told Johnson's private secretary that "the utmost malignity and meanness and ingratitude was manifest." The delegates were "old and prejudiced men of unprogressive minds." The reporter, however, hastily added that "the people are all right. . . . Everybody *loves* and *fears* the President." To complete the work of reconstruction, Truman advised Georgians and Alabamians to guarantee civil rights for blacks in order to forestall the imposition of black suffrage. After two weeks in Florida, he headed north to Tennessee.[9]

Truman may have deplored newspaper sensationalism, but in at least one report from Georgia he engaged in the practice himself. Schurz had already commented on the escapades of General Edward A. Wild the previous August. Wild had extracted confessions concerning a bank robbery by hanging several individuals by the thumbs—a traditional if painful army practice—and had searched the home of Robert Toombs for hidden contraband. For these actions he had been removed from command in September. Yet, three months later, Truman not only dragged up the incident again, but embellished it with details not found in accounts filed at the time. One of the accused felons was hanged by the thumbs "until the entire flesh was torn from the bones"; the search of the Toombs home became lurid, for Wild had "two of the first ladies of the county . . . stripped naked and examined by two colored women, an indignity I have never heard of before the war." Several southern newspapers eagerly reprinted the account—one which did little to bol-

8. New York *Times*, October 31, 1865.
9. Truman to Johnson, November 1, 1865, and to William A. Browning, November 9, 1865.

ster the image of the Freedmen's Bureau, despite Truman's assertions that the institution was doing good work.[10]

Truman's newspaper reports made no secret of his admiration for Johnson. From Nashville he wrote on New Year's Day, 1866, that the President's plan, "so grand and patriotic in its conception, is only clogged in its execution by the disunionist marplots of the extreme Radical parties in Congress." Nor was the reporter above casting slurs at Johnson's other observers. He praised General George H. Thomas, citing the Rock of Chickamauga's refusal to accept "presents of brownstone houses, or carriages and teams"—an indirect reference to Ulysses S. Grant, who had proven very willing indeed to receive several houses and horses tendered him by grateful northerners. In another column Truman dismissed the pro-Radical Memphis *Loyalist* as "edited by disunionists of the Carl Schurz school." Of course, Truman's objectivity was also open to question, as he unwittingly revealed when he related that he sought information "among those who have ever been steadfast friends of Andrew Johnson and the Union."[11]

From Tennessee, Truman traveled to Arkansas, Mississippi, and Louisiana, but if he wrote Johnson any letters, they have not been preserved. Instead, the President had to follow the course of his correspondent through the *Times*. At Little Rock Truman noted that graycoat veterans "all accept the logic and the terms of the situation gracefully and manfully." In Mississippi, Truman noticed much "bitterness and discontent" in the interior of the state, but in general his letters had lost their incisive edge and had ground down to travelogues. This changed once he entered Texas and headed for the constitutional convention at Austin, arriving February 8. To Johnson he reported that the attitude of the majority of convention delegates led him to believe that the debates would not draw the fire of northern radicals eager for signs of southern recalcitrance. Later he recalled, "I talked with men of all classes, in order to be, and I was, very particular in forming conclusions." With the adjournment of the convention several weeks later, he returned to Washington.[12]

"I feel it my duty to represent these things precisely to the reader as they are," Truman assured his *Times* readers, and, despite his own inclinations, in both his letters to Johnson and his newspaper reports he strove for a degree of fairness. After observing affairs in Georgia for a month, the correspondent noted that he had looked into reports of

10. New York *Times*, December 5, 1865; Nashville *Republican Banner*, December 9, 1865.

11. New York *Times*, January 8, 28, 1866.

12. *Ibid.*, January 29, February 4, 1866; Truman to Johnson, February 8, 1866; *Report of the Joint Committee on Reconstruction*, 39 Cong., 1 Sess., 1866, House Report No. 30, pt. IV, 136–40.

atrocities against blacks, and concluded that "in most cases they prove true. But in most cases it is almost always made evident that those who were shot down were thieves and marauders." No doubt this pleased northern conservatives who claimed that such incidents were either manufactured or distorted to serve as Radical propaganda; since Truman apparently never asked blacks for their accounts of such incidents, he relied on southern whites to relate "what really happened." Yet Truman was not so blind as to ignore all mistreatment of blacks. In the same dispatch he concluded that "no candid man can make himself thoroughly acquainted with the new status of the negro, and be opposed to the Freedmen's Bureau." He further remarked that "no jury could be found in the State that would convict a respectable white person upon negro testimony alone." [13]

Moreover, since Truman freely admitted in conversations with white southerners and army officers his double purpose as a reporter for the *Times* and an observer for Johnson, one can probably assume that the people he talked with kept that in mind. Given Truman's notions of the importance of the press in shaping public opinion and molding sectional stereotypes—beliefs shared by others, including Ulysses S. Grant—his reports stressed the positive. Still, he willingly conceded that a continued military presence and the Freedmen's Bureau were essential to maintain order. [14]

While Truman had an enviable reputation as a war correspondent, some people grumbled about his behavior on his tour for Johnson. The unreconstructed editor of the Memphis *Avalanche* complained that Truman searched "the sewers of filth for morsels of petty scandal with which to feed the viciated taste of his readers" and in so doing "he had to manufacture lies." Taken as a whole, his reports were merely the "slanders of a contemptible penny-a-liner." But Truman's enemies were not confined to staunch ex-rebels. Florida carpetbagger Daniel Richards had occasion to observe Truman in action a few months after his tour. "He rather introduced himself by telling me about what kind of disposition he had and his faults were, if he had any, that he was fond of good wine, champaign suppers and the women," Richards wrote Congressman Elihu B. Washburne. "He has demonstrated fully his talents in that direction since he has been here." The carpetbagger thought he had the reporter under control, but he remained cautious: "Still you can not trust a man who is nearly all the time *drunk*, and surrounded by such influences as he has been since he came here. *I should fear these little rebel girls here could get him to report anything they should desire by granting him what he desires.*" To Lyman Trumbull, Richards commented, "It is a burning shame and disgrace to any government worth

13. New York *Times*, October 31, November 23, 1865.
14. *Report of the Joint Committee on Reconstruction*, 39 Cong., 1 Sess., 1866, House Report No. 30, pt. IV, 136–40.

living under that such a man should be sent on such an errand." Johnson supporters had "furnished him with wine, fine parties, and fine women for which he boasts he has a peculiar talent." As a result, "Truman has wandered or staggered about our streets in a maudlin state." [15]

Throughout his trip Truman had consciously sought to counter the impact of Schurz's reports. Like his antagonist, he composed a summary report, submitting it to Johnson on April 9, 1866—one year after Appomattox.[16] Observing that the vast majority of white southerners "are, at the present time, indifferent toward the General Government," he attributed this to "the violent changes of the past few years," which left "the ideas of the populace greatly unsettled." It was "the skulkers," not the average southerner, who were "prolonging past bitterness" by "editing reckless newspapers" which printed "those pernicious utterances that so little represent the thinking, substantial people, and are so eagerly seized out and paraded by certain Northern journalists, who, themselves, as little represent the great North." Rejecting the notion that southern disloyalty and intransigence had increased as a result of "an ill-timed, ill-advised lenience," he asserted that what seemed to be acquiescence in the weeks following Appomattox was rooted in "fearful suspense" and "the silence of submission, of terror, of defeat." Within weeks southerners had recovered from this immobilized state; the "noisy and reckless utterances of late" were nothing more than "the returning wave that followed the depression of defeat—the inevitable and wholesome reaction from despair."

To those who speculated about southerners' loyalty in terms of their allegiance in case of a war with either England or France, Truman replied that such fears "are highly absurd." Most southerners "are tired of war and are anxious to establish and perpetuate peace." Indeed, he pointed out that many prominent Confederate officers, including Nathan Bedford Forrest, William J. Hardee, and Lafayette McLaws, "would offer their services to the United States Government in *any* capacity, even as a private." Confederate veterans would provide "the real basis of reconstruction and the material of worthy citizenship." He dismissed the general impression that northerners were "bitterly persecuted and compelled to abandon the country," suggesting that if northerners refrained "from bitter political discussions and conduct themselves with ordinary discretion, they soon overcome these prejudices, and are treated with respect." Contrary reports were the creation of correspondents "engaged in writing and circulating falsehoods. For some unpatriotic

15. Memphis *Avalanche*, January 24, 1866; Richards to Washburne, June 7, 1866, Elihu B. Washburne Papers, LC; Richards to Trumbull, June 7, 1866, Lyman Trumbull Papers, LC.

16. Truman to Johnson, April 9, 1866, *Sen. Ex. Doc.* No. 43, 39 Cong., 1 Sess., *passim*. All the following quotations are from this source.

purpose, or other, reports of an incendiary character concerning the southern people are transmitted North. To learn the falseness of these reports one needs only to obtain the facts."

Playing down as signs of continued disloyalty the abstract defenses of secession advanced by several southern politicians and editors, Truman argued that it would be difficult to expect such individuals "to reverse their records *ab initio* and declare freely and without hesitation that all their utterances of the past four years had been mistaken." In support of this contention, he quoted Texas provisional governor Andrew J. Hamilton, who told the reporter, "Politicians must have their 'explanations' and their records, they must be allowed to retreat gracefully and to fall gently; but the vast majority of them are all right at heart. They must have time." Many white southerners now accepted the verdict of Appomattox because of the emerging belief "that in the late war the hand of Providence, the decrees of destiny, were against them." It was "a profound and abiding conviction gradually gaining ground in the southern mind that their late struggle was hopeless from the outset—that it was contrary to the will of the Infinite." Little did Truman realize that he had singled out one of the foundations of the mythology of the Lost Cause which would transfix white southerners well into the next century—that defeat was not a reflection upon their honor or an admission of Yankee superiority, but preordained.

Turning to the issues raised by emancipation, Truman suggested that northerners first understand the framework within which white southerners perceived their black counterparts: "Everyone who conscientiously seeks to know the whole truth should not ignore their beliefs, while he censures the revolting practices." Unlike Schurz, who believed that the best way to change white perceptions was vigorously to assert and protect a new order based on free labor, Truman argued that only time eradicated prejudices. While he condemned the "Black Codes" passed by southern legislatures to restrict black mobility and opportunity while maintaining white supremacy, he averred that such regulations were rooted in the fears of poor whites, who saw the freedmen as a threat to their economic security and social status. For the same reason he believed that immediate black enfranchisement would be a "serious detriment" to blacks, for poor whites, "knowing that the suffrage, and a few minor factitious distinctions, are the chief points of their superiority, are jealous over them accordingly," and would respond with more violence. He was convinced that if southern politicians understood that their representation in the House of Representatives would be reduced by non-enfranchisement, they "will convince their constituents that it is necessary and proper to allow the negro to vote, and he will be allowed to do so."

Indeed, to Truman, "It is the former slave-holders who are the best friends the negro has in the south," in part because they, too, had little use for poor whites. He admitted that many "diligently strive to discourage the freedmen from any earnest efforts to promote their higher welfare," and conceded that while slavery may have ended, "glimmerings of its vassalage, its subserviency, and its helplessness linger." Other prejudices remained: blacks' efforts to reunite families or to explore beyond the boundaries of their plantations, while suggesting that the black man's "head is filled with the idea of freedom," and that he would "perceive and resist" any "encroachments" thereon, were regarded by planters as signs of "demoralization." Still, they understood black behavior better than anyone, including northerners working southern plantations, for black workers were "slow, awkward, wasteful and slovenly," frustrating efficiency-minded Yankees. There was "a real attachment" between slave and master, and it would only be a matter of time before the freedman, who "clings to old associations," would return home. Besides, he would always require some form of guardianship, due to "the very nature of his inferiority."

Since white southerners would always be "the guardians of the negro," Truman suggested that the Freedmen's Bureau, which had performed a valuable function as an intermediary and in providing relief to the destitute, "has nearly accomplished the work for which it was created, and the necessity that called it into existence is rapidly passing away"—in short, that it had become a victim of its own success in teaching blacks "self-reliance and self-helpfulness." While federal troops were still required to maintain order in some of the outlying frontier regions of the South, notably Texas, Missouri, and Arkansas, black troops "should be removed as speedily as possible," for "they incite the freedmen to deeds of violence, and encourage them in insolence." White southerners should be left to handle the readjustment in racial relations. Time would erode past prejudices and restore former loyalties—a view which allowed Truman to acknowledge present difficulties while discounting their implications.

These opinions, assessments, and recommendations, summarized in his retrospective report of April, 1866, constituted the third version of Truman's findings based on his southern travels. While his dispatches to the New York *Times* reached the widest audience, the following letters to Johnson, reprising in peace his wartime role as the Tennessean's emissary, embodied his immediate reactions to the postwar South.

Letters

Andrew Johnson,
President of the United States:

Sir: I have visited Huntsville, in North Alabama: Montgomery, Selma, Talladega, and two or three places of lesser note in Central Alabama: Demopolis in Western Alabama, and Blakely and Mobile in Southern Alabama, besides being present at the Constitutional Convention which has just terminated its labors at Montgomery, and respectfully submit the following, which you may implicitly relie upon:

In the fullest extent of the term, there is little or no spontaneous loyalty or love for the United States Government: but that a majority of the people are determined to obey all laws and zealously strive to bring about that harmony which existed between the sections, prior to the war, is a fixed fact. Wherever I have been, and however minute have been my observations, I have noticed one prominent feature in Central and Southern Alabama, to wit: That the original Secessionists are not only prepared to make all sacrifices, and yield gracefully to the powers that be, but they acknowledge their ill-success and complete subjugation with more candor, and accept of, and take hold of, your policy of restoration and reconstruction with more ardor, and seem to have a fuller and juster appreciation of the magnanimity of the soldiers and citizens of the North, than these men of more moderate opinions who were urged into a support of the Rebellion against their own feelings and sense of duty.

Nine tenths of the people in North Alabama, from Stevenson in the East to Florence in the West, are strictly loyal and devoted to the United States Government and its laws, although a small portion of these nine-tenths still linger around the vase of the defunct institution of slavery, foolishly believing that it is but partially destroyed, and that its utter restoration may be brought about by a decision of the Supreme Court of the United States. Twenty-three out of the one hundred delegates in the State Convention were impressed with this silly idea.[1]

Another class of citizens who are disposed to be loyal and circumspect are those who have been in the army. I have talked with officers and soldiers upon the great topics of the day, and they all agree that they have been well-whipped, and magnanimously treated since the termination of hostilities. Among the leading officers of the late C.S.A. from Alabama, I have talked with Generals Clanton,[2] Holtzclaw[3] and Roddy,[4] and Colonels Maury,[5] Cummings,[6] Johnson[7] and others, and they all agree that there is but one thing to do—to acknowledge the power of the Federal Government, and heartily acquiesce in what may be proposed by the officers in power. I am fully prepared to see *all* the virtue these people possess, and to encourage them all I can by kind words and good advice. I shall particularly aim to *see* the polish of returning reason and loyalty, if indeed there *is* any bright side to the picture: but at the same time I shall not choose to deceive you, even though I might imagine you may deem me in error, by misrepresenting the real feeling of the people. In seeking information I have not been wading around in babbling brooks, but I have plunged into the current:—in other words, I have been amongst the strong men of the State: I have observed keenly their actions, and I have listened attentively to their conversations and deliberations, without being led astray by the reticence of pulpit orators, or by the non-committal effusions of half-starved editors, or by the whimperings of imbecile old men, or the pleasantries ⟨and ignorance⟩ of silly young ladies.

Therefore, looking at things precisely as they exist, in the State of Alabama, which, it will be remembered, was the last State in the Union to feel the effects of the war in point of devastation, &c., except a small portion of the State north of the Tennessee river, I am constrained to make the following distinction:—that the people are loyal, but not patriotic. Certainly no patriotism whatever exists south of the Tennessee river—no love of county, the inspiration of which makes the heart bound, is discernible. But the people are loyal: if, as I take it, a perfect willingness to submit to the decree of the sword; a manifest disposition to obey all laws, and a unanimous desire to promote that harmony between the North and South, which once existed, and for a speedy restoration of Alabama with her modern improvements, to the position she once occupied, is loyalty. I need not inform you that your policy and generosity has elicited the approval of the entire South. You have not an enemy, either openly or covertly in Alabama. There is also great respect manifested for Mr. Seward[8] in all quarters, and a growing confidence in the people of the North, as a whole people. This is the best sign I have, that your policy of reconstruction will be a great success; and that the people, in their ardent admiration of, and their unbounded confidence in, you, will make all the necessary sacrifices, and come fully up to the expectations of the great conservative element which you represent. This, in my estimation, is the certain result. The Convention acted nobly and harmoniously—the only question being with delegates whether they were doing precisely as was required or desired of them by you, and expected of them by the North. And this is the same feeling all over the State, with but few exceptions. If then, Congress gives you a helping hand, just as sure as there is a God in Heaven, this great country will be re-united a thousand times stronger than ever before. There can be no mistake about this thing. The perfect subjugation of this people, and their profound realization and unqualified admission of their subjugation, and their willingness to submit to the authority of the Government, bespeaks grand results: and I shall find myself most eggregiously in error, if in a few short months the little bud of submission (or loyalty) does not burst forth into its full development, scenting the hitherto disturbed atmosphere with a patriotic fragrance which shall be inhaled by the whole American people.

Those who seem to be the most disloyal just now are the ministers of the gospel, editors of newspapers, old men and young women.

The ministers of the gospel, with but few exceptions, all over the State are disloyal. Now that doctors of divinity dare not promulgate treason and encourage sedition from the pulpit, the greatest and most flagrant exhibitions of disloyalty are exhibited (not that they say anything disloyal, but from the fact that they will not say anything loyal) in the Episcopal Church. The minister of the gospel in the Episcopal Church will not even invoke the blessings of God and health and prosperity upon the President of the United States, when everybody else admits that you are the great good friend of the South.[9] Besides, a large number of the people composing these congregations desire that the liturgy should be read without the Confederate States "amendment.["][10] I need not say further on this matter, as I understand it has been lain before you.[11] But my private opinion upon this subject is that Gen Wood should be sustained in this matter, and ere long the old salaried hypocrites will offer their services to pray for the President of the United States, or any other man, if they only get well paid for it. I always did have a respect for ministers of the gospel, but some of them have acted in such bad faith during the war, that I am seemingly severe[.]

The editors of newspapers throughout the State, are also disloyal. Not an editor in this city or in Montgomery would permit me to write anything for them at all. The editor of the Selma Times[12] permitted me to write a communication. He informed me, however, that in a short time he should come out strong for the Government. He seemed to understand that it was unwise to be lauding you in one column continually, and slandering everybody else connected with the Government in another. I told Mr. Jno Forsyth of this city that he was deceiving the people south and enraging the people north—and doing untold injury to the cause by his uniform reticence. I think, however, that in a month or more there will be vast improvement among these editors. They deem it dishonorable to make a sudden change, and argue that they cannot spring too much upon the people at once.

I think the Freedmen and the Freedmen's Bureau question is the most important one of all. The people are almost unanimously in favor of getting rid of the Freedmen's Bureau in this State. I am strongly on the side of these Southern people, but there are many bad men amongst them, and I conscientiously believe that the removal of this institution would be a great calamity. I will allow that those who will behave themselves would be well treated. But there are 140,000 sufferers, of this class, including the aged, infirm and children. Now, these people have not enough means to take care of their white paupers, who, according to the Comptroller's report, number 138,000 souls, & yet they wish to get rid of the Freedmen's Bureau, which is feeding and otherwise caring for 140,000 black paupers, a tenth part of whom would ⟨suffer⟩ perish this winter were it not for Government aid.[13]

Alabamians all over the state say they have no money, and complain that they are an impoverished people. So they are. The State has been impoverished

1st By depletion during war:

2d By a rapacious system of taxation:

3d By the annulling of all investments in State and Confederate securities:

4th By the destruction of railroads, crops and buildings:

5th By paralysis of all industry:

6th By the terrible drouth: and

7th By the cancellation of one half of the entire aggregate of property in the State.

This shows conclusively that the people, if they would, cannot provide for, or ameliorate the condition of, the sufferers of this unfortunate class. Therefore, in my opinion, a Freedmen's Bureau must exist, either as a State or National institution, notwithstanding the unanimous opposition to it.

My impression is that

1st The whole pretext of the attack being made upon you and your policy and your friends, is that under it the negro will, by the Legislatures of the Southern States, be deprived of those rights which are essential to social life and well being: and

2d The claim of the attacking party is that negro suffrage, in the choice of the Legislature, is necessary to prevent this.

But this pretext would be removed, and this claim emasculated, if each State were, by organic enactment, to take the whole matter from the Legislature, and secure to the negro the same rights of person and property as other non-voting inhabitants.[14]

This would put Alabama on the same footing as the Northern States. It would remove internal dissension as to the status of the negro. It would reassert the right of the State to control its own suffrage, and it would give the negro himself a fixed status and reliable basis upon which to go to work.

This gives to the negro nothing more than what he already has in this State with the concurrence of the late Constitutional Convention.

Cotton stealing has been going on to an alarming extent in this State by United States Treasury agents.[15] I suppose, however, you have been made aware of these facts.

Yours Very Respectfully Ben C. Truman

ALS, DNA-RG107, Records of the Office of Secretary of War, Misc. Papers, 1804–1867.

1. Although his figures are inaccurate—the actual vote on the issue was 17–66—Truman's report of the unrealistic diehards among the slaveholders is accurate. Thomas W. Coleman of Choctaw County, the principal spokesman, in a well-reasoned speech opposed the majority's resolution to abolish slavery and to recommend amendment of the state constitution to that effect. Arguing that the Supreme Court had yet to rule on the constitutionality of the Confiscation Acts and on Lincoln's Emancipation Proclamation, he expressed a willingness to accept the death of slavery as imposed by bayonets, but a refusal to be a party to a measure signaling Alabama's acquiescence. *Appleton's Annual Cyclopaedia* (1865), 14–15; Fleming, *Reconstruction in Alabama*, 362–63.

2. Whig lawyer James H. Clanton (1827–1871), a Bell-Everett elector in 1860, became a Confederate brigadier in 1863. After the war he gained prominence in Alabama's Democratic party and the Ku Klux Klan.

3. Lawyer James T. Holtzclaw (1833–1893) fought in the western theater, winning promotion to brigadier general in 1864.

4. Philip D. Roddey (1826–1897), a tailor, sheriff, and steamboatman, held several cavalry commands in the western theater.

5. Harry Maury (c1827–1869), a prewar lawyer and politician, commanded several Alabama infantry regiments.

6. Samuel J. Cumming (1821–1893) was a member of Alabama's 1865 constitutional convention.

7. George D. Johnston (1832–1910), another prewar lawyer and politician, actually attained the rank of brigadier by the end of the war.

8. A Whig-turned-Republican, William Henry Seward (1801–1872), secretary of state under Lincoln and Johnson, advocated a fairly conservative approach to reconstruction in marked contrast to his prominence in prewar antislavery politics.

9. After Appomattox, Episcopal bishop Richard H. Wilmer (1816–1900) directed the clergy to omit reference to the President of the United States in the "prayer for all in authority" until the restoration of civil authority was complete. On September 20, Gen. Charles R. Woods, pursuant to orders of his superior, Gen. George H. Thomas, issued General Order No. 38, "suspending" Wilmer and the clergy and forbidding them "to preach, or perform divine service" until they included the chief executive in prayer. The bishop protested, arguing that prayer was a religious act not subject to secular authorities. Fleming, *Reconstruction in Alabama*, 24, 325–27; Wilmer to Woods, September 22, 1865, Johnson Papers, LC; see also Walter C. Whitaker, *Richard Hooker Wilmer: Second Bishop of Alabama* (Philadelphia, 1907).

10. During the war, "Confederate" was substituted for "United" in the wording of "the prayer for all in authority." Fleming, *Reconstruction in Alabama*, 324.

11. Three weeks earlier Governor Parsons had called Johnson's attention to Woods's order, terming it "unwise and impolitic." While asserting that most people disapproved of Wilmer's behavior, he questioned whether the order was not an infringement upon religious liberty. Nearly three months later (December 22), Johnson directed Thomas to rescind Woods's order; three days later Wilmer resumed use of the prayer, including the President once more. *Ibid.*, 327–28; Parsons to Johnson, September 24, 1865, Johnson Papers, LC.

12. Prewar editor of the Louisville *Courier*, Robert McKee (1830–1909) had been elected secretary of state in Kentucky's provisional government. He was wounded at Shiloh while serving as a volunteer aide.

13. According to General Howard, in September the Freedmen's Bureau issued 82,066 rations in Alabama—36,295 to blacks and 45,771 to whites. *House Ex. Doc. No. 11, 39 Cong., 1 Sess.*, 16.

14. The Alabama legislature failed to satisfy Truman's expectations. The redefinition of vagrancy and increased penalties for grand larceny, arson, and burglary were understood as steps to address offenses which whites thought blacks likely to commit, and interracial marriage was prohibited. Blacks were also prohibited in testifying in certain cases between whites before the higher state courts. Governor R.M. Patton vetoed three other bills singling out freedmen for special treatment. Fleming, *Reconstruction in Alabama*, 384; Theodore B. Wilson, *The Black Codes of the South* (University, Ala., 1965), 76–77; McPherson, *Reconstruction*, 21.

15. Confiscation legislation passed in 1862 and 1863 authorized treasury agents to seize and dispose of Confederate property, including government-owned cotton. Many agents also "confiscated" privately-owned cotton, retaining between 25 and 50 percent of the proceeds from subsequent sales. The notorious instances of fraud excited adverse comment at Washington. "I am sure I sent some honest cotton agents South," commented treasury secretary McCulloch; "but it sometimes seems very doubtful whether any of them remained honest very long." In August, 1865, Johnson had called on Gen. George H. Thomas to investigate such frauds, but Thomas failed to uncover any wrongdoing. Fleming, *Reconstruction in Alabama*, 284–303; Reid, *After the War*, 204; Johnson to Thomas, August 13, 1865, Johnson Papers, Ser. 3A; Thomas to Johnson, August 29, 1865, Johnson Papers, LC; see also Truman's report in the November 2, 1865, New York *Times*.

◄►

Milledgeville Ga. Nov. 1. '65

Andrew Johnson,
President of U.S.

The Georgia Convention evinces the most painful hesitation in regard to the repudiation of the State debt. It is by no means in consequence of any disloyal feeling, but, on the contrary, it is the fear for the future credit of the State. In one sense of the word this is commendable: but, looking at it in the light that you and Mr. Seward do, the State debt, or at least portions of the State debt, are as strictly associated with secession as were the State's declarations of war.[1] This is the way I understand it, and I have thus reasoned with many gentlemen of the Convention and influential lobby members,[2] of whom there are not a few, all of them being opposed to the act of repudiation. But there are several reasons why the Convention came very near passing an act to pay this debt. First, several distinguished gentlemen of Georgia just from Washington, informed members that *you* considered the subject only of State importance, and the State should do what it deemed most proper in the premises.[3] Ex Gov. Jos. Brown[4] stated authoritatively, that you had informed him that the disposition of the State debt was of no material consequence. Gen Steadman also informed members, that although an utter repudiation of all State debts contracted in aid of and succoring the rebellion, was looked for by the President and the country at large, he believed that "scaling it down to a specie payment" would give satisfaction[.] Notwithstanding your despatches, the Convention hangs fire tenaciously, and a multiplicity of documents and appeals are industriously circulated beseeching members to declare against repudiation. The Convention means well, however, and will do everything clean.[5]

The Freedmen, so far as I have made myself interested and acquainted, are in a better condition in this State than in Alabama. Not that they are governed with more ability or sagacity than in Alabama. In fact, I think Gen. Swayne, the Commissioner in Alabama, is a gentleman of more enlarged ideas concerning the freedmen, the freedmen's bureau, and all its ramifications, than any person I have met. But Georgia has been longer under Federal rule, and the negroes have more experience regarding their transition state, and are more disposed to work. Gen Tillson made a speech to the Convention a few nights ago,[6] and urged its members to permit the negro to testify in the courts.[7] He also made a speech to the negroes, which was full of good advice, and threats of punishment and imprisonment in case they did not abstain from indolence.[8]

There is a vast improvement in the tone of the people in Macon, Columbus and Atlanta, in the newspaper offices, in railroad carriages and at the hotels. So far as I have been in this State the people are all right. I am disposed to tell you the actual state of things—I will not deceive you—and I can assure you that the people to a man in the three cities I have named, including the one I write from, are sound, and to be trusted. Of course there is no hostility to you—but the people here seem to be in the exercise of enough good sense to know that the only way to exhibit and manifest the devotion they feel for you is to give their unequivocal support to the laws, which they are certainly doing. I have not seen an ill-tempered man in Georgia. Notwithstanding some things, as might naturally be expected, are unpalatable, as a body the people are serene and hopeful. The newspapers in Georgia occasionally devote some of their space to paragraphs of encouragement and advice, and I have no doubt but some of the good effects of your policy of restoration &c. will be to illumine opaque and anxious minds by the reflection of the light which it has infused in the hearts of the prostrate multitudes you are so magnanimously interceding for.

Yours Very Respectfully
Benjamin C. Truman

ALS, DNA-RG105, Washington Headquarters, Office of the Commissioner, Lets. Recd. by President Johnson Relating to Bureau Affairs, 1865–68.

1. As recently as October 28, the President had advised provisional governor James Johnson: "The people of Georgia should not hesitate one single moment in repudiating every single dollar of debt" from the war effort. Secretary of State William H. Seward echoed the President's promptings. Johnson Papers, LC; Conway, *Reconstruction of Georgia*, 49; Seward to James Johnson, October 28, 1865, McPherson, *Reconstruction*, 21.

2. Truman took an active role in the debate over the war debt, furnishing delegate J.R. Parrott of Bartow County with newspaper clippings outlining the President's advocacy of repudiation. New York *Times*, November 17, 1865.

3. Probably a reference to O.A. Lochrane and Joseph E. Brown. Lochrane had visited Johnson on October 12 and 20, and had relayed the results of his interview to several correspondents; one observer complained that the judge spent too much time "edifying his marvel-loving hearers by his pretended knowledge of all the President's plans." In a report for the *Times* Truman commented: "Distinguished Georgians, (with barrels full of bonds and notes,) among them an ex-governor [Brown], lately from Washington, urged delegates to disregard possible disapproval by the northern public. Some went so far as to say that the President had informed them that Georgia could do as she pleased with her debts." A Georgia paper reported that "a gentleman just returned from Washington" had stated, "Nor do we think, if the President were asked his opinion, that he would approve the policy of repudiation." *Ibid.*; New York *Herald*, October 13, 1865; New York *Times*, November 2, 9, 1865; Alexander H. Stephens, *Recollections of Alexander H. Stephens*,

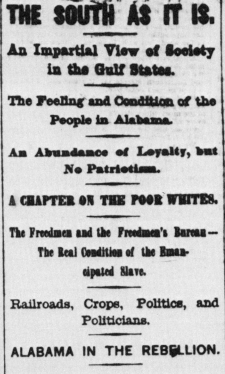

Truman's Other Audience:
New York Times, *October 31, 1865.*

Myrta L. Avary, ed. (New York, 1910), 535; Milledgeville *Federal Union*, October 17, 1865.

4. Georgia's ex-governor Joseph E. Brown (1821–1894), whose rigid adherence to states' rights often set him at odds with the Confederate government, spent a brief sojourn in Repbulican ranks during Reconstruction before returning to the Democrats and taking a U.S. Senate seat.

5. On November 8, by a vote of 133 to 117, the convention passed a resolution "to render null and void all debts of this State created for the purpose of carrying on the late war against the United States." Thompson, *Reconstruction in Georgia*, 138; James Johnson to Andrew Johnson, November 8, 1865, Johnson Papers, Ser. 2, LC.

6. See Watterson to Johnson, October 30, 1865, n.2.

7. See Schurz to Johnson, August 13, 1865, n.28.

8. One Georgia paper echoed Truman's sentiments in an editorial, suggesting that Tillson "will do all he can to make Cuffee a respectable colored gentleman, but if Cuffee will not work, nor listen to wise counsels, then he will reap the whirlwind where he sows the wind." Columbus *Sun and Times*, November 1, 1865.

———— ❖ ————

Milledgeville, Ga, Nov. 9, 1865.

Col. William A. Browning,
Private Secretary President Johnson:

Colonel: The Georgia State Constitutional Convention terminated its session yesterday. The Convention was not composed of the best men in the State, although there were many gifted and prominent Georgians present.[1] There were, of course only three things to be done of National importance, but the utmost malignity and meanness and ingratitude was manifest d[ur]ing the entire proceedings. The fact is the leading men were afraid to show their hands on the question of Repudiation, and they staid at home and sent a delegation of old and prejudiced men of unprogressive minds to act as their cats paw. What was to be done was to declare null and void the ordinance of Secession and all associate ordinances in conflict with the law and authority of the United States: to abolish Slav[er]y and make provisions for the protection of the great mass of people late in slav[er]y, and to repudiate the State debt. Now, the Convention would not declare *null and* void the ordinance, but *repealed* it. The foll[ow]ing is the ordinance:

[The attached clipping reports that the people of Georgia "do declare and ordain" that both the ordinance "to dissolve the Union" and that "to adopt and ratify the Constitution of the Confederate States of America . . . are hereby, repealed."]

As relates to slav[er]y, it was abolished with a most malignant and mean proviso, as follows:

[Stressing their involuntary "acquiescence to the action of the Government of the United States" in the emancipation of slaves, the convention abolishes slavery in Georgia, at the same time reserving the right of Georgians to make "claims for compensation of loss sustained . . . upon the justice and magnanimity" of the federal government.]

But the Repudiation question was the toughest one. It was introduced the second day but was not settled until the last day of the Convention.

Notwithstanding the telegrams of the President and Mr. Seward, and the lobbying done by Gov. Johnson and his friends, there was a tremendous effort made to defeat the bill. I will give it to you in brief. Mr. Chappell[2] one day last week offered the resolution declaring the whole war debt *null and void* &c.

[The appended lengthy account of the debate over the war debt clause details the repeated efforts of delegates to arrive at some measure short of outright repudiation of the debt. These substitutes failing to gain majority support, Chappell's repudiating ordinance passed by a 133–117 vote. Also attached are two documents: a resolution addressed to Johnson urging a rapid reconstruction and expressing the delegates' "entire confidence in your just and kind intentions towards them, and their anticipations of your conciliatory and trustful consideration of their acts and doings in this convention"; and an ordinance establishing congressional districts and providing for elections for state officers, legislators, congressmen, and the mayor of Savannah.]

Notwithstanding this reluctance to do the right thing as manifested by the Convention, the people are all right. I would not say so if it was not a fact, because I do not wish to deceive you. I have been to Albany, Eufaula, Macon, Columbus, Marietta and Atlanta, and I tell you there is a great resolution rife in the feeling amongst the people. The editors are all com[in]g out and telling the people that they must do all they can to promote har[mo]ny and a return of good feeling. One paper in Columbus a few days ago said it would not be long before the Stars and Stripes would again be cherished by the people of Georgia. Another thing the people of Georgia are not unmindful of their great financial and commercial interests. All over the State the people are alive to their advantages. Everybody *loves* and *fears* the President. I tell all such that the only way to strengthen him is to give his policy a sincere acquiescence, and to make laws for the protection of the negroes, giving them all the rights of other non-voting inhabitants, and to send men to Congress who can take the test oath. You have no idea what a good feeling prevails in Georgia.

The Freedmen are in a much better condition here than in Alabama, and so are the poor Whites. I have said all in relation to the freedmen in Alabama and Georgia that is necess[ar]y. Besides, Gov. Parsons and Gen Swayne are in Washington, and they will urge their claims in regard to this all-important subject.[3]

If I am not mistaken the State of Georgia, in giving this evidence of her intention to reinstate herself, and recover her honor, is laying a foundation for a condition of prosperity and strength far beyond what she ever enjoyed before, or could ever reasonably have hoped for under the old system, even had not war temporarily thrown her back.

In conclusion, let me say that you may depend upon it, everything is working well in Georgia. There is an improvement in the tone of the people that bespeaks an unlooked for harmony in feeling and concert in action.

Yours Very Respectfully,
Benj. C. Truman.

ALS, DLC-JP. Although addressed to Johnson's secretary, the contents make it clear that it was intended for the President's eyes.

1. Most of the approximately three hundred delegates who assembled at Milledgeville had opposed immediate secession in 1861 and had supported Bell or Douglas in 1860. Johnson's amnesty proclamation barred several prominent leaders from participation, including Howell Cobb, Robert Toombs, Joseph E. Brown, and Alexander Stephens. Conway, *Reconstruction of Georgia*, 44–45; Thompson, *Reconstruction in Georgia*, 134–36.

2. Absalom H. Chappell (1801–1878), a lawyer and prewar states' rights Whig, aligned himself with Georgia conservatives in 1867.

3. Parsons and Swayne left Montgomery on October 24 and arrived within a week at Washington, reportedly to seek the President's approval of their contemplated policy toward freedmen. On November 1 and 2, Parsons conferred with Johnson; newspaper reports claimed that he protested against the operations of the Freedmen's Bureau. At a meeting for southern relief in New York on November 13, however, Parsons praised the Bureau, asserting that it "had done good service." New Orleans *Picayune*, November 3, 1865; New York *Tribune*, November 3, 13, 1865; New York *Herald*, November 2, 14, 1865; New York *Times*, November 2, 1865.

◆◆◆

Memphis, Tenn, Jan, 5, 1866.

Andrew Johnson, President of the U.S.

As you might have seen I have not prepared any of my letters *a la* Schurz,[1] because I had only intended them for you. But when I return from Texas I will make out an elaborate report.[2] I met Mr. East[3] in Nashville, and he informed me that he was going to Washington, so he will post you on affairs of that section in detail. One thing, I must say, however, in this connection, and that is that the Press & Times is doing more harm than good.[4] And so is Gov. Brownlow.[5]

I can assure you with all my heart, that one can hardly realize the improvement in the tone of the people. In coming from Florida here I had occasion to pass through the same sections that I was in last fall, and I noticed a great change in the people, everywhere. I talk to all the editors in particular. But the fact is the whole people are determined to do precisely what you want them to do, not only because they feel pledged to this, but because they feel that with your support they can break down the extreme radicals whom they hate. With the exception of a very few of our own officers, who want to stay in the service,[6] the whole army endorse you in the warmest manner.

In this city there is an influential Conservative party, made up of reliable Union men, and men who have been in the Confederate army, who are doing the right thing. The Commercial, edited by Mr. J. Keating,[7] is the organ of this party, and it is doing good service. I have had a long talk with Mr. Keating and he feels pledged to sustain you and the

Union party of the North in a manly way. The Commercial is the best and largest circulated paper in the city. Mr. Keating was once a journeyman printer in New York and is an honorable man. The whole country are sure that you will whip the Radicals, and God Almighty will help you do it.

I met old Dan Rice,[8] the clown, who has been in some parts of the States with his circus, and in the guise of a clown, he says he has felt of the people, and they go wild he says, when he mentions you as the savior of the country &c. I only mention this to show the tener, although I have no doubt the great showman is doing more good in one day than Carl Shurz did in a month. By the way what a bombshell Grant threw into Shurz's camp.[9]

As I said above, I am not writing for the public (in these letters) or Congress, but for your private self. I go from here to Little Rock, and then to Texas. Mr. Raymond[10] butted up against a big gun, but he's on the right side.[11] My letters in the New York Times are copied all over the south.[12] Most of the editors seem disposed to do just what I ask them down here. I tell some of them *don't write up the President too much, if you do you will inadvertently write him down*. I tell the people that you are bound to whip the Radicals even if you have to hang Davis.

Yours very respectfully   Ben. C. Truman

ALS, DLC-JP.

1. Probably a reference to the tone of Schurz's final report, submitted by Johnson to Congress on December 19, 1865. Although addressed to the President, Schurz's report more closely resembled a damning indictment of presidential reconstruction designed to gain Radical applause.

2. Johnson submitted Truman's final report, dated April 9, 1866, to Congress on May 8.

3. Lawyer Edward H. East (1830–1904), one of Johnson's close advisers, had assisted the military governor as Tennessee's secretary of state. See *Johnson Papers*, III, 410n; V, 245n.

4. Much to Johnson's dismay, the Nashville *Press and Times* strongly supported Brownlow's policy of excluding ex-Confederates from the ballot box. In his report to the New York *Times*, Truman characterized the paper as edited "in the style of the Cincinnati *Gazette*, and damns everybody as disloyal who does not regard a colored man as *better* than a white person." James W. Patton, *Unionism and Reconstruction in Tennessee, 1860–1869* (Chapel Hill, 1934), 105; New York *Times*, January 8, 1866.

5. Minister-turned-Whig politician and newspaper editor, William G. Brownlow (1805–1877), who had joined former foe Johnson in resisting secession, succeeded the vice president-elect as governor in 1865. His tough stand against former Confederates alienated Johnson and helped provoke the emergence of the Ku Klux Klan.

6. A suggestion that commissioned officers, fearful of losing their employment due to rapid demobilization and reduction of the army, might, as a way to keep their positions, justify the retention of present forces because of continued resistance to the reestablishment of United States authority.

7. Irish immigrant John M. Keating (c1830–1906) had worked for several Memphis papers before founding the *Commercial* in 1865. Thomas H. Baker, *The Memphis Commercial Appeal: The History of a Southern Newspaper* (Baton Rouge, 1971), 122–29.

8. Dan Rice (1823–1900) commenced a forty-year career as a clown in 1844; his performances across the nation, which included humorous comments about public affairs, established him as one of the most celebrated practitioners of that art.

9. Grant's December 18, 1865, letter to Johnson, based on his recent trip through the

South, was submitted to Congress along with Schurz's lengthy report. Like Truman, Johnson chose to interpret Grant's conclusions as offering support for the administration's reconstruction policy, thereby undercutting the impact of Schurz's assessment of southern conditions.

10. Henry J. Raymond (1820–1869), a close associate of William H. Seward and Thurlow Weed, founded the New York *Times* in 1851 as a mouthpiece for conservative Whig and Republican ideology. An advocate of Johnson's vice presidential nomination in 1864, he entered Congress the following year determined to act as the new President's spokesman. Growing dissatisfied with the direction of the administration's reconstruction policy, he finally broke with Johnson in 1866.

11. On December 21, 1865, Raymond took to the House floor to defend Johnson's policies, which Thaddeus Stevens had assailed three days earlier in a "viciously radical attack." During Raymond's response he had to ward off Ohio Republican John A. Bingham's interrogatories on southern representation in Congress. McKitrick, *Andrew Johnson and Reconstruction*, 257.

12. For example, Truman's discussion of Gen. Edward A. Wild's activities in Georgia, printed in the New York *Times* on December 5, 1865, appeared in the Augusta *Constitutionalist* on December 24, 1865.

------◆------

Austin, Texas, Feb. 8, 1866.

Andrew Johnson. President of the U.S.

The Convention assembled to-day, and organized. There are 70 members present. 24 are Radical Union men—have been so all the time. This class are as staunch as the East Tennesseeans and more so than the North Alabamians. Only 12 are rabid secessionists, and the balance are Conservatives. A Mr. Throckmorton[1] was elected President. He voted against Secession in the last Convention.[2] The Texan people are behaving first rate. I think this Convention will incorporate in their new Constitution full rights to the negroes—including the right to sue and be sued, to hold property, and to testify in the Courts, and just as Florida done.[3] I have the Constitution of Florida, and have shown it to several of the members. The repudiation of the War debt will meet with little opposition if any. The President of Convention made very patriotic speech.[4]

Respectfully. Ben C. Truman.

ALS, DLC-JP.

1. Unionist Whig James W. Throckmorton (1825–1894), after opposing secession in 1861, joined the Confederate army in command of Texas troops. Elected governor in 1866, he was removed the following year by Gen. Philip H. Sheridan for obstructing military reconstruction.

2. Throckmorton was one of eight delegates so voting in the 1861 convention. Moneyhon, *Republicanism in Reconstruction Texas*, 28.

3. Article VIII of the 1866 constitution nearly realized Truman's hopes. Blacks were allowed to hold property and to sue and be sued, but they were permitted to testify in court only in cases involving other blacks—all in line with Florida's 1865 constitution. *Ibid.*, 38; *Appleton's Annual Cyclopaedia* (1865), 362–63.

4. In his opening remarks, Throckmorton called on the delegates to act "with a spirit uncontaminated by prejudices and bitterness." He expressed the hope that the acts of the convention "may go far toward making strong again that old feeling which united us." New York *Times*, March 5, 1866.

Washington, D.C. March 24. [1866]

Andrew Johnson, President U.S.

My dear Sir: I have just returned from the South, and bring with me a letter from Gov. Hamilton.[1] The proceedings of the Texas Convention have been slow, but that body has done better than any other. The debates have been protracted, not because the Secessionists were not inclined to do what was required, but because the Union men (seven of whom were in favor of negro suffrage) were so strong and uncompromising. I have attended four Conventions during my trip and have been in all parts of seven of the seceded states, during which time I have written some lengthy letters to the New York Times, and several brief ones to yourself and Mr. East. I have met nearly all of the leading politicians of the south, nearly all of the rebel generals, many of the editors of southern papers, while in all cases I have also made it convenient to call upon our own officers, including those connected with the Freedman's Bureau. In all cases, although I have done all in my power for the cause, &c. such as telling rebel editors how they should write, and telling delegates what was required, &c. I have carefully avoided speaking authoritatively, because I thought it might, in some cases, result injudiciously. I have several very important things which I wish to say to you.

The following I will not do unless you desire, or will permit me. But as Carl Schurz published a report in the Tribune I would like to publish one in the Times, of course, sending it to you first.[2] My observations have been careful, and I think I understand the situation pretty well, and as I have been in the south seven months, my report would not be received with indifference. I wish to get before the Reconstruction Committee, but I am told down town that I can not unless I go into some hotel and damn the President.[3]

I have some very important things to say to you, and will be ready to see you, at a moment's notice, day or night.

In conclusion, I must say I am sorry that you have been so foully dealt with from an unexpected quarter,[4] and I will add that the chances for a great Administration paper in this city are splendid. The Intelligencer means all right probably, but it is old fogy in its style, besides its antecedents are bad.[5]

I have a letter from Gen Miller[6] at San Francisco, in which he tenders me some intelligence which he is desirous should be imparted to you.

Yours Very Respectfully   Benj. C. Truman.

ALS, DLC-JP.

1. Dated March 1, the letter discusses problems providing protection against raids by "Indians aided by desperate white men" along the state's northwest border, and, while representing the majority of the state as "quiet and orderly," requests additional troops to subdue the activities of "desperate characters . . . who have been thrown to the surface and emboldened by the events of the past four years." Hamilton to Johnson, March 1, 1866, Johnson Papers, LC.

2. Schurz's report, *sans* appended documentation, was printed in the New York *Tribune* on December 23, 1865. The *Times* printed Truman's report on May 8, 1866, the same day Johnson furnished the Senate with a copy.

3. On April 5, Truman testified before the Joint Committee on Reconstruction's subcommittee investigating conditions in Florida, Texas, and Louisiana. Most historians agree with Truman that the hearings were intended to gather evidence questioning the wisdom of Johnson's policy. If so, the committee achieved its objective; witnesses summoned to testify presented a rather damning indictment of that policy based on their own observations and experiences. *Report of the Joint Committee on Reconstruction*, 39 Cong., 1 Sess., 1866, House Report No. 30, pt. IV, 136–40.

4. Possibly referring to the recent publication by the Washington *Intelligencer* of Johnson's endorsement of a paymaster's refusal to contribute to a fund to defray the transportation costs of soldiers and federal clerks from New Hampshire coming home to vote. Evidently the President mistook the incident as an effort to force officeholders to make political contributions; not only did his actions indirectly harm the Republican party's chances of victory, but they stood in stark relief to his own efforts to secure transportation for Tennessee voters in 1864. The editors of the *Intelligencer* exacerbated the problem in their inept handling of the story, especially in classifying the resulting Republican victory as a defeat for Johnson, leaving the impression of a Johnson-Copperhead alliance. See the Washington *Intelligencer*, March 21, 23, 1866, and Washington *Chronicle*, March 22, 25, 1866.

5. Once a Whig organ, prewar *Intelligencer* editorials supported compromise efforts, endorsed the Constitutional Union ticket in 1860, and lambasted northern antislavery efforts. A lukewarm supporter of the Union war effort, the paper backed McClellan in 1864. Although disunionism and Whiggery were anathema to War Democrat Johnson, the President persevered in using the paper as the mouthpiece of his administration. William E. Ames, *A History of the National Intelligencer* (Chapel Hill, 1972), 310–38.

6. John F. Miller (1831–1886), who headed the Nashville defenses in 1864, had been appointed collector of the port of San Francisco by Johnson. The letter referred to has not been found.

Ulysses S. Grant:
Warlord Turned Peacemaker

The most visible evidence of federal authority in the defeated South as the presence of the military. Having suppressed the rebellion on the battlefield, Union soldiers and officers now had to administer—and in many cases, create—policy, preserve order, and a host of other duties, until civil governments were reestablished. Johnson's proclamations appointing provisional governors explicitly ordered military commanders to assist them; the Freedmen's Bureau was headed and staffed by army personnel; and the South remained under martial law. Military reports were a prime source of information about southern attitudes; in addition, several prominent generals, most notably Ulysses S. Grant, visited the South during the latter half of 1865 and furnished their civil superiors with accounts of their impressions notable for their moderation, realism, and efforts at even-handedness. Indeed, one Charleston columnist, disgusted with the "misrepresentations" of several northern correspondents, preferred army officers, "who are able to form, from personal observation, a correct estimate of southern life as it now is."[1]

In August, responding to reports that the Freedmen's Bureau was mismanaged and that black troops were proving disruptive, Secretary of War Stanton dispatched George G. Meade, commanding the Military Division of the Atlantic, to Virginia and the Carolinas. The hero of Gettysburg traveled first to South Carolina, where he assisted in resolving a dispute concerning the boundaries of civil and military authority in respect to the continuance of martial law. Meade proposed a compromise, restoring civil rule in all cases not involving blacks, leaving the freedmen under the protection of the army's system of provost courts.[2] He found black soldiers poorly officered and plagued by ill health, but denied that they were encouraging idleness among other freedmen or fomenting friction between laborers and planters. In a concession to the fears and prejudices of white southerners, he recommended that black regiments be stationed on the coast, "where they will be measurably removed from contact with the whites." Provisional governor Benjamin F. Perry, however, reported that the general "expressed an earnest desire to get rid of all negro troops entirely, but said it would have to be done gradually, so as not to offend public sentiment at the North"—a

---

1. John H. Moore, ed., *The Juhl Letters to the Charleston Courier: A View of the South, 1865–1871* (Athens, Ga., 1974), 26–27. Sefton, *Army and Reconstruction*, and Perman, *Reunion Without Compromise*, cover civil-military relations during this period.

2. For Meade's September 20, 1865, report to Stanton, see Appendix I.

marked contrast to Meade's assertion that complaints about the black regiments "are not sufficient in my judgment to justify the discontinuance of this class of troops."[3] Southern whites were happier when Meade halted the confiscation and redistribution of "abandoned" land. Although he doubted the competency of several individual agents, he rejected rumors that Bureau agents were encouraging blacks to leave plantations and recommended that the Bureau be placed under direct military control to "avoid any conflict of authority, arising from the construction of laws and orders."[4]

Having intervened in South Carolina to shape policy to his satisfaction, Meade moved on. In North Carolina, he mediated another conflict between civil and military authority over cases concerning blacks, reaching a similar conclusion. Pleased with the operations of the Bureau in both North Carolina and Virginia, he commended the military commanders in both states, and concluded that the condition of affairs was "on the whole satisfactory," crediting assertions of returning loyalty "within the limits of what may be presumed natural." With the passage of time, Meade believed, the South would adjust to and absorb the result of its defeat.[5]

In October, 1865, Johnson asked Oliver O. Howard, head of the Freedmen's Bureau, to travel to South Carolina, Georgia, and Florida to "endeavor to effect an agreement mutually satisfactory to the freedmen and the land owners" concerning the disposition of land set aside for the use of freedmen and refugees by William T. Sherman the previous January. After a stop at Raleigh, North Carolina, where he witnessed the opening of that state's constitutional convention and urged listeners to treat freedmen kindly, he arrived at Charleston, South Carolina, on October 17. First he met with prominent planters and city officials; then he traveled to the Sea Islands to inform blacks of the President's program. One observer noted, "'Tis the policy of the President to conciliate; & Gen. H. is carrying out his orders."[6]

The blacks did not take readily to Howard's mission. While they were willing to rent land from the planters, they had little desire to return to work for their former masters. Howard made vague assurances that something would be done to secure land for the freedmen; until then, "I urged them to make the best terms they could with the holders of the titles." He left the Palmetto State after establishing a commission

3. Benjamin F. Perry, *Reminiscences of Public Men* (Philadelphia, 1883), 148; Meade to Stanton, September 20, 1865.
4. *Ibid.* General Rufus Saxton was offended by Meade's attitude, telling Oliver O. Howard that the visiting general seemed to believe that "the enemies of the Government in this Department were the agents of the Freedmen's Bureau and not the late Rebels." Saxton to Howard, September 9, 1865, Lets. Sent, Asst. Com., South Carolina, RG105, NA.
5. Meade to Stanton, September 20, 1865.
6. McFeely, *Yankee Stepfather*, 137–39.

composed equally of representatives of the government, the planters, and the freedmen to arbitrate disputes, and appointed Captain Alexander P. Ketchum to supervise the negotiation of labor contracts.[7]

Howard next visited Savannah and Fernandina, where he repeated the painful process of informing blacks of the President's plan to restore land to previous owners. On November 5 he arrived at New Orleans, where the Bureau had been under attack for some time. In a speech to freedmen that night he claimed that he had come to investigate the "precise condition of the freedmen," and stressed the themes of harmony and reasonableness. "Let us be satisfied with what we have, and improve upon it," he concluded.[8] Returning to Washington, he urged Johnson to delay land restoration. At the same time, through both private correspondence and the preparation of his first annual report, he began laying the groundwork for a congressional alternative to the President's policy aimed at not only prolonging the life of the Bureau but expanding its scope.[9]

While Howard was visiting the seaboard, George H. Thomas, commanding the Division of the Tennessee, was traveling through Mississippi, Alabama, and Georgia on a tour of inspection. Johnson thought highly of the Rock of Chickamauga, although the general did not always pander to the President's prejudices. "As a general rule the negro soldiers are under good discipline," he had told Johnson in September. "I believe that in the majority of cases of collision between whites and negro soldiers that the white man has attempted to bully the negro, for it is exceedingly repugnant to southerners to have negro soldiers in their midst & some are so foolish as to vent their anger upon the negro because he is a soldier."[10]

In Jackson, Mississippi, Thomas conferred with department commander Thomas J. Wood, provisional governor Sharkey, and incoming governor Benjamin Humphreys. The President, embarrassed because Humphreys had been elected governor while still awaiting his pardon, had contemplated continuing Sharkey in office, but Thomas advised accepting the result of the election, adding that he had conveyed to the new governor the thrust of administration policy. The general came away from a visit with Col. Samuel Thomas, head of the Freedmen's Bureau in Mississippi, "satisfied that he has administered his office with fairness and impartiality to whites and blacks and that he has been eminently successful in securing a sense of justice towards the negro from the civil authorities." In Alabama one of his aides engaged Episcopal Bishop Richard Wilmer in an ultimately fruitless conversation about

7. *Ibid.*; Oliver O. Howard, *Autobiography of Oliver Otis Howard* (2 vols., New York, 1908), II, 239–41.

8. McFeely, *Yankee Stepfather*, 180–81.

9. *Ibid.*, 196–99.

10. Thomas to Johnson, September 9, 1865, Johnson Papers, LC.

the bishop's refusal to include the President in the prayer for all those in civil authority, an action which had forced Thomas to close all Episcopal churches in the state. The Georgia excursion was cut short, Thomas deciding not to visit the state capitol at Milledgeville lest he cause the same sort of uneasiness among civil officials which characterized his stay at Jackson.[11]

Thomas returned from his trip ambivalent about the temper of white southerners. "The prevailing sentiment seems to be a desire to restore the rebel States to their old relations and functions," he told Stanton, "but many of the people are unfriendly to the people of the loyal States, and to those who have continued loyal to the Government of the United States in the South." His skepticism of white intentions was manifested in his approval of the operations of the Freedmen's Bureau in all three states, because he believed the Bureau essential for the welfare of the freedmen.[12]

The most important inspection tour of the South, however, was that undertaken by Lieutenant General Ulysses S. Grant, the hero of Fort Donelson, Vicksburg, Chattanooga, and Appomattox. Americans would listen to and in most cases heed whatever the nation's foremost military hero had to say about the proper course to pursue toward his former foes, especially since the general rarely shared his political opinions with the public. Nor was Grant exactly unwilling to play a role in the reconstruction process; even while waging war, he was contemplating the peace to follow. In February, 1865, he had been instrumental in the negotiations preceding the ill-fated Hampton Roads Conference; the next month he conferred with Lincoln and Sherman at City Point, Virginia, about peace terms. His successful pursuit of the Army of Northern Virginia was propelled by his desire to prevent Lee from reaching the Blue Ridge Mountains, where the possibility of guerrilla operations not only promised to prolong the war indefinitely but would foment hatreds which would be difficult to overcome in peace. The generous terms offered at Appomattox avoided humiliating the defeated Confederates, commenced economic recovery by allowing soldiers to retain their horses and mules, and forestalled efforts to try Lee and his men for treason by pledging that they would not be disturbed so long as they observed their paroles. As Grant put it in silencing a noisy soldier celebration, "The rebels are our countrymen again."[13]

Although he believed that Lincoln's death was "an irreparable loss to the South, which now needs so much both his tenderness and magnanimity," his initial concern about Johnson's reputation as an advocate of a harsh peace diminished somewhat after several early meetings with the new President. The Tennessean was "a man disposed and capable

11. For Thomas's letter of December 12, 1865, to Stanton, see Appendix I.
12. *Ibid.*
13. Catton, *Grant Takes Command*, 419–24, 449–59.

of conducting the government to its old channels," he concluded. "If so we may look for a speedy peace." Satisfied that "the country has nothing to fear from his administration," Grant suggested that those who were skeptical of the new President's abilities were "unpatriotic." Radical Henry Winter Davis was disgusted with Johnson's reliance on the military hero, "of whom he seemed not exactly to stand in awe of but anxious to conciliate rather than resolved to command."[14]

In the months following Appomattox, Grant advocated leniency toward the defeated South. "The suffering that must exist in the South the next year, even with the war ending now, will be beyond conception," he wrote his wife after a trip to North Carolina to supervise the Sherman-Johnston negotiations. "People who talk now of further retaliation and punishment, except of the political leaders, do not conceive of the suffering endured already, or they are heartless and unfeeling." One of the best ways to secure peace was to display lenity toward Robert E. Lee in the hope that other southerners would follow his example in accepting the results of the war and work toward a lasting peace. Johnson, who had seriously entertained the idea of trying Lee for treason, backed down only when Grant threatened to resign his commission. Putting Lee on trial, Grant believed, might well spark disorder and violence among Confederate veterans and other white southerners. In a sentence subsequently struck from his final report of military operations, Grant asked: "Would it not be well for all to learn to yield enough of their individual views to the will of the majority to preserve a long and happy peace?"[15]

Grant, however, also understood that reconciliation had to be balanced by justice for the freedman. While he did not embrace demands for massive redistribution of property through confiscation or for the immediate enfranchisement of blacks, he was unwilling to side with those who denounced black suffrage as the empowerment of an inferior race. In June the Chicago *Tribune* reported that the general thought that "it is too soon to declare that the loyal blacks in the South shall not be allowed to vote," in part as a practical necessity. "The Government and people may have to choose between keeping a standing army . . . or of enfranchising the blacks, and thereby enabling them to support the white loyalists." But for the present Grant believed that until blacks at-

14. Simon, *The Personal Memoirs of Julia Dent Grant*, 156; Grant to Charles W. Ford, April 17, and to Silas A. Hudson, April 21, 1865, John Y. Simon and David L. Wilson, eds., *The Papers of Ulysses S. Grant* (14 vols. to date, Carbondale, 1967-), XIV, 405, 429–30; John Niven, *Gideon Welles: Lincoln's Secretary of the Navy* (New York, 1973), 501.

15. Grant to Julia Dent Grant, April 25, 1865, *Grant Papers*, XIV, 433; Lee to Johnson, June 13, 1865, and Grant to Johnson, June 16, 1865 (endorsement on Lee to Grant, June 13, 1865), Grant Papers, Illinois State Historical Library; Adam Badeau, *Grant in Peace: From Appomattox to Mount McGregor* (New York, 1887), 25–26; Grant to Stanton, June 20, 1865, Grant Papers, LC.

tained basic literacy, they needed protection more than they needed the ballot.[16]

Through the summer and fall of 1865, Grant's subordinates attended to their responsibilities in the South with mixed feelings. They tried to maintain order, relieve suffering, and assist the Freedmen's Bureau (although some commanders obstructed rather than supported Bureau operations). They clashed with civil officers, especially Johnson's provisional governors, who were intent on reasserting their authority. In New Orleans, Philip H. Sheridan found it "hard to enforce martial law after war has ceased and a form . . . of civil government is in existence." Even so, as the cavalryman assured President Johnson, they could "well afford to be lenient" and ignore "impotent ill feeling," adding that since "it is so hard by any species of legislation to correct this feeling, magnanimity is the safest and most manly course." Others were even more optimistic. George H. Thomas believed that "judicious management" would allow military authorities to restore "perfect order" in Tennessee, Alabama, and Georgia with "but little trouble."[17]

Grant, however, displayed little interest in southern affairs. During the summer of 1865 he escaped the confines of the nation's capital and toured the North, an activity which prevented him from participating in discussions about the role of the military in the occupied South. When he did speak, he advocated reconciliation and the rapid restoration of civil government as the cornerstones of Reconstruction. He worked hard to secure pardons for several Confederate generals, including James Longstreet, and intervened on behalf of imprisoned Alexander Stephens and Clement C. Clay. There seemed to be little harshness now in the man who once waged relentless war.[18]

Grant's emphasis on reconciliation was evident in his stance toward black troops, the Freedmen's Bureau, and black suffrage. In May, 1865, he had ordered the transfer of the all-black XXV Corps from Virginia to the Texas border, partly in response to reports that the ill-disciplined black bluecoats caused friction with white southerners and encouraged idleness and insolence among the freedmen. Of course, any sign of black equality or of former slaves asserting their freedom was viewed by many whites as support for such assertions. By the summer of 1865 these complaints had multiplied; Grant requested the War Department

16. Chicago *Tribune*, June 14, 1865; Michael J. Cramer, *Ulysses S. Grant: Conversations and Unpublished Letters* (New York, 1897), 65.

17. Sheridan to John A. Rawlins, October 7, 1865, Grant Papers, LC; Sheridan to Johnson, November 26, 1865, Johnson Papers, LC; Thomas to Grant, July 1, 1865, Grant Papers, LC. See Perman, *Reunion Without Compromise*, 132–43, and Sefton, *Army and Reconstruction*, 25–59, for an overview of these issues.

18. William B. Hesseltine, *Ulysses S. Grant: Politician* (New York, 1935), 56–58; Badeau, *Grant in Peace*, 27–29, 180–81; Nashville *Republican Banner*, October 5, 7, 1865; *Army & Navy Journal*, October 14, 1865; Grant to Johnson, November 7, 26, 1865, Johnson Papers, LC.

to muster out all black regiments raised in the North. To him, whether the charges were true or not was irrelevant; the mere presence of black troops was destabilizing and inhibited reconciliation, justifying their removal. Grant, however, retained in service black regiments organized in the South, enabling him to control the behavior of part of the southern black population. Had these troops been discharged, they might have compounded the chaotic social situation, and, given their military experience, they could have responded to white provocation with violence. One way to prevent such a possibility was to prohibit black troops from retaining their weapons as they were mustered out, a privilege accorded to white troops.[19]

The operations of the Freedmen's Bureau presented similar problems. Grant favored the idea of some sort of federal agency assisting southern blacks in the transition from slavery to freedom, and supported efforts to staff the Bureau with army officers. But the general proved less patient when he heard reports of misbehavior by Bureau officials. In August he received reports that General Edward A. Wild, supervising Bureau operations in Georgia, was terrorizing white citizens by displaying excessive zeal in carrying out his business. Grant called for Wild's removal, telling Secretary Stanton that he objected to the general's "prejudice in favor of color," and suggested that he send one of his staff officers south to observe conditions and make recommendations to Bureau chief Oliver O. Howard. Guardianship was one thing; advocacy was another, violating Grant's desire for the Bureau to serve as a mediator and harmonizer.[20]

The general-in-chief also opposed immediate enfranchisement of southern blacks, fearing that such a step would only aggravate social disorder in the South. The search for stability was foremost in his mind; Grant did not base his argument against black suffrage on grounds of racial inferiority. He remained in favor of eventual enfranchisement after a period of adjustment and transition. The theme of conciliation was also evident in Grant's concern about offering white southerners relief. Unable to attend a meeting devoted to relief efforts, Grant made his views known in a letter. "How ever we may have differed from our Southern brethren in the events of the past four years, we have now become one people, and with but one interest," he wrote, pledging his support for whatever "is calculated to increase the brotherly feeling between the two sections of our country."[21]

19. Ira Berlin, Joseph P. Reidy, and Leslie S. Rowland, eds., *Freedom: A Documentary History of Emancipation, 1861–1867. Series II: The Black Military Experience* (Cambridge, England, 1982), 733–35; Cresap, *Appomattox Commander*, 220–22.

20. Grant to Stanton, August 30, 1865, Stanton Papers, LC; Nieman, *To Set the Law in Motion*, 13.

21. *Army & Navy Journal*, October 14, 1865; Augusta *Constitutionalist*, December 6, 1865.

Ulysses S. Grant.
Courtesy of The National Archives

Understandably, Andrew Johnson thought that such sentiments confirmed his belief that the general was wholeheartedly behind his policy. With this in mind, he began suggesting that Grant examine southern conditions firsthand in hopes of countering the allegations of Carl Schurz. Staff officer Adam Badeau first made mention of the possibility in October, telling Congressman Elihu B. Washburne, "This is a matter of duty, the President having requested it." Grant did not embrace the idea at first. Given his taciturn nature and reluctance to divulge his reasoning, his terse public statements filtered through the press could give the impression that he agreed with the President's policy, a consensus that was more apparent than real. However, the general's reservations were balanced by his belief that it was his duty to support the President and, as a good subordinate, keep his opinions to himself. On November 22, Grant told staff officer Cyrus B. Comstock that he still had not made up his mind about the trip. Comstock opined that "he had better go so that he might be able to speak decidedly on questions of reconstruction." Two days later, staff officers Orville Babcock and Badeau informed Washburne that their chief was still wavering. After a conference with Johnson on the twenty-fifth, Grant decided to go, and two days later, along with Comstock, Badeau, and Babcock, he left Washington and began what would become known as "Grant's Tour of the South."[22]

The general-in-chief and his staff arrived at the Spotswood House in Richmond in the afternoon and that evening watched blacks parade by torchlight. Convinced that there would be plenty of opportunities to visit Virginia from nearby Washington, they made their way south to North Carolina the next day, as newspapers speculated that the real mission of the tour was to examine the Texas-Mexico border with an eye to future offensives. At Raleigh, the state legislature interrupted its deliberations about the Thirteenth Amendment to welcome the general. Many North Carolinians offered their perspectives on what was to be done, and provisional governor William W. Holden conferred with him. "There seems to be the best of feeling existing," Grant concluded, "and nothing but the greatest desire expressed by original Secessionists and unionists to act in such a way as to secure admittance back and to please the general government." Meanwhile, Comstock huddled with army officers stationed there to discuss the labor situation. The freedmen, he learned, would work for northerners who had emigrated south to establish plantations, but "they distrust their old masters." Many blacks, holding firm to the belief that they would receive land on New Year's Day, 1866, "in spite of efforts to set them right . . . will not make

22. Badeau to Elihu B. Washburne, October 20, November 24, 1865, and Babcock to Washburne, November 24, 1865, Washburne Papers, LC; Cyrus B. Comstock Diary, November 12, 22, 27, 1865, Comstock Papers, LC.

contracts" for the coming year. "Whites fear negro uprisings—both sides wish troops to remain."[23]

Reporters caught up with Grant at Wilmington the next day. He was "dressed in the plainest civilian clothes" and was wearing "a black felt hat." The party boarded a segregated train and discussed, among other issues, "the negro question," as they bounced along the rails (Comstock later complained about the condition of the railroads, overlooking Sherman's role in destroying them). After a stop in Florence, South Carolina, they continued down to Charleston, and a restless Grant went to the car reserved for blacks to smoke a cigar. One reporter noted that the general's "views regarding matters of political import were expressed with the utmost frankness and simplicity," but neglected to discuss what views Grant held.[24]

Arriving in Charleston on the morning of December 1, he was greeted by General Daniel E. Sickles. "Feeling of citizens apparently bad," Comstock jotted down in his diary, after hearing from General Charles Howard, brother of the head of the Freedmen's Bureau and an advocate of black rights, that relations between whites and blacks were tense, "the negroes having no trust in the whites & the latter fearing an uprising." Comstock had a better opportunity to observe white resistance. "As we rode through the city I saw several who called themselves ladies make faces at the Yankee officers with us," he observed. "It is useless to say they are only women—they express openly what their husbands & brothers feel but do not show."[25]

That night, both whites and blacks vied for Grant's favor. Blacks crowded the streets outside Sickles's house to welcome Grant. Inside, whites dined with him and presented their case. James L. Orr, William Aiken, and other prominent South Carolina politicians were eager to ingratiate themselves. At breakfast the next morning Aiken lobbied to have his rice plantation restored. ("The Gov. claims to have always been a union man," Comstock noted.) Grant directed Sickles to investigate Aiken's claim and, if it was true, to restore the plantation "if without prejudice to the negroes." That night Dr. Albert G. Mackey and Judge Andrew G. Magrath joined Orr, Aiken, and Grant and his staff at dinner. Magrath had just been released from Fort Pulaski, and Comstock commented that "the imprisonment has apparently done him good," for the judge "admits & accepts all the results of the war & is perfectly willing to make the most of the present situation." For his part

23. Grant to Julia Dent Grant, November 29, 1865, Grant Papers, LC; Comstock Diary, November 29, 1865; New York *Times*, November 30, 1865. One report out of Washington that day noted that Grant did not necessarily include all southerners in that category. The general-in-chief "is not satisfied with the growth of loyalty at New Orleans," the correspondent wrote, due in part to the rapid revival of pro-secession newspapers. *Ibid.*

24. *Ibid.*, December 11, 1865; Comstock Diary, November 30, 1865.

25. *Ibid.*, December 1, 1865.

Grant came away from Charleston expressing "great pleasure and satisfaction at the general good feeling, spirit and disposition which he had observed along his route, evinced by the Southern people toward the government, and their cheerful adaptation to the new order of affairs."[26]

Few northern visitors to Charleston could leave without also visiting the Sea Islands to observe the black community there, and Grant proved no exception. On December 3, in the company of General Rufus Saxton, a leading advocate of black rights, he left Charleston and traveled to Hilton Head, where, "in his civilian dress and smoking the traditional cigar," he reviewed a regiment of black troops and made a brief inspection of the colony before continuing on his way to Savannah with his staff. Again they bumped along by rail, an observer noting that "they seemed to think it was great fun: they said they were riding on Sherman's *hairpins*." Arriving on the morning of December 4, they were greeted by another throng of cheering blacks. The Savannah *Republican*, anxious to downplay news of southern loyalty, reported that the general's visit was "an event, but a very tame one. . . . There was not the slightest enthusiasm manifested at the arrival, except by the few northern merchants and the colored population."[27]

After a day filled with more interviews, Grant watched a fireworks display that night and attended the theater. News of his presence had leaked out, and some two-thirds of the ticket holders demanded their money back. Unionists had quickly gobbled up the tickets and packed the house. What did the general think of this evidence of southern intransigence? "Oh, nothing at all," he told a reporter. "The close of the war being so recent, a natural soreness is to be expected on the part of certain individuals but it will soon pass away." Besides, he added, "my faith in the future rests on the soldier element of the South. I feel assured that those who did the fighting may be depended upon to restore tranquility."[28]

The next day Grant continued into the interior, visiting Augusta, and slipped through Atlanta so quietly that few people knew he had been in town. One newspaper commented that the general "travels very quietly,

26. *Ibid.*, December 2, 1865; New York *Times*, December 11, 1865. When Sickles and Aiken visited the latter's plantation, Aiken's former slaves were unwilling to enter into labor contracts with their old owner in anticipation of a division and redistribution of lands. The next month, Grant approved the restoration of Aiken's plantation, but, since Congress had yet to act on the status of lands set aside for the freedmen under General Sherman's Special Field Order No. 15, he added: "I would say leave all land to which the Freedmen have obtained possessionary titles, until such settlement is had." Augusta *Constitutionalist*, December 29, 1865; Grant to Sickles, January 26, 1866, Grant Papers, LC.

27. New York *Times*, December 11, 12, 1865; Comstock Diary, December 2–11, 1865; Trowbridge, *The Desolate South*, 263. William S. McFeely's claim in *Grant: A Biography* (New York, 1981), 238, that Grant did not visit the Sea Islands is simply not true. See, for example, the December 1 and 2 entries in the J.W. Saxton Diaries, Saxton Family Papers, Sterling Library, Yale University.

28. Atlanta *Journal*, July 1, 1934; *Army & Navy Journal*, December 16, 1865; New York *Herald*, August 2, 1886.

refuses all public receptions, and demonstrations of every kind—an evidence of a great man, in these days of snobbery and boot-licking." Grant believed that many white southerners were willing to make some sort of settlement. "People all seem pleasant . . . at least towards me," he wrote Julia; they looked "towards the Government to enter faithfully upon a course to restore harmony between the sections." As he journeyed from Savannah to Augusta, he conversed with ex-Confederate general John B. Gordon. Comstock noted that although at one time Gordon was "very bitter," he now seemed "entirely 'reconstructed,' and thinks the war will prove a blessing to the south." Another incident, however, suggested that some whites felt otherwise. Hardly had Grant passed through Augusta when a white policeman shot a black private. Infuriated, black soldiers paraded up and down streets with "bayonets and loaded muskets," disarming whites.[29]

At Atlanta, Grant conferred with General James H. Wilson, a former staff officer. Wilson later recalled that Grant believed Lincoln's death to have been "an irreparable blow to the orderly and conservative reconstruction of the Southern states." The commanding general went on "to discredit the judgment and statesmanship of Andrew Johnson," but added that he "distrusted the senatorial group with which Stanton was associated." Grant's own sentiments were "not only thoroughly conservative, but thoroughly kind" toward southerners, and he hoped "that all classes would frankly accept the situation and devote themselves unselfishly to the restoration of friendly relations" between the sections.[30]

By now the trip was beginning to tell on Grant: he was sick and exhausted. It was time to go back to Washington, especially since Congress had already been in session several days. After a night in Knoxville, Grant returned to the capital via Lynchburg, Virginia, on December 11. Three days later Johnson greeted him at the White House. As Gideon Welles watched, the general related his experiences and impressions. Welles recorded that Grant found "the people more loyal and better-disposed than he expected to find them, and that every consideration calls for the early reestablishment of the Union." The navy secretary took this to be an endorsement of Johnson's policy, characterizing Grant's views as "sensible, patriotic, and wise," and urged the general to compose a written report of his findings and share his views with Congress. Johnson seconded this proposal. Both men believed that Grant was in full accord with their position, though he had simply said that the situation was better than he had expected. Still, these views stood in stark contrast to Schurz's gloomy picture. Since

29. Nashville *Republican Banner*, December 14, 1865; Comstock Diary, December 5, 1865; Grant to Julia Dent Grant, December 4[5], 1865, Grant Papers, LC; Columbus (Ga.) *Sun and Times*, December 12, 1865.

30. James H. Wilson, *Under the Old Flag* (2 vols., New York, 1912), II, 37.

Sumner had already called for Schurz's report, the President could now pair it with Grant's impressions, secure in the knowledge that the public would believe Grant, not Schurz.[31]

Sumner got wind of Johnson's plan the next day when he visited Welles. The secretary told the senator that Grant "had found the people disposed to acquiesce and become good citizens,—that he found those who had been most earnest and active in the Rebellion were the most frank and thorough in their conversion." Sumner was furious. What about the opinions of Chief Justice Chase? Welles responded that Grant's opinions were worth more as "practical common sense from a man of no political knowledge or aspiration, while Chase theorized and had great political ambition." Meanwhile, Grant set about putting his opinions on paper. The short document—merely two printed pages in contrast to Schurz's forty-five-page essay—would nevertheless become one of the most quoted documents of the Reconstruction era.[32]

31. Comstock Diary, December 6–11, 1865; *Welles Diary*, II, 396–97.
32. *Ibid.*, 397–98.

Letter

HEADQUARTERS ARMIES OF THE UNITED STATES,
Washington, D.C., December 18, 1865

SIR:

In reply to your note of the 16th instant,[1] requesting a report from me giving such information as I may be possessed of coming within the scope of the inquiries made by the Senate of the United States in their resolution of the 12th instant,[2] I have the honor to submit the following:

With your approval, and also that of the honorable Secretary of War, I left Washington city on the 27th of last month for the purpose of making a tour of inspection through some of the southern States, or States lately in rebellion, and to see what changes were necessary to be made in the disposition of the military forces of the country; how these forces could be reduced and expenses curtailed, &c.; and to learn, as far as possible, the feelings and intentions of the citizens of those States towards the general government.

The State of Virginia being so accessible to Washington city, and information from this quarter, therefore, being readily obtained, I hastened through the State without conversing or meeting with any of its citizens. In Raleigh, North Carolina, I spent one day; in Charleston, South Carolina, two days; Savannah and Augusta, Georgia, each one day. Both in travelling and whilst stopping I saw much and conversed freely with the citizens of those States as well as with officers of the army who have been stationed among them. The following are the conclusions come to by me.

I am satisfied that the mass of thinking men of the south accept the present situation of affairs in good faith. The questions which have heretofore divided the sentiment of the people of the two sections—slavery and State rights, or the right of a State to secede from the Union—they regard as having been settled forever by the highest tribunal—arms—that man can resort to. I was pleased to learn from the leading men whom I met that they not only accepted the decision arrived at as final, but, now that the smoke of battle has cleared away and time has been given for reflection, that this decision has been a fortunate one for the whole country, they receiving like benefits from it with those who opposed them in the field and in council.

Four years of war, during which law was executed only at the point of the bayonet throughout the States in rebellion, have left the people possibly in a condition not to yield that ready obedience to civil authority the American people have generally been in the habit of yielding. This would render the presence of small garrisons throughout those States necessary until such time as labor returns to its proper channel, and civil authority is fully established. I did not meet any one, either those holding places under the government or citizens of the southern States, who think it practicable to withdraw the military from the south at present. The white and the black mutually require the protection of the general government.

There is such universal acquiescence in the authority of the general government throughout the portions of country visited by me, that the mere presence of a military force, without regard to numbers, is sufficient to maintain order. The good of the country, and economy, require that the force kept in the interior, where there are many freedmen, (elsewhere in the southern States than at forts upon the seacoast no force is necessary,) should all be white troops. The reasons for this are obvious without mentioning many of them. The presence of black troops, lately slaves, demoralizes labor, both by their advice and by furnishing in their camps a resort for the freedmen for long distances around. White troops generally excite no opposition, and therefore a small number of them can maintain order in a given district. Colored troops must be kept in bodies sufficient to defend themselves. It is not the thinking man who would use violence towards any class of troops sent among them by the general government, but the ignorant in some places might; and the late slave seems to be imbued with the idea that the property of his late master should, by right, belong to him, or at least should have no protection from the colored soldier. There is danger of collisions being brought on by such causes.

My observations lead me to the conclusion that the citizens of the southern States are anxious to return to self-government, within the Union, as soon as possible; that whilst reconstructing they want and require protection from the government; that they are in earnest in wishing to do what they think is required by the government, not humiliating to them as citizens, and that if such a course were pointed out they would pursue it in good faith. It is to be regretted that there cannot be a greater commingling, at this time, between the citizens of the two sections, and particularly of those intrusted with the law-making power.

I did not give the operations of the Freedmen's Bureau that attention I would have done if more time had been at my disposal. Conversations on the subject, however, with officers connected with the bureau, lead me to think that, in some of the States, its affairs have not been conducted with good judgment or economy,[3] and that the belief, widely spread among the freedmen of the southern States, that the lands of their former owners will, at least in part, be divided among them, has come from the agents of this bureau.[4] This belief is seriously interfering with the willingness of the freedmen to make contracts for the coming year.[5] In some form the Freedmen's Bureau is an absolute necessity until civil law is established and enforced, securing to the freedmen their rights and full protection. At present, however, it is independent of the military establishment of the country, and seems to be operated by the different agents of the bureau according to their individual notions.[6] Everywhere General Howard, the able head of the bureau, made friends by the just and fair instructions and advice he gave;[7] but the complaint in South Carolina was that when he left, things went on as before. Many, perhaps the majority, of the agents of the Freedmen's Bureau advise the freedmen that by their own industry they must expect to live. To this end they endeavor to secure employment for them, and to see that both contracting parties comply with their engagements. In some instances, I am sorry to say, the freedman's mind does not seem to be disabused of the idea that a freedman has the right to live without care or provision for the future. The effect of the belief in division of lands is idleness and accumulation in camps, towns, and cities. In such cases I think it will be found that vice and disease will tend to the extermination or great reduction of the colored race. It cannot be expected that the opinions held by men at the south for years can be changed in a day, and therefore the freedmen require, for a few years, not only laws to protect them, but the fostering care of those who will give them good counsel, and on whom they rely.

The Freedmen's Bureau being separated from the military establishment of the country, requires all the expense of a separate organization. One does not necessarily know what the other is doing or what orders they are acting under. It seems to me this could be corrected by regarding every officer on duty with troops in the southern States as an agent of the Freedmen's Bureau, and then have all orders from the head of the bureau sent through department commanders. This would create a responsibility that would secure uniformity of action throughout all the south; would insure the orders and instructions from the head of the bureau being carried out, and would relieve from duty and pay a large number of employees of the government.

I have the honor to be, very respectfully, your obedient servant,

U. S. Grant, Lieutenant General.

His Excellency Andrew Johnson,
President of the United States.

Sen. Ex. Doc. No. 2, 39 Cong., 1 Sess., 106–8.

1. Not found.

2. On December 12 Charles Sumner introduced a resolution calling on the President to transmit the reports of Carl Schurz and John Covode to Congress.

3. For example, Grant was aware of the excessive behavior of Gen. Edward A. Wild. See Schurz to Johnson, August 13, 1865, n.22.

4. Gen. Oliver O. Howard, head of the Freedmen's Bureau, shared Grant's opinion and had already taken action. See *ibid.*, n.20.

5. Grant's aide, Gen. Cyrus B. Comstock, noted the same reluctance in his diary account of the trip. November 29, 1865, Comstock Papers, LC.

6. In a circular letter issued on December 22 Howard called attention to Grant's re-

port, and reminded his subordinates that not only was the Bureau part of the War Department, but that Bureau officers were obligated to cooperate with military authorities. Failure to comply with these instructions would result in court martial or dismissal. Circular No. 22, December 22, 1865, *House Ex. Doc.* No. 70, 39 Cong., 1 Sess., 198.

7. A reference to Howard's own tour through the South in October and November, 1865.

Epilogue

"The country is in no state to entertain right opinions, or to act judiciously in relation to the people of the States lately in rebellion, without correct and true information in relation to the real condition of things now existing there," advised one northerner in a letter to the editor of the Boston *Advertiser*, commenting on one of Carl Schurz's published dispatches. Indeed, to many northerners an understanding of the behavior of the defeated southerners was essential to determining the correct course to pursue.[1] As they speculated about the course the President planned to announce when Congress convened in December, many grew increasingly skeptical about the loyalty and submissiveness of white southerners. Not only did they hear tales of violence against blacks and white unionists and of lingering allegiances to the Confederate cause, but the actions of the state constitutional conventions and legislatures gave just cause for alarm. Several states were content to nullify, not repeal, their ordinances of secession; Georgians kicked long and hard before repudiating their war debt, and South Carolinians failed to do so at all; Mississippians grumbled about abolition—indeed, the state legislature failed to ratify the Thirteenth Amendment—while Georgians retained the right to seek compensation for their slaves. State legislatures passed what became known as "Black Codes," severely restricting the civil rights of blacks and delineating punishments for crimes differing according to the race of the convicted. While many Republicans sought refuge in the idea that the President considered his policy "an experiment" which, if it failed, would be discarded by the administration, others prepared to fight, satisfied that Johnson was abandoning the fruits of victory in his haste to achieve reconciliation.

Congressional Republicans commenced their counteroffensive with the opening gavel of the 39th Congress. House clerk Edward McPherson, prompted by Thaddeus Stevens, refused to call the names of any southern representatives-elect—including those from Tennessee, the President's home state. Then Stevens moved for the establishment of a joint committee on reconstruction, to consist of nine representatives and six senators, charged with investigating southern affairs. In the Senate, both Sumner and his Massachusetts colleague Henry Wilson introduced bills looking toward the protection and enfranchisement of the freedmen. The next day Congress received Johnson's first annual message—a masterful document due to its vagueness in delineating exactly what was his policy. The President admitted that his policy's suc-

1. Boston *Advertiser*, August 23, 1865.

cess "requires at least the acquiescence of the States which it concerns," warned southerners that "doubt and jealousy and uncertainty" would characterize politics until they ratified the Thirteenth Amendment, and, while noting that black civil rights required protection, denied that the federal government could provide such protection, let alone enfranchise the freedmen.[2]

Despite the almost universal applause which greeted the message, Republicans were undeterred. On December 12, the Senate adopted Sumner's resolution asking Johnson to transmit the reports of Carl Schurz and John Covode. Over the next week, as Congress waited for the reports, Wilson not only spoke in support of his bill protecting the freedmen but reported a bill extending suffrage to blacks in the District of Columbia; the Senate approved Stevens' resolution for a joint committee (after first removing the provision delaying the seating of southern representatives until the committee made its report); and Stevens attacked the administration's policy. It remained to be seen whether Sumner and Stevens could carry the day, or whether they would have to surrender the helm to moderates, led by Lyman Trumbull and William Pitt Fessenden.[3]

On December 19, Johnson submitted not only Schurz's report but "invited" attention to Grant's far shorter letter; no report from Covode had been filed with the President. Not content with merely submitting the reports, Johnson expressed his opinion that the southern states were adhering to federal authority "with more willingness and greater promptitude than under the circumstances could reasonably have been anticipated." Moreover, "in nearly all of them measures have been adopted or are now pending, to confer upon freedmen rights and privileges which are essential to their comfort, protection, and security"—an unfortunately phrased reference to the black codes, which designed a second-class citizenship for the freedmen. In a reference to Grant's report, Johnson commented that "sectional animosity is surely and rapidly merging itself into a spirit of nationality." Grant's report was then read to the Senate, ensuring its inclusion in many newspapers.[4]

Hardly had the clerk finished reading Grant's report than Charles Sumner jumped to his feet, demanding that Schurz's report be read as well. For months the Massachusetts senator had sought to influence the President to adopt a more comprehensive policy embracing black suffrage. He had encouraged Chase and Schurz to undertake their trips, hoping that their letters would persuade Johnson to adopt the Radical programme. Although resigned to accepting that the President would persevere in his course, several weeks earlier he had made one last at-

2. McPherson, *Reconstruction*, 64–66; Benedict, *Compromise of Principle*, 131–32, 140–42.
3. *Ibid.*, 140–42.
4. For Johnson's message, see Appendix II.

tempt to change the President's mind at a White House interview. The senator had charged the President with having "thrown away the fruits of the victories of the Union army" by allowing southern whites to assault freedmen, only to be rebuffed by Johnson's reply that assaults and murders also took place in Massachusetts. The interview ended in disaster; as Sumner prepared to leave, he picked up his top hat, only to find that Johnson had used it as a spittoon. Having already introduced a series of bills outlining an alternative policy toward the South, he now wanted to give wide publicity to Schurz's report, for it gave credence to his charge that white southerners were unrepentant, rebellious, and determined to mistreat the freedmen.[5]

Other senators were not so entranced with Schurz's prose, and within minutes interrupted the reading and suggested that the report be printed. Outraged, Sumner compared Johnson's message with "the whitewashing message of Franklin Pierce with regard to the enormities in Kansas," described Schurz's report as "accurate, authentic, and most authoritative," and dismissed Grant's tour as "hasty." Other senators objected to his charges of "whitewashing," but Sumner stood his ground and continued in the same vein the following day, illustrating his comments by reading letters from correspondents situated in the South. No one rose to Sumner's defense, while several senators continued to defend the President, deploring the rabid and extreme tone as much as the substance of his remarks. Gideon Welles welcomed Sumner's rashness: "Senator Sumner, by his impetuous violence, will contribute to put things right beyond any other man. The President's message and General Grant's letter seem to have made him demented."[6]

Newspaper editorials and private correspondents weighed the merits of the two reports. The *Army and Navy Journal*, mentioning the trio of reports submitted by Grant, Schurz, and Freedmen's Bureau head Howard, mentioned that all were "very interesting and instructive. . . . The only trouble is these tidings do not all agree." If Grant appeared "very well satisfied," Howard came across as "less confident," and Schurz thought the situation "mixed, and rather bad." Most newspapers praised Grant's report. It "has produced a marvellous effect," recorded a Nashville paper, adding that "great confidence is reposed in Gen. Grant's judgment." Grant's "practical, common-sense view of the whole subject" was refreshing, according to the Springfield *Republican*. The southern press was especially pleased, with the Mobile *Register*'s praising Grant's "great good sense and generous feelings." The New York *Times* added that the general's comments about the Freedmen's Bureau were "surely practical statesmanship." (They also produced results: within days General Howard issued a directive calling the atten-

5. Donald, *Sumner and the Rights of Man*, 236–40.
6. Pierce, *Sumner*, IV, 272–73; *Welles Diary*, II, 400.

tion of Bureau officers to Grant's report.) The Democratic New York *World*, in noting Sumner's response, stated, "never were the MAN and the FANATIC more sharply brought face to face than here." Grant, who "has never trod the crooked ways of politics," had again demonstrated proof of his "solidity of judgment and strength of character." "The people will never stop to weigh the crotchets of such men as *Carl Shurz* and *Carl*[*sic*] *Sumner* against the good sense of General Grant." The Nashville *Republican Banner* closed its account bluntly: "No importance is attached to the repor[t] of Carl Squirt, except as a fulmination from a foreigner of bad temper, bad manners, bad judgment and bad repute."[7]

But Schurz had his champions as well. The New York *Tribune*, which reprinted the report on December 23, commented that the Radical "did his work well. . . . In no case, as we find by comparing his report with his authorities, does he make his case stronger than his witnesses permit him." The Cincinnati *Gazette*, which had featured Whitelaw Reid's account of Chase's May tour, asserted that Schurz had discharged his mission "carefully, conscientiously and well," producing "a fair and well informed report." It concluded: "The state of feeling in the South is a thing about which there can be no dispute save by those who think it necessary to make truth a liar in order to carry out some treacherous plan. No man acts blindly in this matter. We know the facts, and if we do not shape our measures to adequately meet them, it will be because of our unfaithfulness to the country, and not because we lacked knowledge."[8]

Inevitably Radical critics of Johnson's policy wondered how the President could favor Grant's brief letter over the voluminous testimony advanced by Schurz in support of his report. "It don't seem to me that he has been doing everything in the best possible manner," one Illinoisian told Trumbull; "I think he was wise to send Carl Shurz on his southern mission, but I don't think it wise in him to have apparently ignored Shurz' able report as though Gen Grant's mere incidental opinion were better authority." Other Radicals concurred. "It is difficult for one who has accurate and full information concerning the state of society at the South—such information as ought to be lodged at the White House—to read with calmness and just deference to the Presidential declarations," observed the Chicago *Tribune*. "If the President is not informed of the truth, it is a grievous calamity to the country, and an incalulable misfortune to the President personally. If he is fully in-

---

7. Georges Clemenceau, *American Reconstruction, 1865–1870* (New York, 1928), 61–62; *Army & Navy Journal*, December 23, 1865; Nashville *Republican Banner*, December 20, 28, 1865; New York *Times*, December 22, 1865; Springfield *Republican*, December 20, 1865; Mobile *Register*, December 27, 1865; New York *World*, December 21, 1865.
8. New York *Tribune*, December 23, 1865; Cincinnati *Gazette*, December 28, 1865.

formed, as he surely might be, then it is more difficult than one cares to own, to conjecture the logical process by which the Executive mind, starting from certain premises, does at length arrive at certain conclusions." The Radical organ concluded, "it is only necessary to accept the President's report and throw away Gen. Grant's report, and Gen. Howard's report and Gen. Shurz's report; for no man in Congress or out can accept the message unless he rejects these accompanying reports, and *vice versa.*" *Harper's Weekly*, questioning the President's thinking, exclaimed, "How could he expect that General Grant's report of a few days' excursion to Charleston would be accepted as a conclusive statement of the actual condition of public sentiment as against the evidence of prolonged and faithful observation presented by Carl Schurz?"[9]

Radicals grumbled about Grant's report. A North Carolina carpetbagger told Thaddeus Stevens that the general "cannot find out the real Sentiments of the Southern people in a flying visit through the South." William S. Robinson, the Radical correspondent for the Springfield *Republican*, under the pen name "Warrington," assailed the general-in-chief: "Did he ask any of the negroes how they liked the situation? No; they are not 'thinking men'. . . . But no matter for Gen. Grant's opinions. They are made for order and are good for nothing."[10] A careful comparison of the two reports, however, reveals that there were significant areas of agreement between Schurz and Grant, although the tone of the two generals' reports differed greatly. Schurz, as he had promised, questioned the success of Johnson's policy and expressed outrage at southern behavior; Grant, making no reference to existing policy, accepted southern behavior as expected, and joined with Schurz in advocating a continued military presence and the protection of the freedmen. Schurz wanted to spark debate and disrupt administrative policy; Grant preferred to quell controversy, seek middle ground, and encourage a dispassionate environment of reasonableness in which to arrive at a policy toward the South. Neither man thought the time was right to restore full civil government to the South; both agreed that white southerners still lacked the respect for law and order necessary to the establishment of stability and peace; and both called for continued inquiry into southern conditions.

Republicans in Congress had already anticipated this suggestion in empowering the Joint Committee on Reconstruction to take testimony on southern affairs. Over the next several months army officers, northern migrants, blacks, several provisional governors, and a few prominent ex-Confederates, including Alexander H. Stephens and Robert E.

9. Jason Marsh to Lyman Trumbull, January 8, 1866, Trumbull Papers, LC; Chicago *Tribune*, January 6, 1866; *Harper's Weekly*, March 10, 1866.

10. George F. Granger to Thaddeus Stevens, January 11, 1866, Stevens Papers, LC; Springfield *Republican*, December 23, 1865.

Lee, were interrogated by committee members. Doubtless the selection of witnesses and the manner in which they were questioned revealed a bias on the part of committee members, Democrat as well as Republican, moderate as well as extremist, just as Johnson's correspondents were biased; nevertheless, the evidence gathered suggested that the President had underestimated the depth of hostility to blacks, white unionists, and soldiers, and had overestimated the extent of southern loyalty. The committee's majority report reflected Republicans' skepticism about the President's ability to weigh, evaluate, and interpret evidence. While Johnson had "urged the speedy restoration of these States, and expressed the opinion that their condition was such as to justify their restoration, yet it is quite obvious that Congress must either have acted blindly on that opinion of the President, or proceeded to obtain the information requisite for intelligent action on the subject"; readers were reminded of the "impropriety of proceeding wholly on the judgment of any one man." The committee was obligated "to investigate carefully and thoroughly the state of feeling and opinion existing among the people of these States" before deciding whether it would be wise to call reconstruction complete.[11]

Ulysses S. Grant was also questioning the accuracy of Johnson's portrayal of southern conditions. While the President declared that Grant's report constituted a ringing endorsement of his policy, a close reading of what the general said belies this impression, suggesting again that the President merely heard what he wanted to hear. Unwilling to give Johnson's policy a whole-hearted endorsement, he still shared the President's hopes for an early reconciliation between the sections, but his concern about the status of blacks and white unionists was growing. He had expressed his desire to undertake another tour of the lower South, ranging west toward New Orleans and Texas, because he knew he needed to see more to form well-considered conclusions. More importantly, it appears that one of the people who read Schurz's report most carefully was Grant himself, who was persuaded that the issue of violence against blacks required further investigation. Before year's end he issued an order asking his commanders in the South to report "all known outrages . . . committed by white people against the blacks, and the reverse," with an eye toward making the results known to Congress.[12]

The general was moving in step with Lyman Trumbull, who was busy preparing a brace of bills which broached the problem of protect-

11. McKitrick, *Andrew Johnson and Reconstruction*, 331; Patrick W. Riddleberger, *1866: The Critical Year Revisited* (Carbondale, Ill., 1979), 45–46; McPherson, *Reconstruction*, 85–86.

12. New York *World*, December 18, 1865; Grant to George H. Thomas, et al., December 25, 1865, Grant Papers, LC.

ing southern blacks. The first bill extended the life of the Freedmen's Bureau and expanded its powers. Having established this stopgap measure, Trumbull then moved to protect black civil rights in a second bill which defined citizenship and civil rights, outlawed denial of these rights and differing punishments on the ground of race, and empowered federal authorities to enforce the act.[13]

By early January, Grant was convinced that blacks desperately needed the protection he had mentioned in his letter to Johnson. Meeting Schurz, he conveyed his reaction to events in the past month. Schurz was elated to discover that "Grant feels very bad about his thoughtless move and has openly expressed his regrets for what he has done." Nor were blacks the only people requiring federal protection. Union officers, soldiers, and veterans were finding themselves prosecuted by southern state authorities for acts committed under orders during the war.[14] On January 12, 1866, Grant issued General Orders No. 3, directing military commanders in the South to protect military personnel, Freedmen's Bureau agents, and loyal southerners from civil prosecution for acts committed under military authority, and extended the same protection to blacks "charged with offenses for which white persons are not prosecuted or punished in the same manner and degree." Through this directive Grant employed the military to protect the rights which Trumbull sought to secure through his legislation. Three days later, in response to an inquiry from the President about the withdrawal of troops from Georgia and Alabama, he stated: "For the present and until there is full security for equitably maintaining the rights and safety of all classes of citizens in the States lately in rebellion, I would not recommend the withdrawal of United States troops."[15]

To Grant, General Order No. 3 was merely a first step. He dispatched aide Cyrus B. Comstock south once more to confer with military commanders. In New Orleans, Comstock spoke with Generals Sheridan and Canby, and recorded Sheridan's opinion "that if Northerners are protected by martial law & the presence of troops that in a short time all questions will be settled without trouble." If troops were withdrawn, however, Sheridan and Canby agreed that northerners "could get no justice from the courts." Canby, who felt that southern whites' behavior had deteriorated since Appomattox, also warned that blacks "would be far worse off than before the war" if the bluecoats left.

13. Sefton, *Army and Reconstruction*, 66–68.

14. Schurz to wife, January 12, 1866, Schafer, *Intimate Letters*, 356; Alfred H. Terry to Grant, January 1, and Daniel Sickles to Grant, January 6, 1866, Grant Papers, LC; Sefton, *Army and Reconstruction*, 57. Two years later Schurz wrote his wife that Grant said, "I traveled as the general-in-chief and people who came to see me tried to appear to the best advantage. But I have since come to the conclusion that you were right and I was wrong." Schurz to wife, December 20, 1868, Schafer, *Intimate Letters*, 457.

15. McPherson, *Reconstruction*, 122–23; Grant to Johnson, January 15, 1866, Johnson Papers, LC.

Such comments reinforced Grant's increasing skepticism about the depth of southern loyalty.[16]

The general was not reassured when he examined the hostile attitude of southern newspapers. Grant believed that the press could play a powerful role in shaping public opinion, and feared that if southern newspapers proved recalcitrant, they would be "doing more to hinder the work of reconstruction, by keeping alive the spirit of hatred between the two sections, than all the politicians in the land put together." When the Richmond *Examiner* rebuked southern women for attending a ball held by General Alfred H. Terry, Grant, furious at "the dangerously inflammatory course" of the paper, ordered Terry to take possession of its offices, and told the President that he believed "it to be for the best interests of the whole people, North and South, to suppress such utterances." Overruled by Johnson, Grant instructed Terry to allow the paper to publish once more, so long as it would assist "the cultivation of friendly relations between the people of these states." At the same time he ordered military commanders to forward copies of newspapers which "contain sentiments of disloyalty and hostility to the Government in any of its branches."[17]

If the President was dismayed with signs that Grant was not a hearty supporter of his policy, he said nothing publicly, hoping to retain at least the appearance of unity. He showed no such hesitation when it came to confronting Congress' challenge, embodied in its passage of Trumbull's two bills. On Febarury 19, 1866, he vetoed the Freedmen's Bureau bill; two days later the Senate failed to override the veto, and Johnson celebrated the event in an intemperate speech on Washington's Birthday. Emboldened, he next vetoed Trumbull's civil rights bill on March 27, 1866, although he assured Congress that he stood ready to cooperate in protecting black rights "in conformity with the provisions of the Federal Constitution." Trumbull, John Sherman, and other moderates, who firmly believed that the President would sign the bill, were shocked and angered. This time they succeeded in overriding the veto—a major setback to the administration. Undaunted, Johnson on April 2 declared the insurrection at an end east of the Mississippi, an action which severely restricted military authority.[18]

At the end of April the Joint Committee on Reconstruction revealed its alternative plan, embodied in a proposed Fourteenth Amendment to guarantee black rights, repudiate the Confederate debt, disqualify certain former Confederates from voting, and reduce the basis of con-

16. William H. Barnes, *History of the Thirty-Ninth Congress of the United States* (New York, 1868), 119–23; Comstock Diary, January 30, 31, February 2, 6, 7, 10, 1866.

17. Richmond *Dispatch*, February 17, 1866, quoting the Philadelphia *Ledger*; Grant's February 17, 1866, endorsement on Pollard to Grant, February 16, 1866, Headquarters of the Army, Lets. Recd., RG108, NA; Bowers to Terry, February 19, and Grant to Terry, et al., February 17, 1866, Grant Papers, LC.

18. McPherson, *Reconstruction*, 17, 68–81.

gressional representation for states which denied suffrage to a portion of their adult male population. For the next several weeks both houses engaged in lengthy and somewhat acrimonious debates; almost unnoticed was Johnson's submission of Benjamin C. Truman's final report on May 8, in response to an earlier resolution of inquiry offered by John Sherman. While the New York *Times* lauded its correspondent's efforts, other papers, politicians, and the public largely ignored it.[19] In truth, by now both sides had formed their impressions of southern behavior and conditions; the time for inquiry was over. Republicans sought to reconcile internal factions and unite behind a program; Andrew Johnson braced himself to defend the constitutional, political, and social ideals he had always cherished. The resulting clash would reverberate throughout the nation's history to the present day.

In theory, Johnson moved wisely in dispatching men who were sure to provide different, even contrasting, interpretations of conditions in the southern states. However, he failed—and it was a critical failure—to weigh these conflicting assessments in an attempt to form an overall conception of the situation. Perhaps this was rooted in part in the personalities of the correspondents. The President was obviously receptive to information provided by Watterson and Truman when that information was couched in language which openly professed the writer's loyalty to the chief executive. In contrast, at times Chase and Schurz presumed too much on their relationship to Johnson; their letters contain hints of condescension and conceit as they made not-so-subtle suggestions concerning the proper course to be pursued by the President. The Tennessean, always sensitive to any slight, real or imagined, doubtless bristled when he felt he was being lectured. Susceptible to flattery, he warmed far more quickly to the soothing stroking of his supporters.

The oscillation of opinion inherent in the tours suggests that Johnson desired not merely to seek another point of view but to hear from somebody else more likely to share his own attitudes on race and southern society. Watterson's first trip took him over some of the same territory traversed by Chase only a month before; he seemed only too eager to repudiate the chief justice's conclusions. That fall Watterson and Truman roughly followed Schurz's footsteps in investigating conditions in the Deep South. Both men were conscious that their conclusions would controvert the claims made by their Radical counterparts. Perhaps the best evidence that Johnson was looking to substantiate his own impressions is his claim that Grant's report, a fairly dispassionate and balanced document, was an endorsement of his policy—an endorsement which Grant never made.

19. New York *Times*, May 8, 10, 1866.

Each of these select correspondents let his prejudices and preferences shape his perception of conditions. His predilections guided him to different sources of information, which in turn both reinforced and refined those inclinations. Watterson's encouraging representation of the intentions of leading white southerners stemmed in part from his neglect of competing points of view, including those of southern blacks. Indeed, only Chase made any real effort not only to observe the freedmen, but to exchange viewpoints with black leaders, although many blacks did celebrate Grant's presence with public demonstrations. Each envoy conscientiously gathered evidence in support of his contentions, providing Johnson with potentially valuable information. While Schurz, for example, made frank avowal of his bias in private correspondence, he nonetheless produced an impressive array of reports, testimony, and newspaper clippings documenting his case. Too, no one correspondent could have presented all sides of the situation; a complete picture could emerge only after the reports were compared and evaluated. But Johnson would seem to have abnegated this responsibility. Instead his attitude suggests that he was inclined to embrace conclusions which reinforced his own suppositions. Unfortunately, this predisposition negated an ostensible attempt to make a balanced assessment of southern conditions after Appomattox.

Neither Benjamin C. Truman nor Harvey M. Watterson emerged to play prominent roles in shaping reconstruction policy. Truman visited South Carolina and Florida on behalf of the Treasury Department in 1866, and then moved to California as an agent for the Post Office concerned with trans-Pacific mail service. Once on the West Coast he alternated between editing newspapers, occupying minor federal posts, and other labors, while producing several books on California, the Orient, and dueling. He died in Los Angeles in 1916. Watterson maintained a law practice in Washington for a decade, and then alternated between the nation's capital and Louisville, where his son, Henry, was gaining renown as the editor of the *Courier-Journal*. The elder Watterson contributed political commentary and recollections to the paper under the name "An Old Fogy," until his death in 1891.

Salmon P. Chase continued to mix politics and law as chief justice. He often found himself in the minority as the Supreme Court nibbled away at military jurisdiction and test oaths, furthering the President's efforts at a quick and lenient restoration. However, speaking for the majority in *Mississippi v. Johnson* and *Georgia v. Stanton*, both decided in 1867, he rejected southern assertions questioning the constitutionality of the reconstruction legislation passed by Congress in the aftermath of the 1866 elections, thus preserving the introduction of black suffrage in the ten states established through those acts. He also drafted some of the supplemental legislation needed to ensure the effectiveness of the initial Military Reconstruction Act. During his 1865 tour, Chase had refused to visit Jefferson Davis, arguing that it would be an unnecessary act of humiliation; he continued to act in this spirit in delaying Davis' treason trial, and the case was finally dismissed in 1869. By that time Chase's actions while presiding over Johnson's impeachment trial, which made manifest his opposition to the entire proceeding, had revived his presidential ambitions once more. Disappointed when the Republicans closed ranks behind Grant in early 1868, he looked longingly at the Democratic nomination, hoping that his candidacy would remove the acceptance of the blacks' civil and political status as a point of contention. Thwarted once more, he resigned himself to the chief justiceship, which he held until his death in 1873.

In 1865 Carl Schurz was recognized as one of the nation's most prominent spokesmen for the Radical cause. Less than six years later, however, as listeners heard him denounce the use of federal troops to subdue southern violence, they must have wondered whether the leopard had indeed changed his spots. Elected to the Senate with the backing of moderate and conservative Republicans in 1869, he soon dropped reconstruction in his rush to embrace civil service reform, oppose Grant's plan to annex Santo Domingo, and, along with his old compatriot, Charles Sumner, freely assail the general-turned-President. Believing that the ratification of the Fifteenth Amendment and the readmission of all the southern states marked the end of Reconstruction, Schurz attacked proposals to provide protection for black voters and pushed for the removal of all political disqualifications and disabilities imposed on former Confederates through previous legislation. Southerners needed to be conciliated; they could be trusted to protect blacks from the acts of a disruptive few; proposed legislation to suppress violence destroyed states' rights and threatened constitutional safeguards of personal liberty—such arguments, the arguments of Andrew Johnson in 1865 which had earned Schurz's scorn, were now at the heart of his opposition to Reconstruction. One of the organizers of the Liberal Republican movement designed to unseat Grant, he watched it being buried under Grant's landslide reelection victory. Eventually Schurz's liberalism won him a cabinet seat as head of the Interior Department under Rutherford B. Hayes, but he soon left party moorings for good as a Mugwump in the 1880's, enabling him to bask once more in the role of independent iconoclast, urging education as the key to solving the southern race problem. An ardent anti-imperialist and spokesman for German-Americans, Schurz died in 1906.

Although he believed that a politician led a "most slavish" life, Ulysses S. Grant soon became one in spite of himself.[20] During 1866 he found himself increasingly at odds with the President over reconstruction despite mutual efforts to maintain a facade of harmony; the general finally made his displeasure manifest over Johnson's attempt to associate him with the National Union movement. Accompanying the President on the ill-fated "Swing Around the Circle," Grant told his wife that Johnson was "a national disgrace," and confided to others, "I am disgusted at hearing a man make speeches on the way to his own funeral."[21] Believing that Johnson's policy not only disregarded southern violence but threatened to cast away the fruits of victory, the general supported Congress' reconstruction measures and endorsed black suffrage. Through 1867 the President and the general maintained an uneasy truce, with Grant replacing Secretary of War Stanton on an *ad interim* basis to prevent Johnson from obtaining the upper hand in determining policy toward the South. In January, 1868, their dispute became public knowledge when Grant refused to cooperate with Johnson when the latter sought to defy Congress' restoration of Stanton under the Tenure of Office Act. In the ensuing impeachment crisis, Grant urged senators to convict Johnson.

In 1868 Grant was nominated for the presidency on the Republican ticket. To his old comrade Sherman he explained that he was "forced into it in spite of myself," reflecting a sincere disinclination to forego a secure job and popular adoration for the strain and strife of partisan politics.[22] Only the realization that the alternative was to leave Reconstruction to "mere trading politicians, the elevation of whom, no matter which party won, would lose to us, largely, the results of the costly war which we have gone through," persuaded him to accept the nomination. The next eight years saw Reconstruction submerged under the chaos of corruption, economic depression, northern apathy, and southern intransigence. Grant fought to protect blacks within the constraints of limited governance and laissez-faire ideology, but the realist within him finally understood that the effort would be in vain. Leaving the White House in 1877, he embarked on a world tour; in 1880, again against his desires, many Republicans boosted him for an unprecedented third term, but he lost the nomination to James A. Garfield. Engaging in business on Wall Street, he was ruined by an unscrupulous partner in 1884; the following year, he raced against a deadly throat cancer to complete his *Memoirs*, dying only days after completing the manuscript.

20. Catton, *Grant Takes Command*, 109.
21. Grant to Julia Dent Grant, September 9, 1866, Grant Papers, LC; Brooks D. Simpson, "Ulysses S. Grant and the Fruits of Victory," *Essays in History* 23 (1979), 33.
22. Grant to Sherman, June 21, 1868, W.T. Sherman Papers, LC.

Appendix I

Observations of Two Other Generals:
George G. Meade and George H. Thomas

Besides Grant, Schurz, and Freedmen's Bureau head Oliver O. Howard, two other prominent Union generals toured the South in 1865 and filed reports with the War Department. George G. Meade (1815– 1872), who had been named commander of the Army of the Potomac in June, 1863, and had led it from Gettysburg to Appomattox, was head of the Division of the Atlantic when he visited the Carolinas and Virginia late in the summer of 1865. That fall George H. Thomas (1816–1870), a Johnson favorite who had commanded the Army of the Cumberland from Chattanooga to Nashville, traveled through Mississippi, Alabama, and Georgia, all included in his Division of the Tennessee. Their reports, reproduced below, provide the perspectives of two soldiers who were instrumental in bringing about Confederate defeat.

George G. Meade to Edwin M. Stanton

Head Quarters, Military Division of the Atlantic
Philadelphia, Pa. Sept. 20th 1865.

Hon. E. M. Stanton, Secretary of War,
Washington, D.C.
Sir,

In compliance with your instructions dated the 21st ultimo,[1] I proceeded to make an inspection of the States of South and North Carolina, and Virginia, and have now the honor to submit the following report.

1. SOUTH CAROLINA.

I first visited Hilton Head, the Head-Quarters of the Department, where I met and conferred with Major General Gillmore. At this time I found the State was virtually under martial law. The State was divided geographically into three districts, with numerous sub-districts, and the troops distributed over these in such manner as best to preserve order. In each of the districts, Major General Gillmore had organized Provost Courts, consisting of two or more officers, and where practicable had associated with these officers citizens of known loyalty. These courts had cognizance of all cases of disorder and breach of the peace, with authority to impose fines and imprisonment. They also adjudicated all cases of violation of contract between planters and freedmen, and settled the right of possession to property within certain limits, but did not touch the question of titles. Appeals were had to the District Commander in certain cases, and a final appeal to the Department Commander was authorized in the most important cases. For the trial of serious offenses, military commissions were organized by the District Commanders. This system of military law had been in successful operation since the State was occupied by our forces, and as far as I could judge, had worked very well and to the satisfaction of all parties. When Governor Perry assumed the duty of Provisional Governor, his proclamation restored to power all the civil and municipal officers throughout the State, who held commissions under the Confederate State Government at the time of Johnston's surrender.[2] Major-General Gillmore, considering this act of Governor Perry, as virtually abolishing martial law, and not seeing his authority for this step in the Proclamation of the President appointing the Provisional Governor, deemed it his duty to object to these civil officers being qualified, and reported his objections in full in a letter to the Department, dated August 1st 1865.[3] Being advised of the existing condition of affairs, on the 29th August I telegraphed to the Department for instructions, enquiring specifically whether the action of Governor Perry in restoring these civil officers, was by the President authorized or approved.[4] In reply I received from the President the following telegram.—"Governor Perry will not be interfered with in his work of reconstruction by the military authorities, without orders from me, upon presentation of the facts in the case, and nature of interference proposed."[5]

Upon the receipt of this telegram, I proceeded in company with Major-General Gillmore to visit Governor Perry at Columbia. On meeting Governor Perry, I explained to him that the military authorities under the instructions of the President, were disposed to cooperate in every way with him in restoring law and order to the State: but that under the existing organic laws of the State, which was a pure slave code, I did not see how justice could be done to the freedmen, in the courts of the State, and that in my judgment the interests of both races would be best subserved, by leaving for the present the adjudication of all cases where a colored man was a party, to the military courts. Governor Perry having promptly acceded to this proposition, the question at issue was at once settled; and a proclamation by the Governor, and a general order by Major-General Gillmore were agreed upon and issued.[6] A full conference was then had with Governor Perry, and a harmonious cooperation of the civil and military authorities of the State initiated.

It is due to Governor Perry that I should here express my appreciation of his readiness to cooperate with the military authorities, and it was greatly to be regretted that several previous efforts made by both

Major-General Gillmore and himself to meet had failed from causes they could not control.

COLORED TROOPS.

At the period of my inspection, Maj.-General Gillmore had, under the orders of the War Department, mustered out of service the regiments of colored troops enlisted at the north, leaving in his command about five regiments organized in the Southern States.[7] These regiments were inspected by my order, and found to be in not very good condition, owing to gross neglect and fraud on the part of the medical and other officers recruiting them & to the want of efficient subaltern officers, these being generally appointed by the Military Commander of the Department, from such material as he had at his disposal at the time the regiments were raised. Major General Gillmore reported that a large number of the men of these regiments, had been pronounced by a Medical Board, as physically disqualified for service. These he was having discharged, and after he had eliminated all such cases, he would present a plan for consolidating the five regiments into either two or three, according to the number of men left. A careful examination satisfied me that the charges against the colored troops mentioned in your letter of instruction were groundless.[8] It is undoubtedly true that the colored troops fraternize more with the laboring population than white soldiers: their camps, moreover, are a great source of attraction to the negroes, and in this way may produce some evil, by tempting the laborers to leave their work and visit the camps. The superior condition of the soldier in point of pay and physical comfort, over the laborer is perhaps also injurious in its effect on the laboring population, leading to discontent: but all these arguments against the employment of colored troops [are] in the abstract, and are believed moreover to be very trifling in their results; and are not sufficient in my judgment to justify the discontinuance of this class of troops.[9] It is undoubtedly true that the people of the South are very much prejudiced against these troops, that they really believe they are actively employed disorganizing the laboring population, and not to be relied on in the event of being called on to suppress a negro insurrection, the chronic terror of the South, but I could get no evidence to justify these fears and prejudices. Still as I was satisfied from the reasons given above, that these troops were, for the purposes for which troops are now required in the south, inferior to the white troops, I directed Major-General Gillmore, after consolidating the regiments as proposed, to move them to the sea-board, where they can be usefully employed garrisoning the fortifications, and where they will be measurably removed from contact with the whites.

FREEDMEN'S BUREAU.

A thorough inspection as far as practicable was made of the working of the Freedmen's Bureau. For the results of this inspection I beg leave to refer to the report of Brevet Major-General Webb,[10] Acting Inspector General, (marked A) to whom this duty was specially confided by me.[11]

Circular, No. 13, from the Bureau,[12] made its appearance during the period of my visit, and caused, from mis-apprehension of its contents, great excitement throughout the State. A deputation of the citizens of Charleston visited me, and at my request submitted their views in writing. (herewith appended, marked B).[13] Finding subsequently from some of the subordinate agents of the Bureau, a disposition to give a construction to the law, in reference to abandoned lands, more rigorous than was, I am sure, intended by the framers of the law, and certainly more rigorous than was justified by the existing condition of affairs and the policy of the President, I deemed it my duty to direct Brevet Major-General Saxton, Assistant Commissioner, to desist from seizing any lands under this law, beyond those turned over to him by the agents of the War and Treasury Departments, until the pleasure of the President could be made known.[14] The difficulty appears to be that the construction of the law is left to the individual judgments of subordinate agents of the Bureau,—that owners are dispossessed of their lands, or at least could be, without a hearing, and compelled to meet all the power of the United States in their efforts to recover their property. This seemed to me neither just nor politic, and I would recommend the establishment of some tribunal, if the United States courts are not soon organized, before which the agent of the Bureau, should prove the title of the Governt. under the law, before dispossessing the occupant. The difficulties alluded to will be seen by a perusal of the papers submitted by the citizens of Charleston, and of those in the case of William Ravenel of Charleston, whose property, on investigation, I directed returned to him. These papers are annexed, marked C.)[15] In reference to the charge against the agents of the Bureau, that they were inciting the negroes to leave the plantations, and become a burden on the Government, I could ascertain nothing to substantiate it. It will be seen by the report of Major General Webb that some of the sub-ordinate agents were found lacking in judgment and competency. This is nothing but what might reasonably be expected from the hasty manner in which the Bureau has been organized. Indeed, the organization has but just commenced. Most of the agents in South Carolina are officers belonging to the troops stationed there. As a general rule they are discreet, intelligent and active; and I have no doubt the exceptions to this rule will be promptly removed by the Commissioner when his attention is called to their special cases.

In regard to the issue of rations to destitute freedmen, I found that there had been much irregularity, but this was being corrected by the order from the Bureau, requiring rations to be issued only for seven days, and on returns certified to and approved by the Commanding Officer of the District where the issue is to be made.

Undoubtedly, the plan of colonizing the freedmen on the sea coast,[16] which was well adapted to the exigency of a state of war, when the freedmen were flocking in to our lines, is now injurious to the organization of labor, inasmuch as it invites dis-content on the part of laborers, who think if they leave their plantations, they can always secure a home and employment under the Government. Every thing is however being done to resist this tendency by requiring the negroes to return to the districts from whence they came. The negroes have also received the idea that they are eventually, some time towards the close of the year, to receive each forty acres of land; and although this idea is not only, not given them by the agents of the Bureau, but every means taken to dis-abuse their minds, it undoubtedly does exercise an injurious influence on them. In time this evil will be corrected.

The independence of the agents of the Bureau of the military authorities in the State is I think objectionable, and I would suggest the Assistant Commissioner in each State be placed under the orders of the Department Commander[.] This would avoid any conflict of authority, arising from the construction of laws and orders.

REDUCTION OF THE FORCES.

It will be seen by the report of MajorGeneral Gillmore, herewith transmitted, marked D,[17] that in his judgment it would not be expedient at present to make any reduction to the existing force of the State.

So far as regards any attempt to resist the authority of the General Government, I do not think a man is required in the State; but so long as the State is in its present disorganised condition, and the question of free labor is so unsettled, it will in my judgment be necessary for the Government to exercise a quasi military jurisdiction; and for this purpose and to enforce prompt acquiescence to its orders, the existing force will be required. After the action of the convention, now in session, is known, and whenever the acts of the Government and people conform to their now very positive professions of their determination to abide by the result of the war, the number of troops in the state can be very materially reduced if not entirely withdrawn.

In conclusion I desire to express my approbation of the efficient manner in which I found Major-General Gillmore dis-charging the duties of Department Commander. In the numerous delicate questions, often involving complicated law points, he has exhibited great judgment and a most conscientious desire to do justice to both races. Under his system of Provost Courts, order and quiet prevails throughout the State, and such violations of order as are incidental to all communities are promptly noticed and punished. I beg leave to bring to the special notice of the Department, Major-General Gillmore's services.

NORTH CAROLINA.

Having completed the inspection of South Carolina, I proceeded to Raleigh, North Carolina, via Wilmington. From this point after consultation with Brevet Major-General Ruger,[18] I despatched officers to various parts of the State, going myself to Charlotte, Salisbury, Greensboro, and from thence to Virginia.

MARTIAL LAW.

The condition of affairs in North Carolina was somewhat different from those found in South Carolina, though in principle they were essentially the same.

Provisional Governor Holden had reorganized his courts and machinery for extending civil law over the State, but Brevet Major-General Ruger had claimed for his military courts the jurisdiction in cases of the freedmen. The matter in issue had been fully set forth in a correspondence between the parties, which had been referred to the Department, but no decision had been received at the period of my visit.[19] No action was deemed necessary on my part, as I concurred with Brevet Major General Ruger in the course adopted by him. Since my return to these Headquarters, I have received a letter from Governor Holden, from which it will be seen the existing condition of affairs, is for the present satisfactory to him.—(marked E.)[20]

Colored Troops.—The number of colored troops in this Department was much greater than in South Carolina, they amounting to over 5000, and forming nearly one half the force in the State. I found here the same prejudices and erroneous ideas in regard to these troops on the part of the inhabitants, with about as little cause as I had found in South Carolina.

Before any conclusion as to the disposition of these troops could be made by me, orders were received by Brevet Major-General Ruger in a telegram from the Department, directing the muster out of those organizations recruited at the north. As this would take the greater part of the colored troops, I directed the balance to be posted on the seaboard.

Freedmen's Bureau. Very much the same condition of affairs was found in his State as in South Carolina. Owing to the absence of permanent Provost Courts, the agents of the Bureau are called upon to adjudicate in cases where the freedmen are concerned. Not hearing of any disposition to take property under the plea of abandoned, no orders were given on this subject.

The number of rations issued to destitute freedmen was being reduced, under the orders of the Bureau; and every effort on the part of the agents being made to reduce [induce?] the return of the negroes to the districts they formerly lived in, and to urge their going to work on contract.

Issue of rations to destitute whites. I found this was a very considerable item in this State, but Brevet Major-General Ruger had given his attention to the subject, and had fixed a day, after which all such issues would cease, and the county authorities would be called on to provide for their destitute.

Reduction of troops. After discharging the troops ordered to be mustered out, Brevet Major-General Ruger did not think it would be expedient to make any further reduction, until matters were so arranged that the troops could be withdrawn entirely.

Miscellaneous. I had an interview with Governor Holden, who expressed himself satisfied, as he has since done in writing, with Brevet Major-General Ruger and the conduct of military affairs.

Governor Holden seemed confident that the convention about meeting would conduct matters so satisfactorily, that there would be no necessity for keeping any military force in the State. I was fully convinced that all the reports of cruel treatment of negroes by the whites, and all rumours of insubordination and proposed insurrection by the negroes, were equally groundless, and were circulated by designing parties for selfish purposes. By the consent of Brevet Major-General Ruger, in many parts of the State, an armed police had been organized to preserve order. These forces were however under the orders and control of the District Commander. I found the system was working well, and that the fear of having colored troops stationed among them, induced prompt volunteering on the part of citizens to perform this police duty. Brevet Major-General Ruger accompanied me in my visit to the western part of the State, and I take pleasure in commending to the Department, the discretion, tact, and good judgment exhibited by Brevet Major-General Ruger in his conduct of affairs.

VIRGINIA.

On reaching Richmond, I had a conference with Governor Pierpoint and Major-General Terry.[21] Major-General Terry at my request has forwarded a report on the condition of his command, which is herewith attached, marked F.[22] The order directing the mustering out of colored troops enlisted at the north, dis-charged the only colored regiment in Virginia.

The Freedmen's Bureau under the superintendence of Colonel O. Brown,[23] Assistant Commissioner was working well. The question of issue of rations to destitute whites and blacks, was one of greater magnitude here from the number of applicants for the Government Bounty.

But it will be seen, it had occupied Major-General Terry's attention, and that both himself and Governor Pierpoint, were endeavoring to arrange the transfer of this burden from the United States to the State and County authorities. In connection with this subject, attention is called to a difficulty reported by Major-General Terry. In order to decrease the accumulation of negroes on the seaboard and about large cities, it is necessary to furnish transportation to those willing to return to their former residences. This cannot at present be done without a reference of the case to the Commissioner at Washington, and an order from the War Department. To avoid the delays and difficulties now encountered, it is respectfully recommended, that an order be issued giving the Department Commander authority to grant them passes.[24]

The Department is aware of the difficulty which has occurred with regard to the election for municipal authorities in Richmond.[25] In the absence of these authorities, the military have to perform all police duties. A very large garrison, owing to this cause, and the protection and preservation of the large amount of Confederate property collected here, is thus required for Richmond. The great extent of the State, together with the appearance in the mountains of a spirit of disorder, in Major General Terry's judgment, will not for the present admit of any reduction of his force. The satisfactory condition in which I found the affairs of the Department require I should call special attention to the services of Major-General Terry, who has displayed great judgment in the management of difficult questions.

RESTRICTIONS ON TRADE.

The proclamation of the President removing all restrictions on trade,[26] was published soon after my departure from Washington. From all I could learn, this measure was in every way expedient, as there did not seem to be the slightest reason to believe, any of the articles hertofore forbidden, would be introduced for any improper purposes.

In conclusion I have to report the condition of affairs, as on the whole satisfactory. The people are slowly recovering from the shock of war. Every where the most earnest professions of submission to the result of the war were made, and I am disposed to give credit to these assertions within the limits of what may be presumed natural. But it must be remembered that it is not natural to expect a sudden revolution in the ideas in which a people have been always educated.

The great change in the labor question will require time for both races to realize and conform to; and until this period arrives, it will undoubtedly be necessary to retain such military control as will compel mutual justice from both parties. This control should be exercised with judgment and discretion, and every effort made to convince both races that it is exercised only for their mutual benefit. Instructions to this effect were given to Department Commanders, and I am satisfied, there need be no apprehension of any improper interference of the military with the civil authorities.

Very Respectfully, Your obedient servant, Geo. G. Meade
Major-General, U.S.A.

LS, DNA-RG94, Lets. Recd. by the Office of the Adjutant General, Main Series, File 1370-A-1865.

1. Stanton, understanding the President's concern about the conduct of black troops, assured him that "wherever there is any loyal sentiment, there appears to be no difficulty in regard to the presence of colored troops—complaint being confined chiefly to the most rebellious States—South Carolina and Mississippi." However, believing that there was "some ground for complaint or apprehension of collision in South Carolina," he recommended that Meade be dispatched to the state "to ascertain the real condition of things and provide a proper remedy." He instructed Meade to investigate charges of misbehavior among black troops, violence against black laborers, and misconduct by Freedmen's Bureau agents. Stanton to Johnson, August 21, 1865, Stanton Papers, LC; Stanton to Meade, August 21, 1865, Military Division of the Atlantic, Lets. Recd., RG343, NA; same to same, August 21, 1865, Secretary of War, Lets. Sent, Vol. 59, 294–96, RG107, NA.

2. See Schurz to Johnson, July 28, 1865, n. 25.

3. Gillmore, asking whether the several clauses of Perry's proclamation which conflicted with the President's amnesty policy would be allowed to stand, averred that the governor's reestablishment of the civil court system virtually superseded martial law. He was "firmly impressed that the policy indicated, will result in evil consequences" in race relations and the establishment of a labor system, and in support of this contention, cited his July 27 report to Carl Schurz. Gillmore to Lorenzo Thomas, August 1, 1865, Lets. Sent, Dept. of the South/South Carolina, Vol. 15, 393–94, RG393, NA; Schurz to Johnson, July 28, 1865, n. 27.

4. On August 28, Meade telegraphed Stanton: "Is Gov Perry authorized to restore to power the civil officer[s] indicated by him in his proclamation? And is the President willing this restoration take place?" The secretary, vacationing in New York, instructed his assistant that, although no reply was necessary, the President should see a copy of the general's dispatch. Meade to Stanton, August 28, 1865, and Stanton to Thomas T. Eckert, August 31, 1865, Tels. Recd. by the Secretary of War, 1865, Vol. 48, 246, 261, RG107, NA.

5. As recorded in Johnson's letterpress copy of his telegram of August 31 to Meade, the President employed the word "Restoration," not reconstruction. Johnson Papers, Ser. 3A, LC.

6. Issued September 8, 1865, General Orders No. 30 authorized the reopening of civil courts, but reserved to military provost courts and the Freedmen's Bureau adjudication of cases concerning blacks. File 1370-A-1865, Lets. Recd. by the Office of the Adjutant General, RG94, NA.

7. On Grant's urging, the War Department in early September issued orders that all black regiments raised in the North be mustered out. Grant to Stanton, August 30, 1865, Stanton Papers, LC; OR, Ser. 3, Vol. 5, 108.

8. "Complaints have been made that this class of troops are insubordinate, and lax in discipline; that they are discontented, turbulent, and present a threatening aspect to the people of the Department in which they are employed. No specific facts upon this subject have come to the knowledge of this Department, and whether there is any occasion for such complaints is a matter upon which the President desires accurate information." Stanton to Meade, August 21, 1865, Lets. Sent, Vol. 59, 294, RG107, NA.

9. In contrast, Gillmore complained that there were "so many bad men" among his black troops—"men, who by their false representations and seditious advice, have exercised a most baleful influence upon the plantation laborers"—that he had to use white troops to enforce labor contracts. Sefton, Army and Reconstruction, 52.

10. Alexander S. Webb (1835–1911) served in the Army of the Potomac, commanded the troops that withstood Pickett's Charge at Gettysburg, and became chief of staff for Meade in 1865.

11. Webb's report defended Bureau agents from charges that they were discouraging

blacks from working, although he hoped agents would attend to their duties more carefully. Webb to Meade, September 18, 1865, File 1370-A-1865, Lets. Recd. by the Office of the Adjutant General, RG94, NA.

12. On August 19, Saxton reissued Howard's Circular No. 13 of July 28, instructing assistant commissioners to commence distributing land to blacks. The circular was repealed in September. *House Ex. Doc.* No. 2, 39 Cong., 1 Sess., 111.

13. Eight prominent Charlestonians, including leading merchant George W. Williams and former mayor Charles Macbeth, petitioned Meade, and "through you to the consideration of the President," for relief from the "great & grievous burden" of the Bureau. Testifying to their willingness to "deal with the existing condition of things fairly & in good faith," they protested the seizure of "their last resource, of the very *homes* which are . . . all that is left to them." If this policy were pursued, it would become "absolutely impossible . . . for the people & the State to retrieve or mend their shattered fortunes." If Johnson acted quickly to counter confiscation, he "would replace apprehension & dismay with hope & confidence & renewed activity," as well as foster "the growing feelings of loyalty & devotion to the Government." File 1370-A-1865, Lets. Recd. by the Office of the Adjutant General, RG94, NA.

14. He instructed Saxton to "desist from seizing any lands under the plea of 'abandoned,'" and added that Gillmore was informed of the directive. At Johnson's direction, on September 12, Howard issued Circular No. 15, which rescinded No. 13 and outlined a policy restoring lands to their previous owners. Meade to Saxton, September 3, 1865, Lets. Recd. (Registered), Asst. Com., South Carolina, RG105, NA; McFeely, *Yankee Stepfather*, 133–34.

15. Merchant William Ravenel (1806–1888), finding his Charleston house situated "directly under the fire from Morris Island—it was absolutely unsafe," moved his family to Columbia. He allowed a Union officer, Lt. Hy Hagens, to occupy the house until he decided to relocate his family in Charleston. However, a Freedmen's Bureau agent, Capt. James P. Low, moved to seize the property as "abandoned" under Circular No. 13. After an investigation of the facts of the case, Meade directed Saxton to restore to Ravenel his house. Emma B. Richardson, compiler, "Dr. Anthony Cordes and Some of His Descendants," *The South Carolina Historical and Genealogical Magazine*, XLIV (January, 1943), 20–21; Charleston city directories (1866–1868); Ravenel to Saxton, Hagens to Webb, Low to Webb, Webb to Meade, and Meade to Saxton, all September 1, 1865, Lets. Recd. (Registered), Asst. Com., South Carolina, RG105, NA.

16. A reference to General Sherman's Special Field Order No. 15, issued January 16, 1865, setting aside land along the South Carolina, Georgia, and north Florida coast "for the settlement of the negroes." Sherman, *Memoirs*, II, 250–52.

17. Gillmore's report was in the form of responses to Meade's inquiries about black soldiers and troop levels in his department. He informed Meade that the black regiments were in poor condition, advocated the retention of the present occupation forces, and praised the Freedmen's Bureau. Gillmore to Meade, September 8, 1865, File 1370-A-1865, Lets. Recd., Office of the Adjutant General, RG94, NA.

18. Thomas H. Ruger (1833–1907), who had fought in the Shenandoah Valley and with the armies of the Potomac and the Tennessee, had commanded the Department of North Carolina since June, 1865.

19. The administration had supported Ruger's refusal to let North Carolina civil courts try cases involving blacks. Meade told Holden that once blacks were guaranteed a fair trial, military authority would be withdrawn. Raper, *Holden*, 66.

20. Holden expressed his satisfaction at the partial restoration of civil authority, asked for help in maintaining order in the western part of the state, and promised that the freedmen would be protected. Holden to Meade, September 12, 1865, File 1370-A-1865, Lets. Recd., Office of the Adjutant General, RG94, NA.

21. Alfred H. Terry (1827–1890), active in operations along the South Carolina coast and with the Army of the James, had won fame as the captor of Fort Fisher outside Wilmington, North Carolina, in January, 1865.

22. Terry described the distribution of rations to freedmen and concluded that federal aid was essential. He also praised the working of the Bureau, although he urged that blacks be afforded transportation to relieve overcrowding. Terry to George D. Ruggles, September 15, 1865, *ibid.*

23. Orlando Brown (1827–1904) had been a surgeon and quartermaster during the

war before taking the colonelcy of a black regiment. Lets. Recd., Office of the Adjutant General, U.S.C.T. Div., B-430-1865, RG94, NA.

24. Meade was referring to General Orders No. 138, issued by the War Department on September 16, 1865. The War Department made no modifications of the order in line with the general's suggestion, and subordinates continued to adhere to previous policy. See General Order No. 163, November 28, 1865, General Orders and Circulars, Department of North Carolina, 1865, Office of the Adjutant General, RG94, NA.

25. The election in Richmond in late July had resulted in the selection of locally prominent Confederates for municipal offices. These results were overturned by Gen. John W. Turner, and he was sustained by the President. Sefton, *Army and Reconstruction*, 30; *Welles Diary*, II, 347–48.

26. The last and most comprehensive of Johnson's three proclamations restoring trade with the South was issued August 29, 1865. Richardson, *Messages*, VI, 331.

George H. Thomas to Edwin M. Stanton

Nashville, Tenn., December 12, 1865.

Hon. E. M. Stanton:

I reached here night before last. Have during my trip visited Vicksburg, Jackson, and Meridian, Miss.; Mobile, Montgomery, Selma, and West Point, Ala.; Atlanta, Kingston, and Dalton, Ga. The prevailing sentiment seems to be a desire to restore the rebel States to their old relations and functions, but many of the people are unfriendly to the people of the loyal States, and to those who have continued loyal to the Government of the United States in the South. The Legislature of Mississippi adjourned without ratifying the Constitutional Amendment. Suspicion is, that the second clause, if ratified, will empower Congress to interfere in the international [internal?] legislation of the several Southern States affecting the social and political *status* of negroes.[1] I found Governor Humphreys disposed to acquiesce promptly in the decision of the President to continue Governor Sharkey as Provisional Governor,[2] but both feared that a public announcement of such a decision after he (Humphreys) had been inaugurated would be very disastrous to the effort to reconstruct the State. I therefore advised that they and General Wood, who was also present at the interview, have a complete understanding of what I believed to be the policy of the President;—I then explained what I believed his policy to be, in general terms, stating it as nearly as I could remember, in the words of his replies to the delegations from South Carolina, Virginia, and other States,[3] who had called on him;—and cooperate cordially together to carry out its provisions. This advice seemed to be well received by both Governors. I therefore hope that there will be no further trouble. I believe that the recognition of Governor Humphreys as Provisional Governor of Mississippi would have a more beneficial effect in relieving the anxiety of the people on the subject of final reconstruction and recognition. The people of Alabama are either more practical or more loyal than the Mississippians. The Legislature is a dignified body, and seems ready to meet the emergency and to act on the various questions presented fully, and seems sincerely desirous of the reconstruction of the Senate [state?] in complete harmony with the policy of the President. The Governor elect (Patten)[4] will not consent to be inaugurated until he can be recognized by the President. I did not visit Milledgeville, as the President did not express a desire that I should. I believe, also, had I gone, my visit would have caused as much uneasiness in the minds of the members of the Legislature of Georgia as my visit to Jackson did in Mississippi. The last symptom of open rebellion in Alabama is exhibited by the self-styled Bishop of Alabama[5] and the women. I hope to be able to settle the bishop's case in a few days.

George H. Thomas,
Major-General.

Thomas B. Van Horne, *The Life of General George H. Thomas* (New York, 1882), 401–2).

1. In November, citing the potential evils for the expansion of federal power implicit in the second clause, the Mississippi legislature rejected the amendment 45–25, although Johnson had urged its ratification. Harris, *Presidential Reconstruction in Mississippi*, 142; Johnson to Sharkey, November 1, 1865, Johnson Papers, LC.

2. On November 17 Johnson instructed Sharkey to "continue to exercise any and all the functions of Provisional Governor," and urged the state legislature to ratify the Thirteenth Amendment. The same day the President relayed his decision to Thomas, and suggested that he confer with Humphreys. When Thomas visited Sharkey the provisional governor declined to discuss prospects for legislation concerning freedmen, urging the general to talk to Humphreys. On December 14, Humphreys took office. Johnson to Sharkey, November 17, 1865, and to Thomas, November 17, 1865, Tels. Sent by Pres., Vol. 2, Office of the Secretary of War, RG107, NA; Harris, *Presidential Reconstruction in Mississippi*, 117.

3. It is not clear exactly to which interviews Thomas refers. On June 24, Johnson advised a South Carolina delegation to abolish slavery, adding, "Do you know that I believe I am a better States rights man than some of you are?" Two weeks later, he defended the $20,000 clause in his amnesty proclamation in an interview with Richmond merchants. In September he told southerners from several states that he opposed "consolidation or concentration of power,"; and would "do all in my power to restore" the happiness and prosperity of southerners "which they enjoyed before the madness of misguided men . . . led them astray to their own undoing," while assuring another set of Virginians that he would be favorably disposed toward assisting southern recovery. While Thomas was visiting Washington in October, the President rejected a petition from South Carolinians requesting the pardon of Jefferson Davis, assured his visitors that he had no desire to enact a harsh peace, and urged them to pass laws just to black civil rights. Washington *Star*, June 26, 1865; New York *Times*, July 10, 1865; Washington *Chronicle*, September 13, 1865; New York *Times*, September 13, 1865; New York *Herald*, October 14, 1865.

4. Robert M. Patton (1809–1885), Whig and later a Republican, served for over two decades in the state legislature before the war and was a member of both the secession and the 1865 constitutional conventions. He had been elected governor on November 6 in a three-way race, receiving 20,611 of a total of 45,548 votes cast. Patton took office December 13.

5. Richard H. Wilmer. See Truman to Johnson, October 13, 1865, notes 9–11.

Appendix II

The following message, read to the Senate on December 19, accompanied the transmittal of the reports of Carl Schurz and Ulysses S. Grant in response to Senator Charles Sumner's call for information on December 12. It represents the only public record of Johnson's direct response to the information garnered on these tours. Furious with senators who declined to sit through the reading of Schurz's lengthy report, Sumner claimed that Johnson's message "is like the whitewashing message of Franklin Pierce with regard to the enormities in Kansas," a charge which embroiled him in an extensive debate over the meaning and import of the term "whitewashing." The next day Sumner, again maintaining that Johnson's message represented an "attempt to whitewash the unhappy condition of the Rebel States, and to throw the mantle of official oblivion over sickening and heartrending outrages," read from numerous letters testifying to southern violence and disloyalty.

Washington, December 18, 1865.

To the Senate of the United States:

In reply to the resolution adopted by the Senate on the 12th instant, I have the honor to state that the rebellion waged by a portion of the people against the properly constituted authority of the Government of the United States has been suppressed; that the United States are in possession of every State in which the insurrection existed, and that, as far as it could be done, the courts of the United States have been restored, post-offices reestablished, and steps taken to put into effective operation the revenue laws of the country.

As the result of the measures instituted by the Executive with the view of inducing a resumption of the functions of the States comprehended in the inquiry of the Senate, the people of North Carolina, South Carolina, Georgia, Alabama, Mississippi, Louisiana, Arkansas, and Tennessee have reorganized their respective State governments, and "are yielding obedience to the laws and Government of the United States" with more willingness and greater promptitude than under the circumstances could reasonably have been anticipated. The proposed amendment to the Constitution, providing for the abolition of slavery forever within the limits of the country, has been ratified by each one of those States, with the exception of Mississippi, from which no official information has been received, and in nearly all of them measures have been adopted or are now pending to confer upon freedmen the privileges which are essential to their comfort, protection, and security. In Florida and Texas the people are making commendable progress in restoring their State governments, and no doubt is entertained that they will at an early period be in a condition to resume all of their practical relations with the General Government.

In "that portion of the Union lately in rebellion" the aspect of affairs is more promising than, in view of all the circumstances, could well have been expected. The people throughout the entire South evince a laudable desire to renew their allegiance to the Government and to repair the devastations of war by a prompt and cheerful return to peaceful pursuits, and abiding faith is entertained that their actions will conform to their professions, and that in acknowledging the supremacy of the Constitution and laws of the United States their loyalty will be unreservedly given to the Government, whose leniency they can not fail to appreciate and whose fostering care will soon restore them to a condition of prosperity. It is true that in some of the States the demoralizing effects of the war are to be seen in occasional disorders; but these are local in character, not frequent in occurrence, and are rapidly disappearing as the authority of civil law is extended and sustained. Perplexing questions are naturally to be expected from the great and sudden change in the relations between the two races; but systems are gradually developing themselves under which the freedman will receive the protection to which he is justly entitled, and, by means of his labor, make himself a useful and independent member in the community in which he has a home.

From all the information in my possession and from that which I have recently derived from the most reliable authority I am induced to cherish the belief that sectional animosity is surely and rapidly merging itself into a spirit of nationality, and that representation, connected with a properly adjusted system of taxation, will result in a harmonious restoration of the relation of the States to the National Union.

The report of Carl Schurz is herewith transmitted, as requested by the Senate. No reports from the Hon. John Covode[1] have been received by the President.[2] The attention of the Senate is invited to the accompanying report from Lieutenant-General Grant, who recently made a tour of inspection through several of the States whose inhabitants participated in the rebellion.

Andrew Johnson.

Richardson, *Messages*, VI, 372–73.

1. John Covode (1808–1871), a former Whig and Republican congressman, returned to Congress in 1867 as a spokesman for Radical measures.

2. Upon his return to Washington, Covode prepared a report entitled "Louisiana, Politically Considered," which he planned to present to both Johnson and Stanton. When Covode encountered the President, however, he found the chief executive "a great deal fatigued at the time." Promising to look at the report later, Johnson suggested that Covode file it with Stanton. Subsequent conversation between the congressman and the President apparently failed to shake Johnson's support of Wells. Two years later, Johnson expressed a desire to see Covode's report. Grant, then secretary of war *ad interim*, reported on October 25, 1867, that while War Department files contained two reports

dated June 13, 1865, a "careful search" failed to uncover any other reports. Another
search, undertaken in 1889 at the request of Yale Professor William Graham Sumner,
yielded similar results. A partially illegible draft is in the Covode Papers, LC. Covode to
Stanton, July 11, 1865, Lets. Recd., 1865, Office of Secretary of War, RG107, NA;
Grant to Johnson, October 25, 1867, Rutherford B. Hayes Library, Fremont, Ohio;
Sumner to Redfield Proctor, March 11, 1889, and Proctor to Sumner, March 23, 1889,
Lets. Recd., 1889, Office of Secretary of War, RG107, NA; *Report of the Joint Committee
on Reconstruction*, 39 Cong., 1 Sess., 1866, House Report No. 30, pt. iv, 114–19.

Appendix III

New York *Times* Reports of Benjamin C. Truman

Listed below are Truman's reports on southern conditions which appeared in the New York *Times* during the time covered by his letters to Johnson. The datelines provide a rough outline of the course of his journeys, and the dispatches often fill out Truman's increasingly short missives to the White House, as well as providing one of the few accounts of the Texas Constitutional Convention of February, 1866.

Dateline		*Publication Date*
October 25	Montgomery, Ala.	October 31
October 25	Montgomery, Ala.	November 2
November 8 or 9	Milledgeville, Ga.	November 17
November 10	Milledgeville, Ga.	November 23
November 13	Columbus, Ga.	December 3
November 16	Atlanta, Ga.	December 3
November 20	Augusta, Ga.	December 3
November 25	Augusta, Ga.	December 5
December 2	Savannah, Ga.	December 10
December 7	Tallahassee, Fla.	December 25
January 1	Nashville, Tenn.	January 8
January 4	Memphis, Tenn.	January 15
January 13	Memphis, Tenn.	January 28
January 17	Little Rock, Ark.	January 29
January 20	Jackson, Miss.	February 4
February 2	New Orleans, La.	February 25
February 3	Galveston, Tex.	February 19
February 3	Indianola, Tex.	March 5
February 14	Austin, Tex.	March 11
February 26	Austin, Tex.	March 18
March 1	San Antonio, Tex.	March 25
March 24	Houston, Tex.	April 1

Appendix IV

The Observers and the Observed:
Two Humorous Perspectives

If northerners displayed an intense interest in southern conditions, they also could poke fun at the process of gaining that information. The two pieces below provide a humorous perspective on the attitudes of both investigators and white southerners. The first, by David Ross Locke (1833–1888), editor of the Toledo *Blade*, is an example of his use of political satire to advocate Republican policy. Through the character of Copperhead Petroleum V. Nasby, Locke portrayed the Democratic party as foolish, corrupt, racist, short-sighted, and disloyal. In contrast, an unsigned column in the conservative Cincinnati *Commercial*, reprinted here as it appeared in the Richmond *Dispatch*, ridiculed Schurz's report, submitted to Congress the previous month, as well as the dispatches of several northern newspaper correspondents.

1.

A Conversation with General McStinger, of the State of Georgia, which is interrupted by a Subjugated Rebel.

Washington, D.C., Nov. 18, 1865.

Sence the November elections I hev bin spendin' the heft uv my time in Washington. I find a melankoly pleasure in ling'rin around the scene uv so many Demokratic triumphs. Here it wuz that Brooks, the heroic, bludgeoned Sumner; here it wuz that Calhoon, & Yancey, and Breckinridge achieved their glory and renown. Besides, it's the easiest place to dodge a board bill in the Yoonited States. There's so many Congressmen here who resemble me, that I hev no difficulty in passin for one, two-thirds uv the time.

Yesterday I met, in the readin-rom uv Willard's, Ginral MacStinger, of South Karliny. The Ginral is here on the same bizness most uv the Southern men hev in this classic city, that uv prokoorin a pardon, wich he hed prokoored, and wuz gittin ready to go home and accept the nominashen for Congress in his deestrick.

The Ginral wuz gloomy. Things didn't soot him, he observed, and he wuz afeerd that the country wuz on the high road to rooin. He hed bin absent from the Yoonited States suthin over four yeers, wich time he hed spent in the southern confederacy. When he went out the Constooshnel Dimocrisy hed some rites wich wuz respected. On his return wat did he see? The power in the hands uv Radikals, Ablishnism in the majority everywhere, a ex-tailor President,—a state uv affairs disgustin in the extreme to the highly sensitive Southern mind. He had accepted a pardon only becoz he felt hisself constrained to put hisself in2 position to go to Congress, that the country might be reskood from its impendin peril. He shood go to Congress, and then he should ask the despots who now hev control, whether,—

1. They spozed the South wood submit to hoomiliatin condishns?

2. What Androo Johnson means by dictatin to the Convenshuns uv sovereign States?

"Why," sez he, "but a few days ago this boor hed the ashoorence to write to the Georgy Convenshun that it '*must not*'—mark the term—'MUST NOT assom the confedrit war debt.' Is a tailor to say '*must not*' to shivelrus Georgy? Good God!—where are we driftin? For one, I never will be consilliated on them terms—never! I never wuz used to that style uv talk in Dimekratic convenshuns.

"Ez soon ez I take my seet in Congris," resoomed he, "I shel deliver a speech, wich I writ the day after Lee surrendered, so ez to hev it ready, in which I shel take the follerin ground, to wit:

"That the South hev buried the hatchit, and hev diskivered that they love the old Yoonion above eny thing on earth. But,

"The North must meet us half way, or we wont be answerable for the consekences. Ez a basis for a settlement, I shell insist on the follerin condishens:

"The Federal debt must be repoodiated, principal and interest, or ef paid, the Southern war debt must be paid likewise—ez a peece offerin. The doctrine uv State Rites must be made the soopreme law uv the land, that the South may withdraw whenever they feel theirselves dissatisfied with Massachusetts. Uv coarse this is a olive branch.

"Jefferson Davis must be to-wunst set at liberty and Sumner hung, ez proof that the North is really consilliatory. On this pint I am inflexible, and on the others immovable."

An old man who hed bin listnin to our talk, murmured that there wuz a parallel to this last proposishen.

"Where?" demanded the Genral.

"The Jews, I remember," replied he, "demanded that Barrabas be released unto them, who wuz a thief, I believe, and the Savior be crucified, but I forgit jist how it wuz."

The Genral withered him with a litenin glance, and resoomed:

"I shel, uv course, offer the North suthin in the way uv compensation, for the troo theory uv a Republikin Government is compermise. On our part we pledge ourselves to kum back, and give the North the benefit uv our kumin back, so long ez Massachusetts condux herself akkordin to our ijees uv what is rite. But ef this ekitable adjustment is rejected, all I hev to say then is, I shell resign, and the Government may sink without wun effort from me to save it."

I wuz about to give in my experience, when the old man, who wuz sittin near us, broke in agin:

"My name," sed he, "is Maginnis, and I live in Alabama. I want to say a word to the gentleman from Karliny, and to the wun from Noo Gersey."

"How," retorted I, "do yoo know I'm from Noo Gersey, not hevin spoken a word in yoor hearin?"

"By a instink I hev. Whenever I see a Sutherner layin it down heavy to a indivijouel whose phisynogamy is uv sich a cast that upon beholdin it yoo instinktively feel to see that yoor pocket-handkercher is safe, a face that wood be dangerous if it had courage into it, I alluz know the latter to be a Northern copperhead. The Noo Gersey part I guessed at, becoz, my friend, that State furnished the lowest order uv copperheads of any uv em. Pardon me ef I flatter yoo. But what I wanted to say wuz, that I spose suthen hez happened doorin the past 4 years. I was a original secessionist. Sum years ago I hed a hundred niggers, and wuz doin well with em. But, unforchunitly, my brother died, and left me ez much more land, but no niggers. I wanted niggers enuff to work that land, and spozed ef cut off from the North, and the slave-trade wuz reopened, I cood git em cheaper. Hentz I seceshed. Sich men ez Genral McStinger told me the North woodent fight or I woodent hev secesht, but I did it. I went out for wool and cum back shorn. I seceshed with 100 niggers to git 200, and alas! I find myself back into the old government, with nary a nigger.

"But all this is no excoose for talkin bald noncents. Yoo old ass," sed he, addressin Genral McStinger, "yoo talk uv wat yoo will do, and what yoo wont. Hevent you diskivered that yoo are whipped? Hevent you found out that yoo are subjoogated? Are yoo back into the Yoonyun uv your own free will and akkord? Hevent yoo got a pardon in yoor pockit, which dockyment is all that saves yoor neck from stretchin hemp? Why do yoo talk uv wat South karliny will and wont do? Good Lord! I recollect about a year since South karliny would *never* permit her soil 2 be pollutid by Yankee hirelins, yit Sherman marched all over it with a few uv em, and skarcly a gun was fired at em. So too I recollect that that sed State, wich wuz agoin to whip the entire North, and wich wood, ef overpowered, submit gracefully and with dignity to annihilation, and sich, wuz the first to git down on her marrow bones, and beg for peace like a dorg. Ef yoo intend this talk for the purpose uv skarin the North, beleeve me when I say that the North aint so easy skared ez it wuz. Ef its intendid for home consumption, consider me the people. Ive heard it before, and I'll take no more uv it until my stumick settles. It makes me puke. The fact is we are whipped, and hev got to do the best we kin. We are a goin to pay the Federal debt, and aint goin to pay the confederet debt. Davis will be hung, and serve him rite. States rites is dead, and slavery is abolished, and with it shivelry; and its my opinion the South is a d—d sight better off without either of em. I kin sware, now, after livin outside uv the shadder uv the flag 4 yeres, that I love it! You bet I do. I carry a small one in my coat pocket. I hev a middlin sized one waved by my youngest boy over the family when at prayers, and a whalin big one wavin over my house all the time. I hev diskivered that its a good thing to live under, and when sich cusses as yoo talk uv what yoo will and wont do under it, I bile. Go home, yoo cusses, go home! Yoo, South, and pullin orf your coat, go to work, thankin God that Johnson's merciful enuff to let yoo go home at all, insted uv hangin yoo up like a dorg, for tryin to bust a Guverment too good for yoo. Yoo, North, thankful that the men uv sense uv the North hed the manhood to prevent us from rooinin ourselves by makin sich ez yoo our niggers. Avaunt!"

And the excited Mr. Maginnis, who is evidently subjoogated, strode out uv our presence. His intemperit talk cast a chill over our confidencis, and we dident resoom with the ease and freedom we commenced with, and in a few minutes we parted. I didn't like him.

Petroleum V. Nasby,
Lait Paster uv the Church of the New Dispensashun.

Petroleum V. Nasby [David Ross Locke], "*Swingin Round the Cirkle*" (Boston, 1867), 19–26.

2.

A Special Committee Visits Richmond.

As a comic companion to an editorial in today's Dispatch, we publish the following, from the Cincinnati *Commercial*. It is from the Washington correspondent of that paper, and is a fair burlesque of the special reports upon the condition of the South. The hit is both good and humorous:

THE REPORT OF THE SPECIAL COMMITTEE.

The Special Radical Committee on Reconstruction intend, it is said, to visit the Southern States to investigate their condition, and report whether they are fit for admission into full communion in the sisterhood of Union. As most of the gentlemen composing the committee have already made up their minds on the subject, I don't see the use of the contemplated tour, especially as their report has been agreed upon. As the document will be looked for with considerable interest, I have procured a copy of it, for the publication of which I trust I will not be accused of a breach of good faith. Here it is:

Washington, January, 1866.

To the Honorable Senate and House of Representatives:

Your committee, appointed to visit the States lately in rebellion, and investigate and report upon their condition as to loyalty and fitness for re-admission into the Union, have performed the duty assigned to them, and beg leave to make the following report:

"Naturally, the first place visited by your committee was Richmond, Va., the capital of the late Confederacy. Our coming had been heralded in the newspapers there, and the demonstration at the railroad depot on our arrival may be taken as, in some degree, indicative of the popular sentiment in that city. We found a large concourse of citizens of African descent awaiting us, and as we disembarked from the cars, they hailed us with shouts of welcome, mingled with 'This way to the Spotswood House,' 'Here's yer buss for the Exchange,' 'Here's yer cab for any part of the city,' 'Baggage to the hotel, gents,' etc. It was grateful to the heart of loyal men to be thus welcomed in a city so lately the headquarters of rebellion, while at the same time we began to feel convinced already that the only truly loyal people of the South were of the colored race. We could not decline the hospitalities so generously tendered us, and accordingly we selected two carriages from the large number placed at our disposal. We were driven to the Spotswood by our hospitable friends, who charged us two dollars apiece, and half a dollar extra for baggage. After so much kindness from the colored race, we were unprepared for the harsh treatment we subsequently received from the white oligarchs of Richmond. The proprietors of the Spotswood gave us rooms in the fifth story, back, saying to his clerk, as we have been informed by a faithful African who blacked our boots for a quarter a pair, that they were good enough for Yankee Radicals. The same spirit of disloyal hate was manifested to us in the dining-room, where, in response to our repeated calls for codfish and pumpkin-pie, we were served with nothing but bacon and hot cakes. We asked why this was done, and were told by a loyal waiter, to whom we had just given a postal half-dollar, that Mr. Spotswood said he didn't keep a hotel for the accommodation of Yankees, and therefore persistently excluded codfish and pumpkin-pies from the bill of fare. Your committee do not deem it necessary to dwell upon this evidence of smouldering disloyalty, nor to compare it with the hastily formed opinion of General Grant respecting Southern sentiment. Our object was to get beneath the surface of things in the South, to find the true character of the sub-stratum. We remained in Richmond a few days, to study the character of the people. On all hands we found evidences of distinctions on account of color, except in a freedmen's colony, where the blacks received the whites on an equal footing with themselves. We also noticed a disloyal disposition to speak of Stonewall Jackson and General Lee in terms of praise and commendation, while General Butler's name was only mentioned in contemptuous connection with silver spoons, and occasionally a little platedware, and he himself seemed to be better known as the Bottle Imp of Bermuda Hundred than in any other way."

Richmond *Dispatch*, January 13, 1866.

Index

Advice After Appomattox was designed by Sheila Hart; composed by G&S Typesetters, Austin, Texas; printed by Thomson-Shore, Inc., Dexter, Michigan; and bound by John H. Dekker & Sons, Grand Rapids, Michigan. The book was set in 10/12 Monticello and printed on 60-lb. Warren's Olde Style wove.